The Unraveled Plot

A volume in the SUNY series in Contemporary French Thought
David Pettigrew and François Raffoul, editors

The Unraveled Plot

Thinking Literature, Community, and Politics with Jean-Luc Nancy

AUKJE VAN ROODEN

Cover Credit: Regardt van der Meulen, "Unravel" (Deconstructed Series), 2016

Published by State University of New York Press, Albany

Revised translation of L'Intrigue dénouée. Mythe, littérature et communauté dans la pensée de Jean-Luc Nancy (Brill 2022).

EU GPSR Authorised Representative:
Logos Europe, 9 rue Nicolas Poussin, 17000, La Rochelle, France
contact@logoseurope.eu

For information, contact State University of New York Press, Albany, NY
www.sunypress.edu

Library of Congress Cataloging-in-Publication Data

Names: Van Rooden, Aukje, author
Title: The unraveled plot : Thinking literature, community, and politics with
     Jean-Luc Nancy / Aukje van Rooden
Description: Albany : State University of New York Press, [2025] | Series:
SUNY series in Contemporary French Thought | Includes bibliographical references
     and index.
Identifiers: ISBN 9798855803938 (hardcover : alk. paper) | ISBN 9798855803952
     (ebook) | ISBN 9798855803945 (pbk. : alk. paper)
Further information is available at the Library of Congress.

Contents

Abbreviations of Works
by Jean-Luc Nancy

References are included with a citation to both the English translations where they exist and the original French. In all other cases the English translations are mine.

A *Adoration: The Deconstruction of Christianity II.* Translated by John McKeane. New York: Fordham University Press, 2012. *L'Adoration (Déconstruction du christianisme, 2)* Galilée, 2010.

AL *L'Absolu littéraire: Théorie de la littérature du romantisme allemand,* with Philippe Lacoue-Labarthe. Seuil, 1978.

ÀP *À plus d'un titre—Jacques Derrida: Sur un portrait de Valerio Adami.* Galilée, 2007.

BH *The Banality of Heidegger.* Translated by Jeff Fort. Fordham University Press, 2017. *Banalité de Heidegger.* Galilée, 2015.

BP *The Birth to Presence.* Translated by Brian Holmes et al. Stanford University Press, 1993. Translation of essays stemming from several works.

BSP *Being Singular Plural.* Translated by Robert Richardson and Anne O'Byrne. Stanford University Press, 2000. *Être singulier pluriel.* Galilée, 1996.

C *Corpus.* Translated by Richard A. Rand. Fordham University Press, 2008. *Corpus.* Métailié, 2006.

"CC"   "The Confronted Community." Translated by Amanda McDonald. *Postcolonial Studies* 6, no. 1 (2003): 23–36. *La communauté affrontée.* Galilée, 2001.

CO   *Coming*, with Adèle Van Reeth. Translated by Charlotte Mandell. Fordham University Press, 2014. *La jouissance.* Plon, 2014.

CW   *The Creation of the World or Globalization.* Translated by François Raffoul and David Pettigrew. State University of New York Press, 2007. *La création du monde ou la mondialisation.* Galilée, 2002.

DC   *The Disavowed Community.* Translated by Philip Armstrong. Fordham University Press, 2016. *La communauté désavouée.* Galilée, 2014.

DE   *Dis-Enclosure: The Deconstruction of Christianity I.* Translated by Bettina Bergo, Gabriel Malenfant, and Michael B. Smith. Fordham University Press, 2008. *La déclosion (Déconstruction du christianisme, 1).* Galilée, 2005.

DI   *Dies Irae.* University of Westminster Press, 2019. "Dies irae." In *La faculté de juger*, edited by Jacques Derrida, Vincent Descombes, Garbis Kortian, Philippe Lacoue-Labarthe, Jean-François Lyotard, and Jean-Luc Nancy, coll. (Minuit, 1985).

DS   *The Discourse of the Syncope: Logodaedalus.* Translated by Saul Anton. Stanford University Press, 2008. *Le discours de la syncope, Tome I: Logodaedalus.* Aubier-Flammarion, 1976.

EF   *The Experience of Freedom.* Translated by Bridget McDonald. Stanford University Press, 1993. *L'Expérience de la liberté.* Galilée, 1988.

ES   *Ego sum: Corpus, Anima, Fabula.* Translated by Marie-Eve Morin. Stanford University Press, 2016. *Ego sum.* Flammarion, 1979.

EPL   *Expectation: Philosophy, Literature.* Translated by Robert Bonnono. Fordham University Press, 2017. *Demande: Littérature et philosophie.* Galilée, 2015.

"FD"   "Finite and Infinite Democracy." In *Democracy in What State?* (coll.). Translated by William McCuaig. Colombia University Press, 2011. "Démocratie finie et infinie." In *Démocratie, dans quel état?* (coll.). (La Fabrique, 2009).

FS   *Fortino Sámano: Les débordements du poème*, with Virginie Lalucq. Galilée, 2004.

FT   *A Finite Thinking*. Edited by Simon Sparks. Stanford University Press, 2003. Collection of essays stemming from several works.

GI   *The Ground of the Image*. Translated by Jeff Fort. Fordham University Press, 2005. *Au fond des images*. Galilée, 2003.

GP   *German Philosophy: A Dialogue*, with Alain Badiou. Translated by Richard Lambert. MIT Press, 2018. *La tradition allemande dans la philosophie*. Edited by Jan Völker. Lignes, 2017.

GT   *The Gravity of Thought*. Translated by François Raffoul and Gregory Recco. Humanities Press, 1997. Collection of the translations of *L'Oubli de la philosophie* (Galilée, 1986) and *Le poids d'une pensée* (Le Griffon d'Argile-Presses Universitaires de Grenoble, 1991).

H   *Hegel: The Restlessness of the Negative*. Translated by Jason E. Smith and Steven Miller. University of Minnesota Press, 2002. *Hegel: L'Inquiétude du négatif*. Hachette, 1997.

IC   *The Inoperative Community*. Translated by Peter Connor, Lisa Garbus, Michael Holland, and Simona Sawhney. University of Minnesota Press, 1991. *La communauté désoeuvrée*. Bourgois, 2004 [1986].

"Imp"   "L'impossible acte constituant." *Le Monde*, July 29, 2005.

LA   *The Literary Absolute: The Theory of Literature in German Romanticism*, with Philippe Lacoue-Labarthe. Translated by Philip Barnard and Cheryl Lester. State University of New York Press, 1988. Reference is made to the French edition (*AL*) when referring to parts that were not incorporated in the English translation.

"LC"   *La comparution*, with Jean-Christophe Bailly. Bourgois, 2007 [1991].

LP   *Le portrait (dans le décor)*. Villeurbanne: Institut d'art contemporain/ Les Cahiers-Philosophie de l'art no. 8, 1999.

M   *The Muses*. Translated by Peggy Kamuf. Stanford University Press, 1996. *Les muses*. Galilée, 2001 [1994].

MII   *Multiple Arts: The Muses II*. Translated by Simon Sparks. Stanford University Press, 2006. Collection of essays stemming from several works.

MB   *Maurice Blanchot: Passion politique; Lettre-récit de 1984 suivie d'une lettre de Dionys Mascolo*. Galilée, 2011.

"Mét"   "La métamorphose, le monde." Interview by Boyan Manchev. *Rue Descartes* 64 (2009): 78–93.

"NBW"   "Nothing but the World: An Interview with Vacarme." *Rethinking Marxism* 19, no. 4 (2007): 521–53. "Rien que le monde," *Vacarme* 11, no. 2 (2000): 4–12.

"NM"   "The Nazi Myth," with Philippe Lacoue-Labarthe, translated by Brian Holmes. *Critical Inquiry* 16, no. 2 (1990): 291–312. *Le mythe nazi*. La Tour d'Aigue: L'Aube, 2003 [1991].

NT   *Noli Me Tangere*. Translated by Sarah Clift, Pascale-Anne Brault, and Micheal Naas. Fordham University Press, 2008. *Noli me tangere: Essai sur la levée du corps*. Bayard, 2003.

"OBC"   "Of Being-in-Common." In *Community at Loose Ends*, edited by The Miamy Theory Collective, translated by James Creech (University of Minnesota Press, 1991). This essay is included in the French edition of *La communauté désoeuvrée*, but kept out of the English edition.

P   *Portrait*. Translated by Sarah Clift and Simon Sparks. Fordham University Press, 2018. Collection of the translation of *Le regard du portrait* (Galilée, 2000) and *L'Autre portrait* (Galilée, 2014).

PD   *Proprement dit: Entretien sur le mythe*. Interview by Mathilde Girard. Lignes, 2015.

PP   *Le poids d'une pensée*. Le Griffon d'Argile-Presses Universitaires de Grenoble, 1991.

"Qs"   "Quand le sens ne fait plus monde." Interview by Michaël Fœssel, Olivier Mongin, and Jean-Loup Thébaud. *Esprit* 403, no. 3–4 (2014): 27–46.

"Res"   "Responsibility—Of the Sense to Come," dialogue with Jacques Derrida. In *For Strasbourg: Conversations of Friendship and Philosophy*, edited and translated by Pascale-Anne Brault and Michael Naas (Fordham University Press, 2014). "Responsabilité—du sens à venir: Entretien," with Jacques Derrida. In *Sens en tous sens: Autour des travaux de Jean-Luc Nancy*, edited by Francis Guibal and Jean-Clet Martin (Galilée, 2004), 165–200.

"RM"   "Rancière and Metaphysics." In *Jacques Rancière: History, Politics, Aesthetics*, edited by Gabriel Rockhill and Philip Watts, translated

by John Hulsey (Duke University Press, 2009). "Rancière et la métaphysique." In *La philosophie déplacée: Autour de Jacques Rancière*, edited by Laurence Cornu and Patrice Vermeren (Horlieu Éditions, 2006).

RP   *Retreating the Political.* Edited by Jean-Luc Nancy and Philippe Lacoue-Labarthe. Translated by Simon Sparks. Routledge, 1997. *Le retrait du politique*, edited by Jean-Luc Nancy and Philippe Lacoue-Labarthe. Cahiers du Centre de recherches philosophiques sur le politique. Galilée, 1983.

S   *Sexistence.* Translated by Steven Miller. Fordham University Press, 2021. *Sexistence.* Galilée, 2017.

"Sc"   "Scene: An Exchange of Letters," with Philippe Lacoue-Labarthe. In *Beyond Representation: Philosophy and Poetic Imagination*, edited by Ricard Eldridge (Cambridge University Press, 1996). *"Scène,"* with Philippe Lacoue-Labarthe. Bourgois, 2013.

"SV"   "Sharing Voices." In *Transforming the Hermeneutic Context: From Nietzsche to Nancy*, edited and translated by Gayle L. Ormiston and Alan D. Schrift (State University of New York Press, 1990). *Le partage des voix.* Galilée, 1982.

SW   *The Sense of the World.* Translated by Jeffrey S. Librett. University of Minnesota Press, 1997. *Le sens du monde.* Galilée, 2001 [1993].

"TC"   "The Compearance: From the Existence of 'Communism' to the Community of 'Existence,'" translated by Tracey B. Strong. *Political Theory* 20, no. 3 (1992): 371–98. Reference is made to the French edition ("LC") when referring to parts that were not incorporated in the English translation.

TD   *The Truth of Democracy.* Translated by Pascale-Anne Brault and Michael Naas. Fordham University Press, 2010. *Vérité de la démocratie.* Galilée, 2008.

"TP"   "Techniques du present." Interview by Benoît Goetz. *Le Portique* 3 (1999): 1–10.

"UC"   "Un commencement." In Philippe Lacoue-Labarthe. *L'"Allégorie" suivi de "Un commencement"* (Galilée, 2006).

Introduction

Literature, Community, and Politics

There is a voice of community articulated in the interruption, and even out of the interruption itself. A name has been given to this voice of interruption: literature (or writing, if we adopt the acceptation of this word that coincides with literature). This name is no doubt unsuitable. But no name is suitable here. . . . What is unsuitable about literature is that it is not suited to the myth of community, nor to the community of myth. It is suited neither to communion nor to communication.

—Jean-Luc Nancy, *The Inoperative Community*

Unraveling the Mythological

Literature as the voice of community—not the communal voice in which community speaks with one voice, nor a voice communicating the "message" of the community at stake, but the always interrupted and interrupting voice of the plurality of voices every community consists of. This is how Nancy sees the fundamental relation between "community" and "literature" that is at stake in the present book. The historical and philosophical risks of this relation are captured by Nancy under the rubric of "myth," this both vague and heavy-loaded term hinting at totalitarian forms of communal meaning. However, "myth" is not only a risk haunting every attempt to understand the voice of community as literary; it also indicates a particular power, a force that helps to understand the birth or rise of community, each time anew, through literature. "Myth," then, is for Nancy not something to do away with, but a force proper to literature, as he subsequently observes: "Not only is literature the beneficiary (or the echo) of myth, literature has itself

in a sense been thought and no doubt should be thought as myth—as the myth of mythless society" (*IC* 63/157–58, translation modified).[1] Instead of trying to undo literature of its mythic powers, Nancy therefore suggests to carefully listen to the way in which the literary voice of community speaks, and to the way in which the powers of communion and communication find both their echo and their interruption in this literary voicing of community.

Literature, then, should *in a sense* still be thought as myth according to Nancy. But in what sense has literature still something to do with myth? And in what sense is it the myth of a "mythless society"? To what extent is literature thus an *unraveling* of community's myth, that is, *plot*? These are the questions that will accompany my analysis of Nancy's work in the present book. The emphasis placed on myth may come as a surprise, for although Nancy's work is known for its reflections on community and, to a lesser extent, the literary and the artistic, it is not particularly known for its reflection on the notion of myth. Yet, throughout the entirety of his career, Nancy has sought to rethink the relation between the communal and the literary, the sharing of sense, and the necessary recitation of our being-with, in short: issues oftentimes understood in terms of "myth." It can therefore be argued that Nancy is one of the very few among contemporary philosophers who has fundamentally revisited the question of myth.[2]

In Nancy's work, the theme of myth manifests itself according to a double vector, simultaneously repelling and attracting his thought, a double vector that, moreover, is proper to the very structure of myth itself. Indeed, stripped to its essence, myth presupposes a specific, even paradoxical, interdependence of the communal and the literary, an interdependence which is that of a founding fiction or a fictional foundation. According to Nancy, "literature" is at stake at the very moment when this interdependence called "myth" is *interrupted*, or rather *as* its very interruption. Because, as Nancy holds, the paradoxical logic of myth always already interrupts itself—betraying either its foundational or its fictional part—literature is both myth's "beneficiary" and "echo." As we shall see, Nancy's entire philosophical work can be understood as an attempt to understand what remains of what is usually called "myth" after this necessary self-interruption—a remainder that is, indeed, mythical or mytho-poetical rather than mythological. Listening to the literary echoes of myth, Nancy develops an interestingly new perspective not only on the way literature, community, and politics can be conceived in present times, but also on the way to think of their interrelation.

But why are we to revisit the interrelation between literature, community, and politics in present times? And, moreover, why would we still

want to do so in terms of myth? The most telling difference between so-called premodern and modern communities is after all that the latter *no longer* conceive themselves to be the result of some divine or cosmological arrangement. "Modern man," as Mircea Eliade has it in his work on myth, "consciously and voluntarily creates history" and therefore does not wish to rely on a myth of origin in constituting a community.[3] The constitution of a modern community, then, is an invention, that is, a creation of what is not yet given. Or, as Nancy observes in relation to the creation of the European community, a modern people is not a given people, but always "a people in the process of constituting itself, in the process of inventing itself by inventing, precisely, its 'idea' or its 'form' " ("Imp" n.p.).

The difficulty of modern communities—which is, of course, at the same time their most interesting aspect—is that these communities constitute themselves, so to speak, in a *vacuum*, in a chaotic in-between time without foundation, because they constitute *themselves*. In other words, the modern act of constituting a community always amounts to a *self*-constitution because there is no external or transcendent authority that would authorize this act. According to Nancy, the fact that a community—that is, *we*—invent our own idea and form implies that the idea or form of this "we," that is, its original blueprint, is not already given. In the absence of a myth of origin, such an idea and form are always contingent; they are the result of a decision taken in specific circumstances, a decision that could have been otherwise and that is therefore in principle open to debate. This is why, in our modern democracies, the idea and form of community are not produced once and for all, but are to be *repeated*, or even *reaffirmed*, time and again. A modern democratic community does not, in other words, have one unique origin, but must repeat its origin over and over again, and is, therefore, in principle a *work in progress*.

Indeed, we can say that this contingency and open-endedness of our modern communities is precisely the reason why they are *not* mythological in nature. Interestingly, however, one can also argue the opposite, namely that it is *particularly* our contemporary communities that have a mythological structure. This is suggested by Walter Benjamin, perhaps the most rigorous thinker of the role of myth in modern politics, in his essay "Critique of Violence" in which he unravels the hidden structure of our modern political systems.[4] Although Benjamin's essay is "notoriously difficult"[5] and "terribly equivocal,"[6] it makes a diagnosis of our contemporary political systems whose explanatory force is far from being exhausted and to which all contemporary analyses of political communities must relate.

What, then, is this diagnosis? Benjamin's point, to summarize it a little freely, is that contemporary political orders willfully conceal the contingency of their origin and that this concealment takes the form of a mythological structure.[7] In order to grasp the full depth of Benjamin's claim, it should be noted that it is motivated by the observation that the origin of modern communities is not only contingent, but that it is, *for this reason*, also, in a sense, *violent*. Because the imposed order could have been different, its constitution necessarily involves a forced decision. Benjamin points out that the violence of this original decision is not a temporary harm from which one can be freed afterwards, but continues to show itself in the everyday reality of the political order. Executive power, for example, is never a simple application of given laws, but requires in each specific case a new decision concerning the organization of community. One could therefore say that Benjamin's "Critique of Violence" is, above all, a critique of the hidden violence involved in a political order. By "violence" one should therefore not necessarily understand the brute force at stake for example in acts of oppression, but, as the German word *Gewalt* indicates, also simply "authority" or "government" (*walten* = to rule, to govern).

The German word *walten* is a perfect example of how the constitution of modern communities is ambiguous. The ambiguity arises from the fact that the constitution, which establishes authorized power, cannot derive its legitimacy from any previous authority, because it is formed in the void where the distinction between legal and illegal does not exist yet. The point of Benjamin's essay is to draw attention to the continued existence of this a-legal void within political power. The violence of political power, Benjamin clarifies, consists of two dimensions, namely a *law making* violence (*rechtsetzende Gewalt*) and a *law preserving* violence (*rechtserhaltende Gewalt*). According to him—and this is the core of the structure that Benjamin calls "mythical" and that I propose to name "mythological" for reasons that will become clear—these dimensions of "making" and "preserving" are not isolated and successive, but are inextricably *intertwined*, because installing an order anticipates its preservation and, conversely, preserving an order implies the original moment of its foundation.[8]

It is this encirclement of founding and preserving powers that marks the *continuity* between mythological "premodern" communities and our contemporary ones, a continuity that indeed resides in a certain idea of destiny. Just as Greek gods could impose law by a sudden intervention, contemporary political orders are characterized, Benjamin holds, by a "fate-imposed" [*schiksalmäßiger*] violence.[9] That is, just like the law of the Greek gods,

modern political orders may be in a sense contingent, but they are not presented as "accidental," as an order that could have been otherwise, but rather as an order that is *supposed* to be like this. Obviously, presenting an order as a matter of destiny transforms the whole idea of history, replacing the idea of history as an open-ended narrative by that of a *plot* (which is the English translation of the Aristotelian *muthos*), that is, by the idea of a predestined succession of events.[10]

It is in this respect that the *temporal* dimension of myth is most clearly interwoven with a *linguistic* one. For a people does not only invent its own "idea" and "form," as we already saw, but it also generally justifies this idea and form by taking recourse to a *narrative*, a *narrative of origin* that presents the contingent as fate-imposed. This linguistic strategy responds, as Jacques Derrida points out in his essay on Benjamin's "Critique of Violence," to the grammatical category of the *future anterior* which is proper to myth: "In these situations [of a newly founded order, AvR] said to found law (*droit*) or state, the grammatical category of the future anterior all too well resembles a modification of the present to describe the violence in progress. It consists, precisely, in feigning the presence or simple modalization of presence. Those who say 'our time,' while thinking 'our present' in light of a *future anterior* present do not know very well, by definition, what they are saying."[11] While the constitution of a political order necessarily takes place in a vacuum, this vacuum, then, is covered both by a *projection* of what is to come and by an *after-the-fact* legitimization of what is past. In other words, by using the grammatical category of the future anterior, one jumps over this void by presenting a political order that *will have been* so.[12]

In a sense, then, myth thus always consists of a revolt against historical time.[13] Even if the use of the grammatical category of the future anterior seems to be transparent, it nevertheless has the power to represent history as a consistent process, pretending to know the mysteries of the whole historical process—the secrets of the past, the intricacies of the present, the uncertainties of the future.[14] In this pretension, democracies, whose representations are by principle always open to debate, dangerously approach what Claude Lefort calls a "society without history," a description characterizing not only premodern societies, but also totalitarian ones.[15] If we want to interrupt this mythological idea of community and the non-historicity it entails—and this is the ultimate stake of Nancy's work on literature, community, and politics—we must therefore be wary of this linguistic dimension.

In other words, in order to be able to really assume the task of constituting ourselves as a community *in* a sensibility towards the contingency of

our political orders, we need another way of "plotting" the social, a way that would not consist in the encirclement of founding and preserving powers, but should be, on the contrary, an *unraveled* plot, that is, a plotting without myth or rather without mytho*logy*, without myth turned into a *logos*. Or as Nancy has it, we should "*reassert* the whole power of myth and harness it *anew* to a fresh set of rules" (*MII* 82, my emphasis). Reasserting the power of myth, this is what is at stake in Nancy's rethinking of the way politics, community, and literature interrelate and that makes Nancy's work particularly relevant today, because it takes seriously the post-foundationalist condition of our present communities, but without dismissing the all too human desire to plot stories and establish relations.[16]

Outline

As we will see, in this attempt to rethink the relationship between community, literature, and politics Nancy does not return to Benjamin's work directly, but to one of Benjamin's major sources of inspiration: the German Romantics, or more specifically the Jena Romantics and their call for a "*new mythology*." Chapter 1—"The Romantic Heritage"—will therefore characterize Nancy as a neo-Romantic thinker. Despite Nancy's abundant references to Jena Romanticism, especially in *The Literary Absolute: Theory of Literature in German Romanticism*, co-authored with Philippe Lacoue-Labarthe, Nancy himself has always been quite critical of the Romantic tradition. However, as is the case with the notion of myth itself, the Romantic heritage manifests itself in Nancy's work as a double vector, simultaneously repelling and attracting his thought. While recognizing the value of the Romantic heritage for contemporary thought, he emphasizes at the same time the problematic aspects of this heritage. In the end, it is precisely the Romantic heritage that *prevents* us from cutting ourselves loose from traditional ideas of community, literature and myth according to Nancy.

Nonetheless, I believe Nancy's thought can be situated more firmly in line with Jena Romanticism, or a certain interpretation of it, than is generally believed. Otherwise scattered ideas in Nancy's work—about community, politics, the arts, and sense—present themselves in a particularly illuminating cohesion when conceived through the prism of their Romantic heritage. In order to properly highlight this cohesion, I will therefore first sketch the historical moment of Jena Romanticism and contextualize the political, aesthetic, and literary ideas introduced by it, each of which, as we will see,

is rethought, critiqued, and reiterated by Nancy. Before analyzing Nancy's work on politics, community, and the literary, I will thus open chapter 1 with a broad overview of Jena Romanticism. Nancy's own study of German Romanticism, co-authored with Lacoue-Labarthe, is of course the starting and ending point of this overview, but this first chapter will also give room for a more independent reflection on Jena Romanticism in order to pave the way for a more favorable and more fruitful interpretation of the Romantic legacy in Nancy's work, important for a better understanding of Nancy's own view on the relation between politics, community, and literature.

The emphasis in chapter 1 will be on the call for a "new mythology" issued at the end of the eighteenth century by the Jena Romantics. According to them, this new mythology should not be a mere repetition of Greek mythology, but should be *new* in the sense that it should adapt to the achievements of modern times. This implies that myth should be thought of, as Nancy and Lacoue-Labarthe also emphasize, as a process of community's *self*-formation. Importantly, this self-formation was understood by the Jena Romantics according to a *poetic* model, that is, as a *work of art*. Community, in other words, was conceived of by them as a work to be completed, a product to be produced. Importantly, however, the specifically Romantic notion of this work of art at the same time *challenges* its character as a "work." Indeed, what the Jena Romantics prefer to call a "poetic" work is not so much the finished product, but rather the infinite productivity that lies at its source. Thus understood, each poetic work is only a fragmented and momentary manifestation of this infinite productivity.

This poetic model provided by Jena Romanticism later became the very core of modern and postmodern thought, of which the unfinished, the fragmented, and the momentary are key features. This is also the reason why many argue that (post)modern thought is ultimately rooted in Romanticism. Maurice Blanchot, for instance, points out that Jena Romantic poetics has initiated an understanding of community as being inoperative, *unworked* (*désoeuvrée*)—an idea taken up by Nancy in his book *The Inoperative Com-munity*.[17] But, as said, although Nancy recognizes the innovative aspects of Romantic thought, he tends to emphasize above all those aspects that are still, despite everything, *mythological* in nature. According to Nancy, we must therefore move beyond the Romantic horizon in order to think anew, in a non-mythological way, the fundamental relationship between politics, community, and literature.

In chapter 2—"The Work of Community"—I will therefore focus on the reassertion, *beyond* Jena Romanticism, of the question of myth as

proposed by Nancy. This second chapter begins, however, by indicating why Nancy thinks our current reflections on community cannot get rid of the mythological structure inherited from Jena Romanticism. As we shall see, Nancy suggests that we, in our being-with, are somehow still searching for something *common*, something to share, a quest that he believes is revived by the Romantic call for a new mythology. Nancy's specific contribution to rethinking the Romantic heritage consists in the persistent and tireless call to think our being-with *without* resorting to the presupposition of something common. According to him, we must accept that community is nothing more than the fact that we are together, that we *co-exist*, without there being anything else in common than this very co-existence. "Community," then, Nancy stresses, is not something to be invented anew or to be formed, nor is it something from the past that has been lost in modern times, but it is simply what is there when we are there, together.

It is, more precisely, on this *ontological* level that we should begin to rethink the whole idea of community according to Nancy. Not surprisingly, this ontological rethinking of community has major consequences for the way in which we should conceive of the relation between community and literature. If this relation still has something to do with what we used to call "myth," it is in any case not a myth that would define community and determine it. As stated earlier, Nancy incites us to reassert the very power of myth by harnessing it to "a fresh set of rules," that is, not the rules of the old mythological game, but rather to rules that save the mythical power from its old mythological use. As we shall see in chapter 2, instead of explaining *what* a specific community is and why, this power consists of nothing other than a community constituting itself by expressing itself.

This obviously leads to another poetic model of community, a model that is, nevertheless, very close to that of the Jena Romantics. In chapter 3—"An Ontological Poetics"—I will indicate that Nancy developpes a *mythic* poetics that is emphatically distinguished from a *mythological* poetics by a crucial emphasis on what he calls the *sense* of community. Whereas a mythological poetics is situated on the level of *signification*, the mythical poetics developed by Nancy is rather situated on this level of sense, that is, of what is offered to the senses, here and now. In chapter 3, I will also argue that in his poetics, Nancy seems to radicalize the deconstructivist conception of literature of contemporaries like Blanchot and Derrida, taking their central notion of the "literary" or "writing" as the main characteristic of an *ontological* dynamics. By understanding the poetic on an ontological level, Nancy wants to indicate that our existence is in a sense always a poetic

existence, that is to say, that it presents itself in a poetic mode. With this ontological poetics, Nancy follows in the footsteps of Martin Heidegger, for whom *Dichtung*, in the broad sense, is the disclosure of existence as such. Although Nancy, like Heidegger, is first and foremost interested in "poetry" in this broad sense of the word, he nevertheless regularly deals with concrete works of literature. One of the attempts in chapter 3 will therefore be to interrogate the specific status of these concrete literary works in Nancy's ontological poetics.

As an extension of this attempt, chapter 4—"Literature's Unworked Force"—tries to expand Nancy's ontological poetics with a more specific theory of literary language as the language of *fiction*. In doing so, I will put Nancy's work into dialogue, not only, again, with that of Blanchot and Derrida, but also, among others, with Hannah Arendt's, Jacques Rancière's, Mehdi Belhaj Kacem's, and Thierry De Duve's theories of fiction and simulation. Instead of depriving literary works of their fictional status in light of a more fundamental ontological take on poetics, like Nancy does, these theories emphasize the necessity to hold onto granting literary works some exceptional status on the basis of their fictionality. Drawing from theoretical angles that partly stretch beyond Nancy's, these authors suggest that works of poetry and literature, in the ordinary sense of the word, might be able to open up a domain immune to the workings of mythology, precisely *because* of their explicitly fictional status.

As we will see, Nancy's ontological poetics seems to exclude this fictional dimension, at least as far as the sense of our being-with is concerned. According to Nancy's ontological poetics, each enunciation, fictional or not, is a manifestation, even a constitution, of our being-with as it is an utterance, an *expression* of oneself towards others. What is more, precisely the awareness of this overall poetic dimension of our being-with will according to Nancy provoke the interruption of the persistent mythological structure of our political orders. However, as I will argue in this final chapter, in order to *facilitate* this awareness, we must perhaps make room *in* our political orders for "fiction" in the strict sense of the word. Perhaps it is only in this way that we can lend an ear to the echo of myth that is called literature.

Chapter 1

The Romantic Heritage

German Romanticism

Romanticism as the Birthplace of Modernity

As indicated, it is not self-evident to situate Nancy's work in the Romantic tradition. However, in order to understand the specific relation between politics, community, and literature in Nancy's thought, it is essential to trace it back to its sources in Jena Romanticism. Nancy himself, moreover, has repeatedly emphasized the influence of Jena Romanticism on his work and his dialogue with this tradition spans his entire oeuvre, from his earliest to his latest works.[1] Apart from offering certain philosophical themes, the Jena Romantics have, in my opinion, also influenced the poetic-philosophical style of Nancy's work.[2] Although I will sometimes refer to less well-known texts of Nancy's to highlight these "Romantic" traces in his work, I hope to demonstrate that his major works, too, are in constant dialogue with Romanticism when dealing with the issue of community and its expression. The Romantic tradition, in other words, provides the backdrop of Nancy's thought, as it does of modern thought more generally.

It is probably for this reason that Nancy and Lacoue-Labarthe felt the urge to disclose the legacy of German Romanticism to the French public. This is at least one of the main reasons they mention for publishing their collective work *The Literary Absolute: Theory of Literature in German Romanticism*, offering French translations of the so far untranslated major texts of German Romanticism, alternated with theoretical sections in which they explain and contextualize these translated texts. In this way, Nancy and

11

Lacoue-Labarthe not only introduce the Romantic heritage to the French public but also explain why an understanding of this heritage is indispensable for the understanding of our modern condition. To anticipate very briefly, according to them the "modernity" of German Romanticism lies in the fact that it conceives the self-formation of community as an *infinite*, never-ending process. Consequently, what is "common" remains in German Romanticism incomplete, dynamic and elusive, or rather, it is grasped in its ungraspability. For this very reason, Romantic thought can be seen as a questioning of the mythological forms of community discussed in the introduction.

This innovative dimension of Romanticism has strongly and also positively inspired modern and postmodern thought. However, in addition to disclosing these influential texts of Jena Romanticism to French readers, Nancy and Lacoue-Labarthe also want to emphasize what they call the "reverse (or obverse . . .) side" of Romanticism, that is, the side that has *not* been sufficiently noticed by contemporary thinkers (*LA* 15/26). While Jena Romanticism is often conceived as the birth place of modernity, the aim of Nancy and Lacoue-Labarthe is rather to warn us for the risk of over-romanticizing romanticism. They even suggests that the reason we do not succeed in cutting ourselves loose from mythological thinking is that we keep on returning to our Romantic roots: Romanticism is a trap we keep falling into. Romanticism, in other words, has a double face—both modern and conservative—a double face that is reflected by the very ambiguity of the Romantic call for a "*new* mythology."

On the one hand, this Romantic appeal to mythology indeed clearly stems from a feeling of nostalgia, nostalgia for the premodern, primitive, and supposedly "authentic" communities whose origin, essence, and destiny were simply "given." In these premodern communities—as described amongst others in the works of Mircea Eliade and Claude Lefort—everyone would simply have its proper predesigned place and exist in a harmonious constellation with each other.[3] According to the German Romantics, "myth" is what forms the basis of such a constellation, be it openly or more implicitly. As a result of technical and scientific progress during the Enlightenment, this social bond, however, has drastically changed. Though German Romantics partly consider this change as a welcome modernization, they also see the risk of an increasing social *decomposition*, evoking the nightmare of a purely functional assemblage of atomic individuals, that is—to borrow the terms later used by Ferdinand Tönnies—of a *community* turned into a mere *society*.[4] The problem of such a change, according to them, is not only that one would

distance oneself from nature, but also from oneself. The task of modern people, then, according to the German Romantics, is to reinvent their own identity, not only as human beings but also and above all as *social* beings.

In eighteenth-century Germany, the loss of a common social identity is all the more painful because of the French Revolution, which continued to affect all of Europe. Although the French Revolution was in many ways disappointing, it arouses in the German Romantics a jealous enthusiasm that revealed both the desire for *and* lack of the social unity in Germany. The bloody outcome of the French Revolution, however, dashes their hopes of a purely political revolt. As a result, the Romantic aspiration for a social identity is both more modest and more ambitious: According to the German Romantics, this reinvention has to be a total re-figuration of their social being, a re-figuration that would, however, consist of a *slow* and *organic* self-formation from within, an *evolution* instead of a revolution. According to them, a mythology modeled on the classic age would be the most suitable means to reach this goal.

The call for a *new* mythology nevertheless reveals a concern to break with the past and to build another future. Although inspired by the classical age, the German Romantics realize that the mythological worldview is definitely over and that their time demands a different use of myth. Since the mythological worldview gave way, in the course of time and especially during the Enlightenment, to a *rational* one, the new mythology propagated by the German Romantics is above all a mythology *of reason*, that is to say, a mythology constituted and sustained by reason. That it is nevertheless a *mythology* of reason is due to their attempt to reevaluate modern reason by an appeal to myth. The desire for a new mythology was, among other things, a reaction against the unbridled and one-sided rationalization of the Enlightenment, against the tendency of placing Reason—that is to say System, Order, and Classification—to the highest ranks of humanity. The new mythology sought by the German Romantics thus presupposes not only a rationalization of mythology, but, conversely, also a mythologization of reason, that is, as we shall see, its *poeticization*. A new mythology is in other words a means of opening the straitjacket of purely speculative thought to reason's sensibility and creativity, and thereby to poetry and imagination.

Before presenting Nancy's and Lacoue-Labarthe's cautious but ultimately disapproving reading of German Romanticism in *The Literary Absolute*, I will, as announced in the introduction, give a more general, even genealogical, reading of the Romantic heritage, in order to prepare a more favorable and also more

fruitful interpretation of its influence on Nancy's thought. In what follows I will therefore focus in particular on the *modern* face of German Romanticism, that is, on those parts of German Romantic thought that prepare the way for Nancy's philosophy. As we shall see, German Romanticism marks a real revolution in thought: It presents a whole new idea of literature, an idea in which literature ties in with myth and community in an entirely new way.

At the heart of the current chapter, then, will be this renewed relationship between literature, myth, and community—presented in an exemplary way, first, in *The Oldest Systematic Program of German Idealism* (1796, Hegel, Schelling, and/or Hölderlin), and subsequently in the writings of the Schlegel brothers in their journal *Athenaeum* (1798–1800). The focus will be merely on *early* German Romanticism, that is on the so-called *Frühromantiker* or Jena Romantics, referring to the city that at that time was one of the most important cultural centers. This focus entails both a historical and a topographical delimitation, because, as is also stated by Nancy, the Schlegel brothers' journal *Athenaeum* is the uncontested center of the Jena Romantic movement.[5]

The Oldest Systematic Program

The call for a "new mythology" in German Romanticism, as well as the ambiguity of this call as underlined by Nancy, results not only from the political and sociocultural situation, but also from the *philosophical* situation of that time, a situation largely determined by Kant's philosophy. Kant's complex influence can be understood by the fact that his thought resulted in two different and sometimes even contradictory philosophical movements, namely German idealism and German Romanticism, linking them as firmly as it separates them. This is why it is *The Oldest Systematic Program*, although it is the oldest program of German *idealism*, that opened the field of thought of Jena *Romanticism*. What, then, is the common core of German idealism and Romanticism?

Kant, as we know and as he states in particular in his *Critique of Pure Reason*, meticulously distinguishes the domain of thought from that of the sensible, that is, logic from aesthetics. In order to produce knowledge, however, a link should be established between the two domains, a link realized by a "capacity" that Kant calls imagination, *Einbildungskraft*. Imagination, in brief, is the condition of possibility for something to appear to us. Or, to push this line of reasoning to the extreme: If the "something" that appears to us, gives itself as something to be observed and known, that is, as *eidos* or

forma, then imagination is the *formation* of these forms.[6] Well, this formation of forms, is, in Kant, the task of "transcendental aesthetics," which is in fact a double one: the formation of both space and time. Because it is only in space-time, or *as spaced and temporalized*, that things give themselves, the formation of forms has thus a transcendental status.

Broadly speaking, one could say that the difference between a German idealist's and a German Romantic's interpretation of Kant lies in the way they understand this transcendental formation. German idealists, to begin with, understand this transcendental formation of the things appearing to us as a matter of *reason*, as a capacity of our thought. Since this transcendental formation boils down from the subjective constitution of our mind, idealists aim to provide the subject with a foundational status. According to them, then, it is the subject that founds all possible external experiences. German Romantics, on the other hand, take the transcendental formation to be a *poetic* capacity and therefore a matter of *art*. For German Romantics it is not the thinking subject who founds all possible experience, but the *poetic* subject, if at least one can still speak of "foundation." In the end, then, whereas German idealists—notwithstanding the great differences between them—conceive the highest act of mankind as an act of pure thought, German Romantics conceive it as a poetic act. This divergence has led to the persistent prejudice that Romanticism is an artistic movement, while idealism would be strictly philosophical. But this distinction is not only forced and unnuanced, it is quite simply false. "[A]lthough it is not entirely or simply philosophical," say also Nancy and Lacoue-Labarthe, "Romanticism is rigorously comprehensible (or even accessible) *only on a philosophical basis*" (*LA* 29/42, my emphasis). For this reason, according to them, "the birthplace of romanticism is situated in philosophy—in the philosophical question of art and poetry" (*LA* 103/374).

In the end, then, the main question of *both* German idealism and Romanticism is thus a philosophical one, namely the Kantian question: How do the realms of thought and the sensible align? Not only this shared philosophical issue, but also the close kinship of representatives of the two movements, make it quite impossible to clearly distinguish German idealism from German Romanticism. For the same reason, it is impossible to consider either of them as homogeneous movements. Rather, the aim here is to bring to light a number of features peculiar to eighteenth- and nineteenth-century thinking about myth, and thus to sketch out the birthplace not only of Western mythological logic, but also of Nancy's proposed interruption of that logic.

The birth announcement of this Romantic idea of a new mythology, and of its interruption, is thus *The Systematic Program of German Idealism*. The great interest given to this—incomplete—text of barely two pages, is not only due to its programmatic nature, but is also explained by the enigma that surrounds it. While one can be certain that the text's handwriting is that of Hegel's, it is less certain that the content should be attributed to him: It would rather stem from Schelling or Hölderlin, who were both staying with Hegel in Tübingen at that time. Franz Rosenzweig, who discovered this text among Hegel's manuscripts, believes that he can conclude, based on the content and terminology, that this text was originally written by Schelling and then copied by Hegel. This hypothesis is also defended by Nancy and Lacoue-Labarthe who underline that the ideas put forward in the *Systematic Program* do not correspond with those of Hegel, nor with those of Hölderlin (*LA* 28/40).[7] However, it is not only the content that wraps this little text in mystery, but also its form. It is remarkable that the *Systematic Program* is written in the first-person, which weakens the hypotheses of a collective writing or of a copy by Hegel of a programmatic statement belonging to someone else. Apart from that, the first-person perspective is difficult to reconcile with the programmatic stakes of the text.

I prefer not to pursue this research on the author of the program, but to consider it as the expression of a certain relationship between philosophy, poetry, and community that expresses ideas that were already circulating, in various forms, at that time—either under the name of Rousseau's civil religion, or, later, in the work of a Tönnies or a George—a relationship that is made public, in this text, under the name of a "new mythology."[8] Let us start by reading the full text of the *Systematic Program*:

The Oldest Systematic Program of German idealism (1797)

An Ethics. Since all metaphysics will henceforth fall into *morals*—for which Kant, with both of his practical postulates has given only an *example* and *exhausted* nothing, so this ethics will contain nothing other than a complete system of all ideas, or what is the same, of all practical postulates. The first idea is naturally the conception *of myself* as an absolutely free being. Along with the free, self-conscious being an entire *world* emerges simultaneously—out of nothingness—the only true and conceivable *creation out of nothingness*—Here I will descend to the fields of physics; the question is this: How should a world

be constituted for a moral being? I should like to give our physics, progressing laboriously with experiments, wings again. So, whenever philosophy provides the ideas, experience the data, we can finally obtain physics on the whole, which I expect of later epochs. It does not seem as if present day physics could satisfy a creative spirit such as ours is or should be.

From nature I come to *man's works*. The idea of humanity first—I want to show that there is no idea of the *state* because the state is something *mechanical,* just as little as there is an idea of a *machine.*

Only that which is the object of *freedom* is called *idea.* We must therefore go beyond the state!—Because every state must treat free human beings like mechanical works; and it should not do that; therefore, it should *cease.* You see for yourself that here all the ideas, that of eternal peace, etc., are merely *subordinate* ideas of a higher idea. At the same time, I want to set forth the principles for a *history of humanity* here and expose the whole miserable human work of state, constitution, government, legislature—down to the skin. Finally, the ideas of a moral world, deity, immortality—overthrow of everything (superstition) pseudo doctrines, persecution of the priesthood, which recently poses as reason, come through itself.—(The) absolute freedom of all spirits who carry the intellectual world within themselves, and may not seek either God or immortality *outside of themselves.*

Finally, the idea which unites all, the idea of *beauty,* the word taken in the higher platonic sense. I am convinced that the highest act of reason, which, in that it comprises all ideas, is an aesthetic act, and that *truth and goodness* are united like sisters *only in beauty*—The philosopher must possess just as much aesthetic power as the poet. The people without aesthetic sense are our philosophers of the letter. The philosophy of the spirit is an aesthetic philosophy. One cannot be clever in anything, one cannot even reason cleverly in history—without aesthetic sense. It should now be revealed here what those people who do not understand ideas are actually lacking—and candidly enough admit that everything is obscure to them as soon as one goes beyond charts and indices.

Poetry thereby obtains a higher dignity; it becomes again in the end what it was in the beginning—*teacher* of *(history)*

humanity because there is no longer any philosophy, any history; poetic art alone will outlive all the rest of the sciences and arts.

At the same time, we so often hear that the great multitude should have a *sensual religion*. Not only the great multitude, but even philosophy needs it. Monotheism of reason and the heart, polytheism of the imagination and art, that is what we need!

First, I will speak about an idea here, which as far as I know, has never occurred to anyone's mind—we must have a new mythology; this mythology must, however, stand in the service of ideas, it must become a mythology of *reason*.

Until we make ideas aesthetic, i.e., mythological, they hold no interest for the *people*, and conversely, before mythology is reasonable, the philosopher must be ashamed of it. Thus, finally the enlightened and unenlightened must shake hands; mythology must become philosophical, and the people reasonable, and philosophy must become mythological in order to make philosophy sensual. Then eternal unity will reign among us. Never again the contemptuous glance, never the blind trembling of the people before its wise men and priests. Only then does *equal* development of *all* powers await us, of the individual as well as of all individuals. No power will be suppressed any longer, then general freedom and equality of spirits will reign—A higher spirit sent from heaven must establish this religion among us, it will be the last and greatest work of humanity."[9]

From the very first lines of this extremely dense text, which according to Nancy and Lacoue-Labarthe forms the "overture" of German Romanticism (*LA* 27/37), it is clear that it stems from a *concern*. Foreseeing that metaphysics would soon be a uniquely ethical affair, the narrator of the *Systematic Program* indicates, on the example of Kant, that metaphysics should in fact be based on *ideas* and should, more precisely, amount to "a complete system of all Ideas," which, in turn, amounts to a complete system of "practical postulates."[10] As for the objects of these practical postulates, or postulates of practical reason (the immortality of the soul and the existence of God), one can, according to Kant, only *assume* that they exist, because it they are principally beyond knowledge. Although it is necessary, from the point of view of morality, to assume them, there is therefore no intuition of them.[11] If Kant, with these two postulates, has only given an *example*

of a metaphysics turned into morality, the ambition of the narrator of the program is greater: to give a complete system of all practical postulates, that is, of all ideas.

In his analysis of this text, Manfred Frank rightly says that the narrator seems to aspire here to a deductive system analogous to Spinoza's *Ethics*, that is a system whose elements can all be deduced from a first axiom that is itself not deduced from anything other than itself.[12] According to the narrator of the program, this axiom—"the first Idea"—consists, "naturally," in "the conception of *myself* as an absolutely free being." If we take this first idea in the Kantian sense of the term, it is—like all ideas—a conception used by reason to carry out a practical act. Consequently, the conception of myself as a free being not only realizes this freedom, but it does so, as the narrator of the *Systematic Program* says, "*out of nothingness.*" This is why this idea of a free being is indeed the "founding" idea of the new ethics aimed at, not because it would be a foundation of what is given, but because it provides the conception of reality as it should be. It is thus always a practical postulate, which then functions as a *regulating* idea.[13]

It could be said that the *Systematic Program* was the result of a general concern, the concern namely for a mindless automatism in which we are at the mercy of machinery blind to the ends it serves. The new ethics aimed at, which should be constituted by a new mythology, instead starts from the premise of absolute self-determination. It is with this free self-determination, out of nothingness, that the self determines the world in which it finds itself: "Along with the free, self-conscious being an entire *world* emerges simultaneously—out of nothingness—the only true and conceivable *creation out of nothingness.*" The narrator then descends, in his own words, into the field of physics, in order to give it "wings again," because a physics closed in a mechanical chain of causes and effects does not satisfy the "creative spirit" that we have—or should have. In other words, the idea of the free self gives rise to the idea of a nature that is free, not locked in a closed, mechanical chain, and that could become a "physics on the whole" as creative as the creative mind. A similar nonmechanical conception of nature is found among the Jena Romantics under the name of the "organic."[14]

Then the narrator turns to the "man's works," which he also wants to save from the scourge of mechanics. Since the idea of human beings as absolutely free prevents him from thinking of himself as a mechanical cog, we are obliged to abandon the idea of the state, which, according to the narrator, does nothing else. What is more, the *idea* of the State itself turns

out to be impossible, because "only that which is the object of *freedom* is called *idea*." Just as there is no idea of the machine, there is no idea of the state. The program thus criticizes the state, not for political reasons, but for philosophical and ethical reasons. As a mechanical organization, the state is contrary to man as a self-determining being. Again, the narrator opposes creativity to mechanics. He also seems to be implicitly opposing Kant, who in *Perpetual Peace* puts his hope precisely in the state.[15]

Because creativity demands absolute freedom, or rather *consists* in absolute freedom, as Nancy and Lacoue-Labarthe also emphasize (*LA* 33/48), the subject cannot accept any heteronomy, that is to say, any government, authority, domain, or support outside itself. With the overcoming of the State, we must, according to the program, also overcome "the whole miserable human work of state, constitution, government, legislature." But it is not only the ideas of political government that are "pseudo doctrines," but also the "priesthood, which recently poses as reason" the ideas of the moral world, of deity and immortality. Absolute freedom, then, belongs to self-determining human beings and to them alone. There is no need to look for an additional foundation: If free human beings are the condition of creation from nothing, they do not need to "seek either God or immortality *outside of themselves*." The representation of myself as an absolutely free being, then, is not only the first idea, but also the *only* idea that can be first and, as such, the basis from which human work and physics can be founded.

The Last Work

Importantly for us in the second half of the *Systematic Program* (which begins with "Finally"), the self-determination of the self is characterized as an *aesthetic* act, which obviously grants a major role to poetry in the realization of the times to come: As in Antiquity, poetry must become the "*teacher . . . of humanity*." Among the ideas or practical postulates, the idea of beauty is thus the highest, or more precisely, it is the *overarching* idea, the idea that embraces all the others. This is the heart of German Romanticism and the reason why the program is treated—also by Nancy and Lacoue-Labarthe—as the key text of German Romanticism. Everything related to ideas—that is to say to freedom, because "only that which is object of *freedom* is called *idea*"—is, according to the *Systematic Program*, necessarily to be understood as an *aesthetic* act of reason and thus as a form of "beauty." If they want to go beyond the level of "philosophers of the letter" and deal with ideas instead of tables and registers, then philosophers must

have "as much aesthetic power as the poet." True philosophy, then, is not a philosophy of the Letter alone, but of the Spirit: an *aesthetic* philosophy.

According to the author, however, the aesthetic act is not the sole preserve of philosophers. *All* human beings should become poets, that is free, minds. For the great majority, though, it is not the *Systematic Program of German Idealism*, however exciting it may be, that will convince them. Moreover, it is not a question of convincing people, but of letting them think freely, autonomously and for themselves. This is where the importance of mythology comes in. For it is here that the narrator confides an idea "has never occurred to anyone's mind," namely the idea that this aesthetic education of humanity can only be achieved through a *new mythology*. Unlike the mythologies of antiquity, this new mythology does not have to come from on high and hold us by the hand. It must inspire, make ideas sensible, enthuse, but only in order to make people think freely. This is why it has to be a mythology *of reason*, a mythology that is at the service of ideas, given, of course, that the supreme act of reason is an aesthetic act.

This new mythology evoked by the program must be realized collectively, must affect all humanity and lead to an "eternal unity" where no spirit will be oppressed by another.[16] Because of this connecting and unifying function, the program also describes this new mythology as a "sensual religion" and as a "new religion." But once again we are talking about a *new* religion, because it is necessary to put an end to the "blind trembling of the people before its wise men and priests." In the end, everyone will be equal and free, and there will be no one—priest, monarch, or sage—who can rise above them and impose themself as a model. The new mythology will be "the last and greatest work of humanity" *by humanity itself.* The new mythology should therefore be both what constitutes the self-determining subject and what is constituted by it.

With the distance of a good two centuries, we can see that the *Systematic Program* revolves around a modern idea that will become extremely important for Nancy. It is the idea that there is no *intuitus originarius*, that is, no immediate consciousness of an idea. The "conception of *myself* as an absolutely free being" that is the primary idea according to the *Systematic Program*, is always an indirect, mediated representation, obtained by an aesthetic forming and shaping. According to Nancy, this is indeed what the German tradition has taught us more generally, as he indicates in a dialogue with Alain Badiou: "I would say that there is perhaps something that emerges with (and only with) German philosophy—something that is already present yet barely visible in Kant, and becomes increasingly manifest

in Hegel, Schelling, Hölderlin, and then Heidegger—namely a preoccupation with the idea that *the saying of philosophy*, its enunciation—even its voice, if you like—should *be present in what is said*" (*GP* 7/14, my emphasis). This is why, as the program formulates it, ideas *are only aesthetically*. What makes an idea an idea is its being presented by means of an "aesthetic power" similar to that of the poet. This is also why, for the German Romantics, the supreme act of humanity is to make a *work* of itself, or rather to realize itself as a work—the last Great Work of humanity, in both senses of the word. Of course, there are major differences in the various developments of this claim of a necessary "aestheticization," but I would say that it fundamentally motivates the thinking of German Romanticism, as well as, critically, the later philosophies that graft themselves onto Romanticism in one way or another, not only Nancy's but also Heidegger's, Derrida's, or, differently, Lacoue-Labarthe's.

According to the *Systematic Program*—not without reason named *systematic*—humanity would realize itself as a system. The aesthetic idea of myself is the basis of this "complete system of all ideas," a system that extends from the self-determining self, via a "physics on the whole," to the human work of humanity. Of course, it should be noted here that this system should not be understood as the set of tables and registers vilified by the "philosophers of the letter." It will be, instead, a system animated and vitalized—literally made alive—by the breath of the creative spirit. Although Heidegger never commented on the *Systematic Program*, his reading of Schelling's 1809 *Treatise on the Essence of Human Freedom* can shed light on what is at stake here. Heidegger describes the thought of Schelling (one of the supposed authors of the *Systematic Program*) as characterized by what he calls, following Nietzsche, the "will to system," which implies not only a systematization, but also a systematization desired, even carried out, by the subject.[17]

According to Heidegger, thinking in terms of systems follows from a series of premises that have dominated philosophical thought since Plato. Firstly, mathematics has become the main criterion of knowledge. What passes for knowledge is thus determined on the basis of mathematical criteria. In order to found knowledge, one wanted to propose a first foundation, that is to say a foundation which does not need any other foundation than itself. This self-founding foundation is finally located by Descartes in the thinking subject, the *ego cogito*, which ultimately determines what is and what is not. According to Heidegger, the greatest mistake in philosophy is to assume that the *subject* is the basis of the system he calls "*Seynsgefüge*," the jointure that

belongs to the essence of Being in general. In other words, it is through its desire or will that the subject makes the moral system possible.

This is why Nancy and Lacoue-Labarthe, in *The Literary Absolute*, largely inspired by Heidegger's reading of Schelling, speak of a "System-Subject" (*LA* 27sq/39sq) and of a "Work-Subject" (*LA* 55sq/78sq). I would say that in the program the interweaving of system thinking and subject thinking is knotted in a single phrase: that of "man's work"—a phrase that is repeated in the very last sentence with the promise of "the last and greatest work of humanity." The aesthetic act or work is not the affair of nature or of being itself, but is the one and only affair, indeed the *creation*, of *free man*. Because the demythologization of communities has led to a purely instrumental rationality, we need a re-mythologization of the world, or as Nancy says elsewhere, a "symbolization" (*CW* 53/59), in order to free the world from its rational straitjacket.[18]

But how are we to interpret the last sentence of the program? What or who is this "higher spirit sent from heaven" assisting the subject in this creation? In his lectures on new mythology, Frank indicates that this higher spirit reveals the narrator's aspiration to ground reason in a theology.[19] Although there is undoubtedly a religious element in this birth announcement of Romanticism, I would argue that the role of the higher spirit sent from heaven is in fact the thoroughly *modern*, not to say deconstructive, element of the *Systematic Program*. Indeed, if one assumes, as Frank does, that reason is grounded in a theology, the mythology of reason can hardly be called "new." However, rather than a divine entity, the modern superior spirit sent from heaven seems to be the *genius*, namely that strong spirit which creates out of nothing. That it is sent from heaven implies that the creative act is neither to be calculated nor predicted.

According to the program, the new mythology is therefore not something to be planned but is, on the contrary, in a sense, to be welcomed. It seems to require, in other words, a certain openness or receptivity to what is to come, and its possibility can perhaps only be felt in what Friedrich Schlegel will later call, in his *Dialogue on Poetry*, "signs" and "hints."[20] The turn of phrase of the very last sentence of the program thus seems to question or at least weaken the thesis put forward at the beginning of this paragraph, namely that this program links the thought of the system to the *will* of the subject. Although the creative subject is the foundation of the system of the new mythology, it is so in such a way that this mythology seems precisely to lose its founding and systematic value. This ambiguous path is pursued to the end by the Jena Romantics.

The Romantic Notion of Work

ANOTHER MODEL OF THE WORK

It can be said that Jena Romanticism further develops the idea of the new mythology referred to in the *Systematic Program*, and thus continues the modern path taken there. As in the *Systematic Program*, freedom in Jena Romanticism is understood not just as an idea of the subject, but as its *realization* and *creation*. In the same line of reasoning, beauty does not have the status of an indication of what the Romantics prefer to call the "absolute," but is its very realization, here and now, *in* and *as* the poetic act. What is already advanced in the *Systematic Program*, but is reinforced in the thinking of the Jena Romantics, is therefore the passage, or transition, from a certain idealism to a certain *realism*. It is not realism in the sense that poetry is a truthful imitation of reality, but rather in the sense that poetry itself is a form of realization, of becoming real, in the sense that enjoying something beautiful is freedom *in action*.

However, the Jena Romantics do not only intensify the aspirations of the *Systematic Program*, but they also push them to excess, thereby revealing their internal contradiction.[21] This internal contradiction is partly due to the positioning of this mode of thinking at the crossroads of great historical movements. The thinking of the authors associated with *Athenaeum* is in many ways a place of transition, a place where different important philosophical, aesthetic, and cultural traditions intersect, mix, and intertwine. This transitional character can be seen above all in their thinking about art. Broadly speaking, the Romantic poetics can be conceived both as the continuation of the poetics of the Work, that is of the "absolute work of man," of the last magnum opus of humanity evoked in the *Systematic Program*, and as the launch of a poetics that Nancy, following Blanchot, calls "unworked" (*désoeuvrée*), that is a poetics that declares the end of the completed work and rather highlights its interruption and failure.

As Nancy and Lacoue-Labarthe clearly point out, Jena Romanticism, then, "inaugurates another 'model' of the 'work.' Or rather, to be more precise, it sets the work to work in a different mode" (*LA* 39/57). What the Jena Romantics are looking for is thus another way of thinking about the work, another model, which would imply at the same time the systematic completeness of a whole that contains everything *and* a dynamic liveliness that goes beyond the rigidity of tables and registers. One could say, in terms that are not necessarily those of the Jena Romantics themselves, that they

found this other model in a shift of attention from the *work* to the *working*. Or, more precisely, they found the essence of the work in the act of its realization rather than in the realized product. Instead of focusing on the final product of the work after the poetic act, the Jena Romantics fix their attention on the process and dynamics of the act of *formation* itself. For them, the work therefore always needs to be understood as a work *in progress*.

This shift is partially prepared in the *Systematic Program*. It is nevertheless radicalized by the Jena Romantics, in the sense that the possibility of a "last and greatest" work, as proposed in the *Systematic Program*, is repeatedly problematized. Pushing, as it were, to extremes the tension signaled in the last sentence of the *Systematic Program*, Jena Romanticism seems to eternally defer the moment of completion, the moment when the last work will be reached, without giving up the aspiration to reach it. Indeed, if the essence of the poetic work lies in the process of its realization, this essence only becomes apparent if the last work has not yet been completed. In other words, if this is a matter of a will to system, what matters above all is the *will to* . . . , that is, the aspiration, the expectation, the openness. Or rather, the system is perhaps only constituted *in* this will.

Although this aspiration is not so much a weakening as a driving force of the will to system viewed with suspicion by Nancy, it also marks the beginning of a profound questioning of the idea of the work as something completed, total, even totalitarian. It puts the limits of the work under tension and transgresses them to the extent that transgression of these limits becomes itself the main purpose of the poetic work. This not only has repercussions on the reflection on poetry, but also touches on the way poetics and aesthetics interrelate. Indeed, in this Romantic transgression of the traditional model of the work, we can see a reservation towards *aesthetics* as such.[22] For this reason, the Romantic shift from the finished work to its working has set the trend for a dislocation, even a rupture, of aesthetics in the traditional sense of the word; a trend that has intensified in recent decades, with calls for a "para-,"[23] "an-,"[24] "in-,"[25] or "post-"[26] aesthetics—a trend, moreover, of which Nancy's particular poetics is also part. In all cases, it is the juxtaposition of aesthetics and politics in a totalitarian work that forms the target of criticism.

FRAGMENTARY WRITING

As Nancy and Lacoue-Labarthe point out, this questioning of the notion of the work by the Jena Romantics is mainly reflected in their practice

of fragmentary writing, a practice, we can say, that is further cultivated by Nancy in his own writings. According to Nancy and Lacoue-Labarthe, the authors of *Athenaeum* were even the first to present the fragment as a poetic *genre*, which is not to say that they were the first to write in fragments.[27] That the fragment became for the Jena Romantics the poetic genre par excellence means that it was not merely a more or less arbitrary form through which they expressed their ideas, but as it were the very heart, the exemplary expression of these ideas, or as Nancy and Lacoue-Labarthe say: "To an even greater extent than the 'genre' of theoretical romanticism, the fragment is considered its incarnation, the most distinctive mark of its originality, or the sign of its radical modernity" (*LA* 39–40/58).[28] In other words, it is the fragment that is the other "model" of the work, the model that sets the work to work in a different mode.[29]

The fragments published in the *Athenaeum* journal—in general and on average composed of five sentences, although there are also fragments that cover several pages or, on the contrary, a single sentence—are very similar to sayings or aphorisms, given the assurance of their tone and the general absence of arguments. If one examines the fragmentary writing of the Jena Romantics in greater depth, there is, according to Nancy and Lacoue-Labarthe, nevertheless a crucial aspect that stands out: The different fragments do not form a kaleidoscopic whole of parts that are adequately entangled with each other. Rather, it is a conflicting and irreducibly heterogeneous constellation of fragments that seem to contradict and intertwine differently with each new reading.

One obvious explanation for this irreducible heterogeneity could be that the fragments—at least those published anonymously under the name "Athenaeum"—are by different authors. Although anonymity was a criterion and even a condition of possibility for the Romantic ideal of *symphilosophy* or *sympoesy*—thought or poetry as a collective and shared project—we must nevertheless seek a deeper explanation.[30] What the set of fragments in the *Athenaeum* journal shows is that its unity or synthesis is found *outside* their "letter alone," in the formation or reading of the co-presence of the fragments. As Nancy and Lacoue-Labarthe say: "[T]o write the fragment is to write fragments" (*LA* 43–44/64). Fragmentary works are a work in progress precisely because the synthesis of the fragments is never given, because it is never *there*, but always elsewhere. Fragmentary writing, then, is only its promise, but, according to the equivocal tension proper to the will to system, also its realization.

From Ergon to Organicity

Relatedly, the uniqueness of the Jena Romantics' poetics is situated in its "biological" sense, as it involves the process of generation, birth, and pro-creation that, as we will see, also plays a key role in Nancy's ontological poetics. The crucial term here is *organicity*.[31] To say that poetry is organic and that the poetic work is an organism is to compare it to a living body, to something that develops from a certain germinating power. Like the author of the *Systematic Program*, the Jena Romantics thus contrast the organic with the mechanical, which, in their view, largely dominates life and thought. By comparing poetry or the poem to an organism, the Jena Romantics not only emphasize the formative character of the work, but also distance themselves from the dominant view in which the work of art is conceived as a secondary *imitation* of reality. On the contrary, as said, they emphasize that poetry is the name given to a *realization*.

As Nancy and Lacoue-Labarthe repeatedly point out, Romantic poetry is above all a matter of *self*-realization or *self*-creation, or in the terms of the *Athenaeum* journal: "In the ego, all things are created organically and everything has its proper place" (*Ath.* 338). According to the Jena Roman-tics, the reason why this self-creation thus far remained mainly an ideal was that most people lacked the creative force: "[T]hey still lack the strength to procreate them out of their own selves" (*Ath.* 352). In preferring the luxury of an external support, they ignore the fact that "moral man rotates around his axis freely by means of his *own* power." But in thinking that they "have discovered the point outside earth that only a mathematician should try to find . . . they have lost the earth itself" (*Ath.* 355). These formulations emphasize that poetry, for the Jena Romantics, is not a representation of nature, but is in a sense itself nature, natural. Like living organisms, it is a self-generating creativity. Or more precisely, poetry, according to the Jena Romantics, does not imitate nature, but it imitates, so to speak, the (self)productivity of nature.[32]

It is in in line with this organic character of the Romantic work that we must understand the description of poetry, in the famous *Athenaeum* fragment 116, as "progressive universal poetry." Here is the beginning of this long fragment: "Romantic poetry is a progressive, universal poetry. Its aim isn't merely to reunite all the separate species of poetry and put poetry in touch with philosophy and rhetoric. It tries to and should mix and fuse poetry and prose, inspiration and criticism, the poetry of art and the

poetry of nature; and make poetry lively and sociable, and life and society poetical" (*Ath.* 116). The progressiveness of Romantic poetry stems from the fact that its "identity" consists above all in an activity, a gathering and combining activity that has no end, as the rest of the fragment indicates: "The romantic kind of poetry is still in the state of becoming; that, in fact, is its real essence: that it should forever be becoming and never be perfected" (*Ath.* 116). As is the case with all organisms, "there is no absolute fulfillment except in death" (*AL* 291).

Romantic poetry, then, is the expression of the productive and creative power of nature itself, and for this reason, it is infinite and universal. Conversely, one could say that nature itself is poetic. The alternative to the mechanical view of nature and community sought by the *Systematic Program* in the self-determination of the creative spirit is thus deepened and enhanced here and the identification of poetry and nature is the center around which the entire poetics of Jena Romanticism revolves, as *Athenaeum* fragment 43 puts it: "[F]rom this we can deduce equally well that man is by nature a poet, and that there is a natural poetry, or vice versa" (*Ath.* 430). This makes the poetry of poets nothing more than the continuation of the original poetry already present in nature—of that what Nancy thinks of as a "poetic ontology"—a "poetry without form or consciousness that palpitates in plants, radiates in light, smiles in the child, sparks in the flower of youth, blazes in the loving heart of women" (*AL* 290) as Friedrich Schlegel has it in his *Dialogue on Poetry*.

The Romantic Work as a Model Without Model

From Product to Production

So, if it is especially the new model of the poetic "work" that Nancy takes from Jena Romanticism, let us have a closer look at what it consists of. Since the new model of the poetic work proposed by the Jena Romantics is that of a work in progress, of an infinite formation or shaping, it is perhaps better to speak—as Nancy and Lacoue-Labarthe suggest—of *poiesis* rather than of poetry, supposing that "[t]he poietic is not so much the work as that which works, not so much the organon as that which organizes. This is where romanticism aims at the heart and inmost depths . . . of the individual and the System: always *poiesis* or, to give at least an equivalent, always production" (*LA* 48–49/69).[33] In other words, the Romantic fragmentary

work is strictly speaking not the formation of a work, but the formation *of the process of formation itself.* But how does the work *not* imply a halt, an immobilization of this process, and thus its denial or betrayal? How can we isolate a moment or an instant from this infinite flow, while at the same time expressing its infinity? In other words, what is the relationship between the work and its endless working?

This dilemma has resulted in the appearance of an exemplary creature, one of the most peculiar inhabitants of the philosophical zoological garden: the hedgehog. It appears in the other famous fragment of *Athenaeum*, fragment 206. Given that the Jena Romantics emphasize the necessarily progressive or unfinished nature of fragmentary poetry, how then are we to understand this famous fragment: "A fragment, like a miniature work of art, has to be entirely isolated from the surrounding world and be *complete in itself* like a hedgehog" (*Ath.* 206, my emphasis, translation modified)? If poetry is always in the process of becoming and never completed, how could it consist of, or give birth to, a fragment that is complete in itself like a hedgehog? The ambiguity of Jena's Romanticism, with its two faces—modern and conservative—can be found in the two opposing logics of the *Athenaeum* fragments 116 and 206. In the first, there is the indication of Romantic poetry as universal progressive poetry, which develops organically without ever reaching its end. A closure on itself seems impossible, because the activity of poetry—the activity that *is* poetry—consists precisely in a constantly renewed relation with what it is not (philosophy, rhetoric, etc.), and therefore implies rather a dispersion or an opening than a closure on itself.

On the other hand, however, there is the image of the hedgehog, which does indeed seem to imply such a closure. Being "complete in itself," the fragment is in itself a totally detached "miniature work of art." This idea is further reinforced by the notion of "microcosm," which recurs several times in the writings of Jena Romanticism. Undoubtedly, these characterizations serve to underline the autonomy of the poetic work, the fact that it moves freely, by its own force and without relying on external principles. But if a single fragment is already a miniature work of art, why do the Jena Romantics speak of fragments in the plural and write in fragments? Or put more directly, in what sense is a fragment completed and detached from everything, still a *fragment?* What the Romantic poetics demands is thus a new reflection on the relationship between partiality and totality, between finitude and infinity, between form and non-form, and by extension, between fixity and fluidity.

As the *Systematic Program* also hinted, the key to this relationship lies in the Romantic idea of the "self," which proves capable of being

both closed in on itself and in relation to what it is not, both closure and openness. Or more precisely, the solution lies rather in the concept of the "individual" as suggested, for the moment still enigmatically, by *Athenaeum* fragment 415: "Whoever conceives of poetry or philosophy as *individuals* has a feeling for them" (*Ath.* 415, my emphasis).[34] The importance of the concept of the individual is also emphasized by Nancy and Lacoue-Labarthe in their brief commentary on *Athenaeum* fragment 206, which they place in a broader philosophical development: "To borrow a term from a later tradition not unrelated to romanticism, that of Schopenhauer and Nietzsche, one is tempted to say that the essence of the fragment is *individuation*" (*LA* 43/63, my emphasis). Without addressing the question of the heritage of Romanticism in Schopenhauer or Nietzsche, we can say that *individuation* is indeed the shaping of the infinite process of formation.

But what is to be understood by this individuation, by the individual or individuality? Returning to *Athenaeum* fragment 116, we read that poetry "exists only to characterize poetical individuals of all sorts" (*Ath.* 116). Given the opening lines of the fragment, which indicate that the activity of poetry is to bring together different genres and domains, the characterization of poetic individualities then seems to revert to the activity of bringing together or touching of heterogeneous elements. This activity is not unique in the sense that it is to be achieved once and for all: Like poetry, it is progressive, eternally to become and never to be achieved. The poetic individuality of which Nancy and Lacoue-Labarthe speak, the becoming "self" of a self, so to speak, thus seems to require the touch of a non-self. The "poetical individuals" evoked in fragment 116 can be born only in and as the plural co-existence of heterogeneous elements, as is indeed expressed in *Athenaeum* fragment 121:

> In vain did individuals express the ideal of their species completely, if the species themselves, strictly and sharply isolated, weren't freely surrendered, as it were, to their originality. But to transport oneself arbitrarily now into this, now into that sphere, as if into another world, not merely with one's reason and imagination, but with one's whole soul; to freely relinquish first one and then another part of one's being, and confine oneself entirely to a third; to seek and find now in this, now in that individual the be-all and end-all of existence, and intentionally forget everyone else: of this only a mind is capable that contains within itself simultaneously a plurality of minds and a whole

system of persons, and in whose inner being the universe which,
as they say, should germinate in every monad, has grown to
fullness and maturity. (*Ath.* 121)

Romantic poetry—and this is the reason why this poetry is always a matter
of "community" as we shall see—does not stem from an isolated individual,
nor is it the expression of one, but is the expression of the plurality of
humanity and the universe.

THE ART OF COMBINING AND RELATING

Retranslating and expanding this structure, one could say that the "individ-
ualized self" or "poetic individuation" produced by fragmentary poetry is
not a single, fixed substance or identity, but is first of all a *relation*.[35] The
self-forming organic in-dividual must be, precisely in order to be able to
form itself organically, in a sense divided within itself, because it is always
in relation, with others and with itself. This also explains why the poetic
self—of which the hedgehog is the prototype—can be complete, but never
self-sufficient. The center of the hedgehog, "its axis," is only formed by
exposing itself, to use this key word of Nancy's ontology. As it is the case
for the heterogeneous whole of the fragments of the *Athenaeum* journal,
the unifying center is for this reason always *outside*. And the fragments,
consequently, can only express "a few ideas pointing toward the heart of
things" (*Id.* 155).

Significantly, then, the co-existence or co-presence of the parts does
not amount to a whole where the parts would exist autonomously next to
each other, and where they are woven into a certain constellation without
changing themselves, as in a kaleidoscope. On the contrary, it is a whole
where the parts knot, untie, and knot again freely, and where this knotting
in fact changes and, as we could say in Nancyan terms, *intrudes* the parts,
and thus the whole.[36] The whole of the fragments, in other words, is thus
a com-position, a positing together, and this could designate the main functioning of what the Jena Romantics call the "organic" or even sometimes
the "chemical" nature of poetry, which, as we have seen, inevitably results in
a *plurality* of fragments, in the fact that "to write the fragment is to write
fragments" (*LA* 43–44/64).[37]

The necessity of this com-position, of the togetherness of this "*cum*," for
Romantic poetry, the *poiein*, can also be glimpsed in the already mentioned
Romantic ideal of *sympoesy* or *symphilosophy*. True philosophy, that is to say

"poeticized" philosophy, does not occur through the path of mechanical deduction or dry demonstration of facts, but through the path of exchange, mixture, dialogue, and mutual inspiration. The result of such a mixture is what the Jena Romantics call *Witz*, an untranslatable word meaning "wit" or "wordplay," that appears regularly in the texts of the Jena Romantics and more generally indicates the sudden and inventive combination of heterogeneous things that captures Nancy's special attention in his early philosophical works.[38] In one of his *Critical Fragments*, Friedrich Schlegel offers us the following description: "A witty idea is a disintegration of spiritual substances which, before being suddenly separated, must have been thoroughly mixed. The imagination must first be satiated with all sorts of life before one can electrify it with the friction of free social intercourse so that the slightest friendly or hostile touch can elicit brilliant sparks and lustrous rays—or smashing thunderbolts" (*Crit.* 34).[39] The "electrifying" character of the *Witz* underlines once again the "chemical" nature of the universal and progressive poetry thematized by the Jena Romantics. According to them, this capacity of the *Witz* is exemplified in the literary genre of the *novel*, as the novel can bring together highly heterogeneous genres, such as dialogue, poem, story, essay, or song, within a single narrative stream. The synthesis of all these elements is not in the totality of the finished work, but in "the relation of the whole composition to a unity higher than that of the letter—which it does and can often disregard—thanks to the connection of ideas, thanks to a spiritual central point" (*LA* 327).[40]

In his *Dialogue on Poetry*—published in the third volume of the *Athenaeum* journal—Friedrich Schlegel not only thematizes the status of the novel, but also puts it into practice. Moreover, this dialogue is one of the most direct testimonies of the lively intellectual friendship that developed in Jena at the turn of the century. In fact, the *Dialogue on Poetry* is above all a conversation between the Schlegel brothers and their friends who, under different names, discuss the role that poetry could play in their time.[41] This conversation consists of long dialogues between the characters, interrupted by several lectures, including "Ludoviko's" speech entitled "Rede über die Mythologie" [Discourse on Mythology], to which we shall return, and a lecture called "Brief über den Roman" [Letter on the Novel].[42]

Although the idea of the novel discussed in the "Brief über den Roman" is no longer mysterious to us, it was to the Jena Romantics. In those days, there was no such genre, and the Romantics would have had to go back to the Greek epic to invent this literary genre they would call "novel." As said, what they were inventing, however, was not so much a genre as a loosely

defined literary form that could contain and bring together all genres. Unlike existing literary genres such as the fairy tale or the verse poem, the novel has no fixed characteristics, and is rather characterized by an absence of characteristics. The question "What is a novel?" can, according to Friedrich Schlegel, therefore only be answered tautologically: A novel is a novel.

The novel, then, is not a specific literary genre but the "element of poetry" itself, the element that determines how a work is made: not according to an external principle, but by the *ars combinatoria* of poetry itself, this sudden, momentary confrontation of heterogeneous elements that never allows itself to be fixed in a form, but on the contrary undoes each form. That not only the reflection on this formless formation, but also its *praxis*, is an important thread in Nancy's thought, too, is demonstrated by the philosophical-literary texts collected in his *Expectation: Philosophy, Literature,* which span thirty-five years and are almost all inspired by the Romantic style.

In Medias Res

As we have seen, the organic nature of Romantic writing lies not only in its eternal becoming, but also in the fact that it is not an imitation of a model, but something that occurs according to a germinating power of its own. Because of the absence of an external principle, it is impossible to describe or teach Romantic poetry in a neutral or objective way. Romantic poetry can only be understood—and this is at the heart of the idea of literary *criticism* as Nancy and Lacoue-Labarthe also state in the chapter called "Criticism" of *The Literary Absolute*—by *(re)producing* it: "The function of criticism, people say, is to educate one's readers! Whoever wants to be educated, let him educate himself. This is rude: but it can't be helped" (*Crit.* 86).

In other words, to grasp or understand the proper law of Romantic poetry is not done by taking it as a given object whose characteristics could be described, but by reproducing, by putting into action the self-productivity that forms its essence. It is for this reason that Friedrich Schlegel begins his *Dialogue on Poetry* with the paradoxical observation that one *cannot speak about* poetry, or more precisely—as becomes clear in reading the context of this phrase—that one can one can only do so *in poetry*: "Just as life itself has sprung from the depths . . . , so it is, of itself, that poetry blossoms, engendered by the original invisible force of humanity, when the warm ray of the divine sun touches it and fertilizes it. Only contours and colors can, by recomposing the form, express how man is formed; and in the same way, in truth, one could speak about poetry only in poetry" (*AL* 90).

If a reflection on Romantic poetry can only be expressed in poetic form, the result is that art and theory are indistinguishable. This crucial idea of Jena Romanticism is expressed even more clearly in fragment 117 of the *Critical Fragments*: "Poetry can only be criticized by way of poetry. A critical judgment of an artistic production has no civil rights in the realm of art if it isn't itself a work of art" (*Crit.* 117). Crucially, it is the work itself that defines the laws by which it is formed. With no objective criteria or external principles, then, Romantic poetry unfolds upon itself, and is therefore essentially *reflexive*: it is both poetry and poetry of poetry. In other words, every poetic utterance, whatever its subject, is always *also* the utterance of the law of poetry itself, or, as *Athenaeum* fragment 238 puts it, "[i]n all its descriptions, this poetry should describe itself, and always be simultaneously poetry and the poetry of poetry" (*Ath.* 238).

Importantly, this unfolding of poetry on itself is not only a reflexive process, but also an infinite one, a process that generates itself anew, each and every time. So, it is not a question of poetry grasping its own reflected image once and for all, but of a multiplied reflection "in an endless succession of mirrors" (*Ath.* 116). Because the poetic organism has no external principle to direct it in this or that direction, or to determine its end, it never ceases to engender and, in so doing, to present itself. The absence of an external principle means that Romantic poetry is, as we have already seen, *progressive*. As in a palace of mirrors, each presentation evokes others, and themselves in turn, making it impossible to fix a single image, or to attribute an exemplary or final value to it.

The consequence of this infinite reflexivity of Romantic poetry is that it is always in a state of transition, that it is always on the way, *in medias res* as Nancy would say, *between*, at the midpoint, in the meantime, as the passage in fragment 116 preceding the metaphor of the series of mirrors indicates: "And it [Romantic poetry, AvR] can also—more than any other form—hover at the midpoint between the portrayed and the portrayer, free of all real and ideal self-interest, on the wings of poetic reflection, and can raise that reflection again and again to a higher power, can multiply it in an endless succession of mirrors" (*Ath.* 116).[43] This situation of transition, of the intermediate, implies that one never arrives at the last word—or for that matter at the last Great Work of humanity. Poetry is always a *means* of reflection—in the two possible senses of the word, that is to say the means by which thought thinks itself and its milieu, its meantime.[44]

The fact that Romantic poetry always happens *in medias res* is not unrelated to its explicitly *prosaic* character. As has been pointed out not

only by Nancy and Lacoue-Labarthe, but also by Benjamin and Heidegger, there is a tendency inherent in Romantic thought which is indeed that of a "prosaization," of a becoming sober, mundane, even profane of poetry, which implies an important change in poetry's relation to the ideal. A "prosaic" poetry is not the sensible expression of a transcendent idea or truth, but is, so to speak, its own truth—and is for this reason, as Nancy repeatedly points out, ultimately "*tautegorical*."[45] Romantic poetry is not the sensory shaping of an idea or truth that transcends this sensibility, but the emergence of this idea or truth in and from this very sensibility. In this way, the Jena Romantics broke with the tenacious idea of the poet as messenger of the divine. Poetry, for them, is another word for the sensible which forms itself, not on the basis of an idea or model that precedes and exceeds it, but by detaching itself, in a folding and refolding movement, from itself into itself—in short, another word for the *individuation* of a self, which is divided in itself, a self that is, therefore, in relation to itself.

Romantic Politics

POETRY AS A DEMOCRATIC MODEL

As we will see, Nancy draws clear political consequences from the Romantic view on poetry. Indeed, as the last words of fragment 117 of the *Critical Fragments* indicate: "A critical judgment of an artistic production has no *civil rights* in the realm [*Reich*] of art if it isn't itself a work of art" (*Crit.* 117). More precisely, from a political point of view the idea of poetry of the Jena Romantics is essentially *republican*: "Poetry is republican speech: a speech which is its own law and end unto itself, and in which all the parts are free citizens and have the right to vote" (*Crit.* 65).[46] Just as in poetry, where the law is imposed by the work on itself and only on itself, in a republic the law is not imposed from above, but sovereignly imposed by the "body" of the people on itself.

The reason why the Jena Romantics emphasize the organicity of self-formation is thus not only poetic or philosophical in nature, but is also motivated by certain political ideas. This convergence of the poetic and the political is indeed explicitly underlined by the Jena Romantics, whose appeal to a new mythology seems above all to be inspired by a deep dissatisfaction with the political situation. By radicalizing the idea of the self-determining Ego, some Romantics even oppose the idea of the state as such, as is also

the case in the *Systematic Program*.[47] Most of them, however, seek to develop a political form compatible with the ideal of the self-formation of a people.

As already indicated, denouncing the terror that accompanied the French Revolution, the Jena Romantics recoil from a solely political revolution. Although it was a revolution of the people, that is, a bottom-up event, the French Revolution went hand in hand with various forms of enforced and imposed power. In order for citizens to be truly free and to decide for themselves a general and gradual forming of each individual *as* individual is necessary according to the Jena Romantics, that is, an *aesthetic* formation, a *Bildung* as one would say in German. One of the first pleas for this general formation was Schiller's famous *Letters on the Aesthetic Education of Man* (1793/1794), which dates from even before the *Systematic Program*. Although the idea of *Bildung* is conceived differently by each of the Romantics, they agree upon the fact that it should be a matter of adopting a certain both non-imposing and non-serving attitude. According to the Jena Romantics, this attitude is the artist's attitude, and for this reason all citizens should become artists in a sense: "The artist should have as little desire to rule as to serve. He can only create, do nothing but create, and so help the state only by making rulers and servants, and by exalting politicians and economists into artists" (*Id.* 54).

Relatedly, an important aspect of the self-determining political body is that it can ultimately only be a *global* body. Only when there is a free exchange of ideas and means between *all* parties, and when citizens are not obliged to confine themselves within national borders, can a republic effectively be called "organic." This Romantic idea of the world republic should however not be too easily characterized as utopian. As LeBlanc et al. also argue in *La forme poétique du monde* [The Poetic Form of The World], the political ideal of the Jena Romantics must be viewed from a perspective that is no longer linear, but goes *beyond* the usual temporal and spatial schemes.[48] What the Jena Romantics designate repeatedly under the term "republican" is not an *elsewhere* to be reached in a near or distant future, but designates, according to the model of universal progressive poetry, the state of an eternal becoming whose formless shape is that of incessant transformation.

This "poetic form of the world," as LeBlanc et al. point out with reference to the title of their study, "appears when the individual and the whole community are able to develop a living thought, infinitely mobile, a thought that consists in knowing how to continuously 'reform' or transform the real. The form itself is fluctuating, and to think freely is precisely to romanticize, that is to say, to continually offer new conceptual combinations likely to

keep the mind alert."[49] If—and now we are back at the exact point where the Jena Romantics enter into discussion with the *Systematic Program*—the *new* mythology is the last Great Work of humanity, then it is so only if we understand this work as infinitely mobile, that is, as a *working* that never ends and can, for this reason, never be completed.

From Utopianism to a New Form of Realism

Here, in this combination of political and poetic ideas, we see the contours of the Jena Romantic's view on myth that paves the way for Nancy's "reassertion" of the power of myth. What, then, are the consequences of the Jena Romantics' transformation of the idea of the poetic work for the notion of myth? How are we to understand the new mythology they desire? This brings us to the third part of Friedrich Schlegel's *Dialogue on Poetry* published in the *Athenaeum* journal. Four years after the *Systematic Program*, Schlegel's "Rede über die Mythologie" once again calls for a new mythology, and once again in a largely programmatic way. The central thesis of this "discourse on mythology," proclaimed from the mouth of "Ludoviko," is the following: "I affirm that our poetry lacks *this center which was mythology for the Ancients*, and that all the essential in which the modern poetic art yields it to the ancient one holds in these words: *we do not have a mythology*" (*AL* 311–12, my emphasis). Whereas in antiquity "all poems are linked to each other, weave in organically and ultimately form one unified whole" (*AL* 312), modern poetry is, according to Schlegel, empty, ephemeral, and lacks the creative spirit that can serve as an infinite formative force. It has no real formative power, let alone the capacity to educate humanity. What we therefore need, according to "Ludoviko," is a *new* mythology that must be extracted "from the depths of the *mind*" (*AL* 312, my emphasis).

Apparently, the supposed readers doubt the possibility of such a mythology, for Friedrich Schlegel asks them to take this idea seriously and to "exclude disbelief." Certainly, he adds, we lack definite proof of the possibility of such mythological poetry. But in his view, there is nevertheless a remarkable indication. This indication is idealist philosophy: "If it is possible that a new mythology elaborates, as it were out of itself, from the only interior depth of the spirit, then we will find in the great phenomenon of our times, in idealism, a remarkable indication and an admirable confirmation of what we are looking for!" (*AL* 312).[50] This remark casts a clearer light on the relationship between Romanticism and German idealism as regards the project of a new mythology. As we have seen, the *Systematic*

Program of German Idealism was not only the program of German idealism but also of its *overcoming*, since it situates *in* idealism the possibility of a renewed *mythology*, that is, of the *realization* of this idealism. And for this to happen, we need, according to Friedrich Schlegel, not just idealism, but a *new realism*: "Idealism, whatever its form, must somehow come out of itself, in order to be able to come back into itself and remain what it is. That is why an, equally unlimited, *new realism* should, and will, be born out of its womb, and why idealism not only serves as an example to new mythology in its mode of engendering, but goes as far as indirectly becoming its source" (*AL* 313, my emphasis). Just as we need a mythology of *reason*, then, so we need a realism of *ideas*.

This coupling of idealism with realism involves another one that will become central to Nancy's own work, namely that of philosophy with poetry. Because "realism can never again appear in the form of *philosophy*, nor in the form of a *system*," the "organ" proper to this realization can only be *poetry* according to Friedrich Schlegel (*AL* 314, my emphasis). A system, or at least a non-poetic philosophical system, is not enough for a new mythology to emerge: poetry, and poetry alone, is capable of expressing, at the highest level, the unifying force common to all that is.

According to the narrator of "Rede über die Mythologie," one of the preparers of this mythological "new realism" is Spinoza, if we are at least careful not to place Spinoza's system on the "noble throne of *knowledge*" (*AL* 314, my emphasis). The strength of Spinoza's philosophy, which is also dear to Nancy, is that it deliberately situates itself in the penumbra of poetry, where things cannot be clearly distinguished, where passion and enthusiasm reign, and where things dare to stand up to the philosophical desire to overexpose and embellish them with "the bellicose paraphernalia of the system" (*AL* 314). In this way, Spinoza's philosophy has drawn our attention to what a fine mythology should do: make visible and spiritually sensible that which eternally eludes consciousness and the philosophical will to system. Spinoza's philosophy could thus be conceived, as what the *Systematic Program* announced as a "physics on the whole," a physics with the wings of poetry.

In contrast to the system builders who place themselves on the noble throne of knowledge, well sheltered from the chaos of sensible nature, the creators of mythology want to capture nature in the form of a work of art or more precisely a "work of art of *nature*" where everything "is relation and metamorphosis, conformation and transformation" and where nature itself is "its process, internal life and method" (*AL* 215). What is important, then, in

the idea of the new mythology elaborated by the Jena Romantics—and what, as we shall see, is largely ignored by Nancy and Lacoue-Labarthe—is the fact that this mythology is not only a mythology of ideas, an *idealist* mythology, but must be, for this very reason, a *realist* mythology grafted onto the model of nature itself, onto the organic, plural, and fragmentary *poiesis*. Anticipating what is to come, we could already say that Nancy, in his own poetics, pursues this very path, be it by *criticizing* Jena Romanticism, and proposes what might be called an extreme poetic realism where nature, the *res* itself, is poetic. In this attempt to distance himself from Jena Romanticism, Nancy describes this poetic reality or real poetry as "mythical" rather than "mythological."

A System Without a System

What is clear, in any case, is that Jena Romanticism proposes a shift in the thinking of the *system*, a shift that is absolutely modern and that forms the indispensable preparation for Nancy's own ontological poetics. Although the Jena Romantics frequently evoke the notion of "system," it is, as we have just seen, a system without a given center or fixed, univocal coordinates. In other words, the Romantic system, if there is one, does not take the form of a *logic* as such. Better still, the Jena Romantics consider "logic" to be the opposite of philosophy and poetry, as indicated, for example, in *Athenaeum* fragment 91: "Logic is neither the preface, nor the instrument, nor the formula, nor an episode of philosophy. It is, rather, a coordinated pragmatic science opposed to poetry and to ethics and deriving from the demand for a positive truth and the premise of the possibility of a system" (*Ath.* 91). The Romantic system, and by extension the new constructed mythology, is thus not a means of classification and categorization; it is, on the contrary, a *sus-tema*, syn-thesis, sym-poetry, that is, a matter of mixture and combination. If we dissect the whole of life scientifically, say the Romantics, we are sure to lose its "inner life," which is precisely what makes the whole a whole. The Romantic system is therefore always an organic whole, structured by its own processes of relation and metamorphosis, of conformation and transformation. With Frederick Beiser we could say that the Jena Romantics therefore propose a "non-foundationalist, holistic and historical" system of thought,[51] or even more radically a "system" or "logic" that proliferates in all directions like the dissemination or rhizomatic proliferation we know of thinkers like Derrida or Deleuze.

This questioning of an unconditional, invariable, foundational principle leads to what is one of the most characteristic aspects of Jena Romantic

thought: *irony*. Irony, as expressed in fragment 69 of the *Ideas* "is the clear consciousness of eternal agility, of an infinitely teeming chaos" (*Id.* 69). This important role attributed to irony, then, first and foremost serves to *destabilize* every system: "[F]or wherever philosophy appears in oral or written dialogues—and is not simply confined into rigid systems—there irony should be asked for and provided" (*Crit.* 42). Using the instrument of irony, poets or philosopher-poets can guard against proposing a false unity, or to put it more correctly, can demonstrate their awareness of the risk of proposing a false unity. It is through irony, in the final analysis, that a statement is interrupted, relativized, and opens itself up to an infinite number of other possible perspectives. Irony is therefore the medicine against the seriousness, audacity, and hubris of idealism.

Importantly, then, the Jena Romantics realize that their new mythology is a *construction*, a construction moreover that gives itself its own rules instead of receiving them, and that cannot have the dubious political tendency, revealed in the introduction, to conceal its ureal and hypothetical character by passing it off as an unshakable transcendental foundation. What they emphasize is, on the one hand, that we need mythology precisely in order to present ourselves as a "we," and, on the other, that the legitimizing function of myth does not lie in the content of the myth, but in the mythic act itself, which is an ongoing poetic act.

The Reverse Side of Romanticism (*Nancy, Lacoue-Labarthe*)

Nancy's Warning

What characterizes Romantic mythology is, to sum up the preceding sections in a nutshell, its *organic, dynamic,* and necessarily *unfinished* form, as well as its new form of *realism*. Not surprisingly, then, Jena Romanticism is generally conceived of as the origin of all the goods of modernity. So why did Nancy and Lacoue-Labarthe ultimately want to distance themselves from Jena Romanticism in *The Literary Absolute*? It is hard to present Nancy and Lacoue-Labarthe's line of reasoning in all its finesse. I will focus on their main argument, namely their interpretation of the key notion of Jena Romanticism: the *organon*, that is, the "work." Asserting the organic and fragmentary character of Romantic poetry, Nancy and Lacoue-Labarthe indicate that the fragmentary Romantic work is ultimately conceived as a *seed*, that is, as a *germ* that already contains within itself all that it will

become. Nancy and Lacoue-Labarthe deduce that "[f]ragmentation is not, then, a *dissemination* but is rather the dispersal that leads to fertilization and future harvests. The genre of the fragment is the genre of *generation*" (*LA* 49/70, my emphasis).

According to Nancy and Lacoue-Labarthe the notions of "seed" and "generation" thus indicate that the progressive becoming of the fragmentary poetry of Jena Romanticism is not an infinite proliferation without direction, but a development with a certain finality: an origin where everything is already given as well as an end where everything will be realized. According to Nancy and Lacoue-Labarthe, Romantic poetry is always stretched between these two poles, oscillating between recollection and presentiment. What is more, the "eternal becoming" characteristic of Romantic poetry can only be realized insofar as these two poles remain out of reach. The finality of Romantic poetry thus lies according to Nancy and Lacoue-Labarthe in what they call "completion," which indicates "simultaneously the absolutization of the Absolute, a fulfillment of every work in its Work, and the disparity, the surplus, the almost unaccountable excess of one more completion, of a singular remainder of completion" (*LA* 113/386). Such a focus on completion or infinite perfection obviously requires that the final point is never to be reached, because at that moment a further perfection would no longer be possible.

Even if, as we have seen, the Romantic fragmentary *poiein* is an organic process that resists calculable programming, it is, according to Nancy and Lacoue-Labarthe, thus nonetheless a *project*, a project that consists in "the *immediate* projection of what it nonetheless incompletes" (*LA* 43/63).[52] When Nancy and Lacoue-Labarthe say that Jena Romanticism "puts the *work* into action *in a different mode*," they mean to emphasize two things. Firstly, they point out that Jena Romanticism broke with the idea of the work as a finished and complete form, with the idea of a form that contains everything, or conversely, with the idea of a whole that gives itself in a single form. Secondly, they point out that it is still, however, a question of a putting to work of the *work*. The "Romantic origin" deplored and desired in Romantic poetry is, according to Nancy and Lacoue-Labarthe, "the always-already-lost of the Organon" (*LA* 50/72), the all-encompassing Work with a capital *W*. Here, then, there is a direct link between the aspirations of Jena Romanticism and those of *The Oldest Systematic Program of German Idealism*.

What is important, however, is that the "last and greatest work of humanity" referred to in the *Systematic Program* is given a negative form

by the Jena Romantics. It is, in other words, the *absence* of this last work that is posed in and through fragmentary writing, according to Nancy and Lacoue-Labarthe: "The work in this sense is absent from works—and fragmentation is *also* always the sign of this absence. But this sign is at least ambivalent, according to the constant logic of this type of thought, whose model is negative theology. The empty place that a garland of fragments surrounds is a precise drawing of the contours of the Work" (*LA* 46–47/67).

Contrary to what has been pointed out in the above, the Romantic *organon* is thus not, according to Nancy and Lacoue-Labarthe, a proliferation without direction, but rather the growth of what they call a "seminal system" with a direction, or as they prefer to say, with a *center* (*LA* 50/71). It is not only that the fragments are co-present, but also that they are held together by a form *drawn in negative* in, or as, their center. As Nancy and Lacoue-Labarthe point out, "the 'system of fragments'" (*Ath.* 77) is a precise drawing, using the traits of its fragmentary configuration, of the contours of the Work of art, which are no doubt external but nonetheless its own *contours*, its absolute Physiognomy" (*LA* 47/68). The encircled center is itself mainly empty, because it is only because of this emptiness that it can continue to attract. This is why the fragments are never a presentation of something present, but indeed always, as *Athenaeum* fragment 22 puts it, "fragments of the future" (*Ath.* 22).

The Unsurpassable Horizon of Romanticism

Since this negative configuration of Romantic poetry as described by Nancy and Lacoue-Labarthe means that the future totality, though absent, is in a sense already outlined in the work, they conclude that Jena Romanticism is in essence a form of Hegelian idealist thought. "[A]t the risk of a slight exaggeration," they remark, "one could say that art, the work, and the artist [for Jena Romanticism, AvR], are in this perspective what the System, the Concept, and the philosopher himself . . . are in the Hegelian perspective" (*LA* 77/203). What Nancy and Lacoue-Labarthe call the "seminal system" of the Romantic organon thus reveals a conception of art, the work, and the artist that, in their view, is not principally distinguishable from idealist thought, which presupposes a truth accessible in its very infinity. Nancy and Lacoue-Labarthe therefore repeatedly emphasize: German idealism is the unsurpassable horizon of German Romanticism, Jena Romanticism is developed against the horizon of German idealism, only freeing a place for itself *in* German idealism (*LA* 34/49).

More precisely, this unsurpassable horizon is built on what Nancy and Lacoue-Labarthe call an *eidaesthetics*. In other words, the Jena Romantics combined their aesthetics, that is, their thinking about sensible presentation, with an *eidetics*, a thinking about distinctive form, essence (*eidos*). More specifically, they suggest that the Jena Romantics are thus to be placed in the long aesthetic tradition that, since Plato, has been based on an "eidetic" definition of the beautiful in which *eidos* is the form in which being appears and makes itself seen.[53] In spite of their attempts to free themselves from this horizon, to empty, to deform, and to infinitize this form, the Jena Romantics did not succeed, according to Nancy and Lacoue-Labarthe, to detach themselves from this tradition.

With this interpretation of the "seminal system" Nancy and Lacoue-Labarthe place themselves in line with Heidegger's already mentioned analysis of Schelling in his *Schelling's Treatise on the Essence of Human Freedom*, in which Heidegger presents Schelling as the "last of the metaphysicians." Indeed, Nancy and Lacoue-Labarthe suggest that "[f]or the problematic of the System in speculative idealism, see Heidegger's *Schelling* 14–61, which from this perspective is clearly the best possible commentary on the text that concerns us here [*The Oldest Systematic Program of German Idealism*, AvR]" (*LA* 132n5/46n1). In fact, although Nancy and Lacoue-Labarthe refer to Heidegger's analysis of the problematic of the system in German *idealism*, it is clear that Heidegger's book was also a strong inspiration for their analysis of the system in German *Romanticism*, and more specifically in Jena Romanticism, as they point out below: "We refer here to the entirety of Heidegger's crucial analysis of the aims of system and of Absolute Knowledge in his *Schelling* (48 ff.). *Our remarks will continually assume Heidegger's analysis*" (*LA* 134n17/66n3, emphasis added). So what is their analysis of the Romantic "system" based on Heidegger's *Schelling?*

In his book on Schelling, Heidegger argues that the question of the system must be conceived as an *ontological* question rather than as an epistemological one. According to Heidegger, in the philosophical tradition, there has been a "misunderstanding" of the notion of system, described by him as the jointure [*Gefüge*] of Being, a misunderstanding that consisted in the understanding of the system as a "structure to guiding knowledge."[54] Conceived as a matter of *reason*, of *thought*, the system is embraced by philosophy as the way to *absolute knowledge*. Inspired by Kant's notion of the transcendental subject, such an aspiration first arose, according to Heidegger, in German idealism. Schelling's merit among the German idealists is, according to Heidegger, to have opened a trail of thought that helps to

conceive of the system *outside* of the limits of the will to a metaphysical system, because the system, the *Fügung*, is, according to Schelling, the affair of *being itself*. This being, says Schelling, cannot be systematized by logical and rational knowledge, since the latter always comes *after* the original position of being.

In his analysis of Schelling's work, Heidegger nevertheless shows that Schelling's attempt, however revolutionary and courageous, was doomed to failure, because Schelling understood being itself according to the idealist model of *subjectivity*, that is, according to the metaphysical model of the *will*:

> Schelling says (p. 24): "In the final and highest instance, there is no other Being than Will. Will is primordial Being." That means primordial Being is will. Willing is striving and desiring, not a blind impulse and urge, but *guided and determined by the idea of that is willed*. What is represented and representing, the idea, is thus what truly wills in willing. To understand Being as will means to understand it in terms of the idea and thus idealistically.[55]

In Nancy and Lacoue-Labarthe's view, just as Schelling's revolutionary attempt was still developed within the conceptual framework of idealism, so too did Jena Romanticism (*AL* 34/49).

To be sure, like Schelling, the Jena Romantics do not understand the system in terms of a systematic order, but as the *systasis* of being itself, that is, as "that by which and as which an ensemble holds together" (*LA* 46/67). According to Nancy and Lacoue-Labarthe, the Romantic system is therefore less a matter of reason than of creative and productive activity:

> "Systasis" necessarily takes place as the organicity of an organon, whether it be a natural creature (a hedgehog), society, or a work of art. Or rather, *that it be all these at once*, as is indicated by the absence of a specific object for the totality of the *Fragments*. Or more precisely yet, that being all these at once (and in keeping with the "at once" of fragmentation of symphilosophy), it should still exist only as a work of art. (*LA* 46/67)

For the Jena Romantics, then, a system is not a systematic organization per se, but a unifying force, so to speak, which turns out to be the same as that of the work of art: a creative force. But according to Nancy and

Lacoue-Labarthe, the Jena Romantics' interpretation of this unifying force nonetheless reveals the idealist scope of their thought. For, as the authors of *The Literary Absolute* ask, echoing Heidegger: Can the creative, unifying force be anything other than the *subject* itself?

The subject-creator, the Self, conclude Nancy and Lacoue-Labarthe, is the whole that holds together and holds itself together: "What makes an individual, what makes an individual's holding-together, is the 'systasis' that produces it. What makes its individuality is its capacity to produce, and to produce itself, first of by means of its internal 'formative force'—the *bildende kraft* inherited from the organism of Kant, which romanticism transcribes into a *vis poetica*—by means all of which 'in the Self all things are formed organically' (*Ath.* 338)" (*LA* 49/69–70).[56] As indicated above, poetic self-formation is indeed a matter of individuation, and, vice versa, individuation is a matter of self-formation. Now, according to Nancy and Lacoue-Labarthe, the Romantic subject is thus understood as a work or a system to be formed, that is, as what they call, following Heidegger's analysis of Schelling, a "System-Subject," a "Work-Subject," or even a "Work-Self-knowledge" [*Oeuvre-Savoir-de-soi*], that is to say a subject that forms itself as a Work and as a System, as well as a work and a system understood as the subject's self-formation (*LA* 55–56/78–79). The major conclusion they draw—which is the main warning underlying their entire study, as well as the reason why Nancy does not want to call himself "Romantic"—is that with Romantic thought, *"we have not left the era of the Subject"* (*LA* 16/27, my emphasis). On the contrary: the logic of seminal self-formation is, in their view, its "true form" (*LA* 33/70).

A Way Out: Energeia

In sum, then, even though this Romantic subject is not the stable, univocal support that it is in certain idealist philosophies, it is still a Subject according to Nancy and Lacoue-Labarthe, a subject that is hypostased from the world. We might wonder, however, if Nancy and Lacoue-Labarthe are not too influenced by Heidegger's interpretation of Schelling. To reiterate, Heidegger indicates that the "system" or "systasis"—described by him as "the original jointure of Being"—cannot be but the subject of philosophical thought. The error of the metaphysicians—including Schelling, despite his courageous attempt to break with this tradition—consists in the fact that they have taken this "systasis" to be the jointure of the subject and not of Being itself.

Heidegger's analysis is undoubtedly of great value for understanding the metaphysical tradition and Schelling's, along with Fichte's and Hegel's, particular role in it, but its transposition into the project of Jena *Romanticism* is not self-evident.[57] Even if Jena Romanticism develops itself within the framework of idealist thought, as Nancy and Lacoue-Labarthe argue, and even if Schelling is seen by Heidegger as the last representative of idealism and thus in a sense as its overcoming, it is surprising that Nancy and Lacoue-Labarthe rely on Heidegger's analysis of Schelling in discussing German Romanticism, and even more specifically, the *Athenaeum* group of which neither Schelling, Fichte nor Hegel were members.[58] Pointing out that Jena Romantic thought amounts to a certain theory of the subject is undoubtedly defensible and enlightening, but one might wonder whether this interpretation could not just as well have taken a different turn.

More precisely, I wonder whether Nancy and Lacoue-Labarthe in *The Literary Absolute* have not overemphasized the aspect of the *ergon* in the Romantic conception of "organicity," thereby dismissing its *energetic* side emphasized by Schlegel among others in *Athenaeum* fragment 375:

> Of all things, *energy* in particular least needs to prove what it can do. If circumstances require, it can quite easily make a show of being passive and be believed. It's satisfied to do its work silently, without accompaniment and without gesticulations. The virtuoso, the genius, want to carry out some particular intention, create some work, etc. The *energetic man* always makes use of only the moment, and is always ready and infinitely flexible. He has an in finite number of projects, or none at all; for energy is really more than mere agility: it is effective, certainly externally effective, but it is also universal power, through which the whole man shapes himself and acts. (*Ath.* 375, my emphasis)

Unlike the man of genius, the *energetic* man has no goals or projects, or else he has an incalculable number of them, which also amounts to having none at all. His strength is not the force of *will*, but the force before it, that is to say, the energetic and silent force without direction. This active force is not directed towards a future destiny (or a lost past), but is simply agility, flexibility, effective here and now. In other words, it is not a sowing for future harvests as Nancy and Lacoue-Labarthe say (*LA* 49/70), but an active force that simply uses the moment. Not *energeia* opposed to power (*dunamis*), as Nancy and Lacoue-Labarthe have it, but energy *as power*. Because it is a force that is "externally effective," a *nach außen wirkende Kraft*,

a force that realizes itself by directing itself outwards, the energetic man is formed, so to speak, without returning to himself, and for this reason *is* in a sense *without self*—is precisely not *subject*.

Nancy and Lacoue-Labarthe in fact point to this non-subjectivistic interpretation as one of the two possible paths of Romantic thought. The first, ascribed by them to Novalis, concerns the organic assimilation (called "intussusception") by an organism of all the elements of the external world, ultimately leading to the "Great Work" (*LA* 56/79). The second path—effectively called "Schlegelian" by them—is indeed that of the energetic man evoked in fragment 375 of *Athenaeum* quoted above. Too hastily, in my opinion, Nancy and Lacoue-Labarthe however characterize "the fragment on energy"—and thus the entire conceptual path it opens up—as "unique, a single element *lost* in the ensemble of the *Fragments*," an element "never named and still less thought" by the Jena Romantics (*LA* 57/79–80). Remarkably, Nancy and Lacoue-Labarthe do not dwell on this element, or perhaps it is more correct to say that they immediately classify it under the first path, given the rhetorical question with which they close the subject: "But what is this flexibility [of the energetic man, AvR], if not an infinite capacity for form, for the absolute of form; and what is energy, *en-ergeia*, if not the putting-into-work itself, the completed *organon*, whose works (of genius) are mere potentialities? (The Aristotelian is *energeia* as opposed to *dynamis*, potentiality)" (*LA* 57/79). Energy understood in this way can according to them therefore only lead to one thing: "Dissolution and energy, then, the ultimate forms of the fragment, would inevitably lead back to the work-subject" (*LA* 57/79). In contract to this conclusion, the aim of my analysis of Jena's Romanticism in this chapter was to show that there is perhaps a more favorable and fruitful reading of this important "Schlegelian" path in the *Athenaeum* texts, and that it deserves to be taken seriously if we are to better understand the legacy of Romanticism in Nancy's thought.

The Future Is Fragmentary

Rupture of the Romantic Horizon

Although Nancy and Lacoue-Labarthe in their Heideggerian reading have perhaps too brusquely rejected this Schlegelian path in the thought of Jena Romanticism, they have clearly indicated that it is exactly here where we should locate the way out of what they call the "totalitarianism of Cogito and System" (*LA* 15/26), which is, according to them part of the Romantic

heritage. Leaving aside the question as to whether or not the Jena Romantics themselves proposed or noticed this, it is clear that this way out is situated in a renunciation of the work, or the work-subject, as an *intended project*—a renunciation that is perhaps most evident in Romantic irony. Our future, the future of us moderns, can only be opened up if we take this renunciation seriously. We must understand, as Nancy and Lacoue-Labarthe conclude *The Literary Absolute*, that "the future *is* fragmentary—and that a work-*project* has no place in it" (*LA* 124/423). This is the task that Nancy has taken on in his own thought, a task that consists in demonstrating that it is not the work, but *being itself* that is fragmentary. Such a proposition, which is ultimately an ontological proposition, makes it impossible to turn being into a project, for being, as Nancy has it, is always *more than one*.

The "lost element" of *energeia* is an indication of this proposition, of the irreversible dissolution of work, of the impossibility of making it into a project. What it suggests, between the lines of the *Athenaeum* fragments, is the existence of an agility or plasticity, of a plural dynamic that results in the individuation of a self and is a movement directed towards an outside, without return or recourse. The reason for this is that dissolution and energy do not solely lead back to the work-subject, but the dissolution that *is* energy also entails *dés-oeuvre-ment*, that is, *un-working*. In the last paragraphs of *The Literary Absolute*, Nancy and Lacoue-Labarthe refer to this Blanchotian notion of *désoeuvrement* pointing out that this is the "equivocation" that governs and destabilizes all Romantic thought: the equivocation that every project of making work consists in the absence of work.[59]

Indeed, of all the commentators on Jena Romanticism, Blanchot has emphasized this element of Romanticism the most, even to the extent that he has placed it at the heart—a heart that is nonetheless errant, foreign—of this Romantic thought. In his text "The Athenaeum," written in 1964 and published in *The Infinite Conversation*, Blanchot puts it as follows: "One can indeed say that in these texts [of the Jena Romantics, AvR] we find expressed the non-Romantic essence of Romanticism . . . : that to write is to make (of) speech (a) work, but that this work is an unworking."[60] According to Blanchot, the fact that the Romantic *poiein* consists of both the *making* and *unmaking* of the work is due to the fact that the infinitely productive force that poetry is for the Romantics only shows itself "in disappearing." It is indeed a *force*, not a thing, which for this reason is transient, without substance. Using a terminology very close to *Athenaeum* fragment 375 on *energeia*, Blanchot characterizes the poetic act as "an affirmation without duration, a freedom without realization, a force that exalts in disappearing and that is in no way discredited if it leaves no trace, for this was its goal:

to make poetry shine, neither as nature nor even as work, but as pure consciousness of the moment."[61]

The great equivocation of Jena Romanticism is thus that the Romantic, creative spirit, who is destined to refound or firmly establish the properly human, moral community, has no other concern than to express itself through a poetic act that does not serve to communicate things, but consists only of a tautological saying. Originally evoked by the sociopolitical and ethical concern to refound or protect the *Gesellschaft* from its increasing disintegration, the Romantic project seems to have ended up with the presupposition of a creative self that is absolutely sovereign, and this poetic sovereignty does not need, as Blanchot puts it, "to be either socially recognized, nor humanly productive."[62]

Exit

In terms of our shared future, we should note that if the supreme act of the creative mind is to say "I," this "I" must potentially be everything, having "a plurality of minds and a whole system of persons within it" as indicated in *Athenaeum* fragment 121, "in whose inner being the universe . . . has grown to fullness and maturity" (*Ath.* 121). And if the ideal of the creative spirit is to produce a work, this work can therefore be nothing less than a *total* work—not a book that represents reality in its totality, but a book that, like in Jorge Luis Borges's "The Parable of the Palace," contains and replaces this totality. This may be "the most radical irony," as Nancy and Lacoue-Labarthe put it, but only insofar as we are still in what they call the "epoch of the book" (*LA* 127/425). Or, to explain it according to a distinction made by Blanchot in *The Space of Literature*, the fact that the Romantic work is nothing and everything at the same time is ironic *only* insofar as we are in the age of the book and not yet in that of the *work*. For "[t]here is a *work* only when, through it, and with the violence of a beginning which is proper to it, the word *being* is pronounced." This is the case, Blanchot holds, "when the work becomes the intimacy between someone who writes it and someone who reads it."[63] Whereas the epoch of book is that of the finished product, of the product that one can hold and that holds and maintains itself in the course of time, the epoch of the work is opened as soon as there is the event of a beginning, each time new and each time differently, like the nothing that interrupts the course of time.

As Nancy points out, the task of thought, in the wake of and beyond Romanticism, is therefore to think differently about the work of community, in a way that moves beyond the reassuring delimitation of a form, a form

that is given a variety of names, varying from the relatively innocent name of "Grand Art," or the rather neutral "metaphysics of art," to the more complex and loaded name of "onto-typology," and the forever contaminated name of the "aestheticization of politics" to, of course, the name beyond all names: "Auschwitz."

Chapter 2

The Work of Community

Myth Interrupted (*Nancy, Aristotle, Balzac*)

THE WESTERN PLOT

As I argued in the introduction, it is undoubtedly with Nancy that the question of myth is most systematically and thoroughly analyzed in contemporary thought. This may come as a surprise. for although the notion of myth has appeared more frequently in Nancy's work in recent decades,[1] it does not play a major role as it does for example in the works of Ernst Cassirer, Roland Barthes, René Girard, or Claude Lévi-Strauss. Nevertheless, I think it is fair to say that Nancy's work is inspired, throughout and from within, so to speak, by a reflection on what myth might be *today*. The concept of myth will thus serve as a key both to opening up Nancy's own thinking, and to opening up Nancy's thinking to a wider debate, a debate whose contours are sketched in the introduction and chapter 1.

What, then, is the concept of myth that sets Nancy's thinking in motion? Even if the phenomenon of myth is so impenetrable that myth theorists all propose rather different definitions, they all insist on its dual structure, which allows the functions of fiction (i.e., invention, construction, narration) and foundation (i.e., assurance, explanation, justification, revelation) to converge. As Nancy has it in *Proprement dit: Entretien sur le mythe* (Properly Speaking: Dialogue on Myth): "The simple image of myth is the most traditional image, myth as fable or rather as fabulation, *both invention and lie*" (*PD* 30, my emphasis). Of course, this structure itself demonstrates an irreducible ambiguity, especially on a social or political level,

as described by Raoul Girardet in his book *Mythes et mythologies politiques*. Political myth, according to Girardet, "is indeed a fabulation, a deformation or an objectively questionable interpretation of reality. But it is true that a fabled story also has an explanatory function, providing a certain number of keys for understanding the present, constituting a grid through which the disconcerting chaos of facts and events seems to be ordered."[2] Political myth, or the myth of a community, is thus understood according to the model given in Aristotle's *Poetics* in his reflection on the *muthos*. The *muthos*, which in other respects can simply be formulated speech, whatever its precise form, obtains a very specific form in Aristotle's *Poetics*, which requires it to be an *ordered* narrative that is to be conceived as a *whole*.

As the most important element of tragedy, the *muthos* is for Aristotle "unified action," that is to say an arrangement that presents contingent and heterogeneous facts in such a way as to form a "whole" consisting of a teleological development from a beginning to an end: "[I]t is clear that the plots ought (as in tragedy) to be constructed dramatically; that is, they should be concerned with a unified action, whole and complete, possessing a beginning, middle parts and an end."[3] For Aristotle, *muthos* is therefore a narrative in the form of a plot that ties events together in such a way that their succession becomes necessary or plausible.[4] What the Aristotelian *muthos* establishes, then, is what I called in the introduction the temporality of the *future anterior*, which presents the course of events as a foreseeable necessary development that *will have been so*.[5] Hence myth's capacity to be explanatory, prophetic, and mobilizing all at once.

For Aristotle, such a knotting of myth is the special ability of the tragedy. This is why the poet differs both from the epic poet and from the historian, and is also "more philosophical" and "more serious" than the historian.[6] The historian must content himself with a simple report of what has taken place, whereas the task of the poet "is not to say what *has* happened, but to say the kind of thing that *would* happen, that is, what is possible in accordance with probability or necessity," thus dealing with the *general* and not the *singular*.[7] Aristotle's model of myth has been of great importance to Western thinking on poetry and literature, but it also, and even more decisively, laid the foundations for Western thought in general.[8] Historians—but indeed all those who set themselves the goal of revealing the course of history or the logic of the world—all or almost all rely on the Aristotelian model of myth as plot. As Benedict Anderson shows in *Imagined Communities*, this attachment to plots stems from an irresistible desire to construct a grand scheme of the cosmos. This desire persisted

even after the disintegration of the great divine schemes, confronting us with the unbearable contingency and arbitrariness of suffering—disease, injustice, death. "What was then required," says Anderson, "was a secular transformation of fatality into continuity, contingency into meaning."[9] In his view, the most successful form of this transformation was the idea of the *nation-state*, which in turn was built around the idea of a *national novel*.

Indeed, the reason why the nation-state can transform chance into destiny is, according to Anderson, because it is based on the model of the novel, or as Anderson specifies, the *Balzacian* novel, which not only provides a narrative, but knots simultaneous and seemingly independent events (experienced by citizens spread all over the country) into a *common plot* using the concept of the *meanwhile*. Forming the fabric of the Balzacian novel, the "meanwhile" suggests an omniscient narrator, a *cosmotheoros*, who sees all simultaneous events as part of the same plot.[10] On an even more general level, Nancy makes a similar point when he says that "[t]he idea of myth alone perhaps presents the very Idea of the West" (*IC* 46/117). This Western idea of myth, he adds, consists in "the entire pretension on the part of the West to appropriate its own origin, or to take away its secret, so that it can at last identify itself, absolutely, around its own pronouncement and its own birth" (*IC* 46/117). The idea of myth on which the West has grafted itself is indeed the Aristotelian-Balzacian idea of myth as a collective plot.

It is this basic structure that Nancy wants to get rid of. If he rejects myth, then, it is this specific form of myth which pretends to identify our origin and destination. The exhaustion of this way of thinking about myth is what Nancy sets out to demonstrate and what he attempts to deconstruct in his texts on community as well as those on poetry, and sense. But—and herein lies the ambiguity inherent in the structure of myth—myth is *also* what already, of itself, reveals that *there is no* origin, development or destiny. Without the knotting or composition of a plot, Aristotle also says, being shows itself only as an infinity of events and particularities without direction, without reversal, and without us being able to distinguish between the contingent and the necessary.[11]

Myth, or rather the necessity of the recourse to myth, thus reveals that there is no predetermined constellation of meaning, and that before there is myth, there is only a simple succession of events. A necessary succession of events, then, does not come from experience, but presents itself as the effect of poetic invention: Myth requires poetic intervention as a condition of possibility. According to Aristotle, the basis of this poetic intervention is the scene (*opsis*), described by him as a purely technical element, a *parergon*,

and for this reason a "very inartistic" and the "least germane" element of poetry: It is the stage, the set, the sound and light. However marginal, the scene is thus the condition of possibility for a plot to arise.[12]

Now, it is in his attempt to unravel the plot and to deconstruct myth as a constellation of meaning, that Nancy stresses this marginal yet essential element of the scene. Significantly, his analysis of Aristotle's *Poetics* in the form of an exchange of letters with Lacoue-Labarthe, revolves entirely around this notion. While Lacoue-Labarthe expresses reservations about the spectacularity of the scene and argues for the utmost sobriety, Nancy, for his part, is keen to emphasize the scene's spectacular brilliance, that is, as he has put it more recently in his interview on myth with Mathilde Girard, "the fact that 'sobriety' itself can be full of effects" (*PD* 24). If there is anything left of myth that is worth exploring by us in the twenty-first century, it lies for Nancy in this element of the scenic.

From the Mythological to the Mythical

Nancy thus wants to remove the notion of myth from its roots in Aristotelian-Balzacian poetics that presents a certain rationalized order, a *logos*, or better still, presents itself *as logos*.[13] This myth is *mytho-logy* in the true sense of the word: a junction of *muthos* and *logos*. Consequently, trying to remove myth from this traditional understanding would be nothing less than trying to think myth without -logy. Nancy embraces this attempt and wants to think the relation between the poetic and the real not according to a teleological construction knotted together by the *logos* of *muthos*, but on an earlier plane, according to what is there *before* there is a plot, namely, the scene—the *opsis*—itself, the fact *that* something can present itself to sight and/or hearing.[14] Now this scene is what Nancy is inclined to call the "mythical" or simply "myth," trying to maintain the power of myth, without falling back into Western mythological thinking.[15]

Turning away from the mythological towards a new understanding of myth or, more precisely, *against* the mythological *through* myth, Nancy aims at what he calls in *Being Singular Plural* a "sort of 'Copernican revolution'" (*BSP* 57/78). Indeed, in his 2015 interview on myth with Mathilde Girard, Nancy describes this Copernican revolution more explicitly than before as a shift from the *mythological* to *myth*:

> What you [Mathilde Girard, AvR] allowed me to understand
> better, it is how our history is intertwined with an epoch that

> has silently led to the reemergence of a question of myth, because this epoch stopped leaving behind the politico-metaphysical mythologies (if you want to distinguish these two notions) of the communisms, spiritualisms and humanisms. I am saying that "*myth*" should be understood as the opening of a possibility of sense—of a sense not provided with accomplished meanings (that is what I would call "*mythology*") but of a sense, simply, as movement, event, existence. (*PD* 20, my emphasis)

According to Nancy, this Copernican revolution—moving from accomplished meanings to the possibility of sense—should ultimately take place at the level of ontology, and lies in the fact that being must be understood to revolve "around *itself* or turning on *itself*, and no longer [revolve] around something else" (*BSP* 57/78–79, my emphasis).[16] Nancy's aim is thus to show that the world's ordering force can no longer be found *outside* being, outside the hustle of our everyday existence, in an eternal, unchanging principle, whether accessible to the philosopher-king, the poet, or anyone else. It is time to give up not only the idea, but also the desire and mourning for such an external principle that could assign a predestined place to everything. For as long as we cling to the idea of such a principle, whatever it may be, we turn away from the present world, from the here-and-now of the world as such.

According to Nancy, it is this *world as such* that must be the starting point, the place and the stake of all our thinking. In his work, Nancy has set himself the task of thinking about what *remains* when we finally, definitively and unreservedly renounce the idea of such guiding force or organizing principle for the world. And what remains once we have abolished the idea of a constellation that holds things together, is the awareness that the world is, that we are, in a situation of permanent disassembly, or, what amounts to the same thing, that we are assembled *without reason*. Nancy's Copernican revolution consists in making us aware that this disassembly itself is the "center" or "ground" of being.

Although we are not yet fully aware of this, according to Nancy, this radical transformation has already begun with the decomposition of the ancient world, that is, roughly speaking, with the transition from polytheism to monotheism.[17] If Nancy often alludes to monotheism and Christianity, it is because they reveal a structure of thought that is still largely *unthought of* in contemporary days. It is important to note that this structure concerns not only the way in which we relate to the divine, but also—and consequently—the very way in which we *think*. Rather than an inquiry into the

historical reality of religion in the West, Nancy's works about Christianity and monotheism are therefore properly philosophical investigations into the conditions of Western thought in general. The main conclusion of these works, it could be argued, lies in their reversal of the Kantian claim that religion lies within the limits of reason. According to Nancy, a careful analysis of the tangential conditions of thought and religion shows, on the contrary, how reason "opens up to the limitedlessness that constitutes its truth" (*DE* 1/9).[18]

Now, what are the characteristics of monotheisms, and more specifically of Christianity that prove this point? According to Nancy, to grasp the particularity of the monotheistic condition, we must first understand it in comparison with the world of polytheism (which in the West was that of Antiquity, but there are of course many forms of polytheism), which is above all a world animated by the effective presence of the gods, who determine its order and ensure its continuity. Polytheism therefore effectively presupposes a given order, in both senses of the word—offered and present—and for this reason can certainly be called *mythological*.[19] In monotheism—and this is the central thesis developed by Nancy in his work on the "deconstruction of Christianity"—this mythological order is destabilized, not because of the reduction of the number of gods to one, but because of the *mode of presence* of this single god. Monotheism is in fact characterized by the presupposition of a god who is not present as our fellow human beings are, but radically *other*. The Christian God is remote, untouchable, and owes his very divinity to being inaccessible, unpresentable, and unknowable. According to the Christian doctrine, God emptied himself of his divine attributes (this is the doctrine of *kenosis*; *kenos* = emptiness) and incarnated the mortal, finite world of humans. The Christian God is therefore the God who allows himself to be understood according to Spinoza's *Deus sive natura*. The Christian God is thus a God who is both everywhere and nowhere, indeed nowhere *because* everywhere.

Although the name of "God" still represents for us the source of the world's organization and even animation, monotheism has also made this name virtually unpronounceable. Or rather, this name has become the name for the Unpronounceable itself—for that which is principally absent or ungraspable. If "God" is the guardian of the absolute meaning of the world, then the meaning of the world is never given. Since a mythological order is characterized by the presupposition of a *given* meaning, monotheism therefore marks a *withdrawal from the mythological* according to Nancy. The principle on which the mythological order is based, or the center around which the

mythological plot is woven, has withdrawn. In other words, according to Nancy, Christian monotheism thus amounts to a "demythologization."[20] What is more, if one asserts that religion is mythological in principle because it is based on the effective presence of the divine, one must even conclude, as Nancy does, following Marcel Gauchet, that Christian monotheism is a religion that *withdraws from religion*: "[T]he threefold monotheism and, in it, more specifically, Christianity . . . understands itself less and less religiously in the sense in which religion implies a mythology (a narrative, a representation of divine actions and persons)" (*DE* 37/57).[21]

That monotheism in a sense already withdraws from religion logically implies a dissolution of the opposition so ardently maintained between religion and secularization. In fact, according to Nancy, monotheism and secularization (understood as liberation from religion, or even as atheism) *co-originate*. Secularization is not a modern invention that has replaced or will replace the religious era, but an idea that lies *at the very heart* of monotheism and Christianity. Indeed, according to Nancy, the inevitable result of God's withdrawal is a "worldization" (*mondialisation*) of the world, a becoming-world of the world: Left to its own devices, detached from its organizing principle, the monotheistic world has become a world that is *nothing but the world* (see "NBW"). It is therefore not Christianity *or* secularization that is constitutive of the West, nor their succession in the course of history, but the original entanglement of the two in the withdrawal of God from the very heart of religion. What is constitutive of the West is thus, in other words, *a demythologization at the very heart of mythology.*

The Myth of Politics

There are roughly three moments in Nancy's work where the question of myth that inspires his thinking rises to the surface and where he extensively addresses the question of myth: The first moment is in the 1986 essay "Myth Interrupted" published in *The Inoperative Community*; the second moment is twenty years later in the text "Un commencement," published in 2006 as an afterword to a collection of prose poems by Lacoue-Labarthe's entitled *L'"Allégorie"*; then, finally, nine years later, in a retrospective interview on the theme of myth with Mathilde Girard entitled *Proprement dit* (2015).[22]

In the first text, Nancy distinguishes—sometimes in an indecisive terminology slightly different from mine[23]—the ambiguity inherent in the structure of myth, drawing the inevitable conclusion that *myth interrupts itself.* The stakes of this conclusion are high, for, as we have seen, the idea of

myth presents for Nancy the very idea of the West, that is, its pretension to appropriate its own origin (*IC* 46/117), a pretension of which Romanticism has perhaps given the most profound theorization, and National Socialism the most horrific realization. But the Western traditions of idealism, structuralism, or humanism are no less dependent on it, according to Nancy, since in all cases, thought is driven by nostalgia for a "paradise lost," for a mode of existence in which everything has its proper place. In his analysis of the Jena Romantics, Frank described this nostalgia as a desire for an "*Einst*," a former time presented as the community's "Golden Age."[24]

In *Mythes et mythologies politiques*, Girardet also indicates that the Golden Age, that "image of a *legendified* past," is one of the "great mythological ensembles," inspiring "visions of a present and a future defined according to what was or what is supposed to have been."[25] It is precisely because of this nostalgia (and its counterpart, messianism) that Nancy wants to get rid of the Western idea of myth: "[W]e no longer have anything to do with myth," he points out, "I would be tempted to say we no longer even have the right to speak about it, to be interested in it" (*IC* 46/117) for by clinging to the idea of a past or future Golden Age, whatever it may be, we turn away from the present world that *is*, here and now. "The Golden Age has one disadvantage," Schlegel, too, remarks not without humor, "namely that *it does not exist*. But for that very reason it has the inestimable advantage of not having acquired rust in the course of history."[26]

But however much Nancy may want that we no longer have anything to do with myth, of course we have *everything* to do with myth, we cannot get rid of it, because what it constitutes is precisely a political "we"—and therein lies the urgency of thinking about myth. Simply put, there can be no political community without myth, or even *mythology*, at least if we want this political community to have a certain duration. As we saw in the introduction, the paradox of the constitutive act—which is always a political act, whatever the domain in which it occurs—is that it can only be foundational by being conservative. In other words, for a constituted entity (a "we," an order of any kind, a system) to serve as a foundation, it must anticipate its preservation by appealing to its own necessity.

As we saw, this constitutive act is indeed paradoxical, for such an entanglement of foundation and preservation is necessary only because there is no given foundation that could guarantee the preservation of this entity. Indeed, if it is beyond doubt that this order is eternal, that fate has decided, there would be no need to ensure preservation. Such a divinely sanctioned eternal order would be expressed in a simple statement of fact,

whereas our political orders need the performative expression of the future anterior. The mythological encirclement of foundation and preservation by which the contingent is transformed into necessity, is the main feature of politics and a politics that escapes this mythological logic seems impossible.[27]

Indeed, I would argue that "political" is everything (every act, every gesture, every utterance—but differences largely dissolve when they present themselves in a political form) that *claims validity* and, consequently, power. This is the case not only in the exercise of state power or in a demonstration of brute force, but in all cases where we present our acts, our gestures, our enunciations, as true, just, or real, or as *more* true, *more* just, and so on, than others. This last addition—that there is also a claim to power in cases where we present our acts as more true than others—also includes acts generally characterized as *counter-power*, such as those by action committees or subversive groups.[28] Importantly, this definition of "politics" does not yet distinguish between the two "archetypal" forms of politics, namely the politics of "dissociation" in the style of Carl Schmitt, and the politics of "association" in the style of Arendt, since both forms presuppose a claim to validity and, therefore, power. It is for this reason that Nancy, although he had long sought for a definition of "politics" that would withdraw it from the realm of power and that would indicate being-with as such, begins to regard, from the 2000s onwards, the use of the word "politics" as misleading and finishes by abandoning the search for an "other" politics altogether. Or as Nancy puts it in 2014 in *The Disavowed Community*: "Let me state right away that, today, I consider, this use of the term [politics, AvR] misleading [*égarant*] which renders 'political' equivalent to 'ontological'" (*DC* 11/33).

This being the case, an *interruption* of the mythological logic must thus always be *non-political*, or, as I would add, at least *display* itself as non-political.[29] But—and here lies the complexity of the whole problematic of myth—such an interruption is already proper to, indeed constitutive of, mythological logic itself: The fact that we attribute a founding power to ourselves reveals that this power is groundless, and therefore, if we may put it this way, powerless. In other words, mythology itself contains the germ of the possibility of its interruption. It is precisely therefore that we need, according to Nancy, to reassert the power of myth within a fresh set of rules. There is thus a tendency in Nancy's work to consider this "fresh set of rules" in a less and less political way. In his first texts, Nancy still seemed tempted to understand our pure and simple being-with as a *political* affair. It is especially from the 2000s onwards that he declares that he wants to

understand it as something that happens principally *outside* the realm of politics: "The ontology of the common is *not immediately political*" ("NBW" 526, my emphasis).[30]

Myth Without Mythology

A Tautegorical Saying of the World by Itself

But if it is not immediately political, what, then, is the nature of the "we" and the telling of this "we" constituted by myth? Myth, as Nancy has it in "Myth Interrupted," is first of all the *original* story of community, that is, the story in which and with which a community originates, that enables people to come together and recognize themselves as gathered. "Before" that story, "we"—but in what sense can we speak of a "before" and a "we"—Nancy holds, "were dispersed (at least this is what the story tells us at times), shoulder to shoulder, working with and confronting one another without recognizing one another" (*IC* 43/109). In other words, it is only through the recitation of the mythic story that there is a "we," and a world in which this "we" occupies a certain place and plays a certain role. The mythic story thus marks "both the story of the beginning of the *world* [as something that makes *sense*, AvR], the beginning of their *assembly*, or the beginning of the *story* itself" (*PD* 110, my emphasis).

That the story also marks the beginning of the story itself is due to a change in the function of language, a change that ultimately amounts to a substitution of language as mere expression by language a way of *plotting*. To reassert the power of myth therefore according to Nancy also means in a way undoing this change in language, trying to tell the difference "between the *lure* (the mythifying myth [here named 'mythological,' AvR]) and *nascent speech* (*mythos* 'properly speaking' [here called 'mythical,' AvR]) that I had risked to call the 'interruption of myth'" (*PD* 32, my emphasis). Interrupting myth, then, boils down to finding a different access to the language of myth, to "nascent" language: "Now [in 2015, AvR] I understand that 'interruption' was meant to designate the breakdown of the lure and the possibility of a new access to this nascent language" (*PD* 32).

When turned into a luring story, nascent language is no longer a furtive exchange between people, an exposure without explanation, but becomes the means of their reunion, identification and meaning: "The Greek . . . *muthos* that is, speech, spoken expression, becomes 'myth' when it takes on a whole

series of values that amplify, fill, and ennoble this speech, giving it the dimensions of a narrative of origins and an explanation of destinies. . . . In myth world makes itself known, and it makes itself known through declaration or through a complete and decisive revelation" (*IC* 48/123). Simple, nascent, expressive speech is transformed into a plot because it establishes a certain *logic of the world* in which a "we" can find its proper place. In the ancient times glorified by the Romantics, these *muthos* and *logos* were one and the same according to Nancy (*IC* 49/123). Simple speech, spoken expression, was already amplified, filled, and ennobled by a complete and decisive meaning, making myth nothing other than the diction of the world revealing its own logic, or, as Nancy puts it, "the speech and the language of the very things that manifest themselves. . . . [I]n myth, their rhythm speaks and their music sounds" (*IC* 50/126).[31]

But, as the Jena Romantics also pointed out in their call for a *new* mythology, we no longer live in such a mythological cosmos, where the world reveals its own logic, where the ordering structure is unmistakably present in everything we do. In our times, as Nancy formulates it, " 'myth' is cut off from its own meaning, on its own meaning, by its own meaning. If it even still has a proper meaning" (*IC* 52/132). A complete and decisive revelation of the logic of the world is therefore only something to be deplored and desired—without really knowing what we are deploring or desiring. This is why, according to Nancy, our thinking about myth itself composes a myth, the myth of the possibility of mythical speech.

It is time to realize that this myth is indeed a myth, that is, "that myth, as inauguration or foundation, is a myth, that is to say, a fiction, *a mere invention*" (*PD* 31, my emphasis) and that "it is not the task of myth to hold, even less to exhaust language, but only to manifest a presence" (*PD* 54). Myth—as the Jena Romantics already hinted—can therefore only be the name for the figuration of being-with by itself, without a model. Or as Nancy has it, it is "proper speech without owner [*parole propre sans propriétaire*], without possible appropriation. Speech without owner, because it is, on the contrary, that which let emerge—which produces, creates, and 'configures'—the very things of which it speaks or, better, *that it* speaks" (*PD* 31).

Twenty-nine years after the publication of his text "Myth Interrupted," Nancy indicates that he has found a suitable notion to express this self-interrupting mythic self-expression. In his attempt to dislocate mythological thought, Nancy relies on a thoroughly Romantic notion, namely the notion of "*tautegory*" taken from Schelling:

> Perhaps we should argue that interruption belongs to myth: that a myth is not a mythology, that is an entire system of cosmo-politico-theo-gony, but rather a *tautegoric* form of speech as Schelling says, that is to say, a speaking of that which expresses itself and only itself. Speaking (*muthein*) as self-presentation. The world, therefore, presenting itself, not to explain itself (which is already a 'cognitive' interpretation of myths) but to present itself. As a result, this speech remains suspended in or on this presentation. (*PD* 53–54)

We did not come across this notion of "tautegory," which also plays a major role in Nancy's text "Un commencement," in our reading of Romanticism. Nevertheless, it follows directly from it. Tautegory—a neologism that Schelling owes to Coleridge—is, according to Schelling, the very stake of the new mythology and distinguishes myth from what is generally called *allegory*.[32] Whereas allegory is a sensible illustration of an idea already given, tautegory is that which gives substance to what would otherwise not be conceived.[33] Tautegory is therefore not the representation of something else, but is no more or less than what it says.[34] Nancy follows Schelling in this opposition between tautegory and allegory, suggesting that allegory as such has become impossible in our times. Allegory, which is literally the unveiling of something in another register (*allos* = other), rests on the presupposition of the world separated into two (or more) registers, traditionally the intelligible and the sensible. But if there is only this world, nothing but this world, as Nancy never ceases to demonstrate, then there is no other register. There is only one register: that of the world.[35]

Following in the footsteps of Schelling and Romanticism, then, Nancy is emphasizing that there is no such thing as something intelligible (an idea, a form, a model) that would subsequently have to be presented in sensible material. For him, the notion of "tautegory" expresses "that there is *properly nothing* to bring to the sensible" ("UC" 158–59), that everything that *is* is already in a sensible way.[36] In other words, the intelligible—as the *Systematic Program* already proclaimed—can only be given *aesthetically*. If we understand myth according to this *tautegorical* structure, it can neither be a presentation of a general idea (of the common, of origin), nor follow an external principle, nor adapt to any model, and can, for this very reason, never be "amplified," "filled," or "ennobled" speech. Tautegorical speech, one might say, is a performative act that *realizes* what it says, but at the same

time *mediates* and *dislocates* it: "I say myself and I say myself as 'myself'; thus it is an 'I' saying, or rather a 'we' saying" (*PD* 68).

This last formulation reveals the problematic of a community that does not want to think of itself in terms of a given idea or essence: the problematic of self-constitution and self-presentation, or if you like of a *collective autobiography*—since is myth, after all, not the autobiography of a community? According to Nancy, the heart of this problem lies in the fact that this autobiography is at the same time what he calls a "heterography." Tautegorical speech may well be a *graphy* of the self by itself, but it is also a *graphy* that shapes, or even invents, this self, precisely because the self is graphically expressed. Tautegory is thus always a "self-hetero-graphy." In Nancy's words: a "tautegory of going astray [*égarement*] that expresses itself—because in fact it does nothing else but express itself" ("UC" 165; see also *LPD* 50 and 54).

It is this necessity of "going astray" that shatters the ground beneath all mythology. Towards the end of "Un commencement," Nancy proclaims:

> For as much as myth is a story of origin, there is myth here [in the 'allegorical' prose poems of Lacoue-Labarthe, AvR], there is nothing less than myth. . . . *There is myth without mythology,* that is to say without establishing allegories for a causal or rational order of the world and existence. There is myth as a tautegory of a going astray that expresses itself—because in fact it does nothing but express itself, there is nothing else to say but this: "Nothing is more misleading." . . . There is therefore, in the end, no story of origin. But there is the origin as story, the origin always already recited and always already erased in its very recitation. ("UC" 14–165, my emphasis)[37]

Here, in this passage that has already been quoted in part, Nancy formulates what is, in my opinion, the core of his view on myth in the wake of Jena Romanticism: myth without mythology as the expression of an origin that is always already erased in its recitation.

At the start of this section, I said that the Copernican revolution that Nancy brings about lies in the attempt to think of the disassembly of things as the "center" of being itself. This attempt is partly based on the Jena Romantics, who had already tried to reestablish this center in a form that was at once dynamic, emptied, and com-posed, a form they found

in the infinite formation of nature itself. Now, we could say that it is the original de-composition of this composition that Nancy asks us to think about. Referring to Blumenberg, Nancy points out that mythical speech makes us forget "*the* beginning" thanks to "*a* beginning" (*PD* 54). Or in his text effectively entitled "Un commencement" [A Beginning]: "Myth but not mythology—that is to say, not a composition of representations and figures but, on the contrary, a decomposition, the rhythmic unbinding of speech opened by its own lack of origin and to its own indefinite murmur. Myth held at a distance in order to let this opening of a *muthos* emerge and reemerge in a better way? Why not?" ("UC" 162). What Nancy still formulates somewhat tentatively in this 2005 text turns out to be, seen in retrospect in his 2015 interview on myth, a deliberate line of thought tracing "what is maintained of myth against the horizon of its destitution" (*PD* 50).

Sense Without Return

Devoid of mythology, myth is thus not a composition of representations or figures, but it is, as quoted above, "decomposition, the rhythmic unbinding of speech opened by its own lack of origin." Or, as Paul Valéry puts it, it is "the name for everything that exists, or subsists, only to the extent that speech is its cause."[38] Nancy's distinction in "Un commencement" between mythological *composition* and mythical *decomposition* is, in my view, inspired by another distinction woven throughout his entire work as its common thread. It is a distinction that is crucial not only to a proper understanding of Nancy's thinking on myth, but also to a general understanding of his work, namely the distinction between *signification* and *sense*. From "The Forgetting of Philosophy"—in my opinion one of Nancy's most important works—onwards we can see the emergence of a new approach to myth, to myth without mythology, that is, an approach to myth *on the level of sense instead of signification.*[39]

In "The Forgetting of Philosophy," Nancy begins by noting that Western thought is conditioned—with the exception of certain moments—by what he calls "the schema of the return" (*GT* §3). This is a scheme of thought characterized by nostalgia for past times and for the Golden Age, as we have seen. In general, we Westerners are a in search of lost times, and our thinking is motivated by the presupposition of something lost, which we make our main task to recover, reinstall, or reappropriate as our own origin. The thing so ardently desired through this reappropriation is, according to Nancy, nothing less than the *sense of the world.* Understood according

to this schema of the return—and this is the central thesis of "The Forgetting of Philosophy"—this sense necessarily has at least two features: It is conceived as something to be *possessed* (because it can be lost) and to be *desired* (because it is lost).

It is a particularly contradictory matter, according to Nancy, that we so often proclaim a *crisis* of sense these days. Indeed, if we presuppose that the sense of the world is something we can possess, lose, and rediscover, it can never be completely absent. In such a crisis, it is only lost from sight, because we have not been able to interpret it in the right way. In the schema of the return, the so-called crisis is, in fact, only a crisis of the *signification* of the sense of the world, which is indeed the kind of thing one can possess. If we persist in a nostalgic thinking according to this schema of the return, Nancy declares, sense will always be understood as signification, but "sense in the sense of 'signification' . . . is not exactly, or not simply, 'sense' or something that 'makes sense': it is the presentation of sense. Signification consists in the establishment or assignment of the presence of a factual (or sensible) reality in the ideal (or intelligible) mode" (*GT* 22/30, translation modified).[40]

So, *signification* is sense presented in a form that is assumed to be total and decisive, without remainder. For this reason, signification is, according to Nancy "the very model of a structure or system that is closed upon itself, or better yet, [thought] as *closure upon itself*" (*GT* 23/31–32). Signification is the closure of sense (and therefore its denial according to Nancy, as we shall see), a closed sense, and for this reason something that we believe we can possess, desire and search for. Tellingly, in the philosophical tradition, attaining the moment of possession of signification is often placed in a distant future or a distant past, in an *elsewhere*, and this tradition is thus characterized rather by the *aspiration* or the *will to signification* than by its attainment. Nevertheless, Nancy would say, this structure of aspiration or will is not a renunciation of this kind of thinking, but its moving force.

We encountered the same structure in our analysis of Jena Romanticism: Because it is not the absolute presentation itself, but the aspiration to such a presentation that motivates thought, the absolute presentation is deliberately placed at a distance, be it a distant future, an afterworld, or a heaven of Ideas. In other words, and to adopt Nancy's terminology, Western thought is characterized first of all by the *will to present* the sense of the world (*GT* §4) and this will can only exist insofar as what is willed is never completed. On the other hand, it is this endless will that undermines the nostalgic schema of the return as the basis of Western thought, a basis

which, of course, is that of metaphysics: "It is the endless-ness of the will-to-signify (or present or realize) the philosophizing man, that constitutes the end, in all senses of the word, of philosophy as metaphysics" (*GT* 49/72, translation modified).

Although "The Forgetting of Philosophy" does not pose the problem in these terms, I would say that this schema of the return is taken up in an exemplary way by mythology. What is the will to signify the world, the will to present and reappropriate one's own origin, if not the *will to myth*? This is the reason why Nancy in "Myth Interrupted" could say that "the will to mythation is perhaps nothing other than the will to will" (*IC* 56/143). Myth is the representation par excellence (as we might say, following Kant) of a willing of the faculty of the will-to-signify, of the faculty of will to be, by this very will, the cause of its representations and of the reality of these representations. That said, the will to myth is indeed the will to what the *Systematic Program* called the *subject's* work or "man's work": the work that would be the last and the greatest work of humanity.

The main challenge according to Nancy is to rescue what he calls the "sense of the world" from the nostalgic desire that characterizes the schema of the return. The way to do this, then, is to wrest this sense of the world from the will-to-signify, in order to understand the sense of the world not as *less than* signification, but as that which is characterized by something *other* than the human will to present. Nancy thus wants to put forward, as he calls it, "*another sense of the word 'sense'*" (*GT* 43/63, translation modified). This other sense of the word "sense" is sense, nothing more, nothing less: neither the overarching signification of existence nor its purpose, reason, or essence, but simply the sense of existence insofar as it can be sensed. What, then, is this sense of existence, if such a question is still appropriate for what is not to be signified? "Sense," according to Nancy, is "first of all that *by which*, or rather that *in which* or even *as which* there is a being [*être*] of sense, or an entity [*existant*] whose existence is by itself, from the outset, in the element of sense, before any signification" (*GT* 60/92, my emphasis). Now according to Nancy, it is the recognition of *this* elementary sense of the world that is the main task of philosophy today. Like Heidegger, who criticized philosophers for forgetting to think being that gives itself before any being, Nancy thus criticizes them for forgetting to think the sense that gives itself before any signification: "To ignore this," it is not only to forget the sense of the world, but it "is to forget philosophy" (*GT* 52/76).

The forgetting of philosophy is thus forgetting that there is sense that exceeds signification, sense that is simply there, *hic et nunc* and that is, for

this reason, neither to be deplored nor to be desired. It is what jumps out at us, what touches our bodies even before we can form an idea of it, what is communicated to us even before we have discerned a message. When there is being, there is sense, and "to be" means first of all to be exposed to that sense.[41] We see how Heidegger's and Nancy's criticisms fit together: To forget sense is to forget being. Indeed, according to Nancy, Heidegger has opened the door to an overcoming of Western thought clinging to a certain lost origin, signification, or will. More precisely, Heidegger opened the door by indicating that what counts, above all, is the fact *that* there is being before we can say *what* it is. Returning now to Nancy's distinction between sense and signification, we might say that while the latter refers to the *quid* of being, sense would refer to its simple *quod*. The sense of existence, or the sense that existence *is*, is nothing more than "the element in which there can be significations, interpretations, representations" (*GT* 59/90).

Drawing on Adorno's observation that "that which might rightfully lay claim to the name of sense dwells in what is *open* and not in what is closed upon itself" (qtd. in *GT* 9/11, my emphasis, translation modified), Nancy notes that the difference between signification and sense comes down to the difference between closure and openness. The "other sense of the word 'sense'" advanced by Nancy is therefore what we might call an "open sense" or "sense as opening," as opposed to the seized or closed sense aspired to by the metaphysical tradition. This always-already open sense withdraws itself from signification, from the possibility of making a project of it, not because it would be something impenetrable, dissimulated, or enigmatic, but because it is, indeed, by principle open, opening.

But what is an open sense? In what sense can sense be open? Let us return to the formulation by which Nancy described myth without mythology, which is for him the way to think about the sense of the world: Myth does not provide a representation or a figure, but resides in the "decomposition, the rhythmic unbinding of speech opened by its own lack of origin and to its own indefinite murmur" ("UC" 162), or more briefly, as we have already seen, "proper speech without owner, without possible appropriation" (*PD* 31). To understand myth as a matter of sense instead of signification, thus seems to require another reflection on language and the relation between language and sense. Indeed, Nancy holds, "to think another sense of sense demands that one put back into question the entire understanding of language" (*GT* 55–56/83, translation modified). Rather than taking language as a means to provide the shared signification of a community, we should understand it as mere expression, as the very stage on which significations

are produced.[42] Speech opened by its own lack of origin is the ongoing staging itself, the space-time necessary for something to happen.

We have already seen that Nancy's insistence on the scenic element critically redirects Aristotelian poetics. By shifting attention from the plot to the scene, Nancy seeks to shift attention from language understood as a means of telling stories to language understood as the element in and through which these stories come about. It should be noted, however, that the status of the scene, the *opsis*, is largely ambiguous in the *Poetics*, and rather than renouncing Aristotelian poetics, Nancy seems to be inviting us to push its presuppositions to the limit. In Aristotle's view, the scene has a triple status. First of all, it is one of the six parts of tragedy, next to plot (*muthos*), character, diction, reasoning, and lyric poetry. The scene is everything visual shown on stage, not in the imagination of the spectators, but before their very eyes. Thus, this staging is an unmistakable and characteristic aspect of tragedy. This importance of the visual aspect is further reinforced by Aristotle's observation that the scene is not only one of the six parts of tragedy, but that it is the part that *comprises all of them*: "[T]ragedy as a whole necessarily has six component parts . . . and there are no others besides these . . . since the scene *implies everything*: characters, plot, diction, lyric poetry, and reasoning as well."[43]

After having characterized the scene as not only a necessary but also an all-encompassing part, Aristotle nevertheless denounces or relativizes its poetic nature as already noted: "The scene is attractive, but is very inartistic and least germane to the art of poetry."[44] To quickly clarify this ambivalence, we could say that, although it is necessary that there be a staging for there to be theater, a redundancy of spectacle or what we would call today "special effects" distracts from the essence of tragedy, which resides for Aristotle apparently in a certain sobriety of the mise-en scène.[45] In "Scene," an exchange of letters between Nancy and Lacoue-Labarthe dealing with Aristotle's notion of the scene, Nancy however tries to subtract the scene not only from the "spectacular," but also from optics proper. The scene is for Nancy like an "archi-theatre," which is "the transcendental condition of the emission of sense as sense" ("Sc" 286/83, translation modified). The scene is in other words not yet a specific uttering (a plot, reasoning, or a character), but it is the "the opening of the exterior as such, of 'outside' as 'outside': that is, for me [Jean-Luc Nancy, AvR], of that which makes a 'sense' 'sense,' its articulation, its utterance" ("Sc" 286, translation modified). The scene is for Nancy, in sum, "an enunciation rather than a statement": Before there

is statement, there is this enunciation which states nothing other than "the fact *that* it is uttered (stated, phrased)" ("Sc" 286/83).

According to Nancy, the scene must therefore be conceived as nothing more than appearance itself and is thus both necessary and foreign to *what* appears. In other words, it has nothing to do with the appearance of this or that specific being, but only with "the appearance *of* being, indeed *as* being" ("Sc" 285/83). So, if myth without mythology—this scenic part that is both *more* and *part of* the *muthos* as plot—is for Nancy an "indefinite murmur," this is because it is the murmur of being itself, of being that presents itself, that touches us and jumps out at us in an as yet undefined manner. It is through and in this poetic element that we always touch the very fact of reality. According to Nancy, the most important point is that "this is indeed the definition of the real: it is not what is to be signified, but what runs up against or what violates signification—the opening of sense, or its being laid bare" (*GT* 69/106, translation modified). This open sense does not consist in an opening that occurs once and for all, as if it were a *prima causa* that would set everything in motion, but is what is simply there, at every step, at every blow, without provenance and without end.

From Writing to Being

But if we situate language on this plane of sense, what, then, is the point of even talking about language? And if reality is laid bare by language that resists signification, what definition of reality are we talking about? Indeed, the sense to which Nancy is trying to draw attention, and which he is trying to remove from the dominant Western thought obsessed with the signification of being, should be understood as both more and less than language, revealing both more and less than the real. It exposes what he calls a "simple truth," which, in its simplicity, "[questions] truth as something of the thing in language, and as something of language in the thing." Which means, according to Nancy, that it has to be understood as "something that *withdraws from the thing*, and something that *withdraws from language*"—a withdrawal, he adds, that is "presence that withdraws in itself" (*GT* 56/84, my emphasis).

In emphasizing the withdrawal from language, Nancy associates himself with poetic theories that emphasize the materiality rather than the signification of words, that is, their concrete *presence*. When language is understood on

the level of sense, it has a sense that is undoubtedly always *there*, concrete and local, here and now, inescapable. It is a *sensible* presence, a presence with a certain extension and a certain weight that cannot be generalized. This is why Nancy declares: "Sense needs a thickness, a density, a mass, and thus an opacity, an obscurity by means of which it leaves itself open and lets itself be touched *as sense* right there where it becomes absent as discourse. Now this 'there' is a material point, a weighty point: the flesh of a lip, the point of a pen or of a style, any writing insofar as it traces out the interior and exterior edges of language" (*GT* 79/8, translation modified). This "realist" aspect that imposes itself on language is therefore the weight and specific modality that prevents the given signification from becoming ab-solute, from detaching itself from the concrete lip or feather from which it emerges, floating above concrete things.

But what, precisely, is the *language*-aspect of this "realist" sense? If sense is murmuring speech, what is linguistic about it, if it not its signification, that is, the presentation of sense? It is undoubtedly in the answer to this question that the greatest originality of Nancy's thought lies. Through his insistence on the materiality that marks language, Nancy associates himself to a large extent with his contemporaries. And by using the term "literature" or "writing" in this context, he associates himself more specifically with Derrida's and with so-called "poststructuralist" or "deconstructivist" thought in general. And yet, by extending his reflection on sense towards an analysis of its weighty being, Nancy takes a step that Derrida was never able or willing to take—namely, the step that leads from writing to ontology, or to try this formulation, the step that leads to an *ontology of writing* or an *ontological writing* (which I will call, further on, an *ontological poetics*).[46]

In his work, Derrida took small steps towards the enormous task of rethinking ontology is such a way that it would match a deconstruction of metaphysical thought, but as soon as he arrived at that point, he stepped back, cautiously suspending the question of the world in the repetition of his adage: "the world, *if there is any* [*s'il y en a*] . . ." I would say, then, that this ontology is finally offered to us by Nancy.[47] As he makes clear from the very first pages of *Being Singular Plural*, the redoing of the ontology is not so much his personal ambition as the very requirement of our time: "This text does not disguise its ambition of redoing the whole of 'first philosophy' by giving the 'singular plural' of Being as its foundation. This, however, is not my ambition, but rather the necessity of the thing itself and of our history. At the very least, I hope to make this necessity felt" (*BSP* xv/13). This aspiration—and if it's formulated in terms of *feeling*, this is not without

reason—has not only motivated *Being Singular Plural*, but proves to be the main issue at stake in his entire work. An audacious challenge, to be fair, at a time when critics of metaphysics are tumbling over one another. However, this much is clear, Nancy has no desire to subscribe to traditional metaphysics, and—largely in agreement with its criticisms—makes a tireless effort to break out of it. What he seeks to develop is an ontology that escapes the hegemony of the "one" and the "same," and is thus an "ontology of 'Being' radically removed from all ontology of substance, of order and origin" ("TC" 374/57).[48]

Nancy's ontology, then, deconstructs what is generally understood as "onto" and "logy," and sees being as something which is always given in a singular and plural way. Here, being is certainly not understood as a predestined unfolding of things, as an extended and ordered whole to be deciphered like a plot, nor as a single substance that would be the permanent support of things, but rather as the heterogeneous and unpredictable articulation of an infinite number of singular events. According to Nancy, existence is nothing more than this: the arrival or birth, each time singularly, of the event of sense. In other words, he proposes an ontology that is content with (if we can use this term, because it is precisely one of the characteristics of this ontology never to be content with . . .) being and *nothing but* being, without wishing to reveal its ultimate sense, its causes and reasons; brief, without wishing to give it a signification. The ontology he proposes, if I may put it this way, is therefore frankly *superficial*, concerned only with the surface of things, not because it does not want to deal with what is behind them, but because *there is nothing behind*. Any backdrop where Gods or Ideas might reside is absent: What remains, as said, is a *tautegorical* world.[49] The "necessity of the thing itself" that Nancy speaks of at the beginning of *Being Singular Plural* also indicates that there can be no other necessity than that of the thing itself.

Material reality, the *res*, whose inescapable facticity Nancy seeks to think under the name of sense, is here not a ground that could be the ultimate support for the edifice of thought, but an open, a gaping chasm (to nothing) each time with the ever-interrupted arrival of being. This means that material reality itself is to be understood as difference, spacing, wandering—in short, as what in the deconstructivist tradition is called "writing":

> The open is the thing: the *real* itself. What constitutes us is
> the open, or if you will, the uncovered that puts us face to
> face. This uncovered is the space of sense—it is the spacing

> in which and as which there is sense, a sense that precedes all
> signification, and that succeeds it too. That space, that thing, *we*,
> might be identified with the agency of language, the political or
> passion . . . But it is withdrawn from all these identifications,
> of which it is, in old-fashioned parlance, the "transcendental
> condition," or—if we want to use another parlance—the space,
> element, flesh, and difference. (*GT* 66/102)

For Nancy, then, difference is not a matter of the incessant displacement and
iteration of signifiers without a fixed referent, but is, so to speak, "embodied" in existing matter itself. Language, for Nancy, therefore means nothing
other than this opening-up, exposure or *ex-peau-sition* (*peau* = skin) of the
world's sense. As Ginette Michaud clearly demonstrates, this is why the
figure of the *mouth* plays a central role in Nancy's thought and could even
be understood as a "primal scene" of Nancy's work.[50] While in Derrida's case
it is signification that shows itself destabilized, interrupted, and indecisive,
in Nancy's case it is being itself that, as he himself puts it, "undecided." Or
rather, it "*undecides itself*" (*DS* 10/13) by the simple fact that, for Nancy,
to ex-ist means to open up, to ex-pose oneself, to lose oneself.[51]

As Catherine Malabou points out, Nancy follows in the footsteps of
Levinas and Sartre, who following and radicalizing Heidegger, presupposed
not only that there is a difference between being and beings, but also that
existence is itself the reality of this difference, a conclusion that Heidegger was
never able to draw, according to Malabou.[52] To quote Malabou: "Existence
appears in them [in Levinas, Sartre, and Nancy, AvR] as the *real effect* of
ontological difference and not simply as the mode of being of a being that
is not a thing."[53] Yet Nancy also distances himself from Levinas and Sartre,
and doubtless from all Heidegger's other heirs, because of his fidelity to the
notion of *being*.[54] In so doing, he seems to want to put ontology back at
the forefront, a position even more "fundamental" than that of Levinasian
ethics and Sartrean existentialism.

The way Nancy explains it, this ontico-ontological difference comes
close to Derridean *différance*.[55] Strictly speaking, being already deconstructs
itself as it constructs itself according to Nancy, which suggests a certain
post-deconstructive thinking. For if being is already undecided as it constructs
itself, what else can we do with it except affirm it?[56] Nevertheless, and this
is why Nancy's relationship to deconstruction is so complex, he continues to
describe "being" and "sense" with rather linguistic notions proper to deconstructivist discourse, such as "writing," "graphy," or, more often, "poetry" or

"literature." This is thus where something of *language* resides in the thing. It is the exposure, the *articulation*, of being itself, the fact that things are not closed in on themselves, but extend and open up.

Rethinking Communism

STAGING A "WE"

Let us try to pick up the threads laid bare so far and tie them together. I have already indicated that Nancy attempts to reassert the power and particularity of myth by removing it from mythology and by harnessing it to a fresh set of rules. This reassertion boils down to a reassertion of the *kind of* meaning at stake in myth, a meaning that Nancy calls "sense" and that precedes, exceeds, and disturbs the very (will to) signification traditionally characterizing myth. If we are to understand the inextricable link between community and myth, or even their co-originarity, without venturing into a mythology, then, according to Nancy, we must understand the mythic as a matter not of signification, but of sense. In this way, Nancy has made the beneficial effort of freeing thought from what he calls in *Proprement dit* "the politico-metaphysical mythologies of the communisms, spiritualisms and humanisms" and of recapturing myth as "the opening of a possibility of sense [that is] not provided with accomplished meanings" (*PD* 20). Needless to say, these accomplished meanings have given mythology a particularly important role in *political* constellations. According to Nancy, we must therefore remove myth from the political sphere, because this sphere is necessarily a sphere of power—and "power is not myth" (*PD* 116).

But a myth without mythology, a formation without explanation, or in other words, a presentation without a plot, to what extent is this possible? Does myth not inevitably entail the politico-metaphysical? How do the mythical and the mythological relate to each other? The paradox that characterizes the structure of myth seems to imply that they are like two sides of the same coin that cannot exist independently of each other. Or, to try another metaphor, being both fiction and foundation, myth dresses itself in a cloak that can be worn on both sides, without being able to show both sides at the same time. The important thing is that this paradoxical characteristic is particularly true of *political* myths, which have to present themselves as foundational while concealing their fictional or invented side. In order to appear on the political stage and establish a certain order of a

certain "we," myth presents itself as foundational by dressing itself in a logic decorated with the "the bellicose paraphernalia of the system"[57] consisting of a "destiny," an "essence" or a "project to be completed." This is the "lure" of the politico-metaphysical "mythifying myth" that Nancy wrote about in *Proprement dit* (*PD* 32). Dismantled of this *intriguing* dress, myth reveals itself, to return to the formulation that Nancy uses in "Un commencement," as an unbinding of speech opened by its own lack of origin, reason, and ground: a dismantling difficult to accept by a political regime. Or perhaps it is more precise to say that myth shows itself as this very scene of denudement, that is to say as the bare, stripped-down scene of being-with itself.[58]

This scene of denudement is not unlike the famous scene in Hans Christian Andersen's tale of *The Emperor's New Clothes*. For isn't myth like the clothes of the emperor (or any other holder of power), clothes that are even more important than the affairs of state, because it is precisely through these clothes that he is recognizable as the emperor? The two weavers, who boast that they can weave the most splendid fabric imaginable, are not so much swindlers in bad faith as the only "absolutely modern" people who understand that there are no imperial clothes as such, and that the emperor's clothes are therefore always, in a certain sense, fantastic, deceptive. What is more, these weavers are well aware that the splendor of the garments is perfectly compatible with their invisibility. In fact, in their hearts, both the people and the emperor are well aware that the emperor is naked, but this awareness does not prevent them from wanting to see the clothes, and indeed from seeing them in all their splendid beauty.[59] Not to believe in the emperor's clothes would be foolish, since without this faith the emperor, and consequently the political community, would lose credibility. It can only be the unemployed, non-political child who reminds the citizens of the fact that the emperor indeed has no clothes at all.

For us to recognize ourselves as a political "we," we thus need mythological garments that conceal to some extent the staging that makes this community possible. But if we are not to be blinded by the splendor of these garments, we must also realize that there are no garments at all, that community is always a bare exposition of our being-with. Consequently, community has to be understood in two different but connected ways, two ways that Ian James distinguishes as follows in *The Fragmentary Demand*:

> The discussion of myth in *La communauté désœuvrée* invokes two different understandings of the term *community*, the traditional

notion of community as a sharing of identity or essence (requiring a foundational myth), and the sense given to the term by Nancy, a shared finitude which cannot be subsumed into any work of identity or project (and which is therefore always without foundation). If community requires or necessarily appeals to myth as a founding fiction, it does so in order to articulate itself in the first sense, that is as a sharing of identity or essence. Yet, Nancy maintains, community exists always and already in the second sense, that is, as the nonidentity of shared finitude. Thinking these two moments together allows Nancy to address the way in which the latter 'interrupts' the former. If the shared world of sense is that which can be formalized or organized within the signifying systems of mythic narratives, it is also . . . that which, in excess of signification, cannot ever be entirely reduced to or mastered by those systems.[60]

How, then, can we bring together these two different understandings of community? How do we think the tension between them that forms the dynamic of all questions associated with community, such as those concerning common identity, military service, civic disobedience, hospitality, and so on?

As Nancy points out, especially in *The Inoperative Community* and "The Compearance" (with Jean-Christophe Bailly), bringing these two understandings together was precisely what communism was all about. According to Nancy, the emergence of communism was, for this reason, of unparalleled importance in the history of the West. Although communism pursued the mythological Western claim of appropriating its common origin, it was the first not to seek it in a transcendent value, but in community itself, that is, in the community understood for itself, stripped bare. This is why Nancy and Bailly propose to conceive of communism as both the radicalization of Western tradition and its interruption ("TC" 377/16–17). Or, to use this metaphor again, to conceive of communism as a politics that seeks to *dress itself in its nakedness*.

As significant as the emergence of communism, however, was its *failure*, especially in the 1980s and 1990s when Nancy's publications on community came out. So, Nancy's and Bailly's main aim is not or not only to detect the specific idea of community put forward by communism, but to examine what remains of it after its failure. Or, as the preliminary note to the French republication of "*La comparution*" states, they are driven by the concern to think the "aftermath" of communism ("LC" 7). For how

can we still think of community, the common, the "we," if the movement that pushed such thinking to extremes has failed? What, if anything, is the lesson of communism? Is there still an urgency in the communist demand? If an overcoming of mythological thinking lies in an overcoming of Western thinking about community, this is indeed an urgency that cannot be overestimated.

According to Nancy, in searching for the essence of the common not in a transcendent principle, but in the immanence of community itself, communism has drawn the political consequence of a world abandoned by the gods, that is, a world devoid of the evidence of a regulating principle. This is why Nancy argues, in his book *The Truth of Democracy*, that communism is necessarily democratic in nature, as well as the other way around. Or, more precisely, for Nancy, the "communist" demand is a democratic demand, that is, the demand to find "the conditions under which government and organization are de facto possible in the absence of any transcendent regulating principle" ("FD" 59/78). In the end, then, communism reveals nothing less than the basic structure of all modern politics.

And yet we must be careful not to place Nancy too hastily on the side of French left-wing intellectuals. The most important lesson to be drawn from his analysis of the "lure" of politico-metaphysical mythologies is that community must be thought first and foremost at the level of *ontology*, not of politics. For him, "communism" is therefore not a political option, but first and foremost an ontological category, and hereby he distances himself from post-Marxist philosophers such as Badiou, Slavoj Žižek, or Antonio Negri rather than endorsing them.[61] Nancy's ontological communism does not call for revolution, nor for any communist-inspired political model, but merely points to the fact that every political model, whatever its form, is "founded" on a being that is already *in common* before it gives itself in the form of an identity, an institute, a regime, or a program.

The Failure of Communism

What Nancy wants to emphasize—and what he believes communism has emphasized—is that community is not something we share, a common being, but rather a being-in-common of which we are part, but which at the same time divides us before we determine ourselves as a group, as well as an individual. This being-in-common is "without value" (*TD* 17/33) that is, not to be determined. Clearly, Marx is not far off. Being outside any measurable value, being-in-common is naturally also outside any exchange

value. An approach sensitive to this being-in-common should therefore be based not on the principle of equivalence but of *non-equivalence*, "finding, or achieving, a sense of evaluation, of evaluative affirmation, that gives to each evaluating gesture—a decision of existence, of work, of bearing—the possibility of not being measured in advance by a given system but of being, on the contrary, each time the affirmation of a unique, incomparable, unsubstitutable 'value' or 'sense' " (*TD* 24/46).[62] Ultimately, an absolutely modern politics should not have to convert to the principle of strict equality, according to which all opinions, cultures, and beliefs are measured by the same measure, but to the principle of inequality, which makes a general measure impossible.

If there is anything to be salvaged from the ruins of communism, it is thus the path opened up by Marx's attempt to think of community as independent of the measure of a given system. According to Marx, what we have in "common" is the particularity of the here and now of "concrete labor," shoulder to shoulder, a particularity that is denied precisely in the generality demanded not only by capitalism, but also, as we might add, by every other attempt to make a *project* of community.[63] The lesson of communism is therefore, according to Nancy, "that it can no longer be a matter of figuring or modeling a communitarian essence in order to present it to ourselves and to celebrate it, but that it is a matter rather of think-ing community, that is, of thinking its insistent and possibly still *unheard* demand, beyond communitarian models or remodelings" (*IC* 22/59, my emphasis). The demand beyond communitarian models or remodelings is that of our naked being-with, which is only given singularly, uniquely, and incomparably each time, as a matter of sense, not signification. What is more, this sense, which precedes and surpasses all signification, means that community cannot determine itself once and for all, but is forced to revalue itself at every moment in which it arises—a revaluation not in the name of another value, but in the name of the lack of a primary value.

Clearly, despite having laid the foundations for a new way of thinking about community, communism has fallen into the trap that has threatened all Western thought in the past: the pretension of appropriating its origin, a pretension whose sometimes naive, sometimes monstrous manifestations are found throughout our history. In the case of communism, the trap lies in the always ready to get stuck suffix "-ism." And it is at the very moment when we are trying to avoid it that such a trap becomes most obvious. In this respect, the failure of communism is perhaps more instructive than its emergence. According to the introductory note to the French republication

of *La comparution*, "[t]he aftermath of communism . . . can only be found in the 'common' *to come* [*à venir*], untied of any '-ism' but exposed to what is most proper to it and which is neither an essence, nor a destination, but always again an event" ("LC" 7–8). The lesson to be drawn, then, is the following: Although the "common" must indeed form the starting point for any reflection on community, it is not necessary to *determine* what is "common" in order for it to form the starting point. The "common" is what imposes itself each time anew, and each time in a different way.

But if we are to go further than communism, we must first detect why communism did not go far enough down the road it had opened up, why it felt the need to turn our being-in-common into an "ism." According to Bailly, there are two features of communism that bear responsibility for the turn taken by events: firstly "the confidence in the notion of *progress*" and secondly "the determination of a revolutionary *subject* (the proletariat) and its armed meta-subject (the party)" ("LC" 46, my emphasis). Even if communism was content with the naked community, without seeking its substance elsewhere than in this community, it wanted to cover this nakedness by determining it and making it the project of a specific subject. This desire boils down to what Nancy calls an "absolute immanentism" where "human beings [are] defined as producers (one might even add: human beings [are] defined al all), and fundamentally as the producers of their own essence in the form of their labor or their work" (*IC* 2/13). In other words, immanent forms of community wish to produce themselves as their own work and realize themselves as the completion of a self-produced essence. A similar immanentism can of course be found in the *System Program*'s aspiration to produce the Great Work of humanity.

In the end, then, we must conclude that the failure of communism does not result from the fact that human beings form and are formed in common—for there is no other option, as communism has clearly seen—but from the additional fact that they form themselves as a work in order to turn themselves into a project: "[I]t is precisely the immanence of man to man, or it is man, taken absolutely, considered as the immanent being par excellence, that constitutes the stumbling block to a thinking of community. A community presupposed as having to be one of human beings presupposes that it effects, or that it must effect, as such and integrally, its own essence, which is itself the accomplishment of the essence of humanness" (*IC* 3/15). It does not make any difference to Nancy whether this essence of man is realized in economic exchange, in a certain political ideal, or rather in a certain relationship to nature: In all cases, it is a matter of closing off the sense of our being-with.

However harmless such an aspiration may be, it always comes down to a "totalitarian" desire, according to Nancy. As one of the key notions of the *Centre de recherches philosophiques sur le politique* founded by Nancy and Lacoue-Labarthe in the 1980s, the term "totalitarianism" stands for a way of thinking about community characterized by the desire for a *total* formation of the community as a *totality*. Or, as they specify themselves, quoting Arendt, it is a system regulated by the "totally self-fulfilling (and willfully self-fulfilling) logic of an idea, an idea 'by which the movement of history is explained as one consistent process' [so that] whatever happens, happens according to the logic of one 'idea'" ("NM" 293/21).[64] Drawing on the Arendtian definition of ideology already given in the introduction, a totalitarian system is thus for Lacoue-Labarthe and Nancy a system that is based on the historical logic of one idea, that is, on a *plot*, and which attributes to itself the principal role in its completion.

The Lesson of Communism

And yet, through its failure and its scandalous, unapologetic realization, communism has taught us an important lesson. It could be said that, for Nancy, communism played the role played by Nietzsche's madman in *The Gay Science* informing us that God is dead, that the earth is detached from the sun, and that there is no consolation or redemption. As he makes his announcement, however, the madman realizes that he has come too soon. Even though people listen to the announcement of God's death, they still do not *hear* what is being said, and go on living as if nothing has changed, as if there were still a bright and distant horizon to guide us.

Similarly, perhaps we have not yet really heard the unheard message of communism, Nancy suggests. If we really want to draw the consequences of the non-mythological world, we must, as Nancy says several times in *The Inoperative Community*, go *beyond all possible horizons*: "The ultimate limit of community, or the limit that is formed by community, as such, traces an entirely different line. This is why, even as we establish that communism is no longer our unsurpassable horizon, we must also establish, just as forcefully, that a communist exigency or demand communicates with the gesture by means of which we must go farther than all possible horizons" (*IC* 8–9/28).[65]

The political system that seems best suited to current conditions is undoubtedly democracy, especially since Nancy hinted at the essentially democratic nature of communism itself. And indeed, after the collapse of communism, the democratic regime was—with reservations, but nonetheless firmly—embraced as the worst of all regimes excepting all others, in

Churchill's famous phrase; not a perfect regime, but nevertheless the only one worth preserving, defending, and even exporting. Problematically, however, although democracy, in this characterization, is not idealized, it nevertheless seems to stand as an ideal, as a regulative idea, however abstract or formal that idea may be. No matter how reserved our attitude towards democracy may be, if this reservation is not also addressed to the democratic regime as such, the latter is no better than "all others." This, at least, seems to be Nancy's hypothesis in *The Truth of Democracy*. Moreover, as we saw in the introduction, this is exactly where Benjamin, too, located the hidden "violence" of the modern constitutional state.

In supporting this hypothesis, Nancy implicitly returns to his analysis of German Romanticism, first and foremost to characterize democracy as an infinite becoming. But as much as we like to perceive our democracy as a regime forever in the making and resisting any definitive form, it is at the same time based on another aspect detected by Nancy in Romanticism, namely its persistence, despite all its revolutionary claims, in the most tenacious aspiration of the Western philosophical tradition: the will to system, that is, the ambition to form democracy as the Great Work of humanity. A few years after their study of Romanticism, Nancy and Lacoue-Labarthe examined the evils of such politicization of the Romantic idea of self-formation in "The Nazi Myth."

Above all, "The Nazi Myth"—like *The Truth of Democracy*—is an attempt to wake us up from our comfortable satisfaction with the democratic system. Nancy and Lacoue-Labarthe emphasize that a regime like Nazism is not an accidental flaw in the political fabric, but reveals its very structure. At first glance, this claim—also supported by Arendt and Agamben, among others[66]—could be seen as unnuanced and even provocative. It is important to understand, however, that this claim does not imply that Western culture *necessarily* leads to Nazism, that Nazism is its inevitable destiny, for this would imply a finality of history that they refuse to evoke. What Nancy and Lacoue-Labarthe are trying to show, is that a logic like that of National Socialism was possible because it could be grafted onto a more general logic, which is the very Western logic of community: "We wish only to underline just how much this logic, with its double trait of the *mimetic will-to-identity* and the *self-fulfillment of form*, belongs profoundly to the mood or character of the West in general and, more precisely to the fundamental tendency of the subject in the metaphysical sense of the word" ("NM" 312/71, my emphasis). Here we recognize again the absolute immanentism that according to Nancy characterizes the Western view on community. Understood

according to this absolute immanentism, a community realizes itself by completing the form it has appropriated as its own. Like they did in *The Literary Absolute*, Nancy and Lacoue-Labarthe add that this double feature of mythological logic was inextricably linked, in the West, but especially in Germany, to a metaphysics of the *subject*. Compared to other European countries, Germany had long lacked a collective identity of its own, that is, a well-defined identity of the German subject. For the Germans, this lack became the object of their action, an action consequently dedicated to their self-realization: "Germany, in other words, was not only missing an identity, but also lacked the ownership of its means and identification" ("NM" 299/39). After the example of the Greeks, the Germans chose a poetic model for this self-realization: the model of the work of art.

Indeed, the Nazi myth is about a collective subject whose logic leads, according to Nancy and Lacoue-Labarthe, to "a fusion of politics and art," in what they call, following on from their study of German Romanticism, *"the production of the political as work of art"* ("NM" 303/49). What characterizes Nazism more specifically is that the subject finds its collective equivalent not only in the nation or the party, but also in its race. The form to which the Nazi aspired, which would contain his origin and destiny, was a physiological form, namely that of the Aryan.[67] Once again, however, what is at stake in Nancy's and Lacoue-Labarthe's analysis is not so much the clarification of the specificities of National Socialism, or of the turn taken by history in general, as an understanding of the present *through* the National Socialist past, an understanding that, as said, should above all wake us up: "A comfortable security in the certitudes of morality and democracy not only guarantee nothing, but exposes one to the risk of not seeing the arrival, or the return, of that whose possibility is not due to any simple accident of history" ("NM" 312/71).

Rethinking Democracy (*Nancy, Heidegger*)

THE TRUTH OF DEMOCRACY

Of course, such a warning can be found in other thinkers, too, and has been repeated so often that it risks losing its disturbing value. The mere observation that the possibility of Nazism is woven into the very structure of our thinking about community, democracy included, is therefore less important than asking how, and to what extent, our democracies can ward off the risk

of the metaphysical-political mythology they entail. Nancy's answer to this question lies in an understanding of the *sense* of community. But how can we focus on sense without falling back into the trap of communism? In *The Truth of Democracy*, written shortly after Nicolas Sarkozy relaunched the debate on national identity, Nancy looks for the beginnings of an answer in an obvious event: May '68. For Nancy, the student and worker movement of spring 1968 is the quintessential example of a community that does not present itself as a work and that does not aspire to give itself a form, but that is characterized, on the contrary, by *unworking*: The "community" of May '68 manifested itself as a community of those who have nothing in common but their resistance to community.

In this respect, *The Truth of Democracy* does not really stand out from the large number of books that have been published—forty years after the fact—about May '68.[68] However, it differs from other contributions in that it does not defend the specific values of May '68, but the general *Umwertung aller Werte* that took place at that time. According to Nancy, one can only prefer one political system to another if one keeps intact the virtue of "true" politics or "true" democracy. The particular strength of the May '68 movement was its questioning of the very truth of democracy. A "true" democracy, as we can summarize Nancy's central claim, is indeed a democracy whose truth is called into question. Or, as Lefort and Rancière have also demonstrated, the essence of democracy is the perpetual and unde-cidable debate, motivated by an inherent "hatred" of democracy.[69] What is more, since this questioning must never cease, there is no point in talking, thirty, forty or fifty years later, about the "legacy" of May '68. The events of '68 demonstrated precisely that democracy can never, not even after the Second World War, not even after the fall of communism, be taken for granted and cherished.

For Nancy, democracy is therefore necessarily *inadequate* (*TD* 2sq/15sq), not because of the so-called "democratic deficit," but more profoundly because it has no fixed representation against which to measure itself. A "represented" world, as Nancy has it in *The Creation of the World, or, Globalization*, "is a world dependent on the gaze of a subject of the world [*sujet du monde*]. A subject of the world (that is to say as well a subject of history) cannot itself be within the world [*être dans le monde*]. Even without a religious representation, such a subject, implicit or explicit, perpetuates the position of the creating, organizing, and addressing God (if not the addressee) of the world" (*CW* 40/31–32). Put another way, it is because we always perpetuate, in a sense, the idea of a God-creator that the will of the perfect system can

arise, and with it, as Nancy adds in *The Truth of Democracy*, "fore-visions or fore-casts [*prévisions*] of a world transformed—reformed, renewed, indeed, re-created or re-founded" (*TD* 6/16).

In short, to say that democracy is necessarily inadequate is not to say that it never fully meets our expectations, as is often alleged, but it is inadequate because it cannot rely on a truth understood according to the model of *adequatio*, a truth that can be approximately attained. Rethinking the truth of democracy means realizing that this truth is not to be found in the protection of a certain number of values, for example against fascist totalitarian regimes, but that it is an indeterminate, empty truth that can only be glorified by criticizing it (*SW* 90/141). This, according to Nancy, is what May '68 taught us. But criticized in the name of what? What does the beach under the paving stones consist of? If we follow Nancy's analysis, democracy can never be called into question in the name of a certain alternative conception of the world (or, if you like, of the political subject, power and sovereignty). There is no measure by which *demos* or *kratein* can be remeasured. *Sous les pavés*, then, is nothing other than what Nancy calls the bare fact of our existence *with* one another, an existence that has no common denominator.

From Politics to Ontology

Again, indicating this bare fact of being-with, "democracy" for Nancy is not a *political* regime, but "a regime of sense" (*TD* 33/60). What counts in "democracy," "communism," or, more generally, "community" is the sense of singular plural being that constantly interrupts and questions every political regime. Instead of trying to reintegrate Nancy's thought into a political program, we should thus understand notions such as "community" and "being in common" on an ontological rather than a political level.[70] Although his early works seem to suggest otherwise, Nancy aspires to redo fundamental ontology not political philosophy. Most importantly, Nancy's redoing of fundamental ontology demonstrates that the very ground on which various communities model themselves can never be political, but is "anything you like—existential, artistic, literary, dreamy, amorous, scientific, thoughtful, leisurely, playful, friendly, gastronomic, urban, and so on" (*TD* 26/48). In all these areas, what is "in common" is decided in a singular and unique way. These decisions not only precede the political decision-making process, but also undermine it. For Nancy, the radically unequal, ever-changing regime of sense that "community" is, is to sum up his main claim once again *"first of all a metaphysics and only afterwards a politics"* (*TD* 34/62, my emphasis).

This also means that politics is never simply and solely political. Or inversely, referring to his essay "The 'Retreat' of the Political," co-authored with Lacoue-Labarthe, that the *retreat* of the political is for Nancy perhaps the political moment par excellence—that is, its re-tracement, redefinition, each time anew. Given its necessarily anarchic nature, politics can only take the form of a questioning and, consequently, a permanent re-tracement, but for such a re-tracement to take place, it must necessarily come from elsewhere. Or, as Nancy indicates in his contribution to the collection *Democracy in What State?*: "[T]hinking about how politics without foundation, politics in a State of permanent revolution (if that expression can stand) must permit spheres that are, strictly speaking, foreign to it, to expand on their own" ("FD" 64/83).

So, a politics without foundation requires there to be a *non-political sphere*, that is,—and this explains why the retreat of the political implies an exit from totalitarianism—a sphere that prevents that "everything is political," according to the well-known adage by which Arendt characterized totalitarian systems. Indeed, the reason why Nancy and Lacoue-Labarthe interrogate the characteristics of totalitarian politics is the same one that led them to write "The Nazi Myth": Although the tentacles of politics in our democracies are not as visible as in tyrannical regimes, they are, in their view, no less omnipresent, and for this very reason. More precisely, it is because of the absence of a separate, transcendent institution founding and legitimizing politics—as God once did for the king—that politics tend to be *total* in our democracies. Who or what decides, in effect, what the limit of politics is? However boldly it may be formulated, Nancy and Lacoue-Labarthe's thesis put forward in "The 'Retreat' of the Political" is a serious one: Our democracies exhibit a "soft" or "unprecedented" totalitarianism that proceeds from "the dissolution of transcendence, and, henceforth [comes] to penetrate all spheres of life now devoid of any alterity" (*RP* 129/192).[71]

It is this subtle and almost unnoticed penetration of all areas of life by politics that has resulted in the point where the democratic regime itself can no longer be questioned: "*Democracy* has become an exemplary case of the loss of the power to signify: representing both supreme political virtue and the only means of achieving the common good, it grew so fraught that it was no longer capable of generating any problematic or serving any heuristic purpose" ("FD" 58/77). If we are to do justice to the "truth" of democracy, which, as we have seen, consists in being perpetually interrogated, then we must realize that *not* everything is political, but that there is first a simple being together in the world. If there is a "political program" in

Nancy's work, it is, in the final analysis, nothing more, but also nothing less, than the meditation with which he concludes *The Truth of Democracy*: "If we first think the being of our being together in the world, we will see which politics gives this thought a chance" (*TD* 34/62).

Importantly, this also means that we should not entirely remove ourselves from the realm of politics, as Nancy observes in the opening text of the *Centre de recherches philosophiques sur le politique*: "The exit, or liquidation of the political . . . is always about to confirm its domination."[72] Still, while it is perfectly clear that Nancy renounces both the omnipresence and the absence of politics, the hopeful resignation expressed in his advice to "see" which politics gives our being-together in the world a "chance" may come as a surprise. For will there ever be a politics that will give anything a "chance"? Or is it rather in the nature of political power to leave nothing to chance, to eliminate as effectively as possible all that is hazardous and unexpected? I will come back to this in chapter 4.

The Impetus of the "With" (Nancy, Heidegger)

Let us now explore in greater depth the *togetherness* that characterizes our being together in the world, and which, according to Nancy, should be the starting point not only of all politics, but also of all philosophical analysis. For it is precisely this togetherness that makes Nancy's new first philosophy a *social* ontology, an ontology that concerns what he alternately calls "being-together," "being-with," "being singular plural," "co-existence," "sharing," or also "compearance."[73] Within this framework, the notion of "compearance" specifies that the absence of a shared common essence is like the absence of a judge who would decide whether one is part of the community or not: "There would thus be no longer a court to which we should compear. However, we find ourselves still in judgement. . . . Common: banal, trivial: we appear before our banality, before the exceptional absence of a 'condition' which one has always too quickly baptized 'human.' Common: not made from a single substance, but to the contrary from the lack of a substance which essentially apportions the lack of essence" ("TC" 372 and 274/54 and 58). Ultimately, then, we compear only with ourselves, being ourselves the only possible measure for measuring ourselves, not on the day of judgment, at the end of the world, but at every moment, for "we com-pear" means nothing other than "we come together (in)to the world" ("TC" 373/57), naked and without pregiven value. So we are always already in relation with each other before this relation is marked, defined, or appropriated.

Of course, Nancy's redoing of ontology would not have been possible without Heidegger's fundamental preparations. By explaining *Dasein* (being-there) as *Mitsein* (being-with), Heidegger paved the way for the social ontology aimed at by Nancy. What is more, through his analysis of *Dasein*, Heidegger was already demonstrating that we are always *there*, thrown into the world, with the consequence that it is impossible to pose ourselves in front of the world, to take ourselves for a *cosmotheoros*, without already being engaged in it. It follows, as Nancy concludes following Heidegger, that "Being 'itself' comes to be defined as relational, as non-absoluteness, and, if you will—in any case this is what I am trying to argue—*as community*" (*IC* 6/21–22). Although he takes up most of Heidegger's analysis, Nancy criticizes him for not having thought radically enough about the *mit* of the *Mitsein* and even the *Mit-da-sein*. Nancy wants

> to give us to understand that Heidegger's *Mitsein*, and even his *Mit-da-sein*, is not thought out as radically or as decisively as it should be. It would really need to be understood that the "*mit*" does not modify the "*sein*" (as if being could already sustain itself in some way, as if being were itself; that is, as if being were or existed absolutely); and it would need to be understood that the "*mit*" does not even qualify the "*Dasein*" but that it constitutes it essentially. ("OBC" 2)

Although one could object that Heidegger, too, pointed out that being-with is not a qualification of being-there, but its condition of possibility, he undeniably paid little attention to it. By proposing to replace the term *Mit-da-sein* by that of *Sein-da-mit*, Nancy sets himself the task of thinking the "with" more insistently than Heidegger as the very modality of being-there.

Besides the *with* of being-with, it is however also the *there* of being-there that Nancy wants to accentuate with more force than Heidegger did. According to Nancy, we must accept that in being-with, we are not so much *there*, but rather *the there*: "It isn't a question, then, of being there. Rather, it has to do, . . . with 'being the there' . . . The 'there' itself is made only of opening and exposition" (*C* 132–133/124). This amounts to saying that we do not occupy a place in a preexisting world, but we ourselves *are* a place, a spacing, a dis-position of the world. Indeed, the world is nothing else than the exposure of the one to the other; the exposure giving itself each time singularly. In short, being *is* not, but is *born*, and *comes to presence*, like an event.[74]

We might conceive of Nancy's reading of Heidegger as an attempt to fold the later Heidegger into the former, as Christopher Fynsk rightly points out: "Nancy folds the later Heidegger (a Heidegger that Derrida has helped us to think with his elaboration of the concepts of *différance* and 'writing') back into the earlier."[75] Indeed, this is what Nancy programmatically proposes in the opening pages of *Being Singular Plural*: "[I]t is necessary to refigure fundamental ontology (as well as the existential analytic, the history of Being, and the thinking of *Ereignis* that goes along with it) with a thorough resolve that *starts from the plural singular of origins*, from *being-with*" (*BSP* 26/45). It is by linking the thought of the event developed by the later Heidegger to the existential analytic developed in *Being and Time* that Nancy tries to form the social ontology that I will define as a *poetic* ontology.

Following Heidegger, Nancy proposes to think of being as an event, as that which *happens*: "the event of Being, which is in no way Being, [but] is nonetheless Being 'itself' " (*BSP* 164/190). In this way, Nancy explicitly distinguishes himself, for example, from Badiou's position who, in *Being and Event* precisely separates being and event.[76] Nancy argues, on the contrary, that they are in the end the same "thing," for it is being itself that is both singular and plural. Following in Heidegger's footsteps, Nancy describes the event as a "leap," not only *into* being, but also *of* being The event, I would say, is thus the *leaping being* or, as Nancy puts it elsewhere, "syn-coping" being (*DS*). This leap manifests itself both temporally and spatially, and both at the same time. In Nancy's words, it is a "leap into the space-time of nothing," that is "into the space-time of space-time 'itself' " (*BSP* 173/199). Instead of going in search of the main tonality of being, as so many ontologies and metaphysics have done, Nancy posits that being is something *rhythmic*. Being in the world, he says, is thus "being-thrown . . . as if *rhythmed by its going-to-itself in itself* . . . Rhythmed autoheterography of existences" (*FT* 128/63). Given this coming-and-going of heterogeneous presences, which is only triggered by the "between" that separates them, singular beings can no longer refer to a stable entity that ensures their permanence. All that remains is for them to relate to each other, without this relation referring to a more general thing that exceeds them. This mutual relation has no other measure than the unmeasurable singular between, a between that nonetheless exposes beings to an outside.

This rhythmic, eventful way of being is what according to Nancy makes up the sense of the world, a sense that exists both in an *extended* and *exposing* way. To better understand this idea, we need to realize that Nancy's

social ontology is not so much, or not solely, an ontology of *humans*. The being-with described by Nancy is, as he himself puts it, "the juxtaposition of pure exteriorities [. . .] (for example, a bench with a tree with a dog with a passer-by)" (*BSP* 35/55). More than an ontology of humans, Nancy's social ontology is an ontology of *bodies*: "The ontology of being-with is an *ontology of bodies*, of every body, whether they be inanimate, animate, sentient, speaking, thinking, having weight, and so on. Above all else, 'body' really means what is outside, insofar as it is outside, next to, against, nearby, with a(n) (other) body, from body to body, in the dis-position" (*BSP* 84/107–8). Heidegger's ontology was anthropocentric in that, for him, the existence of being-there is always and only *human* existence. According to Heidegger, man alone has a world, whereas other beings—animals, things—are only part of this world, but do not themselves have a world.[77] The reason for this exclusive position of man, according to Heidegger, lies in the fact that only man has a practical relationship to the world: *Da-sein* is not an inert existence in the world, but exceeds it in order to relate to its being as a *concern*. Translated into Nancyan terms, only *Dasein* can expose itself and thus relate to its own being. And it is precisely in this relation that its ex-existence consists.

Although Nancy does not always explicitly thematize the question of Heidegger's "humanism," he clearly opposes it on several occasions. Already in "Shattered Love," Nancy distances himself from Heidegger, because the latter "(despite himself?) [kept] the assignation of this *Dasein* in the apparent form of a distinct individuality, as much opposed as exposed to the other individualities, and thus irremediably kept in a sphere of autonomic, if not subjective, allure" (*IC* 104). It is undoubtedly for this reason that Nancy, in *The Inoperative Community* of the same period, proposes to substitute the notion of "subject" by the notion of "singularity," a notion that anticipates the idea of "singular plural being" developed later.[78]

The starting point of Nancy's ontology is not a specific being like in Heidegger's case, but their position next to each other, with each other. Being is the fact that we weigh, touch, and make an impression on the surfaces of other bodies. For this reason, Nancy concludes, the ontology of being-with can only be "materialist." Focusing on the "matter" or the material body, Nancy thus moves beyond Heidegger's humanism. In Nancy's vocabulary, "matter," like "body," must once again be understood as something absolutely *superficial*, that is, without any subterranean foundational capacity or transcendent value. Nancy's oft-used expression *partes extra*

partes indicates that, as far as matter is concerned, it is only a question of the articulation, in the original sense of the word, of beings with one another, without there being any common substance, organizing principle, or concentric movement. If being is *singular-plural*, as Nancy indicates in his book of the same title, this means that being has no fixed point, but is dislocation, the incessant displacement of singular articulations, and that for this reason it never coincides with itself.

The material body, every material body, is thus *exposed*. What makes the material body a *body* (as opposed to what Nancy calls a "mass") is precisely that it is not closed in itself, but ex-poses and opens itself to other bodies. In this way, we could say that *every* being engages in a practical relation with the world. Or, more precisely, the being of being is nothing other than this relation, a relation that makes that being is always being-*with*. Humanity, then, is no more than a secondary entity: The human, says Nancy, exists only "to the extent that this essence of human beings itself belongs to being-in-common" (*EF* 73/99). The human, in other words, is a status derived from a more fundamental existence that is the shared being of all beings. Being-with is thus the "whole" not only of humans, but also of trees, of houses—"a bench with a tree with a dog with a passer-by" (*BSP* 35/55).[79] Just as there are no commas in this sentence separating one entity from another, there is no categorization distinguishing different types of entity.

In his analysis of Nancy's work, *On Touching—Jean-Luc Nancy*, Derrida moreover argues that Nancy's ontology has its starting point not in vision (which is always unifying) like so many ontologies, but in the sense of *touch* (which is in principle plural). This is why Nancy is largely associated with phenomenological thought, such as that of Merleau-Ponty, who also recognizes the body as the condition of openness to the world. But he distances himself from it too. The weakness, or rather the error, of the phenomenological tradition is, in his view, to have maintained the idea of an interiority or property of the body. For his part, Nancy never ceases to emphasize that the body can never be proper or appropriated, because it is already outside itself, distinct from itself, open: "[T]he body's a thing of extension. The body is a thing of exposition. It's not just that the body is exposed but that the body consists in being exposed" (*C* 124/109). This is, of course, an exposure *without return*. For the body *as a body* is always already open to others, it is so to speak always already "intruded" by them.[80]

Sharing Community in and as Literature (*Nancy, Blanchot*)

Communicating Community

So, our way of existing in the world obliges us, according to Nancy, to radically change the way we have hitherto approached the question of community and to move beyond existing political models of community. If these models are indeed the way in which the West has always understood our being-with, then we need to change the way we think, or think at the limit of our thinking, to be able to think our being-with. In order not to give in to the reflex—not only religious and political but also *intellectual*—of dressing it up with the presupposition of an essence, an origin or a destiny, we should go further down the path opened up by what Nancy calls "communism" and respond even more radically to its demand. To do this, we almost have to force our thinking *not* to think, to exhaust it.

As we have seen, the "aftermath" of communism resides, according to Nancy, in a way of thinking that is free of all "-isms." Now, for Nancy, such a renunciation of "isms" lies in what he calls, for want of a better term, a "*literary* communism." I quote Nancy at length:

> For the moment, let us say that in lieu of a name it is necessary to *mobilize words*, so as to set the limit of our thinking back in motion. What "there is" in place of communication is neither the subject nor communal being, but community and sharing.
>
> But this still says nothing. Perhaps, in truth, there is nothing to say. Perhaps we should not seek a word or a concept for it, but rather recognize in the thought of community a theoretical excess (or more precisely, an excess in relation to the theoretical) that would oblige us to adopt another praxis of discourse and community. But we should at least try to say this, because "language alone indicates, at the limit, the sovereign moment where it is no longer current." (Georges Bataille, *Eroticism*) Which means here that only a discourse of community, exhausting itself, can indicate to the community the sovereignty of its sharing (that is to say neither present to it nor signify to it its communion). An ethics and a politics of discourse and writing are evidently implied here. What such a discourse should or can be, how and by whom in society it should and can be held, indeed what holding such a discourse would call for in terms of the transformation,

> revolution, or resolution of that society . . . this is what we
> will have occasion to look into. This is nothing other than the
> question of *literary communism*, or least of what I am trying to
> designate with this clumsy expression: something that would be
> *the sharing of community in and by its writing, its literature.* (IC
> 25–26/66–67, my emphasis)

With the "clumsy" expression of *literary communism*, Nancy is trying to indicate that we must locate the thought of community in another praxis of discourse, or more simply, in the *praxis of discourse* itself. Instead of presenting or signifying community in all sorts of concepts, forms, and ideas, we will have to share it in the practice of discourse itself. More precisely, we *already* share it in this practice. To *speak* of community, or even simply to speak, is already to share community itself, to communicate it. This is what Nancy calls the "writing" and "literature" of community, namely its communication without there being any communion, representation, or signification of this community. What is communicated is only community itself. "Basically," Nancy says elsewhere, "the question is: *what remains* after the 'interruption' [of myth, AvR]? . . . . What remains is . . . *literature*" (*PD* 33, my emphasis).

What makes Nancy look for a way out of traditional thinking of community in a certain theory of communication and literature, is that the model of *language* is, for him, the model par excellence of what is *in* common without there being something common. Through all its differences, variants, accents, and translations, language does not function because there is, beneath it, a single, original language, an Esperanto or Babylonian language that would be like the common source of all enunciations. What we share in and through language is, ultimately, language itself. We share and are shared by language, not because it is the reflection of a preexisting source or system of signification, but because it exists each time as an event *between* us.

Another reason why Nancy, in *The Inoperative Community*, relies on a theory of communication is that he associates himself with Bataille, who, according to him, wanted to develop a new philosophy of *communication* on the basis of this acutely *modern* experience of community.[81] For Nancy, Bataille "is without doubt the one who experienced first, or most acutely, the modern experience of community as neither a work to be produced, nor a lost communion, but rather as space itself, and the spacing of the experience of the outside, of the outside-of-self" (*IC* 19/50). This specifically

modern experience of community, described by Bataille under the slightly misleading title of "inner experience," is the experience of being exposed to each other, of being outside oneself, in ecstasy, as Bataille puts it. This is where the experience of community and being are mutually constituted, for, as Bataille says, a "being is, I believe, incapable on his own, of going to the end of being."[82] Nancy recognizes this as a strictly modern experience, because it encourages us to think of being as something that determines itself *relationally*—as communication—and not in dependence on some shared horizon.

This is also why, later, and also partially inspired by Bataille, Nancy can establish a direct link between language and sex or *eros*. As Nancy says in his book entirely devoted to this link, *Sexistence*: "Sex and language . . . form the double element according to which we exist as the 'human species'—which is to say, as the species that, in the one way or the other, exceeds any given order" (*S* 43/70).[83] In other words, it is through sex and language—or more precisely, through sex as "communication" and through communication as "sexual"—that we *expose* ourselves, that we are (as) exposed. Indeed, *literature* is perhaps just another name for language that has become sexual or sex that has become language: "More than on couches, it is in literature, in art, and in revolution that sex speaks—and speech makes itself sexual. Simultaneously, a major transformation occurs, that of an entire social and technical praxis which desires to recreate the world, desire's own speaking out and language's desire not to say but to make love" (*S* 40/66). In a similar vein, with the expression "literary communism" chosen by Nancy in the 1980s, he also emphasizes that "literature" is always a kind of *excessive* communication: "What is in fact involved is the following: that there is an inscription of the communitarian exposition, and that this exposition, as such, can only be inscribed, or can be offered only by way of an inscription" (*IC* 39/96–97). Because literature is not, first and foremost, the transmission of a message, but primarily or fundamentally a communication *without* a clear message, literary communication cannot be put to work. "Literature," for Nancy, is that which, by principle, un-works, that which resists being put to work, because it is an exposure without return.

This is why—and this is the heart of Nancy's ontological poetics as we will see in chapter 3—Nancy states that "by 'literature' we will have to designate *this being itself . . . in itself*. In other words, it would designate that singular ontological quality that *gives* being in common" (*IC* 64/161, my emphasis). As beings that *ex-ist*, we are already in common in a literary way. What Nancy calls "literary communism" is therefore as common as

everyday life. The ontological plane on which Nancy proposes to understand community, the plane on which it gives itself as a singular plural being, must therefore be conceived as being graphed and spoken *as* literature. Nancy's specific philosophical move claiming that being exists in a poetic way, obviously places his view of "literature" in line with what the Jena Romantics meant by "poetry" or *poiesie*, and what Heidegger referred to as *Dichtung*: the primary "constitution" of things.

COMMUNITY AS UNWORKED WORK

In Nancy's view, the main characteristic of both literature and community is their unworking. Using the Blanchotian notion of "*désoeuvrement*," Nancy says: "Community necessarily takes place in what Blanchot has called 'unworking,' referring to that which, before or beyond the work, withdraws from the work, and which, no longer having to do either with production or with completion, encounters interruption, fragmentation, suspension" (*IC* 31/78–79). Clearly, for Nancy, the "essence" of community lies not in a work to be completed, in a product to be produced, but in that which does not allow itself to be worked upon, in that which prevents and resists such a work. With this hypothesis, Nancy confronts the traditional Western view of community and aims to definitively remove our being-with from such a presupposition by situating it in what *by definition* resists such a work, that is, by situating it in what he calls "literature."

Although the Jena Romantics are surely traditional in the sense that they too subscribe to this traditional Western view, it is at the same time their poetics that inspires the break with the idea of community as work, as well as the replacement of this idea with the idea of community as something more fragmented, dynamic, and organic. In the final part of *The Literary Absolute*, the "Closure," Lacoue-Labarthe and Nancy indicate that such a break should be situated in a reflection on the "unworking" signaled by Blanchot in Jena Romanticism. It is not surprising, then, that Nancy attributes a major role to this notion in his own thinking about community. What is surprising, however, is that he seems to depart fundamentally from the meaning attributed to this notion by Blanchot, while at the same time suggesting to subscribe to it. In my view, this friction—noted by several commentators[84]—stems from the fact that Nancy develops a fundamentally different idea of literature than Blanchot's.

This difference is important, not only because it seems to have motivated Blanchot's reservations about Nancy's work on community expressed in *The*

Unavowable Community—Blanchot's response to Nancy's text *The Inoperative Community*—but also because it goes to the heart of the relation between literature, community, and politics as conceived by Nancy. To what extent, then, do Blanchot's and Nancy's reflections diverge? First of all, unworking is not, for Blanchot, something *opposed* to the work. Whereas Nancy describes unworking as something that "withdraws" from the work, that is "before or beyond" it, Blanchot stresses that work and unworking are not to be detached, and are even the same thing: "[T]he work *is* unworking," as he puts it in *The Infinite Conversation*.[85] A subtle but crucial nuance here is that Blanchot is not saying that the work is *unworked* [*désoeuvrée*], as Nancy would put it, but that it is *unworking* [*désoeuvrement*]. It follows that, for Blanchot, unworking is not something that precedes or succeeds the work, but something that occurs *as* work.[86]

Blanchot's identification of work and unworking undoubtedly stems from his distinction (introduced at the very end of chapter 1) between *book* and *work*. In this framework, the "book" is what has to do with production, the finished product, while the "work" is what is removed from it, what encounters interruption, fragmentation, and suspension. Does this mean that what Nancy calls a "work" is equivalent to what Blanchot prefers to call a "book"? In some cases, this is indeed the case. Nevertheless, it seems to me that their disagreement cannot be resolved so simply. For even if Nancy's "work" is equivalent to Blanchot's "book," Blanchot's unworking seems to contain a dimension that Nancy's lacks, namely, what Blanchot calls "work." In other words, for Blanchot, unworking seems to be a dynamic or a movement that gives itself *in* a work (albeit a noncommunicative one), or even *as* a work, and is for this reason largely ambiguous, whereas for Nancy unworking seems to be, for want of a better word, more pure or purified. It seems to me that Blanchot's *The Unavowable Community* criticizes precisely this aspect of Nancy's analysis.

For a long time, Nancy did not know what to do with this criticism. In the preface to the Italian translation of Blanchot's *The Unavowable Community*, written eighteen years after the publication of Blanchot's book and published separately under the title "The Confronted Community," Nancy admits: "I have never completely clarified this reserve or this reproach, either in a text or for myself, and not in correspondence with Blanchot either. I am speaking of it here for the first time in this preface" ("CC" 30/38).[87] So it is only after all these years that Nancy begins to formulate a response, moreover to return to it several more times after Blanchot's death, among others, briefly, in "Un commencement" (2006) and in *Maurice Blanchot: Passion Politique* (2011), then in a more detailed way in *The Disavowed*

Community (2014), and then in his contribution to *Les politiques de Maurice Blanchot* (2015) and in his interview on myth, *Proprement dit* (2015). It is from 2011 onward, reading Blanchot's critique in light of Blanchot's political orientation in the 1930s, that Nancy begins to explicitly depart from Blanchot's thought in relation to the question of the work and its unworking.

Let us first examine the first explanation given by Nancy to Blanchot's reservation. What Blanchot wanted to indicate, already by his title, concludes Nancy in "The Confronted Community," is that community, despite or "under" its unworking, is always *also* work, but not in the sense of a work of community: "[W]here I [Nancy, AvR] claimed to reveal the 'work' of community as society's death sentence and, as a corollary, to establish the need for a community refusing to constitute work . . . at that very point, then, Blanchot informs me of or rather indicates to me the unavowable [*inavouable*]. Apposed but opposed to the unworked [*désoeuvrée*] of my title, this adjective proposes to think that beneath the unworking there is still work, an unavowable work" ("CC" 31/39, translation slightly modified). This unavowable work, as Nancy deduces from Blanchot's reproach, is there, even before there is any question of a work of community in the sense of a Party or a State, of a Work of Humanity, and it is for this reason unavowable. It is opposed to this work of community, which is produced in order to be avowed, confirmed, and identified.

According to Nancy, Blanchot's reproach or reservation ultimately amounts to a warning that there is yet another signification of work, another kind of work of community, namely a "work" between inverted comma's: "[T]here has been, already, always already, a 'work' of community, an operation of sharing out that will always have gone before any singular or generic existence, a communication and a contagion without which it would be unthinkable to have, in an absolutely general manner, any *presence* or any *world*, since each of these terms brings with it the implication of a *co-existence* or of a co-belonging" ("CC" 32/44). According to Nancy, the unavowable work that Blanchot wanted to emphasize is not another work of community, but rather the ontological dynamic that Nancy considers to be that of being-with. The unworking of community should therefore not only be explained in a negative way, but also understood as a certain "work." This work may be unavowable, but it "does not cease to be spoken, to speak itself in the intimate silence of those who could but cannot avow" ("CC" 31/40), according to Nancy.

It is this intimate silence, unavowable but nonetheless uttered, that Nancy claims Blanchot wanted to draw attention to:

> I imagine that Blanchot wanted to *intimate* to me this silence
> and what it says: prescribe it for me and introduce it into my
> intimacy, as intimacy itself—the intimacy of a communication
> or a community, the intimacy of a style of intimate *work* more
> deeply buried than any unworking, making that unworking
> possible and necessary but not letting itself be dissolved in it.
> Blanchot was asking me not to settle for the negation of commu-
> nial community, and to think further ahead than this negativity,
> toward a secret of the common that is not a common secret.
> ("CC" 31/41, translation slightly modified)

In short, then, in Nancy's 2001 interpretation of Blanchot's critique, the unavowable seems to be nothing other than the being-with that he himself already thought of as the unworking of the community. The unavowable work or "operation of sharing" that Blanchot would reveal according to Nancy is perfectly compatible with Nancy's idea of being-with preceding any work of community. But if this would be what Blanchot would intimate to Nancy, it would be largely redundant a reproach. For what Nancy is trying to do with the notion of unworking is clearly to *move beyond* a merely negative interpretation. For Nancy, the notion of unworking takes on a rather active, even creative meaning, as Fynsk rightly observes (Foreword, *IC* 154n23). If the unworking and the unavowable of community are roughly the same, why would Blanchot bother to emphasize the latter? So, what *is* his reservation about Nancy's understanding of unworking?

This question seems to have haunted Nancy, for after Blanchot's death he returned to Blanchot's critique—this time in a less conciliatory manner—indicating that "[t]he unavowable of community, if I have understood Blanchot correctly (which I cannot decide), is that which opposes its unworking, or that which at least distinguishes itself from it" ("UC" 130, translation slightly modified). It is this interpretation of the unavowable as something that *opposes* or even *resists* the dynamics of unworking that Nancy intensifies in *Maurice Blanchot: Passion Politique* and *The Disavowed Community*. The crux of this reinterpretation of the unavowable is that Blanchot, according to Nancy, led reflection on community "in a direction—far from, if not opposite to mine [Nancy's, AvR]—that made a multi-faceted (erotic, christic, literary) 'communion' emerge in the dark depths of community" (*MB* 31). According to Nancy, Blanchot's idea of the unavowable does not refer to the ontological "work" of being-with as Nancy initially thought, but the unavowable turns out to be in a sense quite the opposite:

a transcendent work beyond being-with that is so secret, abandoned, and exceptional that it implies the abandonment of the possibility of sharing or communication—an idea of the unavowable that Nancy associates with Blanchot's political preferences and sees theorized in his notion of the "neutral."[88] To avoid this direction of thought, Nancy once again stresses that the unavowable can only be given between us, in the always unworked passage of our being in common.

On (Not) Avowing Community

And yet, what Blanchot wanted to underline with the notion of the unavowable is, in my opinion, not only that there is always something unavowable, but also and above all that—to complicate matters—it *must be avowed in a literary work*. By interpreting Blanchot's unavowable in terms of silence, secrecy, and, to put it another way, the untouchable, Nancy misses what seems to me to be the core of Blanchot's reproach. This core is summarized at the end of his book, in a seemingly banal phrase: "[I]n order to be silent, it is necessary to speak," a remark that touches upon the question of *attestation*.[89] Despite its banality, this phrase contains, I think, the most interesting point at which Nancy's and Blanchot's theories diverge from one another, a divergence based, as I said, on their divergent notions of literature.

In the preceding sections, we have already seen that the originality and added value of Nancy's thinking lies in its extension of deconstructivist insights into the realm of ontology, revealing "writing" and "literature" as the mode of existence of things themselves. Yet this extension is not without consequences. One consequence is that what Nancy calls "unworking" is no longer a matter of literary language in the usual sense, but becomes an ontological affair. The project of putting something into a work (or, if you like, into a book) is resisted not by the work or book itself, but by something else. Or rather, it is the thing itself that resists, the *res*, the reality without which there would not even be a work or a book. For Nancy, this unworking characterizes everything that is, and the literary thing is just one of many things, albeit one that is exemplarily sensitive to unworking.

With this gesture, however, Nancy has profoundly redefined the Blanchotian notion of "unworking." In my opinion, Blanchot's remark that it is necessary to speak in order to be silent implies that unworking does not reside in what Nancy calls the silent murmuring of things or bodies, but requires a certain kind of speech, or even a certain kind of work that, as Blanchot puts it, "let a possibility manifest itself, the possibility—beyond

any utilitarian gain—of a being-together."[90] It seems to me that Blanchot is indicating that being together may only manifest itself in its bare togetherness when this bareness is *staged*. In other words—and Blanchot uses a variety of formulations to address this point—our being together may only manifest itself as something unavowable if one has *explicitly* "*renounced* [one's] renunciation of creating a work"[91] or if one is "*vehiculated* by the requirement of being there."[92] Although this implies a work "without project"[93] and "without any remainder,"[94] Blanchot remains convinced that "the absence of a work . . . *needs and presupposes works* so as to let them write themselves under the charm of unworking."[95]

This is why I suggested that, for Blanchot, the unavowable must be *avowed* in order to be experienced as such. Blanchot, too, turns to May '68 to illustrate such an avowal. But unlike Nancy, who praised the community of May '68 as the quintessential example of a community that did not form itself as a work, that did not aspire to give itself shape and produce itself as a project, Blanchot emphasizes the fact that this unworking was realized only through the work of multiple action committees and quasi-serious associations, always ready to dissociate themselves, yes, but united for a cause nonetheless. The fact that this cause was not transformed into a project was due to their explicit refusal of power.[96] If the community of those who have nothing in common consists in the deprivation of all essence, purpose, and project, if it consists in the deliberate stripping away of the mythological mantle to expose the bare staging of myth, then perhaps it can only manifest itself through a staging, or even a *plot* that unravels itself. This, at least, seems to me to be Blanchot's critical addition, and the reason why, according to him, community gives itself in and as a literary work.

Tellingly, such a work is offered by *The Malady of Death*, the enigmatic story by Marguerite Duras presented and discussed by Blanchot in the second part of his book (entitled "The Community of Lovers"). The community of lovers (or "the world of lovers," to borrow a phrase from Bataille) described by Duras seems to Blanchot to be the unworked community par excellence. Why, then, does Blanchot turn to the figure of lovers, after Nancy, in *The Inoperative Community*, has so clearly renounced it, precisely because it is always a figure of communion?[97] As Blanchot argues, Duras's work demonstrates that such an unworked community can only come about through the construction of a certain plot: a closed room, a time calculated in nights and, above all, a contract, binding a man incapable of love and a woman who lets herself be paid to be loved. So do they, in

spite of this, form something like a community without community, an unworked manifestation of being-with?

Blanchot's answer leaves no room for doubt: "It is rather *because of* this that they form a community."[98] It is the contract, absurd and extra-ordinary, that allows them to experience what community is in its unworked mode:

> They are side by side, and that contiguity, passing through every form of empty intimacy, preserves them from playing the comedy of a 'fusional or communional' understanding. A prison community, organized by the one, consented to by the other, where what is at stake is indeed the attempt to love—but for Nothing, an attempt that has in the end no other object than that nothing which animates them unbeknownst to themselves and exposes them to nothing else than to touching each other in vain.[99]

The Nothing that forms the cause and object of contemporary community is displayed by Duras, according to Blanchot, in the fantastic and deceptive project formed by the contract between the two lovers.[100] Ultimately, what characterizes the exemplary communities described by Blanchot—Acéphale, May '68, Duras's "lovers"—is that their members (insofar as this word still has any meaning), *by means of* the knotting of a "plot," enclose themselves in a self-imposed out-of-place and out-of-time,[101] so that their community eventually exists only in this question: "[H]ad it taken place?"[102]

To return to the implicit disagreement between Nancy and Blanchot, this means, in my opinion, that Blanchot wants to stay away from an ontological interpretation of unworking. For him, unworking is linked to literature, or even identical with it, because the literary is that which questions ontology in being itself *deprived of being*.[103] According to Blanchot, literature is characterized precisely by the fact that what it achieves resides halfway between the imaginary and the real. This is why, according to Blanchot, one of the most important characteristics of literature is its *imposture*, its illusionary character: It is indeed a production, but a production that cancels itself out, fades away, puts itself on hold. In doing so, literature obviously draws attention to its technique—in short, to the fact *that* it communicates—rather than to the message communicated.

Of course, it is precisely this aspect that Nancy pushes to the extreme in his ontological poetics. By understanding literature as the technique by

which things say themselves, the experience of literature becomes the inescapable experience that there is reality, or that there is a realization without there yet being a determinable reality. So, for Nancy, it is never a question of knowing whether the literary event has really taken place, because it *is* the very place, the primary spacing, for there to be something. If literature avows our shared being, then, it is not because of its imposterous or fictitious character, but because of the kind of *realism* that is always already implied: It is nothing but what exists. And so, while Blanchot points out that literature implies a deliberate withdrawal from being, Nancy argues that literature and being coincide in what we have named a *tautegory* or indeed "myth." Stripping literature of its allegorical nature, what remains, according to Nancy, is a self-performance of being itself, a self-performance that is not mythological, but mythical.[104]

The Fable Becoming the Real World (*Nancy, Nietzsche, Lyotard*)

Fiction Beyond the "As If"

The reason, then, why the appeal to literature could become so crucial in Nancy's philosophical project stems from the fact that "literature" for him, is precisely *not* fictitious, but is being-with exposing itself, and it is precisely for this reason that it is, as we saw in the introduction, "the beneficiary (or echo) of myth" that should itself "be thought as myth—as the myth of mythless society" (*IC* 63/157–58, translation modified, my emphasis). For Nancy, the need for a reflection on literature thus follows directly from the need for a new reflection on the relationship between politics, community, and literature, because "[a] politics that does not want to know anything about [literature] is a mythology, or an economy [and a] literature that does not want to say anything about it is a mere diversion, or a lie" (*IC* 81/198).

From the observation that literature is the myth of the mythless society, it then follows that Nancy does not believe in a *beyond* of myth, for the presupposition of this possibility, as we have already seen, has been precisely the greatest error of the West.[105] "The dissolution of the myth of foundation," as Ernesto Laclau puts it, "does not dissolve the phantom of its own absence.[106] Paradoxical as it may seem, in the post-antique world, myth is in a sense the only thing "we" have, since "we" cannot but gather around a narrative that recounts the origin of our coming together, thus shaping, fictionalizing, the foundation of that coming together. Or, as

Nancy puts it succinctly in *Proprement dit*: "There is a point where myth ('being-in-the-world'), speech ('speaking-being') and sense ('being-with') are knotted together. We are in the world by means of speech and by speaking we are with each other. In the world speaking-being speaks for everybody [*tout le monde*], that is for all who do not speak, and in doing so it opens or it operates the 'with' of all beings" (*PD* 102–3). Instead of dreaming of a world *without* mythical speech, it is better to devote ourselves to not forgetting what kind of speech this is, and to preventing it from being taken as an absolute foundation. That is why, according to Nancy, we have to *recite* this foundation again and again each, this foundation in which our speaking-being, our being-in-the-world, and our being-with are knotted, as well as realize that it already interrupted in its recitation. The point is to understand that mythical speech is simply this original interruption that prevents the appropriation of the origin it constitutes.

Significantly, according to Nancy, this interruption in the functioning of myth cannot in turn be appropriated, that is, given as a project or taken as a guiding thread. This is the slippery slope Blanchot's thinking takes according to Nancy. It is also the project of the new mythology of Jena Romanticism: "This is why the idea of a 'new mythology' is not only dangerous, it is futile, for a new mythology would presuppose, as its condition of possibility, a myth of myth that would not be subject to the rigorous logic whose course extends from Schelling to Lévi-Strauss—or else, from Plato to us—and that is composed essentially of this nihilist or annihilating logic (or this *mythics*): the being that myth engenders implodes in its own fiction" (*IC* 56/141–42). The "rigorous" logic of myth, from which no one can escape, is that it is both foundation and fiction, and what it constitutes is always ready to implode in its own fiction. To take myth as a guiding principle is to lose oneself immediately. In Nancy's view, this applies not only to the Romantic project of the new mythology, but also to all thought based on the idea of what he calls a "regulative fiction," including Kant's regulating idea. More generally, according to Nancy, we are dealing here with the myriad of ideas that can be lumped together under the denominator of the "philosophy of the 'As If'" (*IC* 162n33/141n64). Described as such in 1911 by Hans Vaihinger in his book *The Philosophy of "As If,"*[107] according to Nancy, it includes not only Romanticism and Idealism, but also the thoughts of Nietzsche, Freud, and Lyotard.

Still, Nancy's relationship to this thought of fiction and the "as if" is not without ambiguity, not least because it seems to have changed over time. In his early texts, Nancy voluntarily joins the Kantian notion of "as

if" by emphasizing the absence of an origin of law, or even of origin as such. However, it is in discussion with Jean-François Lyotard—a discussion that occurs largely in notes, postscripts, and implicit references—that Nancy seems to have changed his mind and begins to criticize the notion of the "as if." I cannot present here in all its finesse the "marginal" discussion between Nancy and Lyotard, but a brief summary of his main point nonetheless provides a better understanding of Nancy's specific attitude towards this important concept in the philosophical tradition, as well as his specific take on literature.[108] Nancy raised the discussion of the notion of the "as if" in his text "Lapsus judicii," and in his subsequent texts "Dies irae" and "Dies illa."[109] In these texts, which respond above all to the ideas formulated by Lyotard in *Just gaming*, Nancy concentrates on the notion of "as if" to think the possibility of justice or law in a situation where universal fundamental principles are lacking. In such a situation, Nancy argues, "juri-diction is or makes juri-*fiction*" (*FT* 157, my emphasis).[110] Although jurisdiction makes us believe that it renders justice in each singular case, it must in fact invent itself each time.

Lyotard takes up the Kantian notion of the "as if" for the same reasons, in response to the irreducible plurality of modernity. This plurality, as is well known, is expressed by Lyotard in a theory of phrases and the genres of phrases. In the absence of a universal genre, disagreements between phrases can, according to Lyotard, only be decided by appealing to a connection established by the notion of "as if." For Lyotard, this notion constitutes a passage, a temporal bridge, between heterogeneous domains that remain otherwise separate. The "as if," in other words, does not function as the substitution of the missing common origin, but is precisely the indication of the absence of such an origin.[111] In a note to his text "Introduction to a Study of the Political According to Kant," Lyotard admits to having been largely inspired by Nancy's text "Lapsus judicii," but wonders at the same time whether Nancy, for his part, does not still associate himself with a certain philosophy of origin. According to Lyotard, the postulation of an origin is something to be avoided at all costs, as it would imply the postulation of a fixed point of reference for law that synthesizes the irreducible plurality that Lyotard himself so ardently seeks to preserve.

Now, it is true that Nancy proposes a certain way of thinking about origin in "Lapsus judicii"—and this not only explains why he differs from most of his contemporaries, but also why he ventures into a thinking about myth. Nevertheless, as we have seen, origin is by no means conceived by him as a fixed point of reference. So, in his reaction to Lyotard's reproach

(in a postscript to the second version of "Lapsus judicii"), Nancy confirms that he is perhaps less interested in the ends of law than in its origin, but adds that he attempts to think this origin as plural in itself. For him, the "as if" is not a passage between already existing multiple domains, but the very manifestation of the plural origin, indeed of the origin of plurality. The "as if" therefore means "sometimes like this, sometimes like that," a *modality* in other words. According to Nancy—and here he in turn criticizes Lyotard's position—this origin is not plural because it would be an origin that was once unique, and is now dislocated into different areas, but rather because it is an *originary dislocation*, a dislocation that therefore also dislocates the very notion of originarity.[112] Already on the ontological level, then, there is an irreducible plurality of singularities that co-appear, compear, and contrast with one another.

While Nancy still expresses his ideas in terms of "as if" in both versions of "Lapsus judicii," he vigorously departs from this notion in his text "Dies irae," written almost ten years later, as he does in *The Inoperative Community*. It seems to me that it is precisely in reaction to Lyotard's interpretation of the "as if" that Nancy departs from it. What he criticizes Lyotard for in "Dies irae" is simply to have substituted the Kantian regulative idea of *unity* with the regulative idea of *plurality*, which nonetheless always functions as a presupposed and invariable horizon: "In these conditions . . . the Idea [the idea of plurality, AvR] continues to act as a final, unitary and totalizing (but not totalitarian) *Idea*: it remains an onto-theo-teleological Idea, even though it is actually only an '*as-if*-onto-theo-teleology' (after all, how does the '*as if*' change its structure? It inscribes it with the mark of unreality: but isn't that nothing more than a reversal of ontological realism?)" (*DI* 34/14). Even though it is not totalitarian, the Lyotardian idea of "as if" remains a *regulating* fiction for Nancy, directing thought towards an end point, like a mirage that, although imaginary, is nonetheless a guiding horizon.

In "Dies illa," which follows on from "Dies irae," Nancy once again emphasizes that the law (or rather the law of the law), even if it is the law of plurality, can never serve as a horizon, because it has to be invented *anew each time*:

> if the universal is not given, this does not mean that it needs to be dreamt or "mimicked" (the weak version of the philosophy of the "as if"; a more or less latent formulation of so-called "value" philosophies), it means that it is to be invented. In other words, it seems important not to simply pose a "judgment without

> criteria" (another expression from Lyotard), itself defined as a judgment "maximizing concepts outside of any knowledge of reality" (and thus in the first place the concept of final end or of destination of the world and of human beings). But one needs to understand also that knowledge is lacking here, not because of an intrinsic deficiency of human understanding (a finitude relative to the model of an *intellectus intuitivus*) but because of the absence, pure and simple, of "reality," which is effectively not given (the absolute finitude of a *Dasein* who puts into play nothing less than the-infinite-meaning of being). (*CW* 60/69)[113]

As we saw above, according to Nancy, we should go *beyond all horizons*, which also means going beyond the very concept of the horizon, even if it is a provisional or invented horizon, as proposed by Lyotard. It is time to realize that we can no longer act as if there were some horizon, some absolute value or truth somewhere. If we need fiction, according to Nancy, it is only in the original Latin sense of *fingere*—"to shape," "to make," that is, insofar as we always have to make, to invent, from nothing, *ex nihilo*, without model.[114] For Nancy, "fiction" has nothing to do with "doing as if," nor with the imaginary. If the word "fiction" still has a meaning, it does not mean "doing as if," but "doing as such," that is, ultimately, "doing." By abandoning the idea of regulative fiction, Nancy has thus replaced the thought of "as if" with a thought of *patéfaction*, or, if you like, of *truth*, also in relation to myth:

> Myth is also this register of a "*patéfaction*": *what* it says is true because it is inherent to its *saying*. Perhaps this truth—which is unproduced, unproven, unrevealed but uttered—can only be uttered bit by bit [*coup par coup*], here a speaker, there another, here a group, here a legend, there another, there a dream, here a story, there another. . . . But each time a way of saying that *says itself* as much as it says something, that says the proper saying itself and that is therefore not a "proper" saying. (*PD* 120)

Reasserting the Power of Myth

This replacement of the conceptual structure of the "as if" by that of a "true saying" is, according to Nancy, the direct and inevitable consequence of the death of God that marked modern times for Nietzsche. After the death of

Despite Heidegger's prejudice that Nancy describes as a certain attachment to values of the exceptional and heroism, Heidegger's text, according to Nancy, nevertheless enables us to unmask this very value of exceptionalism, for his existential analysis necessarily leads to the conclusion that the distinction between authentic and inauthentic being has been *superimposed* on everyday experience. If Heidegger says that *Dasein* must *decide* to withdraw from the everydayness of the "they," this expression, as Nancy clearly puts it, "*must* signify, according to the deepest logic of analysis, that the 'they' carries disclosedness along with it, gives disclosedness, and even that it is, before everything else, the *site of disclosedness*" (*BP* 118, my emphasis).

Importantly, this does not mean that Nancy is guilty of valorizing the banal at the expense of the exceptional. Rather, it is a matter of realizing that these valorizations are themselves groundless precisely because *Dasein* is thrown into the groundless existence of the "they." Presupposing some kind of privilege results from a contradictory attachment to something *proper* or to be *appropriated*. Nancy, who precisely wants to distance poetry from any mythological connotation, is careful not to attribute such values to it. It is of this caution that one should be aware when reading the following remark, added in another note:

> It is quite remarkable that *"poetic" discourse alone* should have been *privileged* a few pages earlier [before the discussed pages of § 34 of *Being and Time*, where Heidegger speaks of the *Gerede* and the *Geschreibe* of the "they," AvR], as the discourse in which "the communication of the existential possibilities of one's state of-mind can become an aim in itself" (§34, p. 162; 205). We will not inquire here into this privilege, which remains without explanation or clarification in *Being and Time*. We will only note that there *can be absolutely no question* of conferring, without any further deliberation, an *ontological privilege of any kind on any form of speech or communication*, each of these forms being under the power of the "they" and subject to the hearing of the "they." (*BP* 404n29, my emphasis)

The firmness of this remark culminates a few lines later in the following question: "We could then ask with what mode of 'privilege' or 'separation' *Rede* must have been invested, later, in the *Rektoratsrede*, in this discourse proposed, without mediation, to the communal sharing of the originary, in this discourse immediately proposing decision" (*BP* 404n29). Despite his

existential analysis, Heidegger simply reproduced, according to Nancy, "the idea and the ideal of a pure meaning—absolute, reserved, and floating outside the limits of discourse" (*BP* 94).[35] In *The Banality of Heidegger*, written about Heidegger's posthumously published *Black Notebooks*, Nancy insists on this point again. Heidegger, Nancy says, "refused to renounce the grand schema of Geschichte even if henceforth he treated it in a different way. Which means also that to the end he would have (will have?) considered the extermination camps as inscribed in the 'destination'" (*BH* 39/60–61). Put in terms already used here, one could thus say that, for Heidegger, poetic speech ultimately presents itself not as the sharing of singular *voices*, but as the *unique* historical voice of many—and for this reason remains within the realm of mythology. Once again, it becomes clear that the gesture of excepting or privileging a certain form of speech from everyday speech entails for Nancy inevitably the appropriation of what is and must remain inappropriable, the decision of what is and must remain undecidable.

Nancy thus distances himself from Heidegger's poetics on this crucial point, a distancing that results from his wish to avoid a Romantic poetics of the final Great Work. Nancy wants to distance himself from values of exception, heroism, and privilege by pointing out that what poetry expresses is not a hidden meaning, difficult to find, which would require talent or a certain knowledge to reveal, but is nothing more than the decisive/decided openness that *is* the existence of *Dasein* in its everydayness. Because this existence is not only expressed in this or that genre of art, but can be expressed, in principle, in everything, Nancy does not attribute a privileged status to *poetic* speech, or rather, as we saw, he considers existence *itself* as poetic, which means that "poetry" here does not mean "literary genre" but can, in principle, be "any sort of saying, shouting, praying, laughing, or sobbing that holds . . . that infinite suspension of sense" (*DE* 97/146). If authentic—or as Nancy prefers to translate it, "proper"—existence resides in the "decision of existence" as Heidegger has it, this decision, then, is not that of "the intoxication, the enthusiasm of floating ideals, but the simple fact of existence" (*BP* 106). In sum, as I formulated at the end of chapter 2, poetry, according to Nancy, presents the ordinary not as extraordinary, but as the ordinary itself.

Nancy's poetics thus undoubtedly amounts to a revaluation of everydayness.[36] In doing so, Nancy does not draw attention to the everyday *at the expense* of the non-everyday, but rather indicates that the two are indistinguishable. And indeed, especially nowadays, the distinction generally made in reflections on community between the authentic and the familiar on the

one hand, and the inauthentic, the foreign or the *unheimliche* on the other, no longer seems to hold. In this world, at once infinitely shrunken and enlarged not only by immigration and mobilization, but also by increased telecommunication, our being-with does not fit neatly into the model of a "home" in which we would settle once and for all, but is instead constituted again and again, in every encounter, however fleeting and anonymous it may be. Indeed, the nameless faces we meet on the street every day, the countless digital connections that cross time zones and national borders in every instant, the prerecorded voice announcing our destination—these are all fundamental constituents of our being-with.[37]

Poetry's Multivocality

It could be said, then, that Nancy's distance from Heideggerian poetics lies in the fact that he renounces the idea of a unique grasp of being, stressing the fact that being can only be captured *singularly* and in a *particular mode* each time. Apart from the exceptionalism in Heidegger's poetics, Nancy thus also distances himself from its presupposed univocity. This is an aspect Nancy develops in particular where he enters into discussion with Heidegger on the question of *technique*, especially in his essay entitled "Why Are There Several Arts and Not Just One?" (*The Muses*). The answer to the question posed in the title is found by Nancy in the primitive meaning of the word "art," a meaning that links the problematics of technique, univocity, and the way of grasping being: "[T]he primitive meaning of the word *ars*, of this Latin *tekhne*, word that translated is that of 'articulation' (from the Greek *arthron*), and all articulation has the structure of a singular plural. . . . [T]he German *Art* . . . means 'mode,' 'species,' 'particular manner.' Art is always a question of *manner*" (*M* 26 /51, my emphasis). "Art," Nancy concludes, is therefore *in principle* plural.

In other words, we can only speak of art as *mode, manner,* or *style* of being when these are thought as plural, otherwise it would suggest what we might call a "grand style," or—what amounts to the same thing—a "without style." Indeed, Nancy maintains in *The Sense of the World* that this "without style" is the very aspiration of myth: "Myth itself is without style, that is, it is on the near side of style" (*SW* 20/39). In contrast, the task of a *demythologized* thought proposed by Nancy himself is thus to look at "the tension of style as spacing and unsettlement of truth according to truth's own *différance*" (*SW* 20–21/39), that is, at the tension of styles in the plural, for a true reflection on style renounces in principle every *ideal*

or *model* of style. Just as there is no such thing as "art" in the singular, there is no such thing as "style" or "technique" in the singular, that is, in general, "art," "style," and "technique" always mean that there are several of them (*M* 26/50–51).

With this observation, Nancy aims not only to unmask those philosophical discourses that postulate the possibility of pure thought without style, or of a "properly philosophical" style, but also to radicalize, once again, Heidegger's poetics. In short, Nancy is diametrically opposed to Heidegger's declinist interpretation of technique as enframing (*Gestell*). According to Nancy, the essence of art is inextricably bound up with technique, to the point that "[i]t might be that art, the arts, is *nothing other* than the second-degree exposition of technique itself" (*M* 26/51, my emphasis). If art is the coming into presence of being, as we have seen and as Nancy observes following Heidegger, it is by its very essence technical, because " 'technics' is today the mode in which this 'coming' [into presence, AvR] unfolds" (*M* 110n45/49n2).

But in what sense is the coming into presence precisely technical? Despite his distance from Heidegger, Nancy takes up the latter's analysis of the notion of *techne* in "The Origin of the Work of Art." Heidegger demonstrates that the word *techne*, in its Greek sense, implies the unveiling of being. In this interpretation, technics is not a rationalized, calculated means of producing objects, but has an *ontological* meaning: Technics is the first appearance of being, its coming into presence. According to Heidegger, *techne* is thus placed in a particular relationship with nature—*phusis*—, a relationship in which they oppose each other, but at the same time mutually constitute each other. Although *phusis* is what grows by itself, it neverthe-less needs *techne* in order to be revealed as such. Technics, in other words, is that through which something *appears*. And this is why Nancy notes, following Heidegger, that "art" is the presentation of presentation, that is, the presentation of the fact *that there is* presentation.

More radically than Heidegger, however, Nancy emphasizes the co-originarity of *phusis* and *techne*. Faithful to the logic of the original sup-plement as revealed by Derrida, Nancy maintains that there is no *phusis* or original nature that would subsequently be brought to light by *techne*. Rather, it is a question of what Ian James calls the *originary technicality* of being: Being exists *only* mediated and drawn out of itself.[38] By critically revisiting Heidegger's analysis of *techne* and *phusis*, Nancy approaches, according to James, what is in the French philosophy of the last century generally conceived under the name of *writing* or *archi-writing*: "To a certain

extent, when Nancy talks about an originary technicity, he is describing what much French thought since the late 1960s has called 'writing.' Derrida's use of the term *archi-écriture* (archi-writing), for instance, does not describe words on the page, but rather that generalized web of marks or inscriptions, which, as differing/deferring temporal traces of sense, in excess of ontological disclosure, open up or make possible time and space as we know it."[39] Nancy's critical revision of Heidegger's poetics lies of course in an emphasis on these "differing/deferring temporal traces of sense," for if original being is only technically or "artistically" revealed, there can never be any question of a pure, unique, and absolute sense of being, as we saw above. "The *technicity* of art," says Nancy in "Why Are There Several Arts and Not Just One?," "dislodges art from its 'poetic' assurance, if one understands by that the production of a revelation, or conceived as a *phusis* unveiled in its truth" (*M* 37/66).

In other words, it is its essential *technicality* that prevents art from being conceived as a *univocal* revelation of being, that is, as a revelation expressed in a single voice. "Technicality," Nancy continues, "is also the 'unworking' [*désoeuvrement*] of the work, what puts it outside itself, touching the infinite. Their technical unworking incessantly *forces* the fine arts, dislodges them endlessly from aestheticizing repose. This is also why art is always coming to its end. The 'end of art' is always the beginning of its *plurality*" (*M* 37/66, my emphasis, translation slightly modified). The criticism leveled at Heidegger's poetics is that, despite the account of the constitutive interrelation between *phusis* and *techne*, it still presupposes that there is something more original, more fundamental or more hidden to be revealed by art, whereas art can only reveal technicality itself. There is nothing behind it. There is nothing more fundamental to reveal than the technicality of this very technicality, the fact that being *is* in a technical way, that is to say—for this is already a tautological formulation—that being is in one way (or another). The *quod* of presentation, in other words, always already implies a *how*. This clearly explains the central role of art and poetry in Nancy's work. Although even the most "prosaic" expression necessarily has a certain style, it is in art and poetry that style is brought most significantly to the forefront.

This issue of technicality is closely linked to Nancy's reiteration of Heidegger's view on *language* in "Sharing Voices," in which Nancy takes as his starting point the Heideggerian notion of *Auslegung* (literally "explication," "arrangement"). As Nancy points out, this notion must first be understood ontologically, as the explication of what we are as beings by the simple fact of our existence. In his reading of *Being and Time*, Nancy emphasizes that

this *Auslegung* implies a *legein*, a positing, a position or disposition of beings alongside one another, in which *Auslegung* is in fact literarily an explication, an *unfolding* of being, and not its interpretation. "There is nothing to be interpreted" ("SV" 220/31), says Nancy.

Clearly, then, Heidegger's analysis of *Auslegung* is based on a specific meaning of *logos*, designating first and foremost "*letting-something-be-seen*, the unconcealment of a thing as revealed (*alèthés*)" ("SV" 219/31). If *Auslegung* has anything to do with *logos* as language, discourse, or understanding, it is only as its condition of possibility. In Nancy's terms, it forms "the *antici-pation* of language well within explicit expression (the precise expression, it must be said)" ("SV" 221/32, my emphasis). Or, as he says it even more clearly: "Here, language as articulation is not first: There is *first* a kind of language-in-addition-to [*d'outre-language*] which only distinguishes the articulation of *Auslegung in* understanding. Thus, this last articulation *is* the being of being-there, as it is *in*-the-world" ("SV" 221/33).[40] According to Nancy, what we hear on this plane of *d'outre-language* are voices rather than words, as the title of his text "Sharing Voices" also indicates.

The plural in this title is obviously of great importance, and once again implies a critical reworking of Heidegger's thought. Although Nancy largely subscribes to Heidegger's analysis of *Auslegung*, he explains—via a reading of Plato's *Ion*—that this notion has, in Heidegger, a literally univocal character. Even if *Auslegung* is Heidegger's explanation of being by itself as (*als*) being, it tends to be articulated in a single voice, a voice that in the worst case speaks only Greek or German. The core of Nancy's critical reworking of Heidegger's existential analysis in "Sharing Voices" is thus that ontological *Auslegung* is always polyphonic, multivocal: "The sharing of voices responds, as if on a perpendicular axis, to the sharing of hermeneutic instances. In the same way as there is no *one* divine voice, there is no *one hermeneia*. But there is the *hermeneia* of *hermeneia*. Perhaps that signifies a 'receptive spontaneity' *to address* oneself necessarily, essentially, to another receptivity, to whom it communicates it spontaneity" ("SV" 238/81). According to Nancy, there is not just *one* voice of being, but many voices, each sound-ing singularly, each time this once. It is in the sharing of voices, then, that singular plural being gives itself.

Painting Dates

Let us now analyze, on a more concrete level, the aspects of Nancy's poetics that we have just sketched. How does Nancy see them at work in a concrete

*In loving memory of Jean-Luc Nancy,
and with gratitude for all those who helped and inspired me.*

work of art? How do these poetic claims show themselves, let themselves be *felt*, in front of a canvas or confronted with a poem? Let us take the example of one of the artists analyzed by Nancy, the contemporary artist of Japanese origin On Kawara to whom Nancy devoted the text with the significant title, "The Technique of the Present." In this essay, On Kawara's so-called *date paintings* take center stage. For the most part, they consist of a series of paintings with dark, monochrome backgrounds and white dates in the middle. The white dates are in block letters, painted so precisely that they appear to be machine-made canvases. It is only when getting very close that one recognizes the artist's hand. All On Kawara's paintings were completed in no more than twenty-four hours, and most bear the date of the day on which they were made. The date, moreover, is written in the language of the country where the artist happens to be at the time of painting.

Interestingly, On Kawara is one of the few "conceptual" artists treated by Nancy. Although it is clear that his paintings lend themselves unevenly to Nancy's poetics, they still have a remarkable place among the large number of paintings from the fifteenth to the seventeenth century commented on by Nancy. However, even if one suspects that Nancy has a marked preference for certain artistic forms or genres, it would be in flagrant contradiction with his poetics to distinguish between them, let alone valorize them. On the contrary, in "The Technique of the Present" Nancy advances that "art is always conceptual" in the sense that "to conceive" means, literally, "to gather and contain within," or as Nancy adds, "to give rise, to give space and form to a presence" (*MII* 198/18). Whether it is a meticulously depicted religious scene or a black square, a work of art gives place, space, and form to a presence, puts or pulls forward something that otherwise would not be there at all. Or, as we can say echoing Nancy's title, all artists, whatever their school, are "technicians of the presence" (*MII* 194/9).

Strictly speaking, Nancy emphasizes, a work of art can never be "abstract," since art, in essence, "is the concrete itself" (*MII* 198/18). The presence of a work of art is never an abstract, imaginary, or promised space-time, but consists in the exact location of the painting on the wall, seen by me at that precise moment, mutually exposed. This is why an artwork, according to Nancy, does not *represent*—which would amount to the transmission of an already existing space-time—but "*gives* these coordinates" (*MII* 198/18, my emphasis).[41] An artwork, to use a more fantastical or science-fictional vocabulary, is not a time machine, but a portal to an unknown dimension, and the both modest and divine craft of the artist is to produce the coordinates. Linking it to his earlier analyses of portraiture and technique, Nancy describes this craft as a *"techne poietike"*: "Poetry, before being the name of a particular art, is the generic name of art. *techne poietike*: productive technique" (*MII* 191/5). This technique is an operation that produces something "not with a view to something else or to a use," but with a view to the production alone, a production of the thing that "brings it forth, presents and exposes it" (*MII* 191/5). According to the verbal family of the word *poiesis*, the poietic technique is thus the technique which arranges, which positions the presence (*MII* 191/5).

There is no denying that, in the case of On Kawara's paintings, this arrangement is very explicit. His triptych "TITLE," for example, consists of three independent panels with a red background showing successively "ONE THING," "1965," and "VIET-NAM." By its very design, this triptych already refers to a space that can open and close, and thus to a spacing rather than a space, but the arrangement made by this artwork naturally also lies in the date and place indicated, as Nancy notes: "Here, Vietnam opens the present—1965—of a division of spaces that gives rise to relation. It is a matter of knowing how everything—every *one-thing*, the 'one' and the 'thing' inextricably linked—has its place, gives rise to its place, and places everything in equal relation to everything else" (*MII* 197/15). In other words, the tryptic is not a representative reference to the US bombing of Vietnam, nor an attempt to give specific meaning to this historical event: Through this reference, it orders the world in a certain way here and now and in this specific way. This work—but especially the collection of several works by On Kawara, because of the mutual reinforcement of all these dates—makes us feel that presence, our presence, emerges from a set of diverse connections or relationships. Presence, then, is not a property of the thing, but that which is "its birth" as an "unfolding within its relations" (*MII* 191/5–6), an "encounter" (*MII* 206/28), as Nancy says at the end of his essay, referring to this other meaning of the word *date*.

Even more obviously than in "TITLE," the poetic technique as understood by Nancy is demonstrated in the "TODAY SERIES," which are without doubt the *date paintings* in their most emblematic form. By displaying the dates of the very day they were painted, these paintings produced between 1966 and 1995 are the bare manifestation of what I have analyzed as the *quod* and the everydayness of the poetic. In On Kawara's work, these two aspects—or perhaps here we should also say these two "coordinates," for it is not, of course, a question of the qualities of the poetic but of its "condition"—are entangled in the *date*. I quote Nancy at length:

> It is thus and only thus, moreover, that the date speaks in painting, that it actually is (once again availing ourselves of the full ambiguity of the expression *le jour même*) the subject of (the) painting. It does not tell a story; it merely announces itself, puts itself forward. It is nothing other than a point in the vast network of all the world's dates—of all the dates that the world is. And this is why we do not read the date on the canvas. We do not interpret it. It does not cell a story. Rather, we only *hear* it. . . . [W]e hear a voice, a tone, or inflection before any recognizable word. (*MII* 200/21)

The everydayness of this painting is further reinforced by the fact that the paintings in the "TODAY SERIES" are sometimes accompanied by the canvas's protective box, containing the page of a newspaper—a *daily* newspaper, that is—from the day and place of its making. Although Nancy perhaps too quickly overlooks the fact that the tautological character of these paintings is carefully *staged* by the artist, this tautological character is, according to Nancy, the very character of artistic expression, which indicates only this: I am made here and now, this is the given as such, with no past, no future, no provenance, and no mission, only the present, this single instant.

Singular Plural Poetics

BEYOND ROMANTIC FRAGMENTATION

As we have already seen, in addition to Hegel's and Heidegger's theories of art, the poetics of the Jena Romantics is a major source of inspiration for Nancy. This decisive source of inspiration is, however, much less recognized by commentators.[42] It is true that references to the Jena Romantics are sometimes less direct in Nancy's work, but as I have pointed out, his dialogue with the Romantics is nonetheless an extremely important track in his philosophical journey. Not only are many of his early texts explicitly devoted to Jena Romanticism, but it has remained a frequent inspiration in Nancy's work, as is demonstrated by the 2015 retrospective collection *Expectation: Philosophy, Literature*. It is precisely by inscribing himself in the Jena Romantic poetics that Nancy seeks to push beyond mythological Romantic thought, which he believes inaugurated Western thought as such.

Undoubtedly, the main insight borrowed and radicalized by Nancy from Jena Romantic poetics is, as said, that poetry is not allegorical but *tautegorical*, or *realistic*, as James also points out: "Nancy's thinking on art can be qualified, albeit tentatively, with the term *realism*."[43] In no way resembling what is generally understood by this term, namely the truthful imitation of the world, Nancy's "realism" returns instead to the classical signification of *poiesis*—taken up by the Jena Romantics—which is that of a "making *of the real*" or, as we saw above, a technique of the present. This realist poetics, as Nancy himself formulates it, referring to the poetry of Hölderlin, "is not a poetics of the possible and it is not, consequently, a poetics of the poem as oeuvre, or work, that is, as possible world or as world of possibles, other world that imitates and sublimates this world. On the contrary, it is a poetics *of the real*: not 'realism' but a poetics of exteriority to any work, and the work's only purpose is to inscribe or, rather, to exscribe" (*EPL* 106/84, my emphasis). This "realist" poetics or poetics "of the real," then, precedes the traditional distinction between realism and anti-realism, two positions that only concern the things *represented* in the work.

Although Jena Romanticism often forms the unthematized horizon of Nancy's poetics, this horizon is nonetheless obvious when Nancy criticizes it. We are talking here, broadly speaking, about three places: first, *The Literary Absolute* where Nancy lays the foundations of his reading of Jena Romanticism, then the essay "Art, a Fragment," included in *The Sense of the World*, and finally, some smaller essays dealing with Romantic poetry, like the one on Hölderlin cited above.[44] As I showed in my reading of *The Literary Absolute* in chapter 1, Nancy's critique of Romanticism focuses in particular on the Romantic's desire to produce themselves and the world as a work of art, that is, as an *ergon*. This desire, as we have seen, is imbued with a certain idea of myth, an idea "which is none other than that of the joint engendering of reality and its diction/fiction (*Dichtung*), in other words, the *phantasm of myth* as we take it to be, precisely, since Romanticism. Or to put it even more precisely: 'Romanticism' is the obsession with a poetic making/making poetic of the world" (*MII* 71, my emphasis). That is why, as Nancy goes on to observe with an almost playful lightness, we have to get rid of Romanticism: "We, on the other hand, have to contend with something quite different which is: being in the world. Which is why we want nothing more to do with Romancicism" (*MII* 71/105).

Why and how we should rid ourselves of this persistent Romantic fantasy was one of our preoccupations in what preceded. In chapter 1, I already announced that Nancy's decisive departure from Jena Romanticism lies first and foremost in a fundamental revival of the Romantic idea of the *fragment* and its connection with unity. For, as Nancy advances in "Taking Account of Poetry," although the poetics of Jena Romanticism is a poetics of the fragment, it was always motivated by "a will to art *in the singular*" (*MII* 10, my emphasis), a will that aspired to put to *work* "in the strong sense of the word 'work' [an] absolute transcendence beyond all determination" (*MII* 11), thereby expressing, according to Nancy, in spite of everything, a *metaphysics* of art. In this same text—written by the way at the same period as the essay on On Kawara—Nancy argues that there is, however, a fundamental equivocation in Jena Romantic poetics, an equivocation that is revealed precisely if we focus on the technical character of art. For it is, as we saw, this technical character that prevents "art" from being art *in the singular*:

> [O]nce poetry is approached from this "technical" angle, which certainly is not at all a particular angle, it is entirely possible that poetry finds itself acting out on its own behalf the whole scene of the differences between the arts. There is no such thing as "poetry in general," any more than in reality there is a thing called "art in general," since art on the contrary exists by virtue of the differences between the arts. Poetry, however, occurs each time within the difference between what used to be described, years ago, as its diverse genres and forms. . . . There are indeed only 'poems,' as we were once all told in primary school. Of course, I do not at all therefore want to abandon any questioning of the being or essence of poetry; but I do want to say that the plurality of different kinds of poetry is integral to that essence. (*MII* 19)

At the heart of Nancy's critical transformation of the Romantic poetics is thus a shift from one kind of fragmentation to another, from the *fragmentary* to what Nancy prefers to call the *fractal*. It is above all in the essay "Art, a Fragment" that Nancy develops this alternative idea of the fragment in order to "distinguish between two different kinds of fragmentation. On the one hand, there is the fragmentation that corresponds to the genre and art of the fragment, whose history is closing before our eyes, and on the other hand, there is the fragmentation that is happening to us, and to 'art'" (*SW* 124/191). In a way, the history of the first fragmentation—which Nancy sees at work in Jena Romanticism—closes before our very eyes precisely because this fragmentation closes in on itself. Like a hedgehog, Nancy holds, the Romantic fragment "collects itself into itself, folds or retracts its frayed and fragile borders" thus converting "its finitude—its interruption, noncompletion, and in-finitude—into finish" (*SW* 124–25/191). Because it is finished, the Romantic fragment cancels out the fracture, so that the "small work of art" or "microcosm" that is the Romantic fragment is ultimately distinguished from the Great Work of Art only by its size.

Against this idea of the fragment, Nancy puts forward another idea of the fragmentary, which he calls the "fractal" and links to his conception of technique. Although Nancy only uses the term "fractality" in the text "Art, a Fragment," the idea expressed by this term recurs in his work in other forms, such as in terms like *scattering*, *locality*, or *singularity*. To establish the parallel between Nancy's and the Romantic poetics of the fragment, I prefer to use the notion of the "fractal." The "fractal," then, diverting the meaning of the term coined by the mathematician Benoît Mandelbrot, designates "the dynamics and the initiality of diffraction, the uneven tracing of 'fractal curves'" rather than the "contour of the 'fragment,' already outlined" (*SW* 124/190). The fractal does in other words not close on itself, but "is intermingled with the coming, the in-finity of a coming into presence, or of an *e-venire*" (*SW* 126/192). Because fractal fragmentation is the coming into presence of presence itself, fractality is "a 'more essential,' 'more primitive,' 'more original,' and consequently 'more unprecedented' and 'more future' fragmentation" (*SW* 127/194) than the fragmentation of the fragment.

The quotation marks that lift these weighty words show that they do not seek to endow fractal art with a metaphysical signature. Rather, fractal fragmentation expresses what we have seen before, that is, the ever-singular *quod* of *presentation itself*, or the presentation of presentation, as distinguished from what Nancy here calls "the 'presentness' [*la présentité*] of a presence" (*SW* 126/193). It would be wrong to conclude that Nancy simply *replaces* the Romantic poetics of the fragment with a poetics of the fractal. Rather, what he is trying to indicate is that Romantic poetics—as, indeed, all poetics—presupposes an even more "fundamental" or "elementary" poetics.

From Genres to Touches

Against the will to art in the singular that haunted the poetics of the Jena Romantics, Nancy thus constantly emphasizes the essential plurality of art *as* art, that is, art as the plural technique of the present, as the ever fractal staging of the present. But how does this essential plurality of art relate to artistic practice, where there are, for example, different *genres* of art? What, for example, remains of their classification, or even their hierarchization, often so carefully considered by so many philosophers and theorists? The most common explanation for the plurality of artistic genres is the one endorsed by Hegel, among others, who declares that it is linked to, or even derives from, the plurality of the senses. In other words, art is plural because its different forms correspond to different senses: painting to sight, music to hearing, and so on. If we follow this line of thought, however, we are immediately faced with the problem of the absence of a univocal relationship between the five senses on the one hand, and art forms on the other. For, firstly, there are art forms that correspond to several senses, such as poetry, which is visual as well as auditory, and conversely, there are senses to which no art form corresponds, such as the olfactory sense—if at least we exclude minor art forms like cooking or the art of perfume. If, on the other hand, we include the latter, another major problem arises, namely that of the hierarchy of arts and senses.

Instead of venturing down this path, Nancy attempts to think of the plurality of art on a more fundamental level than the genres of art, which is, as I have already shown, that of technique, or more precisely, of the originary technicality of being. This original technicality of being discussed above, implies that being always gives itself in a certain way, in a certain mode. This does not mean, however, that there is a restricted number of possible modes in which being can give itself—for then we would easily fall back into a classification of these modes according to the five senses or according to the tools used. The "modality" of being consists in the fact that it gives itself each time in another mode, a mode that is singular each time, even before we can begin to classify it. The singular fact that there is sense—a facticity in which the *that* and the *how* are tied together, as we have seen—precedes the possibility of any differentiation or classification.

This does not mean that there is a general "something," a sense, a world, that is given each time in a different way. On the contrary, art, or the technicality of art, makes us see "that it is precisely not a matter of a differentiation happening to an organic unity, nor of a differential as continuous variation. It is rather a matter of this: that the unity and uniqueness of a world *are*, and are nothing but, the singular difference of a *touch* and of a *zone* of touch" (*M* 19/38). What art makes us see or feel, then, is that the "world" manifests itself in no other way than as that which touches, each time uniquely. Consequently, there is no such thing as *the* world or *the* sense of the world, nor, more concretely, anything like *the* color red or *the* right tone. The world is the here-and-now of sense, of a color, of a touch, of a local sound, all varying in intensity, duration, context, and dimension, and all interwoven in a singular web of relations. Sense is therefore plural because its touch always manifests itself as singularly plural, in the light touch of my fingers on the keyboard, in the grayish white of the page reflected on my hands, in the flighty cry of the passing bird.

Not surprisingly, the sense of touch plays a special role in Nancy's poetics compared to the other senses. Touch is not simply one of the five senses, but exceeds them and makes them possible. For Nancy, touch is thus nothing less than the *transcendental* sense, the condition of possibility for sensibility as such, because two local surfaces need to touch for there to be sense. Seeing, listening, tasting—in short, *existing*—is not possible without touch. This is also why Nancy argues—amongst others in *Sexistence*—that we can best understand our existence in terms of *sex*. Indeed, sex *is* nothing else that the activity of touching, each time singularly.

This key role of the sense of touch is underlined by Derrida in *On Touching—Jean-Luc Nancy*. In the publisher's announcement of the French version of this book, Derrida notes:

> The best and most economical way to start reading Nancy again today, both diachronically and synchronically, would be, it seems to me, to follow the guiding theme of his "question of touch." Over the years, it unfolds to the point of invading, parasitizing, overdetermining everything. It touches everything. . . . [A]ny meditation has come, in recent years, to thematize this "sense," the touch, what it teaches us and assigns to us as regards sensibility, feeling, sensing, feeling oneself as a matter of touching oneself (but as "self-touch you" he says), and also, by the same token, as regards the sense of sense and the sense of the world, as of "finite thinking" in general.[45]

As Derrida also points out, although for Nancy touch is indeed the primary sense, it in no way constitutes a unifying source of meaning, nor, for that very reason, a foundation on which to erect a "metaphysics of touch" analogous to the metaphysics of vision that has so long dominated Western thought from Plato to Descartes and beyond.[46]

In his reflections on touch, Nancy is undeniably close, at least to some extent, to Maurice Merleau-Ponty, who has amply demonstrated that touch is always *double*, implying both a body-subject and a body-object, that is, both a touching and a being touched. Despite Merleau-Ponty's account of what we can call the necessary *dis-position* of touch, Merleau-Ponty nevertheless maintained an immediate continuity between what touches and what is touched according to Nancy, a presupposition that no doubt stems from his attachment to the idea of a kind of property, *mêmeté* or interiority. Nancy, on the other hand, stresses that the heterogeneity that characterizes, or indeed *constitutes*, touch can never be elevated or appropriated, for, as he says in "Why Are There Several Arts and Not Just One?," touch *is* "heterogeneity in principle" (*M* 18/35–36).[47] This is why Nancy prefers not to speak of an auto-affectivity, but of an "auto-heterology of touch" (*M* 17/36). Touch, Nancy argues elliptically, is what makes us sense what makes us sense, or what makes us sense what it is to sense.

A Poem Like a Burst of Laughter

Now, art, according to Nancy, is precisely highlighting the sensing of sense, for in art, the emphasis is put on the mode of presentation of the work, the way it is produced and the material from which it is constructed. In fact, according to Nancy, artistic presentation is, in essence, *nothing other* than this emphasis: not the emphasis on this or that color or tone, but the colorful and tonal emphasis itself, their singular stroke or touch. This is also why Nancy compares the artwork to an *outburst*, an exploding kind of presence that has no other existence than in this explosion, after which it disappears again. An analysis of this specific mode of presence in relation to that of art is offered by Nancy in the essay "Laughter, Presence" (*The Birth to Presence*) in which he reads Baudelaire's prose poem "The Desire to Paint," about a painter who burns with the desire to paint the evanescent laughter of a mysterious woman.

The point of this essay is to criticize the idea of presence as something continuous and given. Asking "Does laughter have a *presence*?," Nancy concludes that laughter exists only in its outburst, and is then lost. The existence of laughter "which is never *one*, never an essence of laughter, nor the laughter of an essence" (*BP* 368/297) is thus limited to the singularity of the outburst and can, like being, never be presented or represented. However, the "desire to paint" thematized in this poem runs counter this (non)presence of the laughter. In fact, Nancy holds, this desire to paint expresses the *aesthetic desire* "from Plato to (at least) Baudelaire himself," namely "the aesthetic program containing presentation of the infinite desire for an impossible Beauty as the presentation of Beauty itself" (*BP* 372/301). In other words, *desire* here is the metaphysical "will to will" that maintains itself by constantly deferring its point of completion. By analogy with the metaphysical habit of presenting sense *as signification*, aesthetics since Plato could thus be characterized as the desire to paint in such a way that it "paints art, *absolutely*" (*BP* 377/307, my emphasis).[48]

In the final section of this chapter, I will return to Nancy's reading of Baudelaire's poem. For now, it is important to note that one of the strongest aspects of Nancy's poetics is that it avoids the risk of falling into the *other* extreme of this metaphysical aesthetics, namely into the presupposition of an "unpresentable," or, what amounts to the same thing, an "indescribable" or "undemonstrable" so dominant in poetic and aesthetic debates. Although Nancy's poetics sometimes seem close to this kind of poetics, he nonetheless firmly distances himself from it, for example in *Finite Thinking*, where he already anticipates his analysis of Hegel's *Aesthetics*:

> Art, for example, has long drawn the rigorous consequences—often in impoverished fashion, it is true—of the end of art as the representation of the absolute, the Idea, or Truth. But in this way it opens up the question of what 'art' could mean. It is thus the realm of representation in its entirety which spins in the void once the presupposition of complete presence and of a closed circle of sense is exhausted. This presupposition is still lodged, if only in a negative form, in the modern and postmodern tradition of a 'presentation of the unpresentable' . . . Now, if all there is is the finite, then everything is presented in it, but in a finite presentation which is neither representation nor the presentation of something unpresentable. (*FT* 23/42)

Thus, although Nancy renounces the presupposition of a complete and definitive presentation, he does not associate himself with the opposite presupposition that presentation is always flawed, that there is always an unpresentable that escapes it, that withdraws from it and can only be presented indirectly, provisionally or by being betrayed. According to Nancy, such poetics remains motivated by an aspiration to completion, be it one still to come.[49]

I would say that this move away from the poetics of the unpresentable goes hand in hand with a move away from a certain phenomenological presupposition, namely, the presupposition of a presence that hides itself while demonstrating itself. As we know, the founding father of phenomenology, Edmund Husserl, was the first to position both the category of the presentable and that of the unpresentable in the domain of *Erscheinung*, in order to do away with the principally unpresentable domain of the noumenal. By introducing the (impossible) possibility of presenting the unpresentable, Husserl was thus thematizing that which cannot be seen, but is nevertheless presentable in principle, if only indirectly, like the underside of the table. In the course of time, both within and beyond phenomenology, we have moved partially away from this claim by reintroducing a category of the *principally* unpresentable. Here, it is no longer a matter of a distinct sphere of sensible phenomena, but of a kind of experience that is so unexpected and abrupt that it surprises experience in an elusive way. Being a radical caesura, this specific genre of experience interrupts the traditional regimes of presence and identity, and introduces the category of *otherness*—an otherness that is in principle unpresentable, but which never ceases to haunt presentations.

The notion of the unpresentable has thus been gradually transformed: from the hidden immanence of Husserl to the withdrawn transcendence of Levinas. In the field of contemporary French philosophy, Nancy occupies a very special place, for Nancy not only wants to distance himself from Husserl, but also from the Levinassian idea of an unpresentable radical otherness, and he does so motivated by a way of thinking about the world that excludes precisely this radical otherness that we might call with Levinas *"otherwise than being,"* noting, however, that Levinas' "being" is not Nancy's "being." What Nancy calls "the presentation of the presentation" is not the presentation of what is below or beyond what is (presented), but it is *the passage to presence*, to its offering or birth. According to Nancy, to put it somewhat enigmatically, the world has an outside, but this outside is not outside the world. In other words, the world is not closed in itself, but neither is it open to another (of the) world. It opens up to what we might call, and indeed what Nancy calls, its "own outside," that is, an outside *within* the world itself.[50]

It also follows, it seems to me, that Nancy is not proposing what might be called a poetics of "ecstasy," as it is found, for example, in certain mystical traditions, but also in more "profane" poetics of limit experiences.[51] Artistic presentation is not "ex-static," says Nancy in *The Muses*, "but ek-sistant. A 'transimmanence.' Art exposes this. Once again, it does not 'represent' this. Art is its ex-position" (*M* 35/63). In other words, art is not a movement outside of oneself "separate from the senses," but is, to return to our analysis of the portrait, a movement which "puts forward," which draws us out of our skins, ex-*peau*-ses us. One might therefore be inclined to group Nancy's poetics under the poetic doctrine of the *sublime*. Although there is indeed a kinship between Nancy's poetics and those based on a certain interpretation of the sublime in Kant, Nancy nonetheless repeatedly expresses his reservations about this Kantian notion. His reservation lies precisely in the fact that a poetics of the sublime seems to rely again, at least in Kant, on the idea of the "unpresentable." This is why Nancy characterizes the thought of the sublime as the very extreme of metaphysical thought, because the "metaphysical demand for signification" reveals itself unambiguously: "The limit of this unconditioned demand is found in the Idea of the presentation of the unconditioned itself: this is the Kantian sublime" (*GT* 24/34).

In the text "The Sublime Offering" Nancy nevertheless tries to understand the sublime in such a way that it is compatible with his own poetics.[52] This rich text takes up the analysis of the beautiful and the sublime given in Kant's *Critique of the Power of Judgment*, thereby starting from the polemical observation that "the deep logic of Kant's text is not a logic of presentation" (*FT* 224/167), or, as one might add, *if* it is a logic of presentation, it is not a matter of presentation as static presence, but of the very *dynamics* of presentation, that is, of the presentation of presentation. It is the analysis of the sublime that can reveal what is actually the "deep logic" of Kant's text, because the sublime is the "proper" gesture of art as such according to Nancy: "[T]he sublime does not constitute in the general field of (re) presentation just one more instance or problematic: it transforms or redirects the entire motif of presentation" (*FT* 225/163).

Instead of being simply a second form of aesthetics alongside that of the beautiful, the sublime shows aesthetics in a new light that *includes* the form of the beautiful. According to Nancy, this new light is that of an "aesthetics of *movement*" instead of an "aesthetics of the *static* or the state" (*FT* 223/166, my emphasis). Underlying this shift from a poetics of the static to a poetics of movement is a certain conception of the *limit* and the *unlimited*. According to Nancy, we are on the wrong track if we confuse the unlimited with the infinite. To say that the sublime presentation is a presentation of the infinite is to assert that it is indeed a specific kind of presentation, namely one that, being finite, is inadequate in relation to the infinite. However, according to Nancy, the unlimited is to be understood not as a state, but as a *gesture*, namely the "the gesture of formation, of figuration itself (*Ein-bildung*) . . . without itself taking on any form" (*FT* 224/167).[53] It is not a question of the adequacy or inadequacy of presentation, nor of presentation at all, but of the gesture in and through which things present themselves.

The sublime poetics of movement—and this explains the title of Nancy's text—is that of an "offering." The sublime, Nancy argues, can be conceived as the moment of emergence of the work of art as such, and is thus the decisive moment of art in general, of which the beautiful work is only one possible appearance. Hence, and this obviously involves a critical reprise of Kant, there is no beautiful art that is not *also* sublime. Presentation can only be presented as a dazzling movement of interruption as an unexpected burst of laughter, for it is necessarily always a presentation *at the limit*. Or, in a vocabulary dear to Nancy, it *touches* its limit. What is offered in the sublime offering is not installed in presence, but remains at a limit "suspended at the border of a reception, an acceptance" (*FT* 237/185). The sublime offering is thus, once again, the offering of nothing more than "the fact *that* [an artwork, AvR] presents itself *as* it presents itself" (*FT* 225/176). Or in other terms already seen, what is offered in the sublime offering of art is the *quod* of the presentation, a *quod* which is always given in a certain *style*, because it, in the end, always inscribes itself in a singular way.

Poetic Language

LANGUAGE AS OPENING

Until now, I have studied Nancy's ontological poetics mainly through his analyses of art in general, and of the visual arts in particular. Among artistic expressions, we have so far largely neglected expressions *in language*, that is specific artworks grouped under the denominator of "poetry" or "literature." Nevertheless, it is these expressions that deserve a more thorough treatment, because it is in poetic art that Nancy's mythical ontological poetics would most directly confront mythological thought, which, of course, implies a certain view on language and narrative.

So, how does Nancy conceive of literary language? Given the elementary distinction he makes between signification and sense, he certainly does not see it as the bearer of a meaningful message. According to Nancy, a literary text does not require an interpretative reading. In this respect, a literary text is no different from On Kawara's *date paintings*, in relation to which Nancy points out that "we do not *read* the date on the canvas: We do not *interpret* it. It does not tell a story." The "text" of On Kawara's painting, on the other hand, demands that "we only *hear* it. . . . We hear a voice, a tone, or inflection before any recognizable word" (*MII* 200/21, my emphasis). Indeed, I would argue that Nancy conceives of linguistic artworks as inflections or tones that need no interpretation, or whose meaning resides in that very tone that resists further interpretating, like in the case of the *onomatopoeia*. Being a creation (*poiein*) of words (*onoma*) that evoke the thing it names by its very sound, the figure of onomatopoeia fits entirely with Nancy's tautegorical poetics, since onomatopoeic language expresses things not by means of another register, as allegorical language would, but in the register of the things themselves.

It is therefore not surprising that this linguistic figure of the onomatopoeia reappears repeatedly in Nancy's poetic analyses. An interesting text in this context is the one entitled "Borborygmi," written on the occasion of the Cerisy-la-Salle colloquium on Derrida's work, and examining the inarticulate growl of language through the onomatopoeia "borborygmi." As Nancy points out, the onomatopoeia "borborygmi" is not only the medical term for a rumbling in the bowels, but has also developed the figurative meaning of "incomprehensible and inarticulate remarks" (*FT* 112/45). If there is an onomatopoeic side to any linguistic expression—and this is obviously what Nancy wants to argue—it is therefore "something that is, immediately and materially, the unheard sense . . . , a sense more powerful and more remote than all configurations, constellations, or constructions of sense" (*FT* 112/45). In other words, the onomatopoeic side of language is what Nancy calls its *sense* tout court, which is the condition as well as the excess of signification.

Nancy had already contextualized this immediate and material side of language in *Being Singular Plural*, drawing on the distinction between *saying* and what is *said*: "Either as an audible voice or a visible mark, *saying* is corporeal, but what is *said* is incorporeal; it is everything that is incorporeal about the world" (*BSP* 84/108, my emphasis). Although this distinction between the corporeal of the saying and the incorporeal of the said seems at first glance to imply the dualism present in the whole series of oppositions between sensible and intelligible, matter and form, body and soul, this is not what Nancy means. What he proposes is rather a distancing of such dualism, without propagating monism. Or, what he suggests seems to be rather *another form of monism*: not a monism that assumes a world made up of a single substance that coincides immediately and entirely with itself, but a monism that assumes a world made up of a materiality that does *not* coincide with itself, that differs from itself and exposes itself, not to its dualistic counterpart, but to its own outside manifested in the interruption of the same.

Nancy himself, however, takes the opposite route, proposing, in *Corpus*, *another form of dualism*:

> Through the appeal or injunction of what falls under the name of body, we must first of all—and I say this as something of a provocation, but not merely so—restore something of the dualism, in the precise sense that we have to think that the body is not a monist unity (as opposed to the dualist vision), having the immediacy and self-immanence with which we earlier endowed the soul. The body is the unity of a being outside itself. (*C* 133/125)[54]

Whether it is another form of dualism or monism, there is no doubt that the aim of Nancy's onomatopoeic account of language is to destabilize the traditional opposition between the sensible and the intelligible, and, consequently, between the corporeal and the incorporeal. In his discussion of the body and language in *Being Singular Plural* Nancy destabilizes this opposition by pointing out that language is—before it is identifiable by what is said—a way in which the body exposes itself and differs from itself: "Before being spoken, before being a particular language or signification, before being verbal, 'language' is the following: the extension and simultaneity of the 'with' insofar as it is the ownmost power of a body, the propriety of its touching another body (or of touching *itself*), which is nothing other than its *definition as body*" (*BSP* 92/116, my emphasis).

In other words, body and language do so not so much evoke a dichotomy, let alone an opposition, but share the same structure. Instead of distinguishing between "language" and "body" and associating one with the incorporeal and the other with the corporeal, it would be better to distinguish between "closed" corporality and "open" corporality, as well as between "closed" and "open" language. On the one hand, we are talking about what Nancy sometimes calls "mass" in relation to the body, and "signification" in relation to textual expressions: the univocal, closed-in-itself substance and the full, immobile presence of signification that metaphysics dreams of.[55] On the other hand, it would be the "exposed" body that Nancy calls "body" tout court, and the exposed language that Nancy calls "sense." Instead of distinguishing between body and language, between saying and the said, the challenge of Nancy's poetics is thus to distinguish between language as a singular, fractal bodily exposure without return, and language as a full, "massive" signification, closed in on itself.

It is in an attempt to stress the former condition of language that Nancy often insists on the relation between language and sex, that is to say between speaking beings and sexual beings. As we have seen, in both cases it is a question of a being that exposes itself beyond itself, of the opening of one body to another, of the sense that circulates *between* us. In fact, for Nancy the most elementary onomatopoeic expressions are indeed sexual exclamations ("Ah!," "Oh!"), which according to him are but expressions of an overflowing self.[56] Importantly, in order to present this overflowing movement as such, it has to be expressed *linguistically* according to Nancy, since "linguistic sense—or sense conceived on the basis of language—consists in the referral [*renvoi*] presented *as such*: [there] is also sense that does not present itself as such (the sense of sensation, of feeling), [but] a word coming from the mouth is at the same time a referral to an outside and to the word itself" (*PD* 80). It is these exclamatory, excessive, onomatopoeic expressions of language that seem to Nancy to be the exemplary manifestation of language as conceived of in his ontological poetics.

Touching Language

Let us now try to get a clearer idea of this language, and of its relation to what remains of myth. I have already shown that for Nancy the onomatopoeia is the linguistic figure par excellence of the mythical dimension of his ontological poetics, but this figure has also played a central role in the philosophies of language from which he wants to distance himself. These are, Nancy holds in Borborygmi, the philosophies of language believing in a "*genuine* onomatopoeia," that is, an "onomatopoeia of *truth*" (FT 113/46, my emphasis) in which the onomatopoeia is taken as a "nominical essence" or as a "Name taken absolutely" (*FT* 113/46). Such a direct and transparent naming of things by their "true" name—the legendary figure of which is of course Adam in the Garden of Eden—has always been the ultimate aspiration of language, an aspiration "that language . . . brushes up against incessantly: the thing making a name for itself" (*FT* 113/47). The aspiration of representative language is thus the precise, unmitigated coincidence of words and things. Although Nancy does not say so explicitly, such a paradisiacal world can only be a *mythological* world. Yet, this paradisiacal world is not ours, nor is it, strictly speaking, a *world*, since we live in a *worldly* world where both things and language lack a divine origin. And in this worldly language, the very concept of an onomatopoeia *of truth* is "contradictory" according to Nancy, for "either there is a noise, which is precisely not a name, or there is a name, which imitates a noise without being the noise itself" (*FT* 113/47).

In other words, representation in language, however truthful it may be, cannot be confused with the thing itself. The ideal of representative language fails because of the very structure of language. This is why we need to understand onomatopoetic language differently according to Nancy—namely as *tautegorical*, as the saying of things by themselves. It is a question, then, of understanding both things and language differently, not as two stable entities that are coupled in an equally stable way, but as the mutual articulation of the one and the other. This is not a mutual manifestation according to the mythological ideal where things have real names, but, on the contrary, a genesis that can be called *mythical* where the word becomes a thing, flesh: *verbum caro factum*. At this point, we see how the rejection of mythological language in favor of mythical language is based on yet another rejection: that of one incarnation in favor of another. Indeed, Nancy stresses on several occasions that we need to rethink the notion of incarnation.

The key text in this context is undoubtedly the short essay *"Verbum caro factum"* in *Dis-Enclosure*. As Nancy points out, in Christian doctrine the incarnation is generally understood as the incorporation into a body of something incorporeal, like the soul or the Truth. Taken literally, however, the formula *verbum caro factum est* implies something else according to Nancy: "If the verb *was made* flesh, or if (in Greek) it *became* flesh, or if it *was engendered* or *engendered itself* as flesh, it is surely the case that it had no need to penetrate the inside of that flesh that was initially given outside it: it became flesh itself" (*DE* 81–82/126). The fact that the word engenders itself as flesh means that it is not the material presentation of a preexisting idea or spirit, but, on the contrary, that it presents itself *as a thing*, that is, as something finite, situated, historical, in short, not as incarnation, but as *carnation*. This rethinking of the Christian doctrine of incarnation is not only one of the driving forces behind Nancy's deconstruction of Christianity, but also a rethinking of the doctrine of representation largely inspired by Christianity, a doctrine in which the material sign is seen as the support of an immaterial idea. In Nancy's interpretation of the doctrine of incarnation, language is thus shown to be like the Latin *carne*, as that which is made of flesh—flesh that is not ready to receive any content, but which is itself open, opening.

In so doing, Nancy undermines the opposition between the sensible and the intelligible, once again opening the way to a tautegorical understanding of language. By basing his poetics on Schelling's model of tautegory, Nancy not only departs from the opposite model of *allegorical* language, but also follows Schelling in understanding this non-allegorical, tautegorical as *symbolic*. Although for the average person, allegory and symbol are two fairly comparable figures of speech, the eighteenth-century writers took the trouble to delimit them strictly. Whereas allegory, for Schelling, was the sensible, concrete illustration of an abstract idea, *symbols*, on the other hand, were much more special. Unlike an allegory, a symbol cannot be generalized, but is instead always unique and singular, and moreover gives substance *to* this uniqueness. Now, it is this Romantic idea of the symbol that Nancy expands in his ontological poetics. More specifically, he proposes replacing the traditional idea of symbolism with this Romantic-Schellingian one which goes back to the etymological sense of the word "symbol." If "our task today is nothing less than the task of creating a form or a *symbolization* of the world" (*CW* 53/59), as Nancy maintains in *The Creation of the World, or, Globalization*, it is thus according to the Romantic rewriting of the idea of "symbolization."

In its Greek meaning, *sumbolon* designates an object cut in two, usually a piece of pottery, functioning as a sign of recognition when the bearers put the two pieces together (*sumballein*).[57] The symbol was thus not the expression of an abstract, general meaning that transcended it, but a broken thing whose pieces signified nothing other than that they were pieces of that specific broken *matter*. Symbolic language—or language understood according to this model of the symbol—thus indicates two things: firstly, that meaning is a matter of touching materiality, and secondly, that it only functions by being interrupted or broken in itself.[58] For Nancy, the symbol—at least in this specific meaning—is therefore a perfect model for understanding language in its worldly, material form. Language for him is always symbolic in the sense that it is a relation between two bodies, a touching of bodies. "The proper value of symbolism," Nancy sums up in *Being Singular Plural*,

> is in making a symbol, that is, in making a connection or a joining, and in giving a face [*figure*] to this liaison by making an image. Insofar as the relation is imagined [*représente*], and because the relation as such is nothing other than its own representation, the symbolic is *what is real in such a relation*. By no means,

however, is such a relation the representation of something that is real (in the secondary, mimetic sense of representation), but the relation is, and is nothing other than, what is real in the representation—its effectiveness and its efficacy. (The paradigm for this is "I love you" or, perhaps more originally, "I am addressing myself to you.") (*BSP* 57–58/79, my emphasis)

This rethinking of symbolic language, like that of incarnation, is key to Nancy's ontological poetics. In other words, the "symbolic" is for Nancy a way in which being expresses itself. This is why we can speak in Nancy's case of a *symbolic being*, as Anne O'Byrne does,[59] in which, according to Nancy, "the world *symbolizes in itself with itself*, in which it articulates itself by making a circulation of meaning possible without reference to another world" (*CW* 53/80, my emphasis). To return to the theme of myth, we might say that it has become clear, once again, that Nancy's poetics is not concerned with the creation of a meaningful imaginary reality, but with the way in which reality manifests itself.

Resuming now our analysis of the role of concrete literary works in Nancy's thinking, it obviously follows from his view on the symbolic nature of language that reading literary texts is not to be understood as an act of interpretation. Rather, according to Nancy's poetics texts have a literary or symbolic value because they *touch* in the most literal sense of the word:

Bodies, for good or ill, are touching each other upon this page, or more precisely, the page itself is a touching (of my hand while it writes, and your hands while they hold the book). This touch is infinitely indirect, deferred—machines, vehicles, photocopies, eyes, still other hands are all interposed—but it continues as a slight, resistant, fine texture, the infinitesimal dust of a contact, everywhere interrupted and pursued. In the end, here and now, your own gaze touches the same traces of characters as mine, and you read me, and I write you. (*C* 51/47)

As a result, the concern of Nancy's poetics is threefold: firstly, to emphasize that literature is always a matter of touch; secondly, that this touch is always deferred, diverted and interrupted by its own technicality; and thirdly, that what we call "literature" makes us touch upon this touching of being.

Yet the paragraph quoted above also seems to suggest an even more radical proposition, namely that it is pointless to decipher, understand, or even *read* a linguistic text. For a text to be poetic or literary, it seems sufficient to be touched by the hands and eyes without being read. The radical nature of this proposition has not gone unnoticed. Michel Lisse, for instance, concludes that "Nancy invalidates reading as deciphering in favor of touching."[60] To be sure, Lisse argues that Nancy's poetics not only *devalues* reading as deciphering, but also *invalidates* it, that is, nullifies it. Although the idea that the poeticity of language consists only in the touching of the book held is obviously a little caricatured (even if it is a caricature evoked by Nancy himself), this caricatured idea that leads to Lisse's reproach nevertheless touches on an important aspect in Nancy's analysis of literature. If poeticity resides in the material touch, that is, in the *skin* of the text, does this mean that its meaning, its narrative construction, or its plot are of no importance?

The Right Touch of the Poem

To answer this question, we need to look at Nancy's own dealings with literary works, like his essay "The Poet's Calculation" on Hölderlin's poetry. Just as in his analysis of the portrait (published shortly afterwards), Nancy begins to describe Hölderlin's poems as a "touching gaze" (*EPL* 93/67). Poetry is thus immediately inscribed in a visual and tactile vocabulary. Being a touching gaze, a gaze that touches, what the poem does is, according to Nancy, to "[isolate] the point of contact" (*EPL* 93/67). Recalling Nancy's description of the work of art as a concrete surface that gives coordinates, we can imagine why he argues that the portrait's or texts' "gaze" is isolating a point of contact and, what is more, in the case of a text isolates it in the single, momentary act of reading the poem.

Once again, Nancy thus underlines the necessarily singular, zonal, and local character of the poetic. As in a painting, a poem is a touch, a momentary *effleurement* that stirs the senses. From the fact that Nancy describes the poem as a "gaze," we can deduce that the poem does not show itself as an entity that has frozen into a perfect closure with itself, as would the reflection in the mirror alleged by Nancy as the counterpart to the gaze of the portrait. Since it is always the touch of one surface on another, there is no poetic interiority, no truth, no property enclosed in the poem before it crosses the touching gaze of the reader.

A fine demonstration of this poetic touch is offered by a lesser-known contemporary French poet, Virginie Lalucq, with whom Nancy co-authored the book *Fortino Sámano: Les débordements du poème* [Fortino Sámano: The

Poem's Overflowings]. The first part of this cooperation features poems by Lalucq; in the second part of this book, fragments of Lalucq's poems are taken up and commented on by Nancy. Lalucq's poems are inspired by a photo of Fortino Sámano, a Mexican revolutionary who, smoking his last cigar, waits to be shot by a federal firing squad on January 12, 1917, his mouth twisted into a rictus smiling at death. Lalucq's poems display the same bold yet hesitant courage shown by the man in the photo: It is as if these poems were dictated out of breath, a knife to the throat, in an enormous effort to be exact. What is immediately striking about Lalucq's poetry—and what Nancy also notices—is its *meter*. Although every poetic text, indeed every text, is metrical, a large proportion of Lalucq's poems are literally *marked* by this meter, interrupted by a slash.

Here is the very first poem in the book:

How many of my executioners were / char-
ming? / The image says nothing about the regulation of
accounts / central / to the shooting / and the light
trail of blood / that will result / for now /
I'm smiling / for now / my criminal
record / empties itself / and again / without a lasso

[*Combien mes bourreaux étaient-ils / char-
mants ? / L'image ne dit rien du règlement de
comptes / central / de la fusillade / et du léger
liséré de sang / qui s'ensuivra / pour l'instant /
je souris / pour l'instant / mon casier judi-
ciaire / se vide / et encore / sans lasso*] (*FS* 13)

More obviously than in other metered poems, Lalucq's "slashed" sentences stutter the reading and prevent a direct understanding of the poem. In the first few lines, for example, the bars cut through the sentence, simultaneously asking two questions of completely different import, namely "How many were my executioners?" and "How many of my executioners were charming?" The passage from the fourth to the fifth line also evokes several meanings that open up this sentence to different readings, by saying at the same time that the "light trail of blood will result for now" and "for now I'm smiling."

The rhythmic interruption by the slashes suspends the poem's significa-tion once again each time, but at the same time makes possible the infinite flow of significations by allowing the parts to link up in different ways.

Although he does not go into the details of the text, Nancy emphasizes in his commentary that it is the very meter that prevents meaning from being fixed once and for all in a single signification. It is the meter that, according to Nancy, "separates the two possibilities of reading" (*FS* 59) and makes of that poem "always, at every instant, a last word without conclusion" (*FS* 63), which of course boils down to saying that there is "no last word" (*FS* 67). Referring to Nancy's account of "The Poet's Calculation" given in his essay on Hölderlin, we can say that it is the poem's rhythmic presence, the coming and going or simultaneity of the appearance and disappearance of its signification, that constitutes its particular touch of sense.

This idea clearly corresponds to the ontology of singular plural being that underlies Nancy's poetics. Since it is not a permanent given, but a repeated coming into presence, sense manifests itself by interrupting itself, that is to say, *rhythmically* or, as we have seen, in a *syncopating* way. In his analysis of Hölderlin's poetry Nancy indeed notes that "[t]he uninterrupted continuity of the 'living sense' can become tangible only when interrupted" (*EPL* 102/79).[61] And reading Lalucq's first poem, it is not hard to imagine that the interruption created by the metrical rhythm results in poetic elements constantly linking, detaching, and connecting. There is no single moment when everything falls into place, but an infinite series of moments when *ça tombe*, when something falls, something touches. Because of this dynamic, there is no harmonious fusion of elements into a single signification, but rather an incessant interruption of this fusion. In this sense, we should probably say that poetic arrangement—poetry that *is* arrangement—as Nancy sees it, is a *co-existence* of elements, rather than their coincidence.

The singularity of this poetic arrangement is of course also emphasized by Nancy in his analysis of the notion of *calculation* dear to Hölderlin. As any poet can confess, poetry requires "constant precision" (*EPL* 85/55), where the elements of the poem must be carefully composed with an eye to what Nancy calls "the accurate determination of distance—between tones and genres, between metrical quantities and sonorous accents, and between the saying and the said" (*EPL* 90/63). The *poetic*—and this is important—is thus not something inherent to certain works, but is the result of a certain technique of composition. So how do you know if you have achieved the right distance, the right precision? Although it is clear, as Nancy says, that the calculation of the poet "turns out right or doesn't turn out at all" (*EPL* 87–88/59), there is a certain unpredictability around which the whole poetic practice revolves. No wonder we often scoff at the idea of creative writing classes: If not a gift or a stroke of luck, the literary touch is in any case believed not to be planned.

Generally speaking, according to Nancy, a poet's exactitude does not consist in constructing a well-considered, balanced, and complete conceptual assemblage. Instead, the poet's project is what can be called *Witz*: a sudden, unforeseen, and singular touch of spirit, a contraction of elements into a single, extremely concise point, which evokes in one single stroke what the philosopher would willingly explain in a series of books; a contraction that Nancy sees, for example, in Hölderlin's famous phrase "since we have been a conversation." Of course, we can only give *examples* of this unexpected touch. There is no manual to follow for it "to turn out right." Although this is a poetics of precision and exactitude, immeasurability is, according to Nancy, the very essence of it: "[T]he measure of exact 'calculation,' the appropriate unity, is not given and that we should never imagine that it will be, nor that it could be" (*EPL* 88/60). Indeed, the phenomenology of reading teaches us that it is always *this* precise word in *this* poem—where the pronunciation slows down a fraction of a second because of the comma that precedes it—that touches, that gives the thrill.[62]

If Nancy insists on the exactitude of the literary text, he does so no doubt to oppose another poetics of calculation of which Aristotle's *Poetics* forms one of the models. What is calculated in Aristotle, instead, is the *calculable*, even the plausible and the necessary, and not the *incalculable* as it is in Hölderlin's case. The point of divergence, according to Nancy, seems that the "whole" that Hölderlin wants to present in his poetry differs from Aristotle's "whole" in stressing that a poetic work has no measure, is immeasurable, because it is never finished. In Aristotle's poetics, as we have seen, the whole is on the contrary a *measurable* one because it is arranged into a unity with a beginning, a middle, and an end that can "readily be taken in at one view" by means of a *plot*, because, as Aristotle put it: "[P]lots . . . should be whole and complete."[63]

Even though Hölderlin's poetry, too, as Nancy sees it, calculates a whole (*ein Ganzes*), it is not a whole whose development can be predicted because it occurs according to the laws of plausibility, but of what Nancy characterizes as a momentary "passage" (*EPL* 88/61). Or rather, it is a ceaseless passage of sense, its inappropriable coming and going, which is undoubtedly what is most symptomatic for literature or art, as Michaud also points out in *Cosa volante*: "[A]rt, as Nancy conceives it since such a long time, since the immemorial, is what doesn't pass, because it precisely that what doesn't cease to pass."[64] According to Nancy, this passage only takes place because of a radical *interruption* in the narrative sequence, because of that "anti-rhythmic" cut that Hölderlin calls the *caesura*. The caesured whole expressed both by Hölderlin's and Lalucq's poetry thus resides in the local rather than the global, in the singular rather than the general and is, according to Nancy, a "whole as different from every other whole," that is, simultaneously, a "whole different from itself and offering itself as such, as *one*. 'One' is the difference between the whole and the whole. It is this alone that is counted one, always one . . . the truth of sense, its arrival, its event" (*EPL* 90/63). In short, whereas the Aristotelian poetics of the plot is concerned with the *generalizable* "one," Nancy's poetics is concerned with the *singularity* of the "one," which is in principle non-generalizable.

Language Beyond Language (*Nancy, Derrida*)

Reading Beyond Communication

The departure of Nancy's ontological poetics from a mythological poetics thus lies, to sum up, in his recognition that poetic language can only exist by being recited, each time singularly because the truth of its sense can only be offered as this one event, each time singularly. In his own reading of literary texts, Nancy thus seeks to demonstrate how their sense lies in—or rather, bursts forth from—their singular sensibility. By way of example, let us analyze his reading of another poem. It is interesting here to return to Baudelaire's prose poem "The Desire to Paint," which Nancy analyzed by exploring the possibility of what he called, in this context, a "poetics of laughter," a poetics that understands the poem as a burst of laughter rather than as its representation or signification. Here is Baudelaire's prose poem:

The desire to paint

Unhappy perhaps is the man, but happy the artist that desire tears apart!

I burn with the desire to paint her who appeared to me so rarely and who so quickly fled, like a beautiful regretted thing the voyager leaves behind as he is carried away into the night. How long it is now, since she disappeared!

She is beautiful and more than beautiful; she is surprising. Darkness in her abounds, and all that she inspires is nocturnal and profound. Her eyes are two caverns where mystery dimly glistens, and like a lightning flash, her glance illuminates: it is an explosion in the dark.

I would compare her to a black sun, if one could imagine a black star pouring out light and happiness. But she makes one think rather of the moon, which has surely marked her with its portentous influence; not the white moon of idylls which resembles a frigid bride, but the sinister and intoxicating moon that hangs deep in a stormy night, jostled by the driven clouds; not the discreet and peaceful moon that visits the sleep of pure men, but the moon ripped from the sky, the conquered and indignant moon that the Thessalian Witches cruelly compel to dance on the frightened grass!

That little forehead is inhabited by a tenacious will and a love of prey. Yet, in the lower part of this disturbing countenance, where quivering nostrils breathe the unknown and the impossible, bursts, with inexpressible grace, the laughter of a wide mouth, red and white and alluring, that makes one dream of the miracle of a superb flower blooming on a volcanic soil. There are women who inspire you with the urge to conquer them and to take your pleasure of them; but this one fills you only with the desire to slowly die beneath her gaze. (Baudelaire, cited in *BP* 369–30)

The artist portrayed in this poem burns with the desire to paint, to fix once and for all on his canvas this woman who has touched him so much, to capture in paint this mysterious woman who constantly eludes him. The point Nancy is trying to make in his reading of Baudelaire's poem is that the burst of laughter of the woman prevents the artist to act upon this desire. Instead of a possessive seizure, the poem reveals, as if by surprise, another mode of the woman's presence. This other mode of presence is, according to Nancy, that of "a presentation that disappears in presence" (*BP* 382/312), a presence that comes to presence like a burst of laughter, unforeseen, irrecoverable, that catches by surprise. The presence of laughter is not a presence to be desired or sought: It is *offered*, or it is not.

According to Nancy, Baudelaire's poem is such an offer. Or perhaps it is better to say that it is the *reading* of the poem that offers it. And indeed, as one reads the poem, familiarizing oneself with the image of this mysterious woman, with her dark cavern-like eyes, it is the red and white mouth bursting into a brilliant and alluring smile that strikes like a flash of lightning, an explosion in the dark. At the disquieting face of this woman, says Nancy, "bursts, with inexpressible grace, the laughter of a wide mouth, red and white and alluring" (*BP* 370/299). It is this burst of laughter that, according to Nancy, marks the failure of the desired representation and seems to make the poem effectively a *presentation*, not a representation, of the event of laughter itself:

> We read this poem in prose as a presentation of laughter, and as nothing but this presentation—or: we read it as a presence of laughter, as a poem, the poetry of which, in its prose, is composed according to the bursting presence of the laughter of this wide mouth red and white, which the poem longs to paint. We read the poem as composed according to this laughter; we read it as being, itself, this laughter—and we read laughter as the presentation of the poem itself. (*BP* 370/299)

What Nancy wants to demonstrate, then, in a far richer analysis than I can repeat here, is that a poetic text can be conceived as, indeed *exists* as, laughter, that it is composed of the same eruptive presence as laughter. Baudelaire's prose poem is thus put forward by Nancy as an example of his claim that a poetic utterance is always a matter of this one, momentary and fractal event.

If we want to catch this poetic value of a text, we must therefore not necessarily try to understand it, but so to speak *sense* it, get *affected* by it, which would mean, among other things, a reading that does not *interpret*. Although the poem clearly communicates a certain view on beauty or even a poetic program, Nancy even suggests that "there is perhaps *no art of reading*" that can respond to the laughter of the poem, because this laughter precisely *exceeds* what the poem communicates (*BP* 371/298). Nancy thus sets out to detect this point of excess, this "minuscule, infinite difference between beauty and its presentation" (*BP* 373/300), and in accordance with his poetics he wants to locate it especially in the *saying* of the poem and not in the *said*, in the "internal rhythm and rhyme" (*BP* 374/301), in the unique tone and color of the poem created by the word "laugh" and its echoes.

In short, this infinite difference between beauty and its presentation is found in aspects that do *not* allow themselves to be enclosed in a communicable signification, which leads Nancy to conclude that "[t]he poem here is thus no longer a painting as image or representation. It is rather representation passing beyond itself, to its truth, which cannot be represented"

(*BP* 377/307). Applied to Baudelaire's specific poem, this amounts to a conclusion that clearly echoes *and* expands the Jena Romantic account of poetry: "Painting is not understood as imitation but as . . . the *modelization* of the model. (Less the drawing than the tracing, and less the tracing than the color, and less the color than the pigment itself, the flesh or skin of painting: a wide red and white mouth)." (*BP* 387/318, my emphasis). Yet, how can we sense, and not to *read*, this "modelization" in a text written, in a way, to be understood? As Nancy has already pointed out, it is very difficult to adopt a way of reading that does justice to the poeticity of the literary text and traditionally especially philosophical readings of literary texts have risked neglecting it.

This risk is not entirely absent in Nancy's own reading. It is indeed surprising that Nancy, in analyzing Baudelaire's poem, refers in particular to the *signification* of this prose poem to illustrate his poetics. Nancy finds color, brilliance, and radiance in the signification or even the traditional symbolic value of words, and so it is first and foremost on the basis of a *hermeneutic* interpretation of the *content* of this poem that Nancy seems to locate the interruption of metaphysical aesthetics, a content of which the red and white mouth forms the radiant core: "This happens (this pleasure, this modeling) where painting comes in: in the red and white mouth" (*BP* 388/319). But can one still say that "the poem does not paint a *significa-tion*" (*BP* 388/319) when one says, two lines above, "white, the color of innocence . . . , and red, the color of sublimity" (*BP* 388/319)? What are we talking about here if not signification and a philosophical interpretation of this signification?

While Nancy's ontological poetics may tend to *invalidate* the signifi-cation of the literary text in favor of its touch, as Lisse has pointed out, Nancy's *own* reading, on the other hand, reveals a tendency to *validate* the signification *insofar as* it emphasizes the touch. Nancy's analysis of the red mouth and the burst of laughter in Baudelaire's poem thus seems inclined to pass over the *saying* of the said. If there is something like the "pigment" or "paste" of the poem, as Nancy puts it, it is not, it seems to me, the pigment of the paint *named* in the poem and emphasized by Nancy, but the way in which Baudelaire has aligned the words, their rhythm and intonation, the unfolding of a sentence, in other words, the staging of the poem. Even if this is not always the case, I would say there is thus a certain embarrassment on Nancy's part in locating the poeticity of literary works, even though he is perfectly aware of the risk of an overly "philosophical" reading, and repeatedly stresses that the poeticity of literary texts lies in the fact that they exceed and resist such a reading. How, then, can we avoid such a risk and conceive of the color, flesh, and tone of language *in* and *from* reading that very language?

From Text to Voice

In order to find the beginning of an answer, we need to turn once again to what Nancy says about language. We have already seen that he distinguishes between signifying language and what he calls "sense." On the one hand, then, language is a means of communication, a purveyor of signification, and, at the height of its power, the constructor of cosmotheorean visions, of the great mythological plots that explain the secrets of the past, the complexities of the present and the uncertainty of the future. And, on the other hand, we have that "other language" which is—before and through all signification—the always singular sense of our disposition in the world, the "language" by which, in which and as which we are together, which puts us in contact with one another without sharing anything other than this very point of contact, of relation. I also pointed out that the latter is not limited to human beings, but in fact concerns everything that is, since *to be* means nothing other than to relate to others, to share being in this world. This is no longer a linguistic (or anthropological or epistemological), but an *ontological* understanding of language. This "other language" of sense is not just the materiality of signifying language, that is to say, the ink or the voice, but, above all, its *corporality*, that is, language understood as a body or matter that exposes and articulates itself.

Even if Nancy describes this ontological dimension of language in linguistic terms (such as tautegory, symbol, onomatopoeia, or more generally as literature or poetry), its scope goes far beyond what is commonly understood by "language." It also goes beyond the theories of his fellow philosophers. The sharpest indication of this is the role Nancy assigns to the *voice* in relation to the text, a role we have already glimpsed in his insistence on the onomatopoeic dimension of language, and in his interest in the themes of the mouth and laughter. This insistence on orality is also one of the indicators of Nancy's philosophical courage, as it prompts him to take up not only the entire metaphysical tradition, but also the no less conventional critique of that tradition.[65] Nancy is thus perfectly aware of Derrida's deconstruction of the metaphysical opposition between "voice" and "text," and it is rather *in the wake of* this deconstruction, so to speak after traversing it, that he takes up the element of orality.

As we know, Derrida, for his part, distinguished between two types of "writing": On the one hand, *phonocentric* and *logocentric* writing, which is indissolubly linked to *logos*, the subject, voice, and speech, and on the other, what he called writing proper or "archi-writing," which is disseminative and characterized by the movement of *différance*. While the first type of writing is understood primarily in terms of the "voice," the second follows the model of the "text." Because of its supposed immediate and direct presence, the philosophical tradition has generally preferred the living voice to the dead letter, as the latter would introduce the possibility of distance, difference, and displacement. At best, the text is conceived as a secondary, derivative reflection of the original voice. In his work Derrida not only undermined the foundations of this opposition between "voice" and "text," but also sought to demonstrate that these two poles were formed according to the same model, that of the text.[66]

Against this well-known horizon of contemporary French philosophy, Nancy begins to devote a large number of essays to the figures of the voice, the mouth, the song, underlining time and again the infallibility of their corporeal presence.[67] Far from seeking to provoke, these essays seek a way of envisioning the scriptural nature of *being* itself, as we saw earlier. In my analysis of Heidegger's influence on Nancy's poetics, above, I have already indicated that the voice is—or rather, *voices are*—a way of thinking being's original disposition (called *Auslegung* by Heidegger). According to Nancy, these voices anticipate signifying language as a kind of "pre-language" or "language-in-addition-to [*d'outre-langage*]" ("SV" 221/33).[68] Nevertheless, the exact status of these sharing voices is not always clear, nor is its relation to signifying language, and it is in this confusion that I see the risk of Nancy's overly "philosophical" or "hermeneutic" reading of literary texts. What, then, according to Nancy, is the status of the "voice" *in* or *in relation to* language? This question has occupied Nancy over the years. In *The Inoperative Community*, published a few years after "Sharing Voices," Nancy seems, for example, to distance himself explicitly from his position expressed in the latter essay, noting that voice "should be understood not as *linguistic* or even *prelinguistic*, but as communitarian" (*IC* 158n24/73n21, my emphasis). The self-correction implied in this remark is: "Contrary to what this essay ["Sharing Voices," AvR] might lead one to think, the sharing of voices does not *lead to* community; on the contrary, it depends on this originary sharing that community 'is' " (*IC* 158n24/73n21).

Nancy's point, then, is that the sharing of our voices is not situated in a primitive or original language, but on an even more "original" plane, that of our mere being together. Or, as Christopher Fynsk argues in his preface to the English translation of *The Inoperative Community*, Nancy wants to emphasize that "the exposure of singular beings is prior to the 'division of voices' he described in *Le partage des voix*, unless 'voice' is understood as prelinguistic" (Fynsk in *IC* xxiii). Because there is, in my opinion, not a shadow of a doubt that the voice in "Sharing Voices" is conceived as pre-linguistic, I would say that Nancy's remark does not reveal so much a self-criticism as he himself suggests, as a way of emphasizing even more clearly, as Fynsk also argues, that the voice as he understands it is still prior to what Heidegger calls "the voice of consciousness"—the non-linguistic call of *Dasein's* concern that has the effect of *Dasein* evading the "they."[69]

A similar refinement of his theory of language is given by Nancy twenty years later, in the English translation of *Hegel: The Restlessness of the Negative*. In the original French version Nancy made a distinction, as elsewhere, between *sense* and *signification*, explaining that the former is "another language [*autre langue*]" that "is not a mysteriously added language [*langue de plus*]" but "is just as much language itself [*le language même*]" (*H* 51).[70] In the English translation of this book, five years later, this passage, and this passage alone, was however deeply modified by Nancy. The last remark is deleted and replaced by a long passage which says, among other things, that this "other language [says] *within* language what language does not say . . . it is not language: it is *beyond* it," and adds that "at the same time, it *also* is language: it works *like* a language (such as the English or the German languages), as it articulates things in the play of their differences" (*H* 35, my emphasis). Although this is, it seems to me, once again an attempt to dispel the possible misunderstanding of an authentic original language, it is at the same time a largely ambiguous attempt because it says that sense *is* and *is not* (in) language, as well as that it works *like* a language, that is, *as if it were* a language.

While this ambiguous or elusive character is part of the "structure" of sense, it remains an open question how this relates to literary language and the textual construction of the literary text. If, for Nancy, the voice marks the scriptural structure of being itself, how does it give itself in a text? Can the voice of being be specifically heard in a literary text? Can literary texts cultivate it, strengthen it, or, conversely, weaken it? This, of course, brings us back to the question of how Nancy's analysis of orality fits in, so to speak, with the analysis of *textuality* proposed by Blanchot, Barthes, and Derrida, among others. What, then, is the *voice of the text*?

Nancy himself repeatedly emphasizes that, despite the apparent divergence between his own insistence on the voice and that of his fellow philosophers on the text, there is a total concordance between these two modes of thinking: "Contemporary thinking on writing and the text (Blanchot, Barthes, Derrida)," says Nancy in "Sharing Voices," "considers under these words, on their account, what announces itself here under the species of the 'voice(s)' " ("SV"256n47/64n45, translation modified). As we have seen, his own insistence on the voice derives not, therefore, from a rejection of the thinking of writing and the text, but only from his aspiration to distance himself as far away as possible from the idea of a text to be read hermeneutically, as he suggests in the preceding lines: "It will only be a question, in everything that follows, of the voice, never of writing. Without a doubt the poems of Homer [Nancy speaks about the ancient poets, AvR] are written, but they are never valued as this *text* to interpret which always forms, from Schleiermacher to Gadamer, the condition of departure of *hermeneutics*" ("SV" 256n47/64n45, my emphasis, translation modified). What Blanchot, Barthes, or Derrida call "text" or "writing," concludes Nancy, it is thus not the hermeneutic *text*, but *"the voice of the text"*: "[T]he *voice of a text* is that which itself is always perfectly clear in that it gives itself without concern for the transcription of meaning. Every text, as such, even the most hermetic or the most poetic, possesses first of all this perfect 'clarity,' which is not visual (signifying), but 'resonant' " ("SV" 256n47/64n45, translation modified).

Although the text, for Blanchot, Barthes, or Derrida, is not *textual* in the sense of harboring a signification to be hermeneutically deciphered, there is, in my opinion, something in this comparison of voice and text that does not seem to work, precisely because of the residue that separates the "voice" from the "voice *of the text*." Apart from its distance from hermeneutics, it seems to me that Nancy wants to take up the vocabulary of orality because it implies the most intimate relation of sense to being, while avoiding falling back into a metaphysics of immediate presence. For what Nancy demonstrates is that being itself is differentiated, technical, mediated—and for this reason impossible to grasp as full presence. Given this mediated nature, Nancy seeks, one might say, the least mediated, or in other words, the "clearest" expression of this being—bodies or mouths touching, skin on skin—and he finds it in, among other things, the voice—the sonority, tonality, timbre—of the text. The textuality of the literary text—the construction of narrative, plot, fictionalization, wordplay, even the fact that it is *written*—in Nancy's poetics, therefore, seems to be no more than an additional technique on top of the technicality already inherent in being itself, a poietic technique that in no way alters its fundamental structure.

Indeed, we have already seen that Nancy describes art as "perhaps nothing other than the second-degree exposition of technique" (*M* 26/51).[71] Nevertheless, it seems to me that, above and beyond the shared fundamental structure of text and voice, there is an important difference between the two. This difference undoubtedly follows from Nancy's radicalization of deconstructive thought, namely the way in which Nancy conceives difference—or différance—no longer as the displacement and incessant iteration of significations, but as the structure of being itself.[72] Whereas for Derrida, as for Blanchot, the différance of significations is more original than the ontico-ontological difference, in the sense that it is *in writing* that the voice of being lets itself be heard, for Nancy, the différance *is* that of the ontico-ontological, which is consequently more original than the différance of significations, because it is *in being* that the voice of being lets itself be heard.[73] Has the *literary* text, then, for Nancy, lost the function that it has in the thinking of his contemporaries? And if so, does Nancy's ontological poetics still have anything to do with what is generally called literature, that is, with novels, poems, fiction? Indeed, I would argue that Nancy's position is not without consequences for the estimation of the specific technique of the literary text.

What Remains of Literature

It seems that, in the end, the discrepancy between the voice of being and the voice of being *as expressed in a literary text* largely corresponds to the discrepancy noted between Nancy's and Blanchot's notions of "literature." In chapter 2, I pointed out that whereas for Blanchot, unworking as the "essence" of literature is a dynamic or movement that is given *in* a literary work, or even *as* a literary work, for Nancy it is what happens below or beyond the work, or can even be given *without* a work, because it consists in a silent murmuring of things. If there is a tacit disagreement between Blanchot and Nancy as to their conceptions of literature, as I argued in chapter 2, it perhaps follows that "literature" is, according to Nancy, neither principally nor exemplarily, the affair of works of art.

Indeed, my provisional elaboration on Nancy's dealing with concrete works of poetic art demonstrates a certain embarrassment on Nancy's part, one that is also noted by Derrida when he sees in Nancy's poetics the risk of overstating the real at the expense of what we can perhaps call the ambiguity proper to literature or art. Alongside an obvious admiration for Nancy's thought, Derrida's *On Touching—Jean-Luc Nancy* shows a reservation or rather a concern as to whether Nancy's "haptocentric" thought succeeds in evading the metaphysical presupposition of the "divine touch" whose "absolute truth" resides in its "*immediacy*."[74] It is important to note that Derrida in no way intends to argue that Nancy's thought testifies to the presupposition of an *intuitus originatus* of full presence, but he nevertheless seems to want to question the motif of touch, even if we consider it to be a touch "mediated" by an originary technicality, as we have seen.

What, then, is alarming according to Derrida? Derrida provides the answer in a remark as audacious as it is enigmatic. After indicating the leading role of the motif of touch in Nancy's thought, and the innovative force of this motif in relation to the phenomenological tradition, Derrida remarks: "For Nancy, touch remains the motif of a sort of absolute, irredentist, and *post-deconstructive realism*."[75] Although it is not clear exactly what Derrida means by this reproach, it is clear that he would not encourage post-deconstructive thinking, if such thinking is at all possible in his view, not so much because such a thinking would presuppose a full or fully accessible presence, but because it presupposes something that *is no longer to be deconstructed.*[76]

Given this reproach from Derrida to Nancy, it is at least remarkable that Nancy, a few years later, gives, in turn, the very same characterization of Derrida's thought in the text "Borborygmi" already examined: "Derrida's thinking is an *absolute realism* of the pure real, that is, of the real which springs forth from behind everything: realizing everything, while being nothing realized, being nothing, the *res* of realization itself" (*FT* 127/62, my emphasis). With this characterization Nancy indicates that Derrida, too, is trying to hint at the evenemential nature of the real itself, springing forth from behind everything as the "auto-hetero-graphy of truth" (*FT* 114/47). In doing so, Nancy thus fully associates himself with Derrida's "reproach," and seems to emphasize once again that there is no divergence between Derrida's thinking and his own. When it comes to Nancy's poetics, it is not hard to argue that it offers what we might call absolute realism, since, as we have seen, the main point of Nancy's poetics is to conceive of *poiesis* as a "making of the real." This also follows from the critical reworking of Heidegger's notion of *Auslegung* in "Sharing Voices," in which one of the crucial moments of this critical reprise is, as we have seen, the observation that *Auslegung* is structured according to the as (*als* in German), that is, the *in so far as*—and not according to the hermeneutic model where something gives itself as something else, *as if* (*als ob*) it were something else ("SV" 220/81).

Through his poetics, Nancy likes to demonstrate that there is always an element in signification that exceeds or interrupts it, and that is not signifying. For him, this element is the real itself, or more daringly: "the *thing* itself" (*GT* 69/106). Does this mean that Nancy's realism is post-deconstructive, as Derrida suggests? Although it is perhaps more a case of *ante-deconstructive* realism, I believe Nancy himself indeed moves explicitly in this direction. In *Corpus*, where he elaborates on the relationship between body and language, he notes, for example, that "[i]n all writing a body is the letter, yet never the letter, or else, more remotely, *more deconstructed than any literality*, it's a 'letricity' no longer meant to be read. What in a writing, and properly so, is not to be read—that's what a body is" (*C* 87/76, my emphasis). Although he does not explicitly state that a body "more deconstructed than any literality" is no longer or not yet to be deconstructed, Nancy nonetheless seems intent on arguing that deconstruction meets its limit where there is nothing to be read.

But perhaps we should rather say that it is not so much its limit that deconstruction encounters here, but its condition of possibility. This leads us, of course, to Derrida's notion of the *undeconstructible*. The undeconstructible, Derrida points out in *Specters of Marx*, is the condition of possibility for deconstruction, its driving force, because it has the structure of a promise that is constantly slipping away, of the announcement of a possibility that always remains to come—the structure, then, that prevents us from reaching the moment of a *post*-deconstruction. With this in mind, Derrida's reservations about Nancy's motif of touch become a little clearer. By characterizing Nancy's poetics as an irredentist absolute realism, Derrida seems to fear that Nancy's poetics presupposes that everything that is, is real, certain, that is to say, realized. So I would argue—albeit more explicitly than Derrida intended in *On Touching—Jean-Luc Nancy*—that his concern amounts to saying that the *uncertain*, if you like *spectral, deceiving,* or *virtual* dimension seems to be abandoned in favor of the inescapable necessity of the real.

In my opinion, this is confirmed by the postscript added by Derrida to the English translation of *On Touching—Jean-Luc Nancy*. In this postscript, Derrida very briefly and provisionally advances the theme of the virtual, asking whether the virtual is necessarily opposed to the *actuality* of touching aimed at by Nancy: "[This postscript] is a pretext to bring up another challenge, a supplementary one, of the *technical supplement* challenging . . . the assurance that touch is on the side of the act or the *actual*, whereas the *virtual* partakes more of the visual, with the appearing of *phanesthai*, that is, with the phantasm, the spectral, and the revenant."[77] Can we imagine a touch that is non-real, that is to say a touch of something that does not exist, but is *virtual*, as in the example of three-dimensional *virtual reality* advanced later by Derrida? What can we say about cases where the real is not only technical, but also *illusory*?[78] Although Derrida tends towards a positive answer, he leaves these questions open. Posed in this way, however, I believe these questions can be answered perfectly within Nancy's poetics. What counts, for example in the case of virtual reality, is always the real touch of the virtual reality: the sounds, the colors, the sensor-equipped glove—in short, not the fact that what is projected or produced is a virtual world, but only *that there is* a world.

And yet, the notion of the virtual key to literature and more generally to its relation to myth leads us to a problematic of testimony or *attestation*. For does literature, in the narrow sense of the term, bear witness above all to reality as such, to the *res*, the *quod*, of the real? Or does it, perhaps, *also* bear witness to a fictitious reality? Could we not say that we are dealing here—in the categories of virtuality and fiction—with a kind of expression that, without contradicting it, nuances or sharpens Nancy's ontological poetics? And what is the point of doing so? What is the point of distinguishing a *poetic* or *literary* scenography from other ones? What, then, are *poets* for, to repeat Hölderlin's famous question: *Wozu Dichter in dürftiger Zeit?* Or, as Nancy puts it in "How Do Things Still Stand With Poetry?":

> And what if what we call "poetry" (irrespective of whether or not it is between the covers of books of poetry), what if what we call "poetry" were the taking into account and the taking on board of an imperious failure constitutive of sense? (I use the word "poetry," but perhaps in the final analysis we need a different one.)
>
> . . . For the moment I shall simply say that the poetic (or poetico-metaphysical) sense of "poetry" has become, in a coordinated history that is itself the history of our philosophy of History, the sense of an infinite assumption of Sense or, alternatively, of an oversignification. . . . And it is this that has become impossible, untenable, intolerable. . . .
>
> In these circumstances, how do things still stand with poetry? What can be said about poetry that does not poeticize it [the metaphysical state of things, AvR]? And what can one say to acknowledge the need or necessity of the exhaustion of sense, of sense itself when it is exhausted? (*MII* 111–13/44–46)

How, then, can we distinguish poetry or literature in a world where the poetico-metaphysical or mythological sense of poetry has become untenable? And what is the point of doing so? These are the questions that will accompany me in the final chapter, and inspire me to redefine the responsibility of literature in contemporary communities.

Chapter 4

Literature's Unworked Force

The Scope and Limit of Nancy's Poetics

Situating Nancy's Poetics

Let us briefly retrace the path we have taken so far. Starting from Benjamin's analysis in "Critique of Violence," I made a diagnosis of contemporary political orders. The central claim put forward was that modern politics, whatever its nature, necessarily is what I call *mythological*, meaning that a political order, because it has no original foundation, always makes use of a founding story that establishes, explains, and directs it. Even if this founding story penetrates and is impregnated with reality to the point where it can no longer be distinguished from it, its dual nature of being at once a fictionalization and the foundation of an order still demonstrates the dual structure of myth itself. The founding story is never a simple statement or report of fact, but always the creative establishment of a certain state of affairs.

We have also seen that mythological politics leads to two contradictory attitudes towards the interrelation of politics, history, and language. On the one hand, myth demands that we take it at its word, allow ourselves to be shaped by it, and accept it as the explanation of the community's origin and destiny. On the other hand, however, the use of myth reveals precisely that this explanation is not self-evident, that the origin and destiny of the community must in a way be invented, and invented again, anew. As indicated, these two contradictory attitudes are evoked by the grammatical form of the *future anterior* in which myths necessarily present themselves, the tense which declares that things *will have been* so. On the one hand, as

Derrida has pointed out, this future anterior is the structure of a *promise*, of a promise that opens up an unresolved future in the present, making us sensitive to an *à venir*, a "to-come" that leaves room for the unforeseen. On the other hand, however, such a promise disguises that there is no assurance that things will turn out this way. The future anterior therefore both *disguises* and *reveals* the main undecidability of the course of events.

While Derrida has focused on the grammatical form of the future anterior as a way of questioning the metaphysics of presence, we must not forget that it is also the heart, indeed the moving force, of mythological politics. Evoked in the name of a political order, it presents a state of affairs as necessary, inevitable, and unchangeable, thereby not opening an indeterminate future, but precisely aiming at creating a society where things were, are and will forever be the same, a society that Lefort calls, following Hegel, "without history"[1] and whose mythological logic—implicitly or explicitly—forms the core of most, if not all, "totalitarian" or "fundamentalist" political orders.

As I indicated in the chapters 2 and 3, Nancy, for his part, argues that a *mythological* take on community is untenable, while emphasizing the necessary *mythic* dimension of our being-with. For this reason, he has sought to develop an alternative way of thinking about the interrelation of literature, community, and politics, taking it to be not a work to be completed, but as *unworked*. Moreover, removing community's unworking from the realm of politics and understanding it above all as an *ontological* affair, Nancy prefers to speak of "being-with" and "being-in-common" rather than "community," taking as its starting point neither the individual, nor the collective, but the simple fact that we *are* only when we are *together*.

Like Blanchot and Bataille, and like several others who seek to criticize totalitarian, or in Nancy's words "immanentist," interpretations of community, he emphasizes the *literary* dimension of this being-with. As said, to explore this literary dimension of community in greater detail, Nancy returns to the heritage of the Jena Romantics by investigating the possibility of a poetics that draws attention not to the work, to the finished product, but rather to the productive activity itself. It is partly by taking cue from the Romantic idea of poeticity as an *infinite* and *fragmentary* productivity that Nancy develops what I have called his *ontological poetics*, which is a "realist" poetics situated at the edge of language where speaking and being-with coincide.

Like most of his contemporaries, Nancy is moving away from a representationalist idea of language by emphasizing the materiality of language rather than its signification. As we saw in the previous chapter, however, Nancy significantly radicalizes this move. By emphasizing the "linguistic" way in which matter gives *itself*, he no longer focuses specifically on the materiality of the *text*, but on the way in which beings themselves are in and because of their materiality, that is, the way they are exposed, articulated or expressed as bodies. Nancy thus develops a poetic understanding not only of texts, but of being itself, an understanding that focuses not on its signification, but on the modality according to which beings present themselves precisely *as* beings, and not as the bearers of a specific signification hidden within or behind them.

With this ontological poetics, Nancy seems to me to be aspiring to something very ambitious, namely to provide a common ground for two dominant paths in contemporary French philosophy. To simplify, we could say that these paths boil down to presupposing a radical transcendence on the one hand, and a radical immanence on the other.[2] Nancy takes a specific direction by fundamentally joining the planes of immanence and transcendence in his ontology of being-with, thereby combining Deleuze's horizontal bodily immanence with Levinas's ethical call of the Other, the substance of Cartesian *res extensa* with Derridean *différance*, Bataille's transgressive excess with a rigorous everydayness. In doing so, he formulates an ontology that includes and links political, ethical, and poetical aspects, and that can be summarized in the formula "being-with is exposition." The reason for this *tour de force* is to avoid the Scylla and Charybdis of on the one hand the idea of an absolute transcendence withdrawn from the world, and on the other the idea of a total incarnation of transcendence within the course of reality.[3]

An important presupposition in the preceding chapters was that Nancy's poetics can be understood as "mythical" even though he himself uses this notion only sporadically. In his attempt to reassert the power of myth Nancy seeks to remove myth from its Aristotelian meaning of *plot*, that is to say, of the grand narrative, while keeping what in his view forms the very syncopating heart of myth, namely its performative force, the fact that it effectuates *by saying*. As I indicated in the previous chapter, Nancy understands this performativity in a way that is both very restrictive and general: What is effectuated is not a specific state of affairs, with a certain finality and signification, but the "tautegorical" effectuation of a certain staging, a *this-here-now* in the expression of this very this-here-now. This is what Nancy calls "the presentation of presentation" (*SW* 138/207): the presentation of the fact *that* there is something present, that something exposes itself sensibly in the present and as presence, and that we are ourselves exposed with it, in an inescapable presence, unmistakable and without secret.

The Scope of Nancy's Poetics

By bringing together performative, material, and social aspects, Nancy's onto-logical poetics provides an interesting and innovative conceptual framework for the analysis of artistic phenomena, including all contemporary artistic practices such as modern dance, urban art, or body art. Indeed, following and radicalizing the Romantic tradition, Nancy's poetics exceeds not only "literature" properly speaking but also "art" as such, demonstrating that every "articulation"—whether artistic or not—can be called *poetic*, that is, an ex-position, a dis-position of reality. It is perfectly consistent with Nancy's Romantic ontological poetics to say that the touch of a stone on the ground can be as poetic as the meter of a poem.[4]

The absence of an exclusive theory of *literature* is therefore not a sign of incompleteness, but rather of consistency and coherence of Nancy's poet-ics. Nevertheless, as we saw, a certain embarrassment can be perceived in Nancy's reading of literary works proper. In analyzing, for example, poems by Baudelaire or Lalucq, Nancy focuses, in line with his poetics, on the sensible manifestation of a tone or a color, but largely overlooks the fact that these are *described* and *staged* manifestations embedded in a *work of art* in the narrow sense of the term. One reason for this neglect, or so I would like to argue in the present chapter, may be that Nancy's ontological poetics does not imply a theory of the literary *work*, nor, consequently, of the specific functioning of literary *language in* such a work. More than a neglect, this is the inevitable result of his understanding of poetic language as the enunciative structure of *being* itself, which reduces the literary work to a derivative enunciation.

Without in any way diminishing the merits of Nancy's poetics, I would therefore like to propose here to complement Nancy's poetics with a more specific theory of the literary work. I propose this complement in order to understand what I want to call the *distinctive force* of literature in the ordi-nary sense of the word, without, however, burdening it anew with a heroic mission, as Heidegger did. This distinctive force must be understood in both senses of the word, that is, firstly as the force unique to the literary work, the force by which literary practice distinguishes itself from other practices, and secondly as the force to distinguish, to make distinctions, even to judge. The distinctive force of the literary work has a potential that, in my view, could reinforce a key issue of Nancy's poetics, an issue put by him in terms of *the political exigency to resist*: "[C]ommunity, in its infinite resistance to everything that would bring it to completion . . . signifies an irrepressible political exigency, and that this exigency in its turn demands something of 'literature,' the inscription of our infinite resistance" (*IC* 80–81/198). I would say that it is precisely literature in the narrow sense of the word, that is, the literary practice of writers and poets, that is demanded for this infinite resistance to take the form of a political exigency.

At first glance, it may seem surprising to argue that a Heideggerian poetics such as Nancy's leads to a weakening of the distinctive power of literary works. After all, Heidegger, for his part, seems to have attributed the greatest possible power to literature by taking *Dichtung* to be the essence of language and the unconcealment of being as such. Nevertheless, I would like to argue that, in the poetics that Nancy upholds in the wake of Heidegger, the importance of literature goes hand in hand with a diminution of the distinctive force of literary works. This is as already noted at the end of the previous chapter, because this distinctive force resides, in my opinion, in a specific characteristic of these works that Nancy deliberately ignores by colliding literature and ontology, namely their *fictionality*. More precisely, this characteristic presupposes two things that Nancy has carefully banished from his poetics: firstly, the fact that literary practices have a necessarily *deceptive* dimension, and, secondly, the additional fact that this dimension in a sense implies the *denial, questioning, or suspension of the real.*

To be sure, banishing these two aspects forms the specific strength of Nancy's poetics. The avoidance of the first aspect is motivated by Nancy's refusal to distinguish between reality on the one hand and fictionality or virtuality on the other. According to him—and this is a courageous move that perhaps takes us beyond the "linguistic turn" and the "society of the spectacle"—there is only reality, or rather, everything that *is* is real.[5] Subsequently, the avoidance of the second aspect seems to derive from Nancy's attempt to radicalize, or perhaps even move beyond, deconstructivist thinking. This attempt is motivated by his aspiration to find, in or beyond deconstruction, an *inescapable facticity*, a touchstone—within all the "maybes," "*s'il y en a's*" and "specters" that have populated French philosophy in the last few centuries. Although this facticity is by no means a first or last foundation, it is nonetheless what Nancy unhesitatingly calls "sense," "truth," "decision," or "being."

The complement to Nancy's poetics that I propose here reanimates, in a sense, these carefully banished specters, without losing sight of Nancy's ontological project. More specifically, I wish to advance a theory of language that is able to distinguish between *literary* statements and *non-literary* statements—a distinction, moreover, that is not generic but gradual and constantly to be reinterrogated. In doing so, I do not intend to criticize Nancy's poetics, but rather examine its scope and push it slightly beyond its own boundaries. If Nancy's poetics does not explore all its possibilities, or if it shows some internal friction, it is not, therefore, the sign of an unfruitful poetics, but the sign of a courageous way of thinking that opens up its own track. Moreover, as I mentioned earlier, the main concern of this track has never been literature per se. Indeed, what I shall develop in this final chapter is rather a theory of literature that *grafts* itself onto Nancy's poetics, but perhaps at the same time demonstrates its limits.

The Limit of Nancy's Poetics

The limits of a certain way of thinking usually present themselves when adopting an external point of view. But in this case, I would argue, there is also an *inner* limit to Nancy's poetics, a limit illustrated by the hesitant way in which Nancy tends to treat concrete literary works. This limit, in other words, is felt at times by Nancy himself. Apart from the fact that his analysis of literary texts seems to testify to a certain conceptual or theoretical friction, there are also interviews in which Nancy himself mentions a personal unease with the question of art. In an interview with the French philosophical journal *Le Portique* in 1999, he remarks for example: "Thirty years ago, I would never have thought that I would speak about art. For me, it was not in line with philosophical questions" ("TP").

This is an astonishing admission, considering that Nancy's main philosophical question implies nothing less than a fundamental relation between philosophy and its poeticity. In the philosophical tradition to which Nancy belongs, art and literature are not only "in line" with philosophical questions, but are, at least conceptually, always already involved. It is true, however, that although Nancy's thinking has always implicitly or explicitly touched on the question of art, it was not until the 1990s that Nancy began to analyze *concrete works* of art like the paintings of On Kawara or Pontormo, the films of Abbas Kiarostami, and the poems of Lalucq. So it seems not so much art in general, but the concrete artworks that were off his radar. Although the theme of art and literature has always been present in his thinking, he is, in other words, not always completely sure about the role *artistic practice* could play in it.[6]

And indeed, if the dividing line between philosophy and literature becomes blurred, if philosophy always finds itself already involved in the realm of poetics, what is the point of examining an artwork as such, in isolation? In Nancy's poetics, as we have seen on several occasions, there is no a priori, that is, generic, difference between the disposition of the world in or outside a work of art. A poem, a primordial cry or a passing bird are equally "poetic" insofar as they are a singular exposition of sense. Seen in this light, it might even be surprising that Nancy, in so many texts, attributes special attention to specific artworks. For if artistic practices are fundamentally indistinguishable from each other and from other practices in terms of their poeticity, why should they be given a privileged role? And why would certain artworks merit more attention than others?

Like the Jena Romantic poetics, Nancy's ontological poetics deliberately lacks criteria for comparing and evaluating artistic articulations, although this lack causes him daunting problems as he points out in the same interview with *Le Portique*:

> I am not on the same level with everything. *And this causes me daunting problems*, because I know that, at times, I seem to make a gesture welcoming everything—when in fact, in my "sensibility," my judgment of taste, but also in my political judgment, I am not at all happy with this or that thing that I find stupid or ugly . . . I cannot say, for example, that I agree with the use of shit in paintings. But when I have to explain why, I'm embarrassed. Because I understand that art has come to this, but at the same time I think that there is something wrong, that this is wrong. . . . But I don't know very well to what extent I can say it. *And I recognize that here I lack a "regulative idea."* ("TP" 5, my emphasis)

In this passage, whose hesitant tone is quite rare in Nancy's discourse, Nancy reveals what could, in my opinion, be conceived as the limit of his poetics, even if he formulates this limit in a somewhat awkward way, because, strictly speaking, he *cannot want* a regulative idea to tell "wrong" from "right" art. In fact, as we saw, what Nancy strongly rejects in all his work is the possibility of any regulative idea.

What he lacks, however, is indeed the ability to *judge* and *distinguish* artworks, not as to their truth or falsity, but as to their effect, content, or mode. To his own regret, his poetics seems to allow him only to assert *that* there is artistic articulation, and not *what* it expresses, nor what it evokes, that is, whether it disappoints, discomfits, or revolts: "[I] am very often disappointed or discomfited—or sometimes even revolted—by what certain contemporary artists do, *and I see that there is a problem there*" ("TP" 5). What seems to be the problem, then, is the lack of the possibility of *attesting* to the specific effect an artwork might have. Trying to overcome this problem will be the central motif of this last chapter, and the main reason for examining the possible distinctive force—in both senses of the word—of works of art: the force of distinguishing artistic practice from other practices, and the force of making distinctions.

But first it should be noted that the reason why Nancy's poetics does *not* offer a "regulative idea" to judge artistic practices is that poeticity, for him, is not regulated or to be regulated. In other words, there are no "good" or "bad" artworks of art according to Nancy's poetics, since his poetics avoids the very idea of Grand Art. Certainly, in a sense, we could say that an artistic practice is on the wrong track if it aims at producing a closed, finite signification, but the challenge of Nancy's poetics is precisely to demonstrate that such closure is never possible, and that each work is a *birth* rather than a product, a birth that irreversibly opens it up to the world. Thus, art always *resists* its own regulation and what Nancy calls "literature" is, as he puts it in the phrase quoted above, precisely "the inscription of our infinite resistance" (*IC* 81/198), a resistance that is always already there, for it is the resistance to all completion that is proper to our being-with itself. Our task today, he keeps repeating, is to think, under the name of "literature," this resistance which is always already proper to our being-with.

But is this enough in the light of contemporary politics, in the light of all the attempts to close and regulate our being-with? In terms of Nancy's ontological poetics, this question must surely be answered in the affirmative. The very point of this ontology is to make us aware of the fact that our task is precisely to stop asking the disillusioned question "But is it enough?" Nonetheless, we can ask, as Nancy also does, whether his ontological poetics is sufficient to understand the practice of artists, their effect and role in society, just as we might ask, in the same vein, whether the inscription of our infinite resistance is enough for this resistance to be felt, attested, or affirmed. In what follows, I shall touch upon—and I realize I can do no more than this—the hypothesis that the possibility of attestation may reside not in what Nancy generally calls "literature," but indeed in *literary practice* in the narrow sense of the word. In proposing this, I would like to push Nancy's poetics one step further, with the help of a number of interlocutors, by investigating the role that literary practice might play in political communities.

The Distinctive Force of Literature (*Nancy, Rancière*)

Is Literature Exceptional?

As we have seen, one of the main aspects of Nancy's poetics is its insistence on poetry's *everydayness* in the attempt to avoid any assumption of a Grand Art, an art with a historical mission that should form the Great Work of humanity, to which, according to Nancy, not only the author of the *Systematic Program*, but also the Jena Romantics, and not to forget Heidegger, aspired. As we saw in chapter 3, Nancy firmly renounces Heidegger's distinction between authentic and inauthentic forms of speech. According to Nancy, as mentioned, "there can be *absolutely no* question of conferring . . . an ontological privilege of *any* kind on *any* form of speech or communication," since all forms of speech are without exception "under the power of the 'they' and subject to the hearing of the 'they'" (*BP* 404n29/123–24n1, my emphasis). When we speak, *they speak*, or even *it speaks* and it is this *worldliness* of speech that, at the most fundamental level, implies that no articulation can be privileged. Heidegger's desire to provide poetry with such a privilege, results according to Nancy from a false attachment to the value of exceptionalism, and from the desire, one might say, to dramatize history.

In his own ontological poetics, Nancy is determined to remove literature from the values of exception, grandeur, and privilege by freeing it from any historical mission: What it presents is the presentation of the ordinary *as* the ordinary, or as Nancy puts it in "The Compearance": " '[L]iterature' . . . is a matter of that which requires and permits that 'ordinary' be presented, not as the extraordinary (by some sleight of hand) but *in* the extraordinary. It is a matter of that which makes an event and makes it come about from the common. And it is a matter, at the same time, of the communication of a sharing so common that without literature it goes unnoticed" ("TC" 386/88). What literature allows us to notice, then, is not some profound sense hidden beneath things, but the very sense that is most familiar to us, which is always there, and which therefore, in principle, has nothing exceptional or privileged about it. In my analysis in this final chapter, I am nevertheless inclined to attribute an exceptional power to literature, not because literature would be "ontologically privileged," as Heidegger suggested, and certainly not because it would have exceptional inherent qualities, but because, as I will try to show, literary practice has the possibility to put its own ontological status in suspense. It is in this way that it helps to notice what would otherwise go unnoticed.

Before exploring this point further, let us first return to the question of the status of literary or artistic practice in Nancy's poetics. In chapter 3, we saw that Nancy first of all focused on the absence of any fundamental difference between different art forms, that is, between literature, painting, music. and so on. Criticizing philosophy's obsession with separating and hierarchizing art forms, Nancy emphasized the plurality of art as such. There is not *one* art that manifests itself differently in different art forms, but "art" is the name for the always singular and plural presentation of being, for the mode according to which the presentation of being presents itself. Before there is differentiation between different art forms, then, there is the singular plurality of sounds, colors, and gestures. Moreover, this always singular plural "art" is not only given in artistic works but also in the *poetic technique* in general that arranges, positions, and repositions presence, a technique that is given everywhere and always. We could therefore say that "literature" in the Nancyan sense of the word is doubly removed from the exceptional value attributed to it throughout history: firstly, because it is not generically distinguished from other art forms, and secondly, because it is not an exception to ordinary reality, but its disposition. But what are the consequences of these two "indistinctions," of this non-exceptionality?

This seems to be the question that Rancière asks himself in an essay with the telling title "The Use of Distinctions."[7] It is perfectly clear that the purpose of Rancière's essay is to rock the boat. Beginning with a clarification of the distinctions made in his own work, Rancière ends by condemning what he sees as a perversion of contemporary "philosophies of difference." This perversion—not a word used by Rancière, by the way—is that these philosophies, in their reserve towards classifications and hierarchizations, tend to overlook distinctions that are, in his view, crucial. Ultimately, the distinction that matters most to Rancière is the distinction between *art* and *life*, or as he puts it in *The Politics of Literature*, between art and "prosaic life."[8] In opposition to Romantically-inspired aesthetics that presume or desire a coincidence of art and life, Rancière emphasizes that there is always an excess in their coincidence, an excess that can generate a liberating and revolutionary force capable of reconfiguring precisely the relation between art and life.

Like many of his contemporaries, Rancière conceives of art as an exception to the dominant instrumentalist rationality, and consequently as the "model" of a new form of thought or even being. The problem, however, of the poetic theories of many of his contemporaries is, according to Rancière, that they apply the exceptional status of art to life or thought *in general*, as a result of which art's exceptional value is nullified.[9] In other words, they have generalized difference, heterogeneity, the eventual, and dissensus—indicated by the denominator of the "artistic"—as a result of which the artistic has become *omnipresent*. According to Rancière, contemporary French philosophy as a whole therefore suffers from a paradox: Because it understands difference so rigorously, such an understanding risks being reversed into what Rancière calls, perhaps too provocatively, a "fundamentalism of the absolutely other" and an "absolutization of distinction."[10] Distinction thus conceived is no longer an incidentally intervening or liberating power, but rather what Rancière calls a "*superpower* of dissensus or of rupture."[11]

According to Rancière, the presupposition of such "superpower" in the end results from the fact that dissensus is reduced to an *ontological* principle.[12] The configuration of the contemporary philosophical field is therefore, according to him, mainly determined by a debate about the nature of this superpower:

> The philosophico-politico-aesthetic scene thereby becomes that of the conflicts of superpowers: superpower of the multitudes comprising the core of the Empire and the force destined to break it (Negri); of the infinite truth which transits political collectives and artworks (Badiou); of the state of exception determining bare life (Agamben); of the Thing and the Law (Lyotard); of the abyssal liberty experienced in the encounter with the horror of the Thing (Žižek). These forms of superpower-in-competition are all ways of capitalizing on one and the same superpower: . . . that of the truth as irreducible alterity punching holes in the chain of knowledge.[13]

We must follow Rancière's analysis to the end if we are to understand what is at stake. The ultimate aim of this generalizing and rather provocative analysis seems to be to guarantee, to keep open—against this general tendency—the possibility of artistic *intervention* at critical moments, importantly, intervention not as "a necessary activity, inscribed in the order of things and demanded by the quest for Being . . . , but as a chance, *supplementary* activity which, like politics and art, *could just as well not have existed*."[14] Rancière's description of art (and politics) is thus diametrically opposed to Nancy's. Whereas Nancy understands "art" indeed as an inevitable necessity (or resistance) inscribed in the order of things, Rancière underlines that it is something occasional that could just as well not have existed.[15] According to Rancière, the former poetics is problematic, because the inscription of the principle of heterogeneity in the order of things "necessitates conferring the power to distinguish onto a superpower of dissensus or of rupture,"[16] a superpower that cannot *not* be, because it is inscribed in the order of things.

I leave open the question of the accuracy of Rancière's cartography of contemporary philosophy. What interests me here is not, first and foremost, the added value of grouping such different ways of thinking under the given denominator, nor the pressing question whether Rancière has not too easily aligned the notions of (in)difference and (in)distinction. Rancière's analysis is interesting to me because it reveals what is at stake in Nancy's poetics in a very illuminating way, even if Nancy is not mentioned by him. The reason why Nancy is not part of the "philosophico-politico-aesthetic scene" sketched out by Rancière is probably because Nancy refuses precisely the presumption of an "irreducible otherness" that is for Rancière the common trait. And yet, the protagonists in the scene described by Rancière do not so much assert a transcendent otherness, but rather an "embodied" or "immanentized" otherness, that is, a "trans-immanence" as is also proposed by Nancy. This also explains the absence of Levinas. In other words, in Nancy's work like in that of many of his contemporaries we are dealing with the introduction of an otherness, a heterogeneity, a difference, *into* being itself—and thus with the possible risk highlighted by Rancière.

The Power to Distinguish

By way of response, during a colloquium dedicated to Rancière's work in Cerisy-la-Salle in 2006, Nancy gave a talk that critically assesses Rancière's plea for a *distinctive* power of art. The title of this talk already reveals a great deal: "Rancière and Metaphysics." Nancy begins with stressing that Rancière conceives of art as the force that reconfigures the distribution of the sensible, that is, the configuration of the elements that determine what is common. The example of such a reconfiguration—cited by Rancière on several occasions—is Flaubert's literature, which, like Balzac's, by giving a voice to the lower rungs of the social ladder, reconfigures the relation between art and life as it was understood in his time. What Flaubert demonstrated, in other words, is that not just certain subjects, but *everything* deserves to be turned into art.[17]

According to Rancière, art thus has the power to resist and consequently to reconfigure the political distribution of the sensible. Although he agrees with the idea of art as a resisting distribution, Nancy already suggests early on in his analysis that there is, apart from this aesthetic-political (re)distribution of the sensible, also *"another* distribution of the sensible" which "is not . . . politics, religion, or art" ("RM" 87/160, my emphasis). Unsurprisingly, this other distribution of the sensible is, according to Nancy, that of *being* itself. Because the distribution of the sensible described by Rancière results from—or is grafted onto—this other more fundamental distribution, Nancy holds, Rancière's aesthetics requires an extrapolation towards metaphysics or ontology. An extrapolation that perhaps makes it redundant, since if being itself is already a distribution or sharing of the sensible, why, asks Nancy, do we need "this *specific* register," which is the register of *art?* ("RM" 88/161, my emphasis). Indeed, for Nancy, an extrapolation towards metaphysics or ontology has precisely for result that none of the possible registers can have a privileged status, as we have already seen.

Nancy's major concern with Rancière's work is thus nothing other than the concern for *exceptionalism* already mentioned above. According to Nancy, we must "attack this privilege" ("RM" 88/161). In his view contemporary discourse more or less blindly stresses the specificity of art, without really asking what is so special about it. Nancy sees that Rancière's efforts, on the contrary, "are to *dissolve* the specificity of art, and furthermore the exception that is attached to it by a considerable spread of contemporary thought" ("RM" 89/161), but he simply has not gone far enough, according to Nancy: "There remains . . .—in general, as in Rancière's work—something that persists and resists underneath this name 'art'" ("RM" 89/161).

Indeed, if being-with is itself already a distributing, that is, a partitioning or modeling of the sensible, why do we still have to assume that artistic practice distributes the sensible in a different way than being itself does? It is thus the *superfluity* of this presupposition that leads Nancy to reject the privilege of art. In other words, Nancy fully agrees with Rancière on "the necessity for 'that which is common' to (re)present itself" in some way or another, but he believes it is "harder to understand" that this (re) presentation has to be "in an *artistic* mode" ("RM" 164, my emphasis). It is better to affirm, according to Nancy, that the distribution of the sensible is not so much artistic but "a writing *beyond writing* inscribed *everywhere* in the flesh of things" ("RM" 92/167, my emphasis, translation modified) and to draw all the consequences from this.[18]

In my opinion, Rancière, however, has good reasons to stress the specificity of art or of something that remains under the name of "art." What remains and resists in the name of "art," for Rancière, is a specific power to *intervene* and *reconfigure* the distribution of the sensible, a power not written in the flesh of things, but indeed a *supplementary, random* power. And it is precisely for this reason that Rancière seems to refrain from going so far as to "dissolve" the specificity of art and, on the contrary, demonstrates the potential *risk* of such a dissolution. This risk is, as we saw, is that it "necessitates conferring the power to distinguish, to intervene, onto a superpower of dissensus." The word "confer" [*confier*] is of crucial importance here and indicates, I think, the exact locus of Nancy's unease felt in the face of certain artistic or political practices.[19] After all, if we could rely on the primordial resistance of being itself to attempts to reduce or mask it, then—to put it bluntly—there would be nothing to fear.

To be sure, Nancy's thinking is not naively optimistic. Nonetheless, it displays a certain indestructible confidence, for example in the already mentioned concluding words of *The Truth of Democracy* where he, after having enumerated all the threats to democracy, proposes to "first think the being of our being together in the world [and then see] which politics gives this thought a chance" (*TD* 34/62). A similar confidence in the power of thought can be found in his essay "Nothing but the World," in which he relativizes the threat posed by "biopolitics." In reinterpreting Giorgio Agamben's concept of the "bare life," Nancy remarks:

> With the word "nudity," what I say also converges with the "bare life" my friend Giorgio Agamben speaks of, even though I certainly don't share his own dramatization of what he calls "biopolitics," I would instead stress the resistance that is *inevitably present* and diffused *within and even at the heart of the worst threats*. One extreme—of domination, of proliferation—reveals another: laying bare and bringing into relief a disarray whose acuity is also *in and of itself* a testimony to a resistance, and within this resistance the tracing out of a "sense." What remains suspended between suicide and survival—someone might be tempted to characterize our situation in these terms—is also a suspense silently freeing up *unexpected possibilities*. ("NBW" 534, my emphasis, translation modified)

According to Nancy, we are thus tempted to "dramatize" our situation, among other things by focusing on the domination and proliferation of what

Agamben calls "biopolitics," that is, the imposition of political structures on bare life. This dramatization of biopolitics, Nancy states, masks what he calls "unexpected possibilities" hidden within and even "at the heart of the worst threats." Instead of being afraid of inevitable catastrophes, it is better, according to Nancy, to realize the possibility of an ever-present resistance. This possibility is found in "the resistance that is inevitably present," a resistance that can already be seen in the disarray resulting from biopolitical threats. In other words, the fact that we feel a certain resistance to the politicization of bare life is according to Nancy an indication that bare life *as such* resists politicization, and that the enterprise of such biopolitics is doomed to failure.

The Importance of Attestation

Though one might conclude that Nancy's attitude is too optimistic or too passive, this seems to me to be too hasty a conclusion. For, as Nancy points out, it is indeed a *task*, and an extremely important one, for thought to uncover and keep an eye on what we might call, with Françoise Proust the "archi-resistance" of being.[20] When we have decisions to make in life, we should realize that the first decision is already made by our being-with itself, that this decision of existence precedes and interrupts our political and social agendas. By endowing, in the wake of Heidegger, the notion of decision with ontological weight, Nancy attempts to highlight what he calls the "mundanity" of decision (*BP* 82/108). For him, decisions, artistic or otherwise, in other words, are not voluntary and autonomous acts of the subject, but the structure of existence itself, which is decided at each moment it is posed. It is a decision always made before me, by "us," in the broadest sense of the term, but this provides us with the task of abstaining from decisions that "might descend from on high to cut through to specific possibilities and objectives of existence" (*BP* 87/115).

The power to distinguish or intervene that Rancière wants to preserve for art is according to Nancy thus "nothing but the exercise of the *appropriation of decision*, which lets itself be shown that the decision of this appropriation always precedes it, and does not belong to it" (*BP* 87/115, my emphasis). Indeed, for Nancy to say that being decides itself is thus to say that it is fundamentally *undecided*.[21] In the final section of "The Forgetting of Philosophy," entitled "On Passivity," Nancy emphasizes that this obviously implies passivity, not as opposed to activity, but as being *passible* that is, "capable of receiving or welcoming" being, "something like 'to registering'" it (*GT* 69/105). In this Nancy joins most contemporary philosophies that value the passivity, passibility, incalculability, and contingency that derives from the main undecidability of the world.

At the same time, however—and here his (implicit) dialogue with Rancière becomes most interesting—Nancy, too, seems to indicate that the mere existence of this undecidability is not enough to prevent it from being thwarted. What we need, so it seems, is a means to *attest* to it in some way, to make ourselves *aware* of it. The need for such attestation is clearly indicated by Nancy his preface to the English translation of *The Inoperative Community*, where he discusses what will happen when we do not sufficiently notice the unworking of our community. Although "[b]eing-in-common will nonetheless never cease to resist," Nancy holds, "*[its] resistance will belong decidedly to another world entirely*" (*IC* xli). In other words, although there will always be resistance, if we fail to attest to it, if we fail to become sufficiently aware of it, it will no longer have any effect on our daily lives, and can no longer be felt, which will be, as he puts it dramatically, "the end of our communities" (*IC* xli) and will abandon us to "political and technological economies" (*IC* xli) in which being in common will have lost all meaning and "our world, as far as politics is concerned, will be a desert" (*IC* xli).[22] Nonetheless, there is something strange in Nancy's warning here. For if the resistance of our being-with is the law of the world, if things fall under its law without exception, how could it belong to another world entirely, a world, moreover, apparently inaccessible? How could it belong to another world if there is *nothing but* the world?

Even if Nancy's warning must be conceived metaphorically, indicating that it is possible within political communities that this resistance is not experienced, not felt, the question remains as to what precisely could *prevent* it. What, to put it another way, could reinforce this resistance and make it *part* of our political communities? And, equally importantly, why do we run the risk of falling *out of touch* with this never-ceasing resistance? A first explanation could be sociological or anthropological. People seem simply incapable of living together on the basis of radical contingency. The more we feel the ground slipping away beneath our feet, the more tempted we are to resort to some intentional world where things happen for a reason.[23] The already mentioned and more formalistic explanation would be the structure of *politics itself* that is necessarily *mythological* in the sense that it must conceal and deny, as its condition of possibility, the groundlessness of our being-with—a denial and concealment that tends to have an *immunizing* effect on the political order. I would therefore argue that it is very difficult if not impossible to conceive of a *politics* that "gives a chance" to the archi-resistance of our being-with.

But how, then, can we prevent our communities from collapsing into economic-technological machineries? How can we install, so to speak, a kind of emergency brake that can interrupt their course? For now, we can only repeat that such interruption must be, principally, *non-political* or *extra-political* as Nancy also points out, taking place on a level that is anything but political—"existential, artistic, literary, dreamy, amorous, scientific, thoughtful, leisurely, playful, friendly, gastronomic, urban, and so on" (*TD* 26/48), a list that is in principle infinite because it concerns *events* rather than well-defined domains. Hence the more recent echo of this remark: "Anarchy is literature, art, love, cooking, sport, daydreaming and also illness, misfortune, malaise. . . . Of course *politics must oppose it*. . . . Anarchy cannot be institutionalized of course. We must therefore think differently" (*PD* 118–19, my emphasis). And yet, I would argue that among this endless list of practices the practice of *literature* is more *adjusted* than others, not only to express the resistance of our being-with, but also to make us more sensitive and aware of it, because it consists of a certain way of speaking.

A Certain Way of Speaking

Taking Responsibility by a Certain Way of Speaking

This is suggested by Nancy himself in an interview with Derrida on the themes of responsibility, response, and decision, published under the title "Responsibility—Of the Sense to Come" ("Res"). The central question posed by Derrida, not only in this interview but indeed in his entire work, is "Can we make ourselves responsible for an event?," ("Res" 59/169) a question that is transformed in the course of the interview into "How to *respond* to what happens?," or more specifically "[How] to respond in a *fitting* [*ajustée*] way?" ("Res" 62/171). Nancy's answer comes as no surprise. According to him, it is *being itself* that is "already given as an element of the response," an element of response, moreover, beyond the question-answer structure, and that always resonates within our own responses ("Res" 61/171). Nancy thus understands responsibility first and foremost in negative terms, suggesting that responsibility is "that I cannot be responsible in the sense of a programmatic, calculated, and calculating appropriation" ("Res" 63/173). Formulated in a positive way, this amounts to saying that "I am at least responsible for the *capacity*, for the *condition of possibility*, of the response [within] the resonance" ("Res," 173, my emphasis). Our concern must therefore be to arrange ourselves in such a way that we are capable of receiving the response given by being.

Here, however, Nancy's seemingly active task (to arrange ourselves in such a way that we are capable of being susceptible), turns out to be less an *action* than a *condition*: We are capable of it by the very fact that we exist. To exist already means to be susceptible to what we can call the archi-response of being. This is also illustrated by the English translation of the title of the French collection of philosophical-literary essays *Demande* by *Expectation*. Nancy explains: " 'Expectation' responds better to what '*Demande*' says to me in French," because "unlike the constraint expressed by the word '*demand*' in English, '*demande*' waits, hopes, wishes" (*EPL* vii). We *are* already the condition of possibility of resonance, because our singular plural existence makes it "resonate." For this reason, as Nancy points out, *silence* is in a way the most adjusted mode of responsibility: "[S]ilence is not simply non-response: it is in some way resonance itself" ("Res" 63/173). What I seek to define in this final chapter—partly by returning to the divergence between Nancy and Blanchot discussed in chapter 2—is, nevertheless, the possibility of responding in a *speaking* way, or, rather, of seeking silence *in* speech, for, as Blanchot rightly writes, "[T]o be silent is not always the best way of being silent."[24] It is thus a matter of inscribing a moment of affirmation, action, and initiative in Nancy's predominantly Heideggerian poetics of concern and expectation.

This is also the path that Derrida and Nancy explore in the conversation quoted above. When asked once again by Derrida how we can respond in a *fitting* way, Nancy refers to the pattern of Zen stories:

> The general pattern of Zen stories, which present their wisdom in the form of a joke, is, for example, the disciple who asks, "Who is Buddha?" and the master responds, "Shitty stick." He doesn't even say, if I am to believe my Zen masters, "he's a shitty stick." Indeed, he doesn't even say "he is," he says "shitty stick," which is a response that is both incongruous, incoherent and asyntactical, therefore disappointing in many regards. . . . But in Zen stories, the response is always made up of both surprise and disappointment at the same time. This is obviously related

to Zen archery, in which one hits the target without aiming at it, the kind of non-intentional and therefore non-phenomenological paradigm that we have perhaps never produced within the West. ("Res" 62/172, my emphasis, translation modified)

The paradigm of the Zen story is, according to Nancy, that of "the *non-satisfaction* for both the question and the response" ("Res" 62/171, my emphasis), or of the deliberate non-satisfaction of answering an unanswerable question. The Zen answer is in other words deliberately *misleading, misdirected,* and for that reason a *joke* rather than an informative answer. Nevertheless, and this is of course what Nancy wants to indicate, it is precisely *because* of this that it is the most fitting answer. The answer is disappointing because it is an answer that nobody needs, a random answer—an answer that *could just as well not have existed,* to borrow Rancière's formula.[25]

What I want to indicate by referring to Nancy's account of the pattern of Zen stories is that there is a possibility here in Nancy's thinking, given almost in spite of himself, of an attestation—or in his own terms, of a *responsibility* and *susceptibility*—which would be more than a silent resonance of the response of being itself, and which is perhaps the possibility of an *affirmative responsibility*—without criteria, without measure, without end. This possibility lies not in a form of silence, but in a *certain way of speaking.* As in the Zen response, it is a way of speaking that evades the communicative pattern, that has no intention of conveying a message, and not even of referring to anything real. What is more, it is a way of speaking that is essentially *deceptive* and *disappointing,* because it is clear that it could have said *whatever, n'importe quoi.*[26] As I shall argue, this is the way of speaking proper to literary practice, that is, not an inherent characteristic of literary texts, but a characteristic that occurs *in practice* when an utterance is judged, at the moment of expression and by those who receive it, *as* literary.

The Role of Deception

When I say that we are dealing here with a way of speaking that is specific to literary practice, I am providing the word "literature" with a meaning that is largely neglected by Nancy, namely as a manner of speech that presents itself in a *simulative, fictitious,* or even *illusory* way. In so doing, I have no intention of reintroducing the opposition between the fictive and the real that Nancy so ardently sought to avoid by focusing on the mythical dimension speech, which is neither fictive nor real or both at the same time. Nancy's innovative turn is undoubtedly to do away with this opposition by rethinking "fiction" in terms of the real. In this, he draws on the original conceptual proximity of the various meanings of the Latin word *fingere*; a proximity also revealed by Lacoue-Labarthe: "The Latin *fingere* . . . is the equivalent of the Greek *plassein/plattein*: to fashion, to model, to sculpt—thus, to figure. But a nuance also already exists in Greek: to fake and to simulate, or to forge by imagination."[27]

In Nancy's ontological poetics myth is a modulation or figuration of *reality*, in which the notion of *fingere* loses the dimension of fakeness and simulation. It could be said, then, that Nancy's poetics adapts to a very literal interpretation of Gustave Thibon's adage "the earth does not lie."[28] In my examination of literary practice, however, I want to draw attention to the fact that we are dealing with a form of speech that *presents itself* as simulative, untrue, and fictitious, *even if* its distinction with the real no longer holds. In this context, a question arises that may seem a little strange at first glance, namely the question posed by Nancy at the end of his short account of the Zen story: "Can I deceive you?" ("Res" 62/172, translation modified). In other words, is the Zen answer a form of *deception*? Is something like deception, strictly speaking, still possible in Nancy's poetics?

Tellingly, in Nancy's poetics this possibility of deception seems to be excluded. Whether it is offered in a diary or in a literary novel, whether it concerns the words of a trustworthy person or of a liar, according to Nancy's ontological poetics, speaking is always a speaking *of the real* and is consequently what Nancy sometimes calls a matter of "veri-diction" or "veri-fication"—a speaking or making of truth.[29] From this point of view, the content of what is said, as well as the intention of the speaker, derive from the main fact *that there is* diction. This fact is what Nancy calls poetic speech, a matter of *"area-lity"* instead of "a-reality," the articulation of a *place* rather than a non-reality. The parenthetical question "Can I deceive you?," is therefore important and revealing because it opens up a dimension that is not given in Nancy's poetics. In this ontological poetics, deception, cheating, or lying are situated on an additional and, from his point of view, irrelevant plane.

So why detect and reinstall this dimension after Nancy has gone to so much trouble to avoid it? Here, we have to ask ourselves once again *why* Nancy wanted to avoid it. In my opinion, the most important reason why he wanted to ban the fictional dimension of utterances from his poetics is to avoid the idea of any *regulative* fiction. We might recall, in this context, Nancy's critique of the philosophy of the "as if" in *The Inoperative*

Community: "[T]he Kantian model of a 'regulative Idea' is up to a point only a modern variation on the function of myth: it knows itself to be the fiction of a myth that will not come about but that gives a rule for thinking and acting. Hence there is an entire philosophy of the 'as if' . . . which is not to be confused with a mythology but which nonetheless bears comparable markings" (*IC* 161n33/141n64). As we saw in chapter 2, according to Nancy, the philosophy of the "as if" does not escape mythological logic, because it always provides, in one way or another, a fiction that functions as a *foundation*. The new mythology to which the Jena Romantics aspired is in his view a case in point according to Nancy, because it regulates community in the direction of an end point where it will be completed, even if this point is inaccessible in principle.

Nancy, on the other hand, constantly emphasizes that our being-with is not to be measured or directed by something unreal or fictitious. Being-with is not something to be projected, desired, or attained, but something that always happens already, at every moment, and is never absent, past or forthcoming. It is, in other words, an inescapable reality that imposes itself here and now, rendering the whole idea of fiction *superfluous*, at least if it implies the ideal, the imaginary, or the unreal. If Nancy continues to use the term "fiction" on several occasions, it is only in the sense of the shaping or formation, at every moment and without model, of being-with, a formation that resists everything that seeks to complete it. In the wake of Nancy's account of the pattern of the Zen story, however, I would like to explore the possibility of reinstalling this dimension of *simulation* within Nancy's poetics by taking cue from the work of Benjamin, Arendt, and Derrida, who in "Critique of Violence," "Truth and Politics," and "History of the Lie," respectively, have analyzed the specific role of the *lie* in political communities. My point is that if we wish to attest to our being-with in a *non-mythological* way, we may need to take recourse to a form of speech that, *in contrast to* political mythological speech, does *not* claim validity. In other words, if a modern political order must claim validity in order to manifest itself *as* political, we must perhaps claim the opposite in order to interrupt it.

Undoubtedly the word "lie"—central to the texts I shall be analyzing—is misleading and susceptible to all forms of misuse and misunderstanding. What is meant, as we shall see, is rather a form of "lying" beyond the opposition of truth and non-truth, a form that boils down to an openly stated deception or non-seriousness. As Benjamin, Arendt, and Derrida suggest, it is the deliberately deceptive and misleading use of language proper to the lie that can, in certain circumstances, open up the possibility of a non-political intervention of politics.

A Non-Political Intervention of Politics (*Nancy*, *Benjamin*)

So, let us analyze the role that lies can play in a mythological political order. In Benjamin's "Critique of Violence" lying—or rather the *impunity* of lying in ancient times—plays an important role in his critique of what he calls the mythical violence of modern political orders.[30] As Benjamin points out, in Antiquity, lying was seen as incongruous, perhaps even immoral, but not as illegal. Lying, and the possible conflicts that might ensue, were rather conceived as part of "a sphere of human agreement that is nonviolent to the extent that it is principally *inaccessible to violence*: the proper sphere of 'understanding,' *language*."[31] According to Benjamin, the sphere of language is principally inaccessible to violence because it has itself "*no trace of power*,"[32] it only deals with sympathy, love, and trust.[33] Strictly speaking, then, even if a lie were to challenge the political order, it is not enclosed within a political logic.

According to Benjamin it is only in modern times, "in a peculiar process of decay,"[34] that lying and deception were politicized and began to be perceived as illegal, that is, as fraud. The reason for this decay lies in the mythological violence discerned by Benjamin in modern political orders: the violence by which all measures taken have as their ultimate end the maintenance of the political order. A similar process is highlighted by Roberto Esposito and Derrida, and in a sense also by Nancy, under the name of the risk of *self-immunization* of a political order. As they argue, in line with Benjamin's analysis, a political order tends to immunize itself against potentially disastrous attacks, but in doing so runs the risk of autoimmune disease, that is, of infecting its own elements. A heathy, viable political order must thus be open to the possibility of intruding attacks of all sorts, be it internal or external.[35]

According to Benjamin, it is a sign of the weakening of the vitality of modern political orders that an incongruous act of language such as lying is considered a crime against that order. The main point of Benjamin's text thus seems to be the search for a form of incongruity that could interrogate the political order without being assimilated in its mythological logic. Because the modern political order no longer leaves room for such interrogation, Benjamin seeks it—under the enigmatic name of "divine violence"—in a form that removes itself entirely from the ordinary community of human beings, but, as said, he also gives the impetus to a reflection on ordinary practices of simulation like lying, or more specifically, literary fiction, which help to analyze more ordinary forms of non-political intervention of the mythological political order.

It is important to note that these practices are "non-political" only if they abstain from claiming validity. In chapter 2, I indicated that, in my view, *any* act or utterance that makes a claim to validity is political—a claim that is not only at stake in the exercise of state power, but also whenever we present our acts, gestures, or utterances as true, just, powerful, or real, or as *more* true, more just etc. than others. As noted, this also includes acts and utterances generally characterized as forms of *counter-power* or even as *anti-political* or *anarchist*, such as those of certain subversive or activist groups. Inversely, it is important to note here that if a particular form of speech does *not* claim validity and, consequently, power, this does not necessarily imply that it is without effect. On the contrary, its particular power may lie precisely in its impotence. But how can an act or utterance have effect if it is deprived of power? What is its specific force in the political order?

A good illustration of the nature of this specific force is Blanchot's comparison between the literary act and the act of political revolutionaries.[36] According to Blanchot, these two acts are similar in that they deny the status quo and seek to replace it with another state of affairs. The crucial difference between a literary act and a revolutionary political act, however, seems to be that the former replaces the status quo with a *fictitious* one, while the latter attempts to install a new, *real* order. Although one might be inclined to conclude that, ultimately, it is the act of the political revolutionary that is effective, while that of the writer evaporates into vanity, according to Blanchot, the opposite is true. For him, the political act and the literary act are not opposed in the way that reality is opposed to fiction, for the new state of affairs envisioned by revolutionaries is just as fictitious as the one proposed by the literary writer. According to Blanchot, the crucial difference between the two acts lies in the *recognition of this fictional dimension*. What characterizes the political revolutionary act, or the political act in general, we might say, is that it *veils* the fact that the order to be installed is not yet given, that it is in fact only an imaginary projection to be realized. In other words, it veils the fictitious dimension of its regulative fiction, or, better still, the effectiveness of political power consists precisely *in* this veiling and in the—mythological—claim that the installed order *will have been so*. In the case of mythological discourse, then, speech ascribes to itself the right to speak.

Unlike the political revolutionary act, the literary act does not, in Blanchot's view, veil the fact that the fictionalized state of affairs is without substance, legitimization, and power. According to Blanchot, literary practice makes no claim to validity, and thus denies itself power entirely. It has no rights, no interests, no ends of its own—and it is precisely for this reason that it can break the intimate link between violence and sovereignty proper to politics.[37] Its deliberate powerlessness thus interrupts the mythological logic of political practice and it is precisely in this interruption that we can locate its responsibility.

The Exigency of "Lying" (*Nancy, Arendt, Derrida*)

THE TRADITIONAL LIE

In order to further unpack the potential force of literary practice in political communities, we have to conceive it as a specific form of "lying." In order to do so, I turn to the relatively little-known text of Derrida, "History of the Lie," that brings together the different lines of enquiry that have been pursued up to now. In his text, Derrida sketches what he calls a *pseudology*, a logic of the *pseudos*, that leads us according to him from a traditional concept of the lie to its inscription in a modern register. This modern register is the register of *performativity*, a register that evades the opposition between truth and non-truth, and approaches that of literary fiction. Importantly, the inscription of the lie in the register of performativity is largely analogous to Nancy's inscription of myth in this same register.

Traditionally, according to Derrida, there has been a "classical and dominant" concept of the lie in philosophy spanning from Plato and Saint Augustine to Rousseau and Kant, among others.[38] This concept understands the lie as the *non-saying of the truth*. It is worth noticing that lies are thus not opposed to truth as such, but to the *saying* of the truth or rather the *intention* to say the truth as Derrida specifies. Lying is "not a fact or a state, it is an *intentional* act."[39] Consequently, lying is not opposed to truth, but to *veracity* or *veridicity*, that is, to truth-saying or true-meaning-to-say.[40] Based on this traditional concept of the lie, there are various variants as to the nature of this intention. For Aristotle, for example, something is a lie when the non-saying of the truth is done on purpose; for Rousseau, it is only a lie when the intention is to do harm. Importantly, however, although lies in this traditional concept are not opposed to truth as such, truth is nevertheless *presupposed*. After all, a "non-saying of the truth" can only be detected if we determine what is true.

According to Derrida, one of the first authors to breach this traditional concept of the lie was Nietzsche, who paradigmatically in his already mentioned text "How the 'True World' Finally Became a Fable" cuts the tie between falsehood and truth. Having abolished the idea of a true world, as well as that of a world of appearances, Nietzsche opens up, already through the form of his text, a genre of speech irreducible to this opposition: the *fable*, that is to say, *myth*. And it is in this domain that Derrida, through his critical gesture, proposes to house the act of lying from now on. The reason for wanting to remove lying from the register of (non)truth and for placing it in the register of fable or myth is, according to Derrida, that one never knows whether someone has the intention of not wanting to tell the truth. Or, as Derrida puts it, "[I]t will always be impossible to *prove*, in the strict sense, that someone has lied even if it can be proved that he or she did not tell the truth."[41] Even the most ruthless defender of veridicity, Kant, pointed out that the motives for our actions are always *"gänzlich verborgen,"* since, even if what we say is untrue, we can always claim that we were acting in good faith, that we did not mean it that way, that we said something else in our inner voice.[42] If lying comes down to the intention not to tell the truth, then we can never determine when a person is lying.

Yet, although we can never be certain when a person is lying, our culture persists in conceiving of the lying according to the traditional concept of not telling or not wanting to tell the truth. What is more, our culture *depends* on it, as Derrida also points out: Without it, "no ethics, no right or law, and no politics would survive."[43] The most important domain that depends on the traditional concept of the lie—a domain that forms, as it were, the fabric of all the others—is that of our *language*, for our language's main condition is the promise of truthfulness, the promise that when using language we will tell or want to tell the truth. Every word uttered and addressed to another person is accompanied by the at least implicit promise to tell the truth, "the truth, my truth, that is, my veracity."[44] Were it not for the ever-imminent possibility of *lying*, this promise of truthfulness would not have been necessary. We thus find ourselves in the paradoxical situation where the possibility of an unprovable lie forms the condition of possibility of language as such and where the traditional concept of the lie remains dominant. Nevertheless, especially in the context of modern politics, as Arendt has shown, the tables are turning.

The Absolute Lie of Modern Politics

In the opening lines of her essay "Truth and Politics," Arendt begins by emphasizing that lying has always been part of political practice: "Lies have always been regarded as necessary and justifiable tools not only for the politician's or the demagogue's but also of the stateman's trade."[45] Arendt notes, however, that lying over time has transformed from a necessary and justifiable tool into the very machinery of politics. This transformation goes hand in hand with the transition from a time when there was still some truth hidden and concealed by lies to a situation where the lie has become *complete* and where truth, as a consequence, has been "maneuvered out of the world altogether."[46] As in the Orwellian Ministry of Plenty, in our hyper-mediatized societies lying has nothing to do anymore with falsifying facts, according to Arendt. It has become the very element in which we operate, having "no connection with anything in the real world, not even the kind of connection that is contained in a direct lie."[47]

In this latter situation, Derrida, too, argues, the lie has become an "*absolute* lie,"[48] because no-one, including the "liar," can distinguish truth from falsehood. With the dissolution of this distinction, the traditional concept of the lie is obviously also undermined, enabling a situation that Arendt describes as follows:

> Such completeness and potential finality [of the lie, AvR], which were unknown to former times, are the dangers that arise out of the modern manipulation of facts. Even in the free world, where the government has not monopolized the power to decide and tell what factually is or is not, gigantic interest organizations have generalized a kind of *raison d'état* frame of mind such as was formerly restricted to the handling of foreign affairs and, in its worst excesses, to situations of clear and present danger. . . . Images made for domestic consumption, as distinguished from lies directed at a foreign adversary, can become a reality for everybody and first of all the image-makers themselves.[49]

Whereas in the past, manipulation of facts was not something that the average citizen could do, in our society it has become a daily practice, practiced not only by interest organizations but by everyone, at all times.[50] The result is a hyper-mediatized space where images compete without their origins being recognizable. Although one might be inclined to situate this sort of Orwellian rejection of truth in the form of omnipresent lying in dictatorial regimes, Arendt suggests that it is especially in the "free world" that this phenomenon can arise, because no one has a monopoly on determining what is true and what is false. In other words, the situation of the absolute lie is the situation where the power to manipulate facts has become democratic, where anyone can manipulate facts, to the point where there are no more facts.

To be sure, although Arendt indicates that there is, in modern societies, "mass manipulation," a "rewriting of history," and a "complete substitution" of reality by images,[51] all these formulations reveal the indignation of someone who has witnessed a true story being obscured by a veil that is not recognizable as such, where "*Niemand zeugt für den/Zeugen.*"[52] In other words, in her description of the complete lie, Arendt still seems to hold onto something of a touchstone, that is, the prospect of a *true story*, of truth, and does not seem to be able to let go of this traditional concept of the lie as much as Derrida did. Nevertheless, Arendt's analysis raises, perhaps partially in spite of herself, an important issue further elaborated by Derrida in his text, namely the issue of the possibility of *lying to oneself* implied in the idea of an absolute lie. For if the lie is absolute, it is necessarily also a lie to oneself. If even liars themselves can no longer distinguish truth from falsehood, they must indeed be capable of deceiving themselves.

This issue is addressed almost in passing by Arendt in the following remark: "[U]nder fully democratic conditions *deception without self-deception is well-nigh impossible.*"[53] The possibility of lying to oneself, of self-deception, is interesting because it is precisely here that the traditional concept of the lie is abandoned, for a crucial aspect of this traditional concept is precisely the *impossibility* of lying to oneself. If lying is the *intention* not to tell the truth, lying *to oneself* is impossible: Either you believe you *are* telling the truth and therefore intend to tell it, or you believe you are *not* telling the truth, and then you cannot be deceived by yourself. In other words, lying according to the traditional concept always means, according to Derrida, "to deceive the other *intentionally* and *consciously* and while *knowing* what it is that one is *deliberately* hiding, therefore while not lying to oneself."[54] If something like self-deception is really possible, it can therefore only occur in modernity where it is no longer a matter of concealing the truth, but of a "destruction of reality or of the original archive."[55] Or, as Arendt puts it, "the difference between the traditional lie and the modern lie will more often than not amount to the difference between hiding and destroying."[56]

One could say that the destruction of reality or of the original archive—that is to say, of the original as such—has its reverse in the *production* of an original, or more precisely of originals in the plural. That is to say, in contemporary societies, things we say are not measured according to the rule of truth, but *become* true. In modernity, then, we are dealing with what we can call, in Nancy's words, *verification*. "Truth" is no longer an incontestable measure, but is what Derrida calls a "performative violence,"[57] which, in political communities, takes the form of "the location of a boundary, the installation of a state . . . which if the conditions of the international community permit it, create the law, whether durably or not, where there was no law or no longer any law."[58] A political "truth," then, and examples of this abound, is a created state of affairs that is held to be and imposed *as true*. The most important claim of "History of the Lie" is that the deliberate lie, consequently, is a performative act too. Just as truth becomes something to be made—verification—so deceitful speech is deceitful only if it is constructed as such: *pseudo-fication*, we might say by analogy. This is the register of the performative in which Derrida proposes to inscribe the kind of lie that we are about to discuss.

Two Modes of Performativity

Even if Derrida stresses that, in order to understand the phenomenon of the modern lie, we need a register other than that of truth/falsehood, another register which is that of *performativity*, he nonetheless chooses to retain the word "lie." But shouldn't we replace it, as Nancy has indeed done, with another concept, such as "poetry" or "creation"? There are indeed good reasons for advocating such a replacement, and we have discussed them in the preceding chapters. However, I would like to point out that there are *also* good reasons for distinguishing the possibility of "mendacious" speech, not in order to finally recognize the truth, but in order to retain the specific force that can emanate from such speech. It is for this reason that I propose to distinguish between two categories of performative acts, or more precisely, between two *modes* in which a performative speech act can occur. I am not seeking to distinguish between different forms of performatives, but argue that the same performative can occur in *two different modes*, namely:

(1) The *political mode* of the performative. Most performatives take place in this mode, since every claim, personal or collective, to *validity*, whether by force, authority, or persuasion, is political. They can be found everywhere, from the opening of a meeting or the declaration of a marriage,

to everyday conversations and promises. And of course, they also include the performatives employed by political authorities. In such cases, we are dealing with what Derrida called "the location of a boundary," producing, when they succeed, "a truth whose power sometimes imposes itself forever."[59] Crucially, the political mode of performatives depends negatively on the *denial of their performative dimension*. In other words, the very essence of performative acts that are produced in the political mode consists in imposing their validity precisely by denying their performativity. The more a speech act denies to be a performative act, and therefore to lack an obvious truth, the more validity and power it acquires—or, in Austin's terms, the more *felicitous* this speech act is. The success of this political mode of performative speech therefore depends on the success of its denial. It is, moreover, the preoccupation with its success that makes this political mode of performativity necessarily *mythological* and which has the consequence of reinforcing the performed state of affairs by means of a recourse to legitimation, conservation, and immunization. As Benjamin recognized, state politics can only function according to the logic of this mythological violence. In other words, the political order *must* act as if its order is true. The "self-deception" Arendt refers to as necessary and specific to democratic systems therefore consists in denying its performativity on the pretext that the traditional truth/untruth schema of truth and falsehood is still in force.

(2) The *unworked mode* of the performative. The second mode according to which a performative can occur is what we can call, for want of a better term, its "empty" or vain mode. These are the rare cases where a performative occurs *without making a claim to validity*. By explicitly renouncing validity, a performative speech act in the unworked mode also renounces the claim to legitimation, conservation, or immunization that validity demands and thus deconstructs political logic rather than establishing it. Importantly, then, by *not* claiming validity, the unworked mode of performative is in principle *non-political* and by renouncing validity, and therefore power, it also does not *contest* any given power. We might say, then, that speech performed in this mode is simply not conceived of as serious, harmful, or threatening, just as the lie in Antiquity before its modern "decay," as described by Benjamin. These performative acts in the unworked mode are the acts that Derrida describes as acts that are normally excluded from theories that rely on the classical and dominant concept of the lie, namely "the innocent, inoffensive [stories], simulacra unsullied by perjury and false witness."[60]

It is important to note that performativity in its unworked mode is not only defined negatively, as if it were everything that is not produced according to the political mode. On the contrary, it is a mode of performativity that must delimit itself positively because, in order *not* to claim validity, one must *deliberately* renounce it. Indeed, because the claim to validity is always tacitly presumed when using language, a performative speech act that does not claim it must *draw attention to this renunciation*. Another crucial point is that the distinction between these two modes is not to be determined in a strict sense, nor once and for all. Precisely because they are performatives, their realization depends not only on the intention of the enunciator, but also on reception and context—a combination whose outcome is not always predictable.

Now, importantly for us, performatives produced in the unworked mode generally correspond to artistic practices. An artwork is characterized precisely by the fact that it does not impose its truth, its idea, its message, if there is one. But this second mode of performativity cannot be identified with artworks as such, because what is decisive for a performative to occur in the unworked mode is for it to be *conceived* as unworked, as a speech act that does not claim any validity, not only on the part of the performer, but also on the part of the receiver. A telling historical example of the fact that an artwork can also *not* be conceived as unworked is Orson Welles's adaptation of H. G. Wells's science fiction novel *The War of the Worlds* for the American radio station CBS, on October 30, 1938. Despite the clear warnings at the beginning and end of the radio emission, and the fact that it was presented on the eve of Halloween, many listeners were panic-stricken into believing that an alien invasion was taking place. And while we may nowadays have become more familiar with the science fiction genre, there is nonetheless a clear tendency towards taking literary writers at their word, and thus politicizing their work. Not only is there a strong demand for authentic and "truthful" fiction, such as autobiographical and historical novels, but literary writers are also regularly accused for deforming the facts.

Although this claim obviously requires further examination, this tendency may well be explained by a weakened sensitivity to the unworked mode of literary texts.[61] For now, the point is that even if an utterance is not intended to be taken seriously, it *can* be taken as such and become a performative in the political mode. The opposite situation, where an utterance claiming validity is *not* taken seriously and set aside of course also occurs—and perhaps always to some extent occurs in cases of works of fiction, that, to writers themselves are oftentimes more than valid. The dividing line between the political and unworked mode of performative speech is the subject of ongoing controversy, and it is precisely for this reason that the unworked mode has its own responsibility.

Literature as Unworked Performative

Performing Powerlessness

To be sure, the demarcation line between these two modes of performativity is not fixed, because, in the end, performatives occurring in the political mode have as little validity as performatives occurring in the unworked mode. But only in the case of the former are we inclined to (re)inscribe them in the register of truth. This is why Arendt's and Derrida's analyses on politics and the lie focus solely on the political mode of performatives. Although Arendt and Derrida avoid analyzing performative acts that do not claim validity, both nevertheless allude to them. What is more, both Arendt and Derrida—like Nancy—stress the vital importance of a realm *beyond* the reach of politics, that is, the importance of the fact that there is resistance against the "limitless extension of the region of the political."[62] I would say that the unworked mode of performatives is worth studying, precisely because it contains the possibility of such resistance.

As argued by Benjamin, in Antiquity lying could be conceived as a remedy against political-metaphysical mythology that tends to subordinate everything to political logic, because it resists the order without undermining it. Deceptive speech is not a struggle *for* power—which is always also a struggle *against* the existing power—but it is a resistance that owes its power precisely to the fact that it is, as Benjamin says, "in principle non-violent."[63] Rather than as revolutionary or anarchistic, lying can thus perhaps best be described as a form of *civil disobedience*.[64] Tellingly, Derrida describes civil disobedience in "History of the Lie" as "the right to *secrecy*,"[65] that is, as the right to a space *sheltered from* political logic. In the end, this right to secrecy is the right to *opacity* more than secrecy per se, because it results not so much from the desire to conceal things, but rather from the impossibility of total transparency or total testimony.[66] The opposite situation would be a totalitarian state of absolute transparency, the *polis* as a glass house.[67] Making room for the necessary possibility of opacity, secrecy, and disobedience, then, boils down to acknowledging the political right not to be political.

This right not to be political inscribed *in politics* refers, or rather taps into, what I repeatedly indicated as the "void" or vacuum in which modern political orders are necessarily erected, the paradoxical moment of their "origin" to be recited time and again but never to be appropriated. Although all those who wish to challenge the order tap into this void, it is this same void that makes room for arbitrary executions of power, which can manifest itself under the denominator of the "state of exception." Like civil disobedience, the state of exception does not so much create a situation of anarchy where there is no longer any law, but rather a situation where the legitimization of the given order is put on hold, and where, strictly speaking, the law is neither executed nor transgressed. So, the inability to appropriate our origin incites politics on the one hand to a profound discretion and restraint, but on the other hand also leads to deliberately opaque constructions, like smokescreens designed to conceal the contingency of the legislative order. One could say that, in this case, opacity takes the form described by Rancière in his "Ten Theses on Politics" under the police formula: "Move along! There's nothing to see here!"[68]

It is in this situation that lying, that is, deliberate deceitful speech, can play a particular role. While generally, and especially from the point of view of the traditional concept of the lie, lying is conceived as an obstruction of normal speech conventions, Arendt was one of the first to point out that the modern lie should be seen as an *act*, and a powerful one at that, which can transform things and set them in motion. Derrida says: "She [Hannah Arendt, AvR] often recalls that the liar is a 'man of action,' and I would even add: par excellence. Between lying and acting, acting in politics, manifesting one's own freedom through action, transforming facts, anticipating the future, there is something like an essential affinity. The imagination is, according to Arendt, the common root of the 'ability to lie' and the 'capacity to act.'"[69] In other words, precisely *because* it originates in imagination, the modern lie seems to be able to open up new perspectives and possibilities, a change of reality, a change which, according to Arendt, "would be impossible if we could not mentally remove ourselves from where we physically are located and *imagine* that things might as well be different from what they actually are. In other words, the deliberate denial of factual truth—the ability to lie—and the capacity to change facts—the ability to act—are interconnected."[70] What prompts us to develop a theory of the lie, or more generally, of explicitly deceitful speech, is, in short, the fact that the regime of truth and truth-saying is already confiscated by political discourse. Consequently, every utterance that inscribes itself into the regime of truth—including Nancy's at points—inscribes itself, by this very gesture, also into political discourse—where it will be greeted, in the best of cases, as a competing claim to truth or, in the worst of cases, as an untruth and therefore as hostile. If one wants to short-circuit this operation of political discourse, the only option seems to be to refrain from claiming the truth and to openly present oneself as "liar."

When applied to literary practice, this means that literary writers should not so much present themselves as elliptic pursuers of truth, nor as revealers of the fictious or constructivist nature of reality as such. Even if this is the case, this only *works* if literature is affirmed as such, if fiction is recognized as fiction, if the deception is recognized as deception—as we saw in the Zen story evoked by Nancy.

In the Interstices of Politics

In a text that in many ways follows on from "History of the Lie," namely "The University Without Condition"—inserted within the same volume *Without Alibi*—Derrida elaborates on the act of imagination implied in lying. Although this text does not deal with the issue of deceitful speech as such, but is a reflection on the task of the university in general and the humanities in particular, there are close links between the two issues. The defining feature of the university, as Derrida concludes, should be to be "heterogeneous to the principle of power," and, for this reason "without any power of its own."[71] It is on the basis of this powerlessness that he believes the university can take on the critical task of challenging the status quo. In explaining this task, Derrida once again refers to the right to civil disobedience, which he explains as the right to say anything and question anything.[72] In his view, such disobedient questioning is concentrated in a single question, a question that must be asked again and again: "What if things were quite different?," or, in Arendt's words, "What if we imagine that things might as well be different from what they actually are?"

Given the political importance attributed to these questions by Derrida and Arendt, it is clear that this kind of powerless speech or questioning is by no means *private* speech, but indeed entrusted to *a public*, an audience, and shared without being imposed. This is why we can say, according to Derrida, that the "What if . . . ?" question is the *literary* question par excellence. Echoing, but in a positive way, Plato's reproach that poets produce *whatever*, literature, like civil disobedience, is "resistance against and beyond the order of the political,"[73] because it is a resistance always expressed, so to speak, from the margin, from the threshold, which also explains why a literary work produced by a politician, for example, can hardly be exempt from political discourse, despite its possible literary qualities. On the contrary, literature holds the possibility of an intervention of politics *within* the limits of the political order, but *without itself being political*, an intervention, in other words, which, precisely because it is not political, is capable of shifting the limits of the political order. Or, more precisely, it is an intervention that seeks to situate itself *at the limit* of the political order, but which, by this very attempt, reveals and questions the difficulty of locating this limit.

In doing so, literature is what Simon Critchley calls, in his 2012 book *Infinitely Demanding: Ethics of Commitment, Politics of Resistance*, "a distance from the state *within* the state":

> It is, we might say, an *interstitial distance*, an internal distance that has to be opened from inside. What I mean, seemingly paradoxical, is that *there is [today, AvR] no distance within the state*. In the time of the purported "war on terror," and in the name of "security," state sovereignty is attempting to saturate the entirety of social life. The constant ideological mobilization of the threat of an external attack has permitted the curtailments of traditional civil liberties in the name of internal political order, so called "homeland security," where order and security have become identified. Such is the politics of fear, where the political might be defined with Carl Schmitt as that activity which assures the internal order of a political unit like a state through the more or less fantastic threat of an enemy. Against this, the task of radical political articulations is the *creation* of interstitial distance within state territory.[74]

According to Critchley, the problem of our contemporary societies is the fact, or at least the risk, that state sovereignty saturates social life entirely, increasing the political realm to the extent that politics has permeated everything. No longer leaving any interstitial distance within the state, this is a situation that lacks room for maneuver, room necessary for things to move, to breathe.

In a 2009 interview with Boyan Manchev, Nancy seems to endorse this vital importance of the interstice. In other words, but with the same issue in mind, Manchev poses the question I posed above, namely the question as to how to know the difference between a world where the archi-resistance of things is *discernible* and a world where this resistance is *indiscernible* because it "belongs to another world entirely."[75] In his reply, Nancy indicates that the difference lies in the *distance*, in the *gap* or rather the *spacing*: "The difference lies in the spacing [*écartement*]. Either one suffocates, as you [Boyan Manchev, AvR] say, and it is because there is no more gap [*écart*], no more distance to take breath and make sense (if the sense is in the reference), or one can breathe. . . . It is the gap as such . . . that must be—how can I put it?—thought, certainly, but also desired and practiced" ("Mét" 88). It is the desiring and especially the *practicing* of this breath-giving gap that is crucial here. According to Critchley this desiring and practicing of the gap should take place through certain articulations, which he calls "radical political articulations," the task of which is to create an interstitial distance in the state logic. Although I would not call these articulations *political*, for reasons already given, I want to underline, with Critchley, the possibility of *creating* these kinds of gaps.

Critchley also gives an indication of the kind of articulations that might create interstitial distance. The best form of articulation—a form increasingly popular in the early 2000s to his delight—is what he calls the "powerless" form of "humorous," "creative," or "theatrical" resistance, such as that of groups like the White Overalls, the Rebel Clown Army, the Pink Bloc, or the Cacophony Society.[76] What these groups have in common, according to Critchley, is that they all "[perform] their powerlessness in the face of power in a profoundly powerful way."[77] To my mind this formula summarizes very aptly the responsibility of unworking performative acts, a responsibility that has already been indicated in a similar way by Judith Butler in *Excitable Speech: A Politics of the Performative*, where they looked for it in a *parodic* performative play with power, especially in the case of racist and sexist affairs: "The possibilities of genre transformation are to be found precisely in the arbitrary relation between such [performative, AvR] acts, in the possibility of the failure to repeat, a de-formity, or a parodic repetition."[78]

Although neither Butler nor Critchley really indicate *why* these kinds of parodic or theatrical articulations would be the best forms of powerless resistance, they have given, through their formulations, a very adequate description of the unworking performative act that I am trying to analyze. More emphatically than them, however, I would consider resistance by counter-power, as found in the acts of various revolutionary, emancipatory, or protest movements as forms of *political* performance because they claim validity. Instead, as said, performatives presented in the unworked mode open the possibility of non-political subversion, which, for this very reason, could unmask the close relationship between politics and truth. As I have argued, the workings of politics can never be unmasked in the name of truth itself, for speech in the name of truth is always already enveloped in the political operations it seeks to unmask.

THE "NON-SERIOUS" PERFORMATIVE OF FICTION (NANCY, AUSTIN, DERRIDA)

How, then, are we to understand the *effect* of unworked performatives, among which I wish to include literary works? In seeking to ascribe a certain effect to these performatives, we are, of course, partially distancing ourselves from Austin's founding theory of speech acts developed in *How to Do Things with Words?* Distinguishing between statements that describe the world—"constatives"—and those that perform an action—"performatives"—Austin claims that constatives can be true or false, while performatives can only be "felicitous" or "infelicitous," depending on the success of the speech act.[79]

While being widely praised for having extended the theory of language beyond the domain of truth, Austin was also criticized, among others by Derrida, for not having gone far enough. In "Signature Event Context" Derrida famously emphasizes that not only so-called performative statements, but *language as such* is essentially performative. Instead of distinguishing two separate domains, the constative and the performative, he argues that the latter forms the basis of *all* utterances, since in addition to its communicative function, a linguistic act always realizes a certain situation. Strictly speaking, then, language is always performative and this being the case, we need to reconsider the notion of *truth*. For if every utterance is performative as Derrida also concluded from his "pseudology," a distinction needs to be made not between true/untrue utterances on the one hand, and felicitous/infelicitous utterances on the other, but between (in)felicitous utterances *that present themselves as true* and those *that present themselves as untrue*. In my opinion, literary statements fall into the latter category.

Nancy undoubtedly associates himself with the Derridean idea that all utterances are performative, and develops, as an extension of this, the idea that all utterances are also "self-performative" (*ES* 24/11) in the sense that they also bring into presence, that is, "perform," the being of the enunciator, as he puts it, for example, in *Ego sum*:

> [T]he event [created by the performative utterance, AvR] is here nothing other than the performation itself, or rather the *being* coextensive with this performation: *I am*. Such a being *is*—as certain and true being—only through and for the duration of its pronunciation. Hence *Cogito*, or from now on *for* (I say, I fabulate, I discourse, I perform, I am performing) is the performative of performation: the *self-preformation*, even the self-formation through the statement of the being of the one who utters as being of truth. (*ES* 85/122–23, my emphasis)

By stressing that the performativity of an enunciation is always a self-performation, Nancy's ontological poetics once again proves to be a tautegorical one, since, as we have seen, in a tautegorical performative, saying and being coincide, because saying is always a matter of saying *oneself* and saying oneself is always a matter of *being* or even *true* being.[80]

Derrida, in his analysis of Austin's speech acts, however, chooses to stress another aspect, namely Austin's move to exclude so-called *non-serious* performative utterances from his theory of speech acts, that is performatives uttered, for example, on stage or introduced in a poem. Let us reread Austin:

> A performative utterance will, for example, be in a peculiar way hollow or void if said by an actor on the stage, or introduced in a poem, or spoken in a soliloquy. This applies in a similar manner to any and every utterance—a sea change in special circumstances. Language in such circumstances is in special ways—intelligibly—used *not seriously*, but in ways parasitic upon its normal use—ways which fall under the doctrine of the etiolations of language. All this we are excluding at present from consideration. Our performative utterances, felicitous or not, are to be understood as issued in ordinary circumstances.[81]

According to Austin, on the contrary, a performative becomes "parasitic" and "void" as soon as it is uttered in a fictional context such as that of a theater or a work of fiction, because pronounced in these contexts, the declaration "I do take this woman to be me lawful wedded wife," for instance, in no way obliges the characters to share their daily lives, and therefore loses its performative force.[82] Yet, Derrida holds, the exclusion of non-serious artistic performatives is nothing less than *impossible*, because it is precisely these performatives that mark the condition of possibility of language as such. This condition of possibility, as Derrida has amply indicated, is the possibility of *iteration*, that is to say, the possibility for statements to be taken up again, quoted, repeated, in different contexts, and this without end. The non-serious repetition of performatives in a poem or on stage thus touches upon the very condition of possibility of the performative and consequently of language: "For, finally, is not what Austin excludes as anomalous, exceptional, 'non serious,' that is, *citation* (on the stage, in a poem, or in a soliloquy), the determined modification of a general citationality—or rather, a general iterability—without which there would not even be a 'successful' performative?"[83]

Though Derrida is right in suggesting that the possibility of non-serious performatives should be key to any theory of performative language, Austin, for his part, is not wrong, to my mind, in suggesting that what these non-serious performatives "do" is quite *different* from what so-called "serious" performatives do. In contrast to Nancy, and more strictly than Derrida, I therefore propose to emphasize and maintain the distinction between language in its everyday "serious" use and in its "non-serious," "fictional," or "literary" use.

The Language of Fiction (*Nancy, Blanchot*)

Giving and Taking

This distinction between the performative in its everyday serious use and the performative in its literary use is, in my opinion, best analyzed by Blanchot, even if he does not use the notion of performativity at all.[84] In his essay "The Language of Fiction" (*The Work of Fire*), Blanchot deals with this distinction by analyzing one and the same sentence in two different modes, two modes in which we recognize the two modes of performativity I have just distinguished, one political, the other unworking. The sentence in question is "The head clerk called," which, Blanchot points out, undergoes a radical transformation depending on whether it is a note I find at the office where I work, or a sentence I read in a story by Kafka. In the first case, "I know who my supervisor is, I know his office, I know many things having to do with who he is, what he says, what others say about him, what he wants, the difficult nature of our hierarchical relationships, the intolerable sense of hierarchy for me, etc.; my knowledge is, in a way, infinite. As new as I may be, I am pressed on all sides by reality, and I attain it and meet it everywhere."[85] The everyday performative—or, more generally, everyday language, because the sentence in question is not a performative in the strict sense—is immediately "within the well-defined context," and thus immediately connects me "to an event in the midst of the world," as Anne-Lise Schulte Nordholt also observes in her analysis of Blanchot's text.[86] The everyday performative phrase functions as a precise reference that incites action by arranging the real and putting it at my disposal. We could say, to return to the distinction between the two modes of performative made above, that this is a performative that claims validity, a performative in its political mode.

But when we encounter this same sentence in Kafka's novel *The Castle,* what effect does it have? According to Blanchot, "as a reader of the first pages of a story, I am not only infinitely ignorant of all that is happening in the world being evoked, but this ignorance is part of the nature of that world, from the moment when, as an object of a narrative, it is presented as an *unreal world*, with which I come into contact by *reading*, not by my ability to *live*."[87] Whereas language normally evokes a specific event in the world, fictional literary language places us in an "unreal" world in which we are powerless, and which is only accessible in and through reading.[88] In both cases, we are dealing with one and the same linguistic sentence, but its effect is transformed according to the circumstances that determine its mode of performativity.

In his theoretical texts and, differently, in his narratives, Blanchot tirelessly seeks to describe this literary experience. On the face of it, Blanchot's poetics is very close to that of Nancy. Blanchot recognizes in fictional language the same power that Nancy attributes to it, namely the power to evoke things, to let them arise around us, in us, without why and without expectation, in a strange familiarity.[89] According to both authors, language is not essentially a means of communication, nor a system of signs secondary to the real world, but the positioning and bringing into presence of a world. As Blanchot puts it, the language of fiction, that is, *fictionizing* language, is language that "aspires to become *more real*, to be made up of a language that is physically and formally *valid*, not to become the sign of beings and objects already absent (since imagined), but rather to *present* them to us, to make us *feel* them and *live* them through the consistency of words, the luminous opacity of things."[90] Although this is a passage that Nancy could have written, Blanchot and Nancy nevertheless differ in the way they understand this literary presentation of things, as I have noted in the preceding chapters. Contrary to what Nancy would declare, the aspiration to become *more real* than a sign, to make us *feel* beings and objects and *live* them, is according to Blanchot "rigorously *contradictory*"[91] and therefore *fails*, because fictional language precisely does *not* give us the sense of the world where we are there *with* things, in the midst of the world, but on the contrary *sidelines* this sense of the world that everyday language gives us.

Whereas everyday language is a form of making and doing, according to Blanchot, the language of fiction distinguishes itself because it *renounces every form of doing*.[92] Even if such an identification of speaking and acting—which is a *mythical* identification—is what literary language aspires to, the language of fiction never achieves it. For Blanchot, literary language is not a saying, a *legein* of being, as it is for Heidegger or Nancy. On the contrary, in his view, what literature says *is* not. Here, Blanchot refers to the idea of language developed by Mallarmé, who is arguably both the most rigorous defender and the most rigorous destroyer of language's mythical aspiration. This idea is summed up by Mallarmé most concisely in this well-known passage from "Crisis of Verse": "I say: a flower! and outside the oblivion to which my voice relegates any shape, insofar as it is something other than the calyx, there arises musically, as the very idea and delicate, the one absent from every bouquet."[93]

Significantly, in *Sexistence*, and in indirect conversation with this passage, Nancy puts forward what can be taken as the main claim of this book on "the real of language and sex" (*S* 38/63): " '[L]ook here!' (actual infinity). A flower, you or me, sometimes us, an image, a contact, a cadence, a life-and-death . . . the gift that existence itself gives to itself, between coming and lifting away, each time alone and exposed to every other one. If this is what it is . . . then it is worth thinking anew the real of language and sex—or rather, how we address one another" (*S* 37–38/62–63). While Blanchot discusses Mallarmé's verse as follows: "*I say a flower!* But in the absence where I mention it, through the oblivion to which I relegate the image it gives me, in the depths of this heavy word, itself looming up like an unknown thing, I passionately summon the darkness of this flower, I summon this perfume that passes through me though I do not breathe it, this dust that impregnates me though I do not see it, this color which is a trace and not light."[94] Comparing these passages, we can say that while Nancy deliberately passes over the fact that Mallarmé *says* a flower by indicating that he *shows* it ("look here!"), Blanchot, for his part, underlines that those words, even in their heaviness and materiality, are far from a coming into existence of a shared sensible reality between us. What these words evoke instead, according to Blanchot, is an "unknown" and suspended reality that imposes itself *as suspended*, a reality that cannot be breathed or seen, and whose color does not touch our eyes.

Blanchot's analysis seems to be written as the anticipated response to Nancy's analysis of concrete literary works, in which Nancy describes literature precisely as that which brings forth the kind of existence that touches our senses. Indeed, in "To Open the Book," Nancy declares that when opening a book "we have *entered* the book. . . . So there is a state, a relation in which the book is not only open before us but we are *in* it. . . . That world is around us, within us; it is impossible to distinguish between them: *we are there, in a place*" (*EPL* 72/98, my emphasis), a "there" and a "place" that are, ontologically speaking, in no way different from other singular moments of thereness. Here lies, in my opinion, the disagreement between Nancy's poetics and Blanchot's, or more generally, between a poetics that focuses on the ontological poeticity of being as such, and a poetics that focuses on the poeticity of what is more traditionally called literature, or, again, between a Heideggerian-inspired poetics and a Mallarméan-inspired poetics.

Literature and Ontology, Revisited

This tacit disagreement between Blanchot's and Nancy's poetics is worth returning to one last time, not least because Nancy regularly draws on Blanchot with regard to the relation between literature, community, and politics. As a result, commentators generally situate Nancy's work in line with Blanchot's, and points of divergence are often characterized not as disagreements, but rather as differences in emphasis.[95] This sense of kinship is reinforced by the fact that Blanchot and Nancy share a deconstructivist or differential theory of language in which they, more than Heidegger, and partly against Mallarmé, both stress the need to abandon the idea of a primary, original language in favor of that of language as a constantly singular supplement of origin. Yet, however similar the stakes, the fundamental difference between Blanchot's and Nancy's poetics nonetheless reveals a disagreement that to my mind ultimately concerns the question of the relation between literature and ontology.

This difference can be summed up in two exemplary remarks by Blanchot and Nancy. Perhaps the central formula of Blanchot's poetics is "the word gives me being, but it gives me it *deprived of being*" from his programmatic text "Literature and the Right to Death,"[96] whereas the central formula of Nancy's poetics would be its shortened version "the word gives me being," or rather "to speak is to be in the world." Nancy thus emphasizes, and in a way rightly so, our being in the world, even where it is believed to be suspended, concealed, or idealized. Yet Blanchot's formula seems to add an interesting perspective, namely that as soon as our being in the world is "parasitized" by the language of fiction, its ontological value is bracketed. The reason why Nancy is not particularly concerned with the "non-seriousness" of the performatives of fiction, that is, the performatives that present themselves as non-true, is that he is primarily interested in the self-performativity of being as such—and this self-performativity is at work, or even *true*, in every utterance, whether it presents itself as true or non-true, real or deceptive.

As we saw above, Nancy thus focuses on the "performative of performation" (*ES* 85/122–23), that is, on the *being* coextensive with that performation, rather than on the modes in which and the contexts in which that performation occurs. The advantage of this insistence on being coextensive with linguistic performativity is that Nancy escapes the uncertainty, suspense, and spectrality that have dominated theories of language of recent centuries. Instead, his poetics makes room for the inescapable facticity of the world, for its abundant everyday evidence. This is undoubtedly Nancy's most important contribution to contemporary thought. Nonetheless, it is worth concentrating on the workings of performativity in literary practice, and this, as indicated, because it involves the possibility of creating interstices in this world that could prevent everything from becoming political.

So let us take a closer look at what Blanchot's claim that "[t]he word gives me being, but it gives me it deprived of being" could mean. Why, according to Blanchot, is being, evoked by literary speech, *deprived* of being? First of all, we need to realize that this claim is motivated by an idea of language formulated by Kojève, the idea, namely, that language denies reality in order to name it. Put another way, according to Kojève, naming a thing erases its uniqueness and facticity in favor of a general sign. The negation of reality in language could thus be said to be analogous to the negation by means of labor, in which the negated reality is dialectically taken up in a final product. For Blanchot, however, there is a crucial difference between the negation effected by labor and the one effected by literature, and the difference lies in the *scope* of the negation. In his view, labor negates a concrete part of reality, some pieces of raw material, in order to transform it into an instrument or a product. The negation of literature, on the other hand, is not local, but *global*. Literature is according to Blanchot always the negation of the world *in its totality*, because it replaces it not by another world, but by what he calls "the other of all worlds."[97]

Yet—and this is important—it is the totality of negation that also renders it *unworked*, that is, *empty* and *ineffectual*. Writers may well be the inventors of new worlds, but what they achieve is in fact nothing, because by refusing the world in its totality, they are precisely denying the time and space—of what Nancy would call its "coordinates"—in which their creation could become reality. I quote Blanchot from "Literature and the Right to Death": "If negation is assumed to have gotten control of everything, then real things, taken one by one, all refer back to that unreal whole which they form together, to the world which is their meaning as a group, and this is the point of view that literature has adopted—it looks at things from the point of view of this still *imaginary* whole which they would really constitute if negation could be achieved. Hence its *non-realism*, the shadow which is its prey."[98] From this non-realist, imaginary point of view "as at the end of time,"[99] a real intervention is impossible, simply because the *whole* does not give itself as real, is never a world in which we can live. For this reason, as Françoise Colin rightly says, it is "too weak to say that the character of the novel has no other existence than that which the novel confers on him, it is necessary to add that this existence is not an existence at all."[100]

In this respect, it is important to note that, if literary practice has a certain effect, that effect is always *unforeseen*. Very rarely does a literary act foment revolt, change the course of history, seduce that mysterious lover. If the writer or artist really wants to change things and have an effect, it is far better—at least in democratic states—to be a journalist, to found a political party, or to set up barricades. Writers, in other words, are perfectly aware that their actions count for nothing and that they therefore have no claim on reality, or at least no direct claim. This is why, for Blanchot—and this, in my opinion, is the particular strength of his poetics—literary practice "is not reality, but the realization of a point of view which remains unreal."[101] What is realized in the literary practice lacks presence, withdraws from our being in the world, is at the point of disappearance.[102]

As a result, for Blanchot, the effect of literary practice lies precisely in the inefficiency, uselessness, and superfluity of the world evoked. The literary act might as well not have been, to borrow Rancière's formula again in this context, and is for this reason always an empty gesture. By adopting a global point of view, by putting ourselves in an untimely and a-topic position, we can only *pretend* to create a world. In fact, what we achieve turns out to be an empty state of things, deprived of *being*, so deprived of being that we are not even sure that the literary act has taken place, as Colin observes:

> The writer's uncertainty is radical because it does not only con-
> cern the fact of knowing if he is a true artist—a concern already
> sufficient to shake a man—, but even if something like art exists.
> For the one who is certain of the world and of history, who is
> heir of the past and tends towards the future, for this person,
> the answer to the question "Is there art?" is assured. But for the
> creator himself, for the one who is dedicated to the proximity
> of art, the nearest becomes the most distant, the most certain
> becomes the most doubtful. Because art for him is not assimilable
> to any reality. . . . To say that perhaps art does not exist, does
> not mean that art does not exist yet, or that it does no longer

> exist: it is the very idea of a realized art, or of art taken in the movement of its possible realization . . . which is ungraspable. Art is what is never given, never assured, neither to the author, nor to the reader.[103]

The success of the unworked performative is therefore essentially undecided. The paradox of the formula "the word gives me being, but it gives it to me deprived of being," then, reveals the essence of literature, which is for Blanchot, like in the case of literary *community* described with reference to Duras, the question "Did it take place?"

This, in a nutshell, is why Nancy in his ontological poetics wants to get rid of all the thinking of the "as if" and the imaginary, as well as the possibility of a "global" or "cosmotheoric" standpoint, since they have nothing to do with the world, with our world, which by principle is always local, and precisely *takes place* here and now. What Nancy wants to retain from what he calls "literature" is the facticity of exposure, the very spacing of what is there, here and now, never graspable, but nonetheless incontestably there: "The question is always perhaps the question of the taking-place: what takes place only takes place by (re)presenting its taking-place" (*PD* 105). Or as he says it in *Dis-Enclosure*, "literature" is a matter of "letting the real—*res*, the thing—*realize itself*, that is, be what it is, and above be *that it is*. This 'letting be' is its task" (*DE* 135/197). So for Nancy, "literature" is not a matter of a certain phenomenological reduction, but first and foremost an ontological affair, the poetic technique that arranges or deploys being.[104] In "literature" as Nancy understands it, there is no being deprived of being, no world deprived of world, there is only being in the world as such. As we saw in chapter 2, Nancy therefore takes pains to exclude from his poetics the dimension of the "as if," the imaginary and the feigned, because he does not want to duplicate reality by postulating some other reality, a reality "otherwise than being" that might serve as a foundation or guiding principle.

However, if we are to understand the performativity specific to literary practice and analyze the role it might play in the interruption of mythological politics, this requires, in my view, the reintroduction of this dimension of the "as if," as well as its variant encountered above, the "what if . . . ?," excluded by Nancy's ontological poetics.[105] This reintroduction, as I understand it, does not, however, imply the reintroduction of a regulative or foundational fiction, nor of the idea of another world, more or less real, alongside our own. Rather than as a regulative fiction, the "as if" needs to be plotted or staged in such a way that it *deregulates* every regulating fiction.[106]

The Performance of Fictionality

But what does this fictional dimension have to offer? What does the speech act of fiction *do*? To answer this question, we need only open a literary book. Take, for example, *The Earthquake in Chile* by the Romantic writer Heinrich von Kleist. From the very first lines of this text, we are troubled as to its exact status, as the reality of the events described seems to impose itself inescapably:

> In Santiago, the capital of the Kingdom of Chile, at the very moment when the great earth tremors of the year 1647 struck, in the wake of which many thousands found their doom, a young Spaniard by the name of Jeronimo Rugera, accused of a crime, stood beside a pillar of the prison in which he'd been incarcerated and wanted to hang himself. Don Henrico Asteron, one of the wealthiest noblemen in town, had about a year before chased him out of his house, where he was at the time employed as a tutor, because he had been found to have a tender entanglement with Donna Josephe, Don Henrico's only daughter.[107]

First of all, because of the omniscient narrator, Kleist's text presents itself as a journalistic account of the events surrounding the great earthquake in Santiago de Chile in 1647. However, being a literary text, whatever the author's possible realistic intentions, this narrative is not a reportage of given events, but is itself an event. Being a performative act, this narrative does not recount things already given, but creates them, *puts them into act* by recounting, and we, then, do the same by reading it. In this sense, the date 1647 referring to the Chilean earthquake functions in the same way as the date 1965 referring to the bombing of Vietnam painted by On Kawara.[108]

Nevertheless, what is enacted in this presentation of the Chilean city, its prison and some of its inhabitants has a particular status that differs from the performative act of concluding a marriage, for example. What is presented or performed, as Blanchot stressed, is not a well-defined state of affairs for which we can take responsibility. What, then, is performed? What, in other words, is *acted out* in the performative act of literature? To answer this question, we can turn to Derek Attridge's *The Singularity of Literature* in which he distinguishes literary performativity from performativity in general, indicating that the former is not only a performance of situations, characters, feelings, ideas, but *also* and *at the same time* a "performance of fictionality."[109] This performance of fictionality is given, according to Attridge, "as the experience of an event or a series of events whereby the characters and occurrences apparently being referred to are in fact, and *without this fact being disguised*, brought into being by language."[110] It is in this phrase "and without this fact being disguised" that the heart of the unworked performance, characterized by Austin as "non-serious," lies and that distinguishes them from serious or, as I have indicated, *political* performances.

But it is also in this phrase that the fundamental ambiguity of literature lies. On the one hand, the literary text acts out, realizes, performs, through a performative gesture, what it narrates. The city, Jeronimo, the impending earthquake, are, in a sense, effectively present; they appear before our eyes, in our veins. With their evocation, what Nancy calls "the *being* coextensive with this performance" (*ES* 85/122–23) is performed. On the other hand, however, the text emphasizes that what is thus enacted, realized, exists only in the fabric of language, and bursts forth—perhaps—only in the fleeting moment of reading. As Blanchot pointedly asserts, the literary act thus consists of a necessarily dual movement in which the left hand removes what has just been given by the right hand. In other words, if the literary act is an offering of being, it is of a being that at the same time is not. In a way, Nancy's performance of the "real" is precisely that, and also includes a dimension of fiction or invention. It is, after all, a forming, an inventing of something that is not yet given, but that becomes real in and through its enunciation, something that is therefore obviously brought into presence by a formative act. This is why Nancy uses the words *fictionalization, poiesis*, and *myth* to describe his ontological poetics. Nevertheless, Attridge's formula points to a specific aspect of this fictionalization, namely that in statements presented as "literary" there is *also* a fictionalization *of fictionality*: The fictional character of fiction is brought to light. This, it seems to me, is not part of Nancy's poetics.

Let us return once again to the example of concluding a marriage, which is an almost caricatural illustration of what happens in language in general. Already in the case of a marriage performed by a registrar, it is clear that the matrimonial bond is brought into being by language and by language alone. In the case of a marriage performed on stage, as in Chekhov's *The Wedding*, it is also clear that it is performed by language, but this performance is accompanied by the performance of fictionality, so that the performative by which there *is*, normally, the reality of a marriage, is "arrested,"[111] halted, or put in brackets. Of course, literary texts vary according to the measure of fictionality (just compare a fairy tale with an autobiographical novel), but the fact that they are *presented* as literary texts, for instance by the label "literature," cannot *not* draw attention to this fictionality. In what follows, then, I want to argue that the way this fictionality is performed is ultimately always the same, namely by the subjugation of the unworked performative to what I propose to call a *meta-performative*. This meta-performative is both the reason why a literary performative obtains an unworked "non-serious" status, and the reason why it can have an exceptional force.

Being Responsible for Literature

The Meta-Performative "This Is Literature"

Previously, we identified the two modes in which a performative can occur: the political mode and the unworked mode. The first mode consists in claiming validity, while the second renounces it. We have also pointed out that this renunciation requires an *explicit maneuver*, because in language the claim to validity is always tacitly presumed. Now, I want to take the analysis of this second mode one step further by suggesting that the renunciation of validity arises from the fact that the performative is subjected to another performative, one that operates at a meta-level. The function of this meta-performative is to bracket the performative in question, to let it fail before being realized. In other words, the performative termed "unworked" owes its specific status to its being framed by another performative. If it is true that performatives only function as such in a specific context, then the context required for this second mode is the utterance of what I call a "meta-performative."[112]

This meta-performative consists—and this is the hypothesis I will support in what follows—in the declaration "This is literature." This statement is performative not only because it realizes a certain state of affairs, but also because it requires both a speaker and a listener. This simple statement "This is literature," or more generally "This is art" or "This is poetic," is enough to transform any object into a work of art, as if it were a magic formula. The peculiarity of our modern times is that, whereas in the past mastery of this formula required a certain expertise or reputation and was reserved only for an elite of critics, today it is totally "democratized" and can be used by anyone for anything. In other words, the literarity of an object lies not in the object's characteristics, nor in the author's intention, but in the *judgment* of the one perceiving it, including writers themselves.[113]

A literary text is distinguished from a journalistic article or a commercial advertisement not because it is of higher aesthetic value, because it bears witness to a certain finality or morality, but because its reader has decided to regard it as a literary text. In other words, it is only because of the meta-performative, the performative that says "This is literature," that an utterance can function *as* a literary utterance. If literature differs from other practices in that it is also a performance of *fictionality*, as Attridge observed, we must add that this performance of fictionality is a performance performed by the reader or listener. Just as the conclusion of a marriage can only be performed within a conditioned framework, represented among other things by a civil registrar, a literary text is only performed as such if it is situated within a framework that indicates that it is indeed literature and not, for example, the word of a madman or an insignificant note on a forgotten umbrella.

Without the judgment "This is literature," then, there is no art—and this is the very essence of art in modernity. Without this judgment, Duchamp's *Bicycle Wheel* is just a bicycle wheel; without this judgment, Khlebnikov's poem "Invocation of Laughter" just a linguistic exercise, and *The Earthquake in Chile* just a false historical testimony. Moreover, each of us has the right, or even the duty, to pass this judgment, yet without having the criteria to do so, as Thierry de Duve argued in what is one of the most pertinent and accurate analyses of modern art, *Kant After Duchamp*: "[A]rt, what one universally calls art, must be *whatever* and be named as art by *whomever*. This is the modern imperative stripped bare."[114] The judgment "This is art," after which there is art, then, is an intervention which, to associate ourselves once again with Rancière's claim regarding the *non-necessity* of art, is not "a necessary activity, inscribed in the order of things and demanded by the quest for Being . . . , but as a *chance, supplementary activity which . . . could just as well not have existed,*"[115] but which is nevertheless imperative.

The consequences are massive, for it not only follows that really *anything*—any utterance, gesture, or object—is a candidate for being art, but also that art always is or should be something *arranged*, if not *dramatized*. "Art" is not a quality intrinsic to a certain kind of thing, nor something that is spontaneously felt, but is always the result of a judgment—a judgment undoubtedly directed by a certain tradition and certain labels, but which is nonetheless absolutely *free*, without criteria. Conversely, this implies that we can also always judge that something is *not* art, even if circumstances seem to suggest otherwise. Even if an object is placed in a museum, we can judge that it has nothing to do with art; even if a book is advertised as "novel" or "fiction," we can decide to read it as a journalistic text and accuse the author of not having correctly represented the facts. An obvious example is the fatwa against the writer Salman Rushdie.

Let us now revert once again to the unease Nancy expressed in an earlier quote when faced with certain artworks: "I cannot say, for example, that I agree with the use of shit in paintings. But when I have to explain why, I'm embarrassed. Because I understand that art has come to this, but at the same time I think that there is something wrong, that this is wrong. . . . But I don't know very well to what extent I can say it. *And I recognize that here I lack a regulative idea*" ("TP" 5, my emphasis). Although we noted above that recourse to a regulative idea is opposed to Nancy's view, we can now conclude that there may well be a regulative idea that fits in with Nancy's poetics, namely the meta-performative judgment "This is (not) art," a judgment that is in fact named a "regulative idea" by De Duve himself.[116] The answer to Nancy's unease would then be that he *himself* is the regulator, the one to judge. Because art can, in principle, be anything, nothing authorizes us to judge something as such, or, as De Duve puts it: "[T]he regulative Idea of modern art, after Dada, is the *whatever*."[117] Obviously, the judgment that this or that object (a painting composed of shit, for example) is or is not art cannot be a rule to which all cases can be submitted. On the contrary, it is a judgment that is passed each time anew, here and now, with respect to this particular work, oftentimes ad hoc, instantly.[118] Nothing *authorizes* Nancy to judge that this or that is art, and he may as well refrain from judging as he is tempted to do,[119] but nothing *prevents* him either from judging that it is art or not. Better still, by disapproving it, he has already passed this judgment.

The fact that the particular performativity of literature depends on the meta-performativity of another utterance ("This is literature") leads to the inevitable conclusion that literariness or poeticity can—and should—be conditioned, dramatized, that is, *enacted*. At first glance, this seems a problematic observation, for if we maintain that the experience of literature is an *event*, as we have done, then this would suggest the possibility of a conditioned event. And indeed, even if the event is usually considered as something that cannot be created, prepared, or even foreseen, I want to support the idea that the resistance, intervention, or interruption called, for want of a better word, "literature," can only have an effect when accompanied by the meta-performative that is the judgment "This is literature." What is conditioned by this judgment is, however, nothing more than a certain *sensitivity* or *susceptibility*, a predisposition required for acts and statements to be conceived as literary. Perhaps we should even argue that the judgment "This is literature" offers us what we might call a literary *gaze*, a gaze that sees things in a certain light, a gaze, as Nancy holds in an already quoted and fairly Romantic formulation to be sure "which requires and permits that the 'ordinary' be presented, not as the extraordinary but *in* the extraordinary" ("TC" 386/88).

It should be noted, however, that the insistence on such a literary gaze implies a crucial shift of emphasis in thinking about literature, namely the shift from determining the characteristics of certain literary *objects* to determining the characteristics of a certain *attitude*. This shift follows from Nancy's poetics that presents the "literary" not as the characteristic of things, but of the way they present themselves. But even if being-with itself is to be conceived as literary, as Nancy maintains, it may well be that this goes unnoticed, that this literarity "belongs to another world entirely" as Nancy predicted. So, even if a poem could, in principle, strike us like a burst of laughter, even if a painting could touch us as we look at it, even if completely ordinary events of shouting, praying, or sobbing could be, singularly, momentarily, that "infinite suspension of sense" that Nancy ascribes to it,[120] it could just as well be that we no longer sense this suspension of sense, that we lack the capacity to experience it as such. It is therefore perhaps rather a certain judgment, a certain gaze, that is needed for it to be sensed as such.

This does not mean that this judgment is always the result of a considered choice. No doubt its expression generally takes place at the *very moment* when we are confronted with a work, and takes us by surprise rather than being the result of deep reflection. For, like literature itself, this judgment, or rather the criterion on the basis of which it is expressed, is *whatever*.[121] The judgment "This is literature" is not accompanied by a norm, which, of course, would again presuppose an intrinsic literarity, but is a performative linguistic act that instantiates what it declares.

Fictionalizing Being (Nancy, Belhaj Kacem)

Let us now, in a final movement, return to the "lying" or deceptive nature of literary utterances. If we start from the idea that language as such is performative, and for this reason a *fingere* in the sense of "forming"—as

Nancy and Derrida do—then the meta-performative implies, so to speak, a meta-fingere, a *second-degree "forming,"* a forming of the forming. Using Attridge's formula that literature is a performance of fictionality, we could thus say that it not only performs this or that, but that it also performs the fact that it is a performance. An example of this structure is Kleist's story, whose opening lines we have already read, and that was, of course, not chosen arbitrarily. The story *The Earthquake in Chile* is often commented on by literary theorists and political philosophers alike. It thus forms a fertile casus for illustrating what is at stake, not only in terms of literary theory, but also in terms of its sociopolitical consequences. Significantly, *The Earthquake in Chile* was written by Kleist while he was imprisoned in France and tells the story of two lovers, Jeronimo and Josephe, who are trying to escape the legal-state violence that pursues them. Having discovered his daughter's relationship with Jeronimo, Josephe's father sends her to a convent, pregnant. Jeronimo, for his part, is sent to prison.

Things get even worse: While Josephe is condemned to death for giving birth on the church steps, Jeronimo decides to commit suicide. But just as Josephe is about to be executed and Jeronimo is about to hang himself, an earthquake shakes the city. Not only does the prison collapse, but so does the legal process. As if by a miracle, Jeronimo and Josephe find each other again, and try to cross the border to escape the violence sanctioned by the state. Nevertheless, the tentacular power of Josephe's father spreads in all directions, and everywhere they travel, Jeronimo and Josephe encounter the rage of the people. Among the few people sympathetic to them is Don Fernando, since the lovers helped his family out during the earthquake. At some point, Jeronimo and Josephe attend a church mass dedicated to the victims of the earthquake. During the mass, the priest accuses the lovers of being the cause of the earthquake, and of having brought down upon themselves the wrath of God through their condemnable behavior. When one of the churchgoers recognizes Josephe, the crowd goes wild. They throw themselves at Don Fernando, seated next to Josephe holding Fernando's child in her lap. Obviously, the crowd mistakes Don Fernando for Josephe's lover Jeronimo. To save Don Fernando, the real Jeronimo reveals himself, announcing that *he* is the real Jeronimo. But then Don Fernando puts on a kind of play:

> Flustered by Jeronimo's remark, the seething mob stopped short; several hands let go of Don Fernando; and since at that very moment a marine officer of high rank came rushing forward,

> and, after shoving his way through the throng, asked: "Don Fernando Ormez! What happened to you?," the latter, now set free, replied with truly heroic composure: "You see there, Don Alonzo, those murderous blackguards! I'd have been done for if that worthy gentleman had not *given himself off as Jeronimo Rugera* to still the raging rabble. Please be so kind as to take him into custody, as well as this young woman, for their own protection," and grabbing hold of Master Pedrillo, added, "and arrest that no good scoundrel who stirred up this whole uproar!"[122]

First of all, we can see that, despite its realistic, almost journalistic beginning, Kleist's story takes on the typical form of a tale that develops around two heroes: Jeronimo and Josephe. The story's fictionality is thus already apparent in its form. But it is also the little theater play described in the quoted passage that—as if in miniature—confirms this fictionality. Through this enactment, Don Fernando offers Jeronimo the opportunity to take shelter from state violence in his own name, in fictional language. It is a refuge because of the theatrical framing provided by the "stage director" Don Fernando, as Peter Fenves also suggests in his analysis of Kleist's story: "In the mise-en-scène of this deadly serious play, Don Fernando is not entirely dishonest, for Jeronimo does in fact give himself out as Jeronimo, but his arrest order is the first of his 'false pretences,' since Jeronimo *is* Jeronimo after all. By giving Jeronimo out as the one who gives himself out as Jeronimo, he transforms Jeronimo's honest, upright and self-sacrificing self-impersonation—'If you seek Jeronimo Rugera: here he is!'—into sheer semblance."[123]

Thus, on the level of the story we could say that Don Fernando is the personification of the meta-performative, the one who proclaims "This is (he is) literature." This hypothesis is reinforced by a detail pointed out by Fenves. Although Kleist's entire narrative is presented as a play, presenting direct speech with a colon, Don Fernando is the only character whose phrases are surrounded by quotation marks. Read as a frame story that doubles what happens in literature in general, we could say that Don Fernando's staging has as a result that the realization of the speech act "I am Jeronimo" fails or is put on hold. This is all the more interesting given that the statement "I am . . ." is, in a sense, the performative par excellence, the statement that evokes the very *existence* of the person as Nancy observed. Jeronimo's existence, in other words, is *pretended*, while being there and being himself.

The example of Kleist is also important from a political point of view. The double performative played out offers Jeronimo and Josephe the possibility of escaping, at least for a while, from political violence, but without undermining the political order. Rather, it is a *shelter* provided by the order itself, a claim supported by the fact that Don Fernando is a representative of the ruling elite. The shelter offered by the order itself is ultimately nothing more than the shelter provided for performatives that occur in the unworked mode of "non-serious" performatives. Or in the terms of Anderson's *The Emperor's New Clothes* mentioned above, Don Fernando's staging consists in transforming Jeronimo's speech into a child's speech, lending him a child's voice. This childlike shelter is created by the judgment "This is literature" that accompanies his speech, with the result that it no longer makes any claim to validity and is therefore not a competing force to the established power.

It is with regard to the possibility of such a shelter, which consists in the possibility to feign or ironize one's own being, that the work of Nancy can be questioned, and indeed has been questioned. In *Théorie du Trickster*, Mehdi Belhaj Kacem asks precisely this question "Can I pretend to *be?*"[124] This book by Belhaj Kacem, who in addition to novels has published numerous essays on the relation between politics, aesthetics and the body, is interesting because it links the linguistic problematic of feigning or lying to the more general philosophical problematic of the subject and its ontological status. As Nancy explains in *Ego sum* on Descartes, we may well lead a life made up of lies and impostures, but our ontological status—the fact that we are—is impossible to feign. The subject's *being*—and here Nancy agrees with Descartes—is in principle that which cannot be feigned, "*the point of the impossible feint or fiction*," the point "where it 'withdraws' itself in *truth*" (*ES* 79/116).[125]

This has important consequences for one of the issues discussed at the beginning of this chapter, namely that of the possibility of *self-deception* in modern political orders. Both Descartes and Nancy rule out the possibility of self-deception, at least in the most radical sense which concerns one's own existence and thereby ultimately inscribe their ontologies in the same regime of truth-beyond-truth in which modern political orders operate. From the viewpoint of ontology, according to them, we can feign many things, but we cannot feign to exist, because every "I feign" necessarily implies an "I exist" and even a *verification* of my existence. The feigned and feigning subject is therefore always a subject that *is*.[126] Because, as we have seen with Arendt and Derrida, it is the phenomenon of self-deception that characterizes contemporary politics, and more precisely mythological politics, this phenomenon deserves to be studied within, but probably also beyond, Nancy's ontological poetics.

Indeed, it is precisely on this point that Belhaj Kacem questions Nancy's poetics. The central thesis advanced by Belhaj Kacem is as follows:

> In the end, feigning feigning can connote a meaning, and wouldn't this be the most exact definition ever given of *irony*? Within ontology, of the subject or the object or thing—here it is all the same thing—the being-feigned is a given fact, implied in the donation of the singular. The *feigning of the feigning*, the irony, acquires its meaning only *beyond the onto-logic* understood as the logic of the being-given of each thing, notably the subject. The feigning of the feigning, the principle of irony, takes only place beyond, *in the incorporeal that is language*, to continue in a stoic vein. But in the order of bodies, there is only the being-feigned and an annulment of the feigning of the feigning. In the incorporeality of language, and only there, the epiphany of a possibility occurs, that of irony, of a feigning to feign.[127]

Nancy's ontological poetics excludes the possibility of irony understood as a feigning to feign, because it is of the order of bodies—and one cannot deny the very being of a body, feigned or not. This, of course, marks Nancy's entire project, and is undoubtedly also the reason why irony plays no part in his poetics, even if it is strongly inspired by Jena Romanticism.

In his attempt to break with the mythological political structure of communities, Nancy detects a more original articulation of being-with than that of the Romantics, and it is on the basis of an ontological analysis that he points out that every mythological politics is, so to speak, a stillborn project, because it is our very being-with that resists this politics at its ever-renewed birth. It is not, therefore, with a political program, nor with any sociocultural or artistic project, that politics can be prevented from becoming mythological, but only with the awareness that such mythology is always already interrupted and deconstructed at its roots.[128]

If we leave behind the ontological order of bodies, however, a new perspective opens up, the political significance of which is already fleetingly indicated by Kleist's story and which I have termed the "distinctive force" of literary works. This perspective is that of a specific responsibility to be attributed to works of fiction. As indicated, this responsibility lies in the *attestation* to the "original" resistance examined by Nancy. This perspective, examined here with the help of the various theories discussed so far, does not so much explain how mythological logic deconstructs itself, but rather indicates how this self-deconstruction can be affirmed, and how it can be attested, as it were, after the fact, in such a way that this attestation is not again incorporated by mythological logic.

So, how to take this responsibility? If it lies in a form of self-deception deliberately expelled from Nancy's poetics, how, then, to deceive ourselves? The mechanism of this self-deception is always something at work *between* us as stated by Belhaj Kacem in his provocative style, and illustrated by him with the following example: "So I go to Club 88, a porn supermarket full of four-screen viewing booths, jerking off to SM, male, 'lesbian' and bi all in bulk. Let's say. At the first signs of exhaustion, I head out, and at the exit I bump into a girlfriend that is quite familiar with my recreational activities. I say to her that I was there for professional reasons, doing some location scouting for one of my art house films."[129] The point here is that both people know very well what really happened, and also know that the other knows. Despite this, the "I" tells a "lie." The "I," more precisely, Belhaj Kacem explains, "tells a lie on a superficial level, pretending to be there for 'scouting'; but says it *knowing not to be believed.*"[130] Thus, the feigning of this all-too-obvious lie is not intended to conceal the truth, or even to conceal unease. Rather, the "I" plays an ironic game in which he does not aspire to be believed, and therefore does not ask his performative statement to succeed. On the contrary, he aims for the *failure* of this performative by pointing out that he is *talking nonsense* (he could just as easily have said "my grandmother sleepwalks and I thought she might be here" or "they sell Milky Way candy bars here and they're my favorite").

The fact that he could have said anything at all is not to say that there was noise on the line, as communication scientists say, but that, from the outset, what is said is not to be taken seriously. The point of a liar in the traditional sense is precisely to be taken seriously, to be *believed* and the fact that the success of the performative is linked to the seriousness of the utterance is a direct result of the essence of language, namely its promise of truthfulness. Language only works if we can believe what is said, and believe that what is said is said to be believed. The act of language therefore always includes an act of *faith*, necessary, indeed, because this truthfulness can never be proven, for there is always the possibility of false testimony or a false witness. In the "it is necessary to believe me" that accompanies our linguistic communication, says Derrida, "the 'it is necessary,' which is not theoretical but performative-pragmatic, is as determining as the 'believe.' . . . The witness marks or declares that something is or has been present to him, which is not so to the addressees to whom the witness is joined by a contract, an oath, a promise, by a pledge of sworn faith whose performativity is constitutive of the witnessing and makes it a pledge [*gage*], an *engagement*."[131] According to Derrida, the act of faith is thus always involved in the act of language.

But the situation becomes more complicated in the case of "non-serious" performatives, which happen in the unworked mode. Whether uttered on stage or in a work of fiction, this performative does not imply the imperative "it is necessary to believe me," or at least not directly. Rather, it implies the opposite: it is uttered precisely so as *not* to be believed. This counts for all the examples given of this performative, perhaps the clearest of which is Nancy's little Zen story. The Zen master's answer "shitty stick" to the question of Buddha's identity is nonsense, and undoubtedly given so as not to be believed. It is plainly and clearly *whatever*. Yet—and for this reason things get even more complicated—this statement is also based on an act of faith. It is the act of faith that disciples have in their Zen master, despite the ridiculousness of his answers, the act of faith of children warning marionettes of danger, the act of faith of the reader who is moved to tears—in short, it is the act of faith required for *believing*, at this very moment, that *even if* we know it is *whatever*, it is and can only be this specific event: We have to believe that whatever is happening is really and *necessarily* happening.[132]

This faith is also emphasized by Nancy when speaking about art:

> As in the stronger spiritual tradition, works of faith or those of love—they are the same—are nothing other than the exercise and effectiveness of faith and love. Works of what we call "art" follow at least the same formal logic, even if they do not harbor true content. In truth, it is precisely a confidence that is realized; a *fidelity that is confirmed in action*, not as the apotheosis of a fulfillment—which would no longer have to be faithful to anything—but as the never resolved, never satisfied tension of a confidence whose object cannot be guaranteed. (*EPL* 69/95, my emphasis)

The unworked performative of literary practice therefore also requires a certain fidelity, confidence, or commitment—an *engagement*—which takes place at the moment when we say "This is literature."[133] Only with this fidelity can such performatives be "felicitous," or to misuse Austin's formula, be felicitous in their infelicity.

This is the greatest enigma of literary experience, the enigma that makes it one of the most fascinating experiences in life. Although the characters' existence is in a sense not an existence at all, there is nevertheless something realized, here and now, in our world. It is something that, at the same time, is not. This is how we can understand the kind of existence, like Madame Bovary's, for example, who exists only as a name without reference, even though everyone knows her as if she were a much-loved relative, and K.'s in Kafka's novels, who does not even have a proper name, or the unknown laughing woman described by Baudelaire. These characters seem to become beings, these texts come to life, because we are willing to believe in them.

Putting Faith in Fiction

Nevertheless, faith in this case is a rather special kind of faith. It is not a whole-hearted faith where there would be "no difference between an assured disposition and its realizations" (*EPL* 69/95), but rather a half-faith, a quasi-faith. Imagine an audience in a theater, captivated by the performance on stage: Puccini's *La Bohème*. As we reach the final act, Mimi, with whom we have shared joys and sorrows, is slowly dying. Although the actress' persuasiveness is so convincing that a large part of the audience reaches for a tissue, no one comes to the poor woman's aid. Apparently, the audience is swaying between two convictions or has both at the same time: On the one hand, they believe what is happening on stage and are touched by it as if it concerned a real person;[134] on the other hand, however, they realize that it is a simulation, which prevents them from taking action.

In my opinion, it is the ethnologist, philosopher, and psychoanalyst Octave Mannoni who found the most adequate formula for this double attitude towards a fictional performance: "I know well, but all the same . . ." Although Mannoni refers in particular to psychoanalytic practice, it seems to me that this belief is at the heart of the experience of fiction.[135] In his eponymous text, Mannoni explains that there is no real contradiction between knowing that something is false and believing it. One of the examples Mannoni gives is drawn from the Hopi tradition, where children's fathers and uncles dance, wearing masks called Katcinas, and give the children piki, red-painted cornballs. What happens when a child discovers the dissimulation? Mannoni quotes one of the Hopis, Talayesva:

> "Once," Talayesva tells us, "when there was to be a Katcina dance within two days, I found my mother in a nearby house, baking piki. I had entered unexpectedly and discovered that she was making red piki. When I saw that it was red piki, I was upset. That evening at supper I ate almost nothing. The next day, when the Katcinas were distributing their gifts to us I did not want any of their piki. But to my surprise they gave me not red but yellow piki. Then I was happy."[136]

What this example demonstrates—which no doubt corresponds to our personal experiences—is that the belief in fiction can survive the denial of experience, only because we want to believe in it.

Importantly, it is not simply a matter of denying reality. The phenomenon is more complex. If it were a simple denial, the phrase "I know well" would suffice. But if this is followed by "but all the same," the belief contradicted by reality is thus both abandoned *and maintained*, that is, one is able to believe in a fiction *and at the same time* recognize that it is only a fiction. If we understand that the act of faith is inherent in every act of language—namely, the leap of faith that language is a perfectly transparent medium and that my interlocutors all intend to tell the whole truth and nothing but the truth—it is not surprising that some have characterized language as a fetish which suggests that the mechanism of "I know well, but all the same" is not an exceptional one that occurs in the minds of naive children or neurotics, but concerns all linguistic beings.[137]

Let us conclude and tie up these last remaining threads. As shown, the possibility of lying to oneself is only opened up by the abandonment of the traditional concept of the lie, understood in terms of the register of truth and falsehood—at the moment when, in Nietzschean terms, the fable itself becomes the true world. With Nancy, I proposed replacing this register of truth and falsehood with that of performativity, and understanding speech as a saying that *becomes true*, or, in other words, that realizes itself tautegorically. Now, we can add that the performativity of speech in its unworked "non-serious" mode that is proper to literature requires a particular act of faith or belief that keeps intact the fictitious nature of the utterance. Whereas, as we have seen, every act of language is in a sense based on an act of faith, the faith implied by the ordinary act of language is not explicitly attributed, but rather the *implicit* condition of possibility of ordinary language. In the speech act of literary works, on the contrary, this act of faith does have the form of a *deliberate* gesture in the form of the meta-performative "This is literature." Because this meta-performative is the result of a judgment that *might just as well not have been passed*, the literary performative act is never implicit, but always the result of an intentionality, however instinctive it may be.

In modern and contemporary theory of literature as well as in Nancy's poetics, the concept of "intention" and certainly that of "will" is perhaps out of place and certainly unwanted. Following the Heideggerian idea that poetic language is non-appropriable, literature is generally conceived as the exemplary form of this non-possession of language. It is in the murmur of literary speech that our essential and inappropriable belonging to language is exemplified, a belonging that precedes acts of will and, what is more, undermines them. Nancy's poetics therefore stresses that the event of language is not within the writer's power, and that there is no point in trying to discover the author's intention. Though this idea is equally at the basis of the present study, I have, however, tried to argue that this non-possession may at the same time require a certain form of intentional plotting or enactment.

This enactment does not re-stage a subjectivist will but rather its non-subjectivist echo, an echo that is only that of a *presupposed* or *ascribed*—that is, in the end, *performed*—intentionality that we can call with a term coined by Attridge, *authoredness*, which is "the presupposition that the words we are reading are the product of a mental event or a number of such events whereby the processes of linguistic meaning are engaged."[138] This concept of "authoredness" in no way implies that the meaning of a literary work lies in the recoverable intention of its author. Strictly speaking, there *does not even have to be an author*, since what matters for a statement to be considered *as* literary is only the decision that this—*whatever*—is a literary utterance. Since, as we have seen, for an utterance to be conceived as a literary utterance that makes no claim to validity, there must be an explicit maneuver, a *decision* to refrain from validation.

The literarity of a text—I repeat this essential point—lies not in the characteristics of the text, nor in the author's intention, but in the meta-performative judgment of the receiver. Only the judgment "This is literature" thus distinguishes a literary statement from borborygmi of the belly or a presidential speech. Importantly, borborygmi or a presidential speech *can* become literary statements if this judgment is applied, since this judgment can be applied to *anything*, thereby transforming its sense. Attridge puts it this way: "Another way of putting this argument of authoredness is that to read a text in the fullest sense is to treat it not as [an] assemblage of words but as 'written' or even better as *a writing*."[139] In other words, in order for there to be a performance of *fictionality*, and for it to occur as *unworked*, this needs to be a *staged* form of unworking.[140] If in our mythless societies, we are to reassert the mythical force of our speech, as Nancy announced in *The Inoperative Community*, and to reassert it in a non-mythological way, it must be by listening to the "literature," the ongoing poetic formation of our being-with. However, by way of concluding our analysis in this last chapter, we can say that it is perhaps not sufficient to *hear* this poetic formation, but that we need the literary arrangement or plotting of literary practice in order to be able to *listen* to it.

Conclusion

The main impetus of Nancy's work is to bring to the fore the singular plurality of our being-with, to accentuate it, to make room for the plurality of singular voices, sounds, chatters, and laughs that rise when we are together, we, beings in the broadest sense of the word. Being at heart nothing but the articulation of this resounding being-with, "myth" has always been a means to designate this sharing of voices, a putting into language or poetry of the mere fact of our being-with. Functioning within a *political* constellation, however, myth easily—even inevitably—turns the sharing of singular voices into one single voice, subsuming the singular sounds, chatters, and laughs under one form, principle or logic—a mythologic.

In a longstanding, multifaceted and courageous attempt to reassert the power in which poetry, sense and our being-with are mutually constituted, Nancy has aimed at soaking off this mythical power from its mythological political form, thereby thinking "community" and "literature" in a different political vein, or, rather, beyond politics altogether, though not without interruptive or subversive force. In chapters 1 and 2, I have argued that Nancy's reflection on myth can be conceived as an attempt to remove the notion of myth from the Aristotelian interpretation of *muthos* as a narrative organization of elements in a totality, inscribing it instead in the Jena Romantic interpretation of myth as *tautegorical* speech, that is, as the saying of the world by itself. As we saw in chapter 3, Nancy subsequently, and moving partly beyond the Romantic tradition, places this stripped-down notion of myth within the larger framework of an *ontological poetics* inspired by Heidegger. Following Heidegger, Nancy adopts the view that being presents itself, as such, at every instant anew, by enunciating or articulating itself, an articulation that can be described as "*Dichtung*," "poetry," or "literature." As indicated in the final chapter, if the very articulation of being itself is a poetic affair, there is no reason to circumscribe a privileged domain where being is articulated in an exemplary fashion. The inevitable consequence of Nancy's ontological poetics—a consequence that Heidegger did not draw according to Nancy—is therefore that the *exceptional* character hitherto ascribed to literature is dissolved.

I hope to have shown, however, going further than and partially against Nancy, that given the way politics, community and literature interrelate, there are good reasons for attributing a certain exceptionality to literary practices, an exceptionality that is based on the specific *performativity* of a work of fiction. As I have argued, the exceptional character of literary practice can be located in the performance of its fictionality that turns the literary utterance into an *unworked* one renouncing every form of validity and therefore power. It is perhaps only because of this renunciation that these practices escape becoming part of a mythological political logic and can become a means to attest to the fundamental unworking of our being-with.

As indicated, this attestation requires the reintroduction, in Nancy's ontological poetics, of the fictional or deceptive dimension of literature that is perhaps too easily rejected by Nancy. If literary speech resists the political mythological logic, it is indeed because it is an echo of what Nancy calls the unworked mode of our existence itself, but, if so, only in the form of an after-the-fact attestation that makes it possible for this echo to be heard as such. To seize this possibility, we need to delimit or rather, indeed, *exempt* a domain of non-serious speech. And in order to exempt it, we have to *judge* it as "literary," instead of being satisfied, as Nancy is inclined to do, with trusting that politics, in due course, will give the unworked mode of our existence a chance. In the final analysis, this is not an ontological exception, but rather a sociocultural one: It is the political order that must make room for and guarantee the possibility of a non-political power within politics, an interstitial power that remains beyond the reach of its power.

Today, this seems perhaps more relevant than ever. With the global tendency towards nationalist and sometimes even outright authoritarian forms of community—forms of community, moreover, that tend to employ fiction in order to achieve their goals—insight is needed into the ways politics, community, and literature can interact. It seems like today we are less and less capable of experiencing fictional utterances as a form of *unworking* and it is precisely for this reason that we need to highlight this unworking "power" in and of literary practice. It is, in other words, precisely because we are in danger of losing what I referred to as the "literary gaze," that it must be preserved and even reconstructed. This book has therefore sought not only to outline Nancy's poetics and situate it within the philosophical tradition, but also to understand this poetics as stemming from a political and cultural concern. This concern, as we have seen, is the fear that there is no longer an interstitial space, the fear of suffocating, as Nancy puts it, because there is "no more distance to take breath and make sense" ("Mét" 88). Since the interstitial space of literary speech is deliberately impotent or without power of its own, this distance must be noticed, preserved, and guaranteed. If we have a responsibility to assume, it is to tirelessly defend this interstitital space of literature.

Notes

Introduction

1. The English translation contains an error that adds unnecessary complexity to the meaning of this already complex sentence, since it accidentally speaks of "the myth *of the myth* of mythless society."

2. Although the theme of myth plays a key role in Nancy's work, with the exception of Mathilde Girard in her interview with Nancy on myth (Jean-Luc Nancy and Mathilde Girard, *Proprement dit: Entretien sur le mythe* [Lignes, 2015]), the few other commentators who present Nancy's thought as a thought of myth do so only in a *negative* way, understanding his thought as that which repels the notion of myth. See, for example, the preface "Between Nihilism and Myth" by Jeffrey S. Librett in the English translation of *The Sense of the World* (University of Minnesota Press, 1997), vii–xxvi; and Oleg Domanov, *Between Myth and Nihilism: Community in Jean-Luc Nancy's Philosophy* (Verlag Dr. Müller, 2008). The latter chose his title for obscure reasons, because the notions of "myth" and "nihilism" play almost no role in his analysis.

3. Mircea Eliade, *The Myth of the Eternal Return: Cosmos and History*, trans. Willard R. Trask (Harper & Brothers, 1959), 141.

4. Walter Benjamin, "Critique of Violence (1921)," in *Reflections: Essays, Aphorisms, Autobiographical Writings* (Schocken Books, 1986).

5. As Judith Butler characterizes it in "Critique, Coercion, and Sacred Life in Benjamin's 'Critique of Violence,'" in *Political Theologies: Public Religions in a Post-Secular World*, eds. Hent de Vries and Lawrence E. Sullivan (Fordham University Press, 2006), 202.

6. Jacques Derrida, "Force of Law: The 'Mystical Foundation of Authority,'" in *Deconstruction and the Possibility of Justice*, eds. Drucilla Cornell, Michel Rosenfeld, and David Gray Carlson (Routledge, 1992), 63.

7. For a more elaborate analysis of the theme of myth in Benjamin's essay, see my "Interrupting Mythological Politics? On the Possibility of a Literary Intervention," *Theory & Event* 12, no. 1 (2009); and "Le cercle mythique: Walter Benjamin

sur la politique et son interruption," *Anthropology+Materialism: A Journal of Social Research* 2, special issue, The Persistence of Myth (2014): 2–16.

8. For this intertwinement, see Walter Benjamin's "Critique of Violence," 278 and 202, where he speaks of a "circular argument" and a "cycle," respectively. In his analysis of Benjamin's text, Derrida suggests that Benjamin himself did not explicitly recognize this intertwining of law making violence and law preserving violence and claims this to be his own proposal: "I shall propose the interpretation according to which the very violence of the foundation or position of law [*Rechtsetzende Gewalt*] must envelop the violence of conservation [*Rechtserhaltende Gewalt*] and cannot break with it. It belongs to the structure of fundamental violence that it calls for the repetition of itself and founds what ought to be conserved, conservable, promised to heritage and tradition, to be shared." Derrida, "Force of Law," 38. Although I do not think that this interpretation leads *beyond* Benjamin's statement, Derrida is in my opinion nonetheless right to point out that we are dealing here with an inevitable *structural* intertwining and not an intertwining resulting from a certain historical decline as Benjamin suggests.

9. Benjamin, "Critique of Violence," 297.

10. See Aristotle, *Poetics*, trans. Malcolm Heath (Penguin Books, 1996), chap. 5.

11. Derrida, "Force of Law," 35, my emphasis. The double meaning of the future anterior is indicated by Derrida in *Psyche: Inventions of the Other*, vol. 1 (Stanford University Press 2007), 175sq.

12. My interpretation goes further than Judith Butler's, who describes the constitutive act as the claim that "*This will be law*" or, more emphatically, "*This is now the law.*" Butler, "Critique, Coercion, and Sacred Life," 202. In Butler's terminology I would say that the claim is that "*This will always have been the law.*"

13. See Mircea Eliade, *The Myth of the Eternal Return*, especially the chap. "The Terror of History."

14. Note that I am quoting Arendt's definition of ideology here. See Hannah Arendt, *The Origins of Totalitarianism* (Harcourt Brace Jovanovich, 1973), 469.

15. Lefort borrows this notion of "society without history" from Hegel. Lefort, "The Question of Democracy," in *Democracy and Political Theory*, trans. David Macey (University of Minnesota Press, 1988), 16. See on non-historicity also Raoul Girardet, *Mythes et mythologies politiques* (Seuil, 1986), 101 and 129. The non-historicity of mythological society can also be expressed in cyclical terms of the eternal return, as Eliade does. See Mircea Eliade, *The Myth of the Eternal Return*.

16. Oliver Marchart, *Post-Foundational Political Thought: Political Difference in Nancy, Lefort, Badiou and Laclau* (Edinburgh University Press, 2007).

17. Contrary to the translation of Nancy's seminal work *La communauté désoeuvrée* as *The Inoperative Community*, I have chosen to translate *désoeuvrement* more literally as "unworking" rather than "inoperativity," or, for that matter "idleness" or "undoing," in order to keep its (critical) resonance with the poetics of the "work" central to the theoretical angle of the present book.

Chapter 1

1. Apart from *The Literary Absolute*, Nancy's early texts on German Romanticism include Jean Paul's translation "Sur le Witz" (with Anne-Marie Lang), *Poetics* 15 (1973); "Le dialogue des genres" (with Philippe Lacoue-Labarthe), *Poétique* 21 (1975); "Menstruum Universale," *SubStance* 21 (1976) (republished in *Expectation: Philosophy, Literature*, 2017); and the translation of Brentano, "Entretien sur le romantisme" (with Anne-Marie Lang and Philippe Lacoue-Labarthe), *Po&sie* 8 (1979). See for a collection of Nancy's texts on or inspired by Romanticism the collection *Expectation: Philosophy, Literature*.

2. For a contextualization of Nancy thought and writing style within the Romantic tradition see my "Jean-Luc Nancy: A Romantic Philosopher? On Romance, Love and Literature," *Angelaki: Journal of the Theoretical Humanities* 26, no. 3–4 (2021): 113–25; and Ginette Michaud, "Jean-Luc Nancy's *Expectation*: Rephrasing 'Philoliterature,'" in *Understanding Nancy, Understanding Modernism*, ed. Cosmin Toma (Bloomsbury, 2023), 17–38.

3. See, for example, Mircea Eliade, *The Myth of the Eternal Return*; and Claude Lefort, "The Question of Democracy." Both underline the fact that it is a question here of societies that believe themselves a-historical, non-contingent, and eternal.

4. Ferdinand Tönnies, *Community and Society*, trans. Charles P. Loomis (Dover, 2002).

5. Despite this delineation, the group of Jena Romantics remains extremely heterogeneous—including philosophers, philologists, writers, and poets—and commentators are far from agreeing on who belongs to it. A very broad definition of its composition would include Friedrich Schiller, Dorothea (Schlegel-)Veith, Caroline (Schlegel-/Schelling-)Böhmer, Karl Gustav von Brinckmann, August Ludwig, Friedrich Daniel Ernst Schleiermacher, August Ferdinand Bernhardi, August Wilhelm Schlegel, Friedrich Schlegel, Ludwig Tieck, Friedrich Wilhelm Joseph Schelling, Friedrich Hölderlin, and Novalis (born Friedrich Leopold von Hardenberg). Although the journal *Athenaeum* was founded and largely edited by the Schlegel brothers, it was the product of the intellectual exchange of the brothers with their future wives Dorothea Veith and Caroline Böhmer, Schelling (who married Caroline after her divorce from August-Wilhelm Schlegel), Schleiermacher, Tieck, and Novalis. The Romantic ideal of an organic intellectual community thus seems to have been partly inspired by this circle of friends. Shortly after the publication of the fifteenth and last volume of the journal, the Jena movement dissolved.

6. On the formation of forms, see also the work of Nancy's former student Juan-Manuel Garrido, *La formation des forms* (Galilée, 2008).

7. See also Manfred Frank, *The Philosophical Foundations of Early German Romanticism*, trans. Elizabeth Millán-Zaibert (State University of New York Press, 2004) and Frank's lectures on new mythology in *Der Kommende Gott* (Suhrkamp, 1982).

8. The *Systematic Program* is not the first call for a new mythology. Following the decomposition of the German kingdom at the end of the eighteenth century, Herder, Schiller, and Goethe were already arguing that a powerful myth might be needed to unite the people.

9. "The Oldest Systematic Program of German Idealism (1797)," trans. Diana I. Behler, in *Philosophy of German Idealism: Fichte, Jacobi and Schelling*, ed. Ernst Behler (Continuum, 2003), 161–63, translation slightly modified. See also Jean-Luc Nancy and Philippe Lacoue-Labarthe, *L'Absolu littéraire*, 53–4. In the French edition of *The Literary Absolute*, Jean-Luc Nancy and Philippe Lacoue-Labarthe included their own translations of "The Oldest Systematic Program" as well as of all the *Athenaeum* fragments. Since Nancy and Lacoue-Labarthe translated these texts themselves (with the collaboration of Anne-Marie Lang) and presented them as a key part of their study, the French translations can be taken as an integral part of their analysis.

10. According to some, the first two italicized words of the *Systematic Program*—*"An Ethics"*—are not the last words of the previous sentence, but the title of the entire text. This will of course give an even greater role to ethics. See Franz Rozenzweig, "Das älteste Systemprogramm des deutschen Idealismus: Ein handschriftlicher Fund," *Sitzungsberichte der Heidelberger der Akademie der Wissenschaften* (1917), 84.

11. See Immanuel Kant, Preface and §4 and §5 of *Critique of Practical Reason*, trans. Mary Gregor (Cambridge University Press, 2015).

12. Manfred Frank, *Der kommende Gott*, 156. In his detailed reading of the *Systematic Program*, Frank puts a strong emphasis on the *finality* [*Zweckmäßigkeit*] proper to the system of ideas. According to this Kantian reading, in which Frank repeatedly refers to Habermas, to act according to ideas is to act according to a rationality of ends [*zweckrationalen Handeln*]. See Manfred Frank, *Der kommende Gott*, 153–87. If, in my reading, I emphasize the *creativity* of the act of reason rather than its finality, it is not only because the *Systematic Program* itself does not pay much attention to finality, but also because it is in the emphasis on the creativity of the act of reason that I believe the *Romantic* significance of the program lies, and thus also the significance of the Romantic heritage present in Nancy's thought.

13. See Frank, *Der kommende Gott*, 158.

14. See also Friedrich Voßkühler, *Kunst als Mythos der Moderne* (Königshausen & Neumann Verlag, 2004), 15. See for the Kantian heritage of the notion of organism also Frank, *Der kommende Gott*, 160sq.

15. It should be noted, however, that Kant understands the state as a machine, but distinguishes between two forms of state-machine, namely the despotic one, governed by a single and absolute will, like a "hand-mill," and the organic one, governed democratically. See Immanuel Kant, *Critique of the Power of Judgment*, §58.

16. The values of unity and legality propagated here seem to reveal a sympathy for the republic, which obviously does not correspond well to the abolition

of the idea of the state as such. As we shall see, it is perhaps rather a question of thinking *differently* about the state.

17. Martin Heidegger, *Schelling's Treatise on the Essence of Human Freedom*, trans. Joan Stambaugh (Ohio University Press, 1985), 29.

18. To quote Nancy more extensively: "One could say that worldhood is the *symbolization* of the world, the way in which the world symbolizes itself with itself, in which it articulates itself by making a circulation of meaning possible without reference to another world. Our task today is nothing less than the task of creating a form or a symbolization of the world" (*CW* 53/59). By the formula "symbolization of the world" Nancy associates himself in a sense with this Romantic appeal, as we shall see.

19. Frank, *Der kommende Gott*, 190. It is surprising that, apart from Frank, almost none of the commentators on the *Systematic Program*, including Nancy and Lacoue-Labarthe, have drawn attention to this last sentence, the meaning of which, it seems to me, is not at all obvious.

20. Friedrich Schlegel, *Gespräch über die Poesie, in Kritische Friedrich-Schlegel-Ausgabe*. Vol. 1, *Kritische Neuausgabe*, Bd. 2 (1967), 284–90. Schlegel's *Gespräch über die Poesie* first appeared in the journal *Athenaeum* in 1800 and consists of four parts: "Epochen der Dichtkunst," "Rede über die Mythologie," "Brief über den Roman," and "Versuch über den verschiedenen Styl in Goethes früheren und späteren Werken." A selection of this text appeared in English translation in *Dialogue on Poetry and Literary Aphorisms*, trans. Ernst Behler and Roman Struc (Pennsylvania State University Press, 1968). Nancy and Lacoue-Labarthe included their own French translation of the four parts in *L'Absolu littéraire*. Here, English translations are mine, with reference to Nancy's and Lacoue-Labarthe's French translation. I come back to this issue of the "signs" and "hints." In this same *Dialogue on Poetry*, Friedrich Schlegel uses the word "heaven" as a synonym for new mythology and indicates (by the mouth of a character probably referring to Schelling) that contemporary poetry lacks "a mother earth, a heaven," that is to say a unifying place which he names later "mythology" (*AL* 310). Attributing divine qualities to the creative spirit, like the author of the *Systematic Program* does, was not at all unusual at the time and is done in a large number of texts dating from the same period, such as Novalis's *Christianity or Europe* (1799), Schleiermacher's *On Religion* (also 1799), and the seminars Schelling gave from 1802 to 1805 in Jena, published posthumously under the title *The Philosophy of Art*.

21. The hypothesis of an *internal* ambiguity in Romantic thought has been revealed especially in the twentieth and twenty-first centuries, among others thanks to Nancy. Nevertheless, even among the defenders of this hypothesis, there is a lack of consensus as to whether the Jena Romantics themselves ever intended to emphasize this internal tension, or whether they presented it *in spite of themselves*.

22. The term "aesthetic" coined by Alexander Gottlieb Baumgarten (*Aesthetica* 1750) also aroused the suspicion of the Jena Romantics. See, for example, *Critical Fragments*, 40.

23. See among others David Carroll, *Paraesthetics: Foucault, Lyotard, Derrida* (Methuen, 1987); and Jay M. Bernstein, *The Fate of Art: Aesthetic Alienation from Kant to Derrida and Adorno* (Pennsylvania State University Press, 1992).

24. See Jean-François Lyotard, *Heidegger and "the Jews,"* trans. Andreas Michael and Mark S. Roberts (Minnesota University Press, 1990).

25. See Alain Badiou, *Handbook of Inaesthetics*, trans. Alberto Toscano (Stanford University Press, 2004); and Mehdi Belhaj Kacem, *Inésthétique et mimésis: Badiou, Lacoue-Labarthe et la question de l'art* (Lignes, 2010).

26. See Krzysztof Ziarek, "Reproducing History: Benjamin and Heidegger on the Work of Art in Modernity," in *The Historicity of Experience: Modernity, the Avant-Garde, and the Event* (Northwestern University Press, 2001), 36–37; and Jacques Rancière, *Aesthetics and its Discontents* (Polity Press, 2009).

27. In 1796, Chamfort had published his *Pensées, maximes, anecdotes, dialogues*, translated into German a year later by August Wilhelm Schlegel. Before him, Pascal and Montaigne, among others, had already written in fragments.

28. Charles LeBlanc et al. suggest that the fragmentary nature of Romantic texts was initially unintentional, and that it was only over time that it developed into a poetic principle. This development is even historically locatable: from 1795 to 1796, Novalis and Friedrich Schlegel exchanged fragmentary texts that served only as brief notations for other texts. From 1798 to 1799, the fragment was to become a specific genre, among others in *Athenaeum*, and only then was it indicated as a method of writing. See LeBlanc et al., *La forme poétique du monde* (Galilée, 2008), 364–65.

29. The collection of fragments published in the journal *Athenaeum*—translated by Nancy and Lacoue-Labarthe in *L'Absolu littéraire*—is divided into three. The first set, called *Critical Fragments*, concerns the fragments published by Friedrich Schlegel in the journal *Lyceum* before the foundation of the journal *Athenaeum*. They were then published in the second issue of *Athenaeum*. The second set, simply called *Athenaeum Fragments*, was also published in the second issue of the journal and consists largely of anonymous fragments. The third set consists of *Ideas* by Friedrich Schlegel and was published in the penultimate issue of the *Athenaeum*. Although these last fragments are really fragmentary—and much shorter and more concise than the fragments of the first and second type—Friedrich Schlegel did not want to call them "fragments." Apparently, August Wilhelm Schlegel, having had problems with this notion from the beginning, finally convinced his brother to give up this term. The three sets of fragments are included in *Friedrich Schlegel's Lucinde and the Fragments*, trans. Peter Firhow (University of Minnesota Press, 1971). I refer to the fragments of the three sets, in text, respectively as *Crit.*, *Ath.*, and *Id.*, followed by the number of the fragment. In addition to the fragments, the journal *Athenaeum* also contains sonnets, letters, and essays, of which Friedrich Schlegel's *Dialogue on Poetry* is most interesting for us.

30. Nancy and Lacoue-Labarthe have tried to trace the authors of all 451 *Athenaeum Fragments*. According to them, a large part was written by August Wilhelm Schlegel. Schleiermacher also made an important contribution. The provenance of most of the other fragments, however, remains doubtful or unknown. See Jean-Luc Nancy and Philippe Lacoue-Labarthe, *L'Absolu littéraire*, 178. For an index, see also Friedrich Schlegel, *Kritische Ausgabe*, Bd. 2 (Schönigh, 1967).

31. For an analysis of this organicity both in Jena Romanticism and in Nancy's work, see Stefanie Heine, "*Fort-Pflanzung*: The Literary Absolute's Botanic Afterlife," in Toma, *Understanding Nancy, Understanding Modernism*, 39–56.

32. This is the basic structure of *Bildung*.

33. Nancy himself pursues this path in his own poetics as I will demonstrate in chapter 3. Nancy and Lacoue-Labarthe seem to unite in the word *poiesis* or *poiein* the two sides of the Greek opposition between *poiesis* and *praxis*. The produced work is only the realization of the act itself.

34. For a more elaborate analysis of the role of the notion of the "individual" in German Romanticism, see my "Reconsidering Literary Autonomy: From an Individual Toward a Relational Paradigm," *Journal of the History of Ideas* 76, no. 2 (2015), 167–90; and the chapter "The Romantic Paradigm" in my *Literature, Autonomy and Commitment* (Bloomsbury, 2019).

35. I am grateful to Antonia Birnbaum for suggesting this line of thought.

36. The logic of the hedgehog is perhaps less paradoxical if one realizes that it consists in what Schopenhauer, and then Freud, have indicated under the name of the *dilemma of the hedgehog*. This dilemma, above all psychological or sociological, indicates the paradoxical situation of the hedgehog, who, in order to unite with his fellow creatures, has to injure himself, getting scratched by the pines of other hedgehogs. See also *Ath.* 336.

37. For this chemical nature see also *Ath.* 366 and 426.

38. See, among others, Nancy's translation of Jean Paul, "Sur le Witz" (with Anne-Marie Lang) and "Menstruum Universale." For a more elaborate analysis of the role of *Witz* in Nancy's thought see my "Jean-Luc Nancy: A Romantic Philosopher?"; and Jean-Michel Rabaté's "'Wet the Ropes!' Poetics of Sense, from Paul Valéry to Jean-Luc Nancy," in *Expectation: Philosophy, Literature*, by Jean-Luc Nancy, trans. Robert Bononno (Fordham University Press, 2017), ix–xx.

39. The phenomenon of *Witz* is closely related to the Kantian *genius*. For Kant, the genial work of art results from a free play between understanding and the imagination that reconciles nature and freedom. It is therefore not surprising that Friedrich Schlegel calls *Witz* a "fragmentary genius" (*Crit.* 9) evoking "the categorical imperative of genius" (*Crit.* 16).

40. Nancy and Lacoue-Labarthe quote from Schlegel's "Brief über den Roman" (part of his *Dialogue on Poetry*). This idea of the novel is of course one of the reasons why the members of the Jena group are called the "Romantics," although

the Jena Romantics themselves never characterized themselves as such. Originally, the word "Romanticism" referred to the *Romance* languages, which, compared to clerical Latin, were perceived as vulgar. Romantic literature therefore refers to books written in these languages and can be compared to so-called romance novels. It is only in the eighteenth century, with the theoretical reflections discussed here, that Romanticism acquired a positive meaning. See for a detailed list of the meanings of the word, Friedrich Schlegel, *Kritische Ausgabe*, Bd. 2, liii.

41. There is disagreement about what character refers to whom, because the opinions voiced can often be attributed to several people. According to Nancy and Lacoue-Labarthe, Lotario is modeled on Novalis, Ludoviko on Schelling, Marcus on Tieck, Andrea on August Wilhelm Schlegel, Amalia on Caroline, Camilla on Dorothea, and Antonio, finally, on Friedrich Schlegel himself. See Jean-Luc Nancy and Philippe Lacoue-Labarthe, *The Literary Absolute*, 273 and 371: 1n. In his translation of Friedrich Schlegel's work, Hans Eichner indicates that Antonio can refer not only to Friedrich Schlegel, but also to Schleiermacher. According to him, the characters of Ludoviko, Andrea, Marcus, and Lotario also proclaim the ideas of the author himself. See *Kritische Ausgabe*, Bd. 2, lxxxviii.

42. Moreover, Nancy and Lacoue-Labarthe note that a last, fifth, exposition is announced several times in the dialogue, namely a poem by "Lotario," but that it is missing in the text. According to them, it is precisely this lack that deliberately destabilizes the magnum opus that this text claims to be.

43. It should be noted that the *Systematic Program* also spoke of the wings that the author wanted to give to "our physics." There too, these wings turned out to be the wings of poetic reflection.

44. For this hypothesis see also Walter Benjamin, *The Concept of Art Criticism in German Romanticism* (1920) where he describes Romantic poetry as "the center of reflection." See also Béatrice Hanssen and Andrew Benjamin, eds., *Walter Benjamin and Romanticism* (Continuum 2002); and especially Lacoue-Labarthe's "Introduction to Walter Benjamin's *The Concept of Art Criticism in German Romanticism*," 9–18.

45. I will return to the tautegorical nature of poetry in chapter 2.

46. Friedrich Schlegel also devoted an essay to the question of the republic, namely "Essay on the Concept of Republicanism Occasioned by the Kantian Tract 'Perpetual Peace'" (1796), in *The Early Political Writings of the German Romantics*, ed. Frederic C. Beiser (Cambridge University Press, 1996), 93–112. Although during his time in Jena, Friedrich Schlegel was convinced that this ideal could be realized in the republic, later, living in Vienna and being introduced to the Austrian court, he believes it should be realized in the monarchy. The same applies to Novalis, who initially favored the republic, but later, under the spell of King Frederick William III of Prussia, his wife Louisa von Mecklenburg-Strelitz and the unifying force of this symbolic couple, became favorable to the monarchy. See also his essay "Faith and Love" (1798) in the same volume.

47. Fichte's ideas also played a considerable role. See Johann Gottlieb Fichte, *Beiträge zur Berichtigung der Urteile des Publikums über die französische Revolution* (1793).

48. LeBlanc et al., *La forme poétique du monde*, 687sq.

49. LeBlanc et al., *La forme poétique du monde*, 689.

50. I have already drawn attention to this clue in the last sentence of the *Systematic Program*, where it was stated that the new mythology needs a superior spirit sent from heaven who offers us the possibility.

51. Frederick C. Beiser, "Friedrich Schlegel: The Mysterious Romantic," in *The Romantic Imperative: The Concept of Early German Romanticism* (Harvard University Press, 2003), 123–26.

52. This structure—which is that of the will to system—is also demonstrated by Jean-Luc Nancy, "The Forgetting of Philosophy," in *The Gravity of Thought*, trans. François Raffoul and Gregory Recco (Humanities Press, 1997). I will come back to the will to system in chapter 2.

53. See also Martin Heidegger, *Nietzsche*, vol. 1, *The Will to Power as Art*, trans. David Farrell Krell (Harper & Row, 1991), 211–20; and Philippe Lacoue-Labarthe, "Sublime Truth," in *Of the Sublime: Presence in Question*, ed. Jean-François Courtine, trans. Jeffrey S. Librett (State University of New York Press, 1993), 76.

54. Heidegger, *Schelling's Treatise on the Essence of Human Freedom*, 32.

55. Heidegger, *Schelling's Treatise on the Essence of Human Freedom*, 95, my emphasis.

56. This idea will return in another form in chapter 4 with the notion of "authoredness" borrowed from Derek Attridge, where I will suggest that what holds the whole together is not the transcendental subject, but the self *presupposed* in the literary text

57. In his text, Heidegger presents Schelling, along with Fichte and Hegel, as a representative of German idealism. See Heidegger, *Schelling's Treatise on the Essence of Human Freedom*, 16.

58. See also Marc Redfield, "Romanticism, *Bildung* and the Literary Absolute," in *Lessons of Romanticism*, eds. Thomas Pfau and Robert Gleckner (Duke University Press, 1989). Redfield questions Nancy's and Lacoue-Labarthe's reduction of the poetic act to an act of the subject. According to him, the reflexive character of Romantic poetry already entails that it is to a large extent non-subjective, as Benjamin's "The Concept of Criticism in German Romanticism" has demonstrated.

59. That *The Literary Absolute* ends with the same conclusion that Blanchot drew in his text on the *Athenaeum* does not imply, however, that Nancy and Lacoue-Labarthe's book is but a repetition of Blanchot's text, as is suggested by Simon Critchley: "[I]t is difficult to see in what respect *The Literary Absolute* conceptually surpasses Blanchot's short and limpid 1964 essay 'The *Athenaeum*.'" Critchley, *Very Little . . . Almost Nothing: Death, Philosophy, Literature* (Routledge, 1997), 116–17.

To overstate the case, according to Critchley, Nancy, and Lacoue-Labarthe have simply replaced Blanchot's term "ambiguity" with the term "equivocation." To my mind, however, Critchley passes over the fact that the conclusion of *The Literary Absolute* is itself a "lost" element in the ensemble of this study, which is otherwise a reading quite *contrary* to Blanchot's as I have tried to show.

60. Maurice Blanchot, "The Athenaeum," in *The Infinite Conversation*, trans. Susan Hanson (University of Minnesota Press, 1993), 357. The third part of this book, entitled "The Absence of the Book (the neutral, the fragmentary)" of which the text "The *Athenaeum*" is a part, deals entirely with the Romantic theory of the work.

61. Blanchot, "The Athenaeum," 353.

62. Blanchot, "The Athenaeum," 401.

63. Blanchot, "The Essential Solitude," in *The Space of Literature*, trans. Ann Smock (University of Nebraska Press, 1982), 22–23, my emphasis.

Chapter 2

1. The notion of myth plays an important role in many of Nancy's works, but especially in *Dis-Enclosure: The Deconstruction of Christianity I* (2008 [2005]); in Nancy's introduction called "Un commencement" to Philippe Lacoue-Labarthe's *L'"Allégorie"* (2006); and in *Proprement dit: Entretien sur le mythe* (with Mathilde Girard, 2015). It was also central in "The Nazi Myth" (with Philippe Lacoue-Labarthe, 1990) and *The Inoperative Community* (1991 [1986]).

2. Raoul Girardet, *Mythes et mythologies politiques*, 13. See from the point of view of the historian, among others Mircea Eliade, *The Myth of the Eternal Return*, 3–6.

3. Aristotle, *Poetics*, chap. 10: "Plot."

4. This is why the translation of the Aristotelian *muthos* by "story" would be less accurate. A translation of *muthos* by "story" would conceal the important distinction Aristotle makes between historiography and poetics, and the importance he attributes, in the latter case, to the aspect of *composition* or *knotting* in the poetic act. Another possibility would be to translate *muthos* as "fable" as among others Jacques Rancière has done in *Film Fables*. Strictly speaking, yet another translation of *muthos* is possible, a translation that opens a completely different track, i.e., the Heideggerian translation of *muthos* by *Sage*. Although Heidegger himself did not develop a theory of myth, Lacoue-Labarthe is right to assert that Heidegger's *Sage* is nothing other than a translation of the word *muthos*. Philippe Lacoue-Labarthe, *Heidegger and the Politics of Poetry*, trans. Jeff Fort (University of Illinois Press, 2007), 33sq. With this word *Sage*, Heidegger wanted to emphasize the "apophantic" nature (*phanis* = to reveal; *apo* = from) of language, that is the fact that language is the showing of being itself. Nancy's interpretation of myth is very close to what

Heidegger meant by the term *Sage*, which he uses as a synonym for *Dichtung*. Although I recognize the merits of the translation as "fable" or "*Sage*," I prefer the conventional translation by "plot" in order to bring Nancy's poetics more clearly in discussion with the political-metaphysical tradition of thinking about the "Work."

5. For an analysis of the political dimension of the "future anterior" in Nancy's and Blanchot's work see my "Le moment révolutionnaire: Sur la temporalité de la littérature chez Maurice Blanchot et Jean-Luc Nancy," *Revue Philosophique de Louvain* 115, no. 4 (2017): 675–90.

6. Aristotle, *Poetics*, chap. 5: "Universality."

7. Aristotle, *Poetics*, chap. 5: "Universality." Aristotle's coupling of the necessary and the probable leads to the conclusion that the two are different modalities of the same law. Indeed, the probable turns out to be what happens most frequently and presents itself in relation to a particular case as a general law: The necessary and the probably thus represent, the first from the objective angle of statistical reality, the other from the subjective angle of expectation, an attenuated form of necessity. It is, moreover, because of the *plot* that tragedy differs from (and exceeds) epic. While epic only describes the succession of events, tragedy describes why they necessarily or probably happen.

8. It is worth noting, however, that in the field of literature, attempts have been made for some time now to move beyond plotted stories, beyond the order of the plausible and the necessary, in order to express the particular, the unique, and the singular.

9. Benedict Anderson, *Imagined Communities: Reflections on the Origin and Spread of Nationalism* (Verso, 2006), 11.

10. Anderson, *Imagined Communities*, 12. See also Jonathan Culler, "Anderson and the Novel," *Diacritics* 29, no. 4 (1999): 20–39.

11. The characteristic reversal within the tragic plot is the reversal of happiness into misfortune. See Aristotle, *Poetics*, chap. 6: "Reversal."

12. See Aristotle, *Poetics*, chap. 4: "The Ranking Completed." I am already interpreting here this extremely complex passage of Aristotle's on *opsis*, referring in part to the exchange of letters between Nancy and Lacoue-Labarthe on this subject. Although Nancy's and Lacoue-Labarthe's intuitions about the role of *opsis* diverge, they agree that what is at issue here is that by which something is presented (be it in a visible and spectacular way, or soberly, that is, only audibly in reading aloud). See Philippe Lacoue-Labarthe and Jean-Luc Nancy, "Scene: An Exchange of Letters," in *Beyond Representation: Philosophy and Poetic Imagination*, ed. Ricard Eldridge (Cambridge University Press, 1996), 273–300; and Nancy's reiteration of this exchange in *Proprement dit* (especially 24 and 42sq). The notion of *parergon* is not used by Lacoue-Labarthe or Nancy, but borrowed from Jacques Derrida's *The Truth in Painting*, trans. Geoffrey Bennington and Ian McLeod (University of Chicago Press, 1987). For an analysis of the ambiguous status of the scene in

Aristotle's *Poetics,* see Esa Kirkkopelto, *Le théâtre de l'expérience: Contributions à la théorie de la scène* (Presses Universitaires Paris-Sorbonne, 2008), 75–88. I will come back to this theme of the "scene" in Nancy's work in the next section.

13. See Jean-Luc Nancy's work: "The greatness of the Greeks—according to the modern age of mythology—is to have lived in intimacy with such [mythical] speech, and to have founded their *logos* in it: they are the ones for whom *muthos* and *logos* 'are the same'" (*IC* 49/123). Nancy cites Heidegger; see also *PD* 74sq.

14. This is why Nancy and Lacoue-Labarthe, in "Scene: An Exchange of Letters," decide, albeit hesitantly, to translate *opsis* by "scene," or also by "primitive scene" or by "archi-theater," emphasizing the fact *that* there is enunciation, even prior to anything that is generally called "spectacle."

15. Something similar seems to be proposed by Lacoue-Labarthe in his essay "*Il faut,*" where he, too, distinguishes between the mythological and the mythical, indicating that the mythical implies the "collapse" of myth or mythology because it is the simple, sober and literal naming of things. Philippe Lacoue-Labarthe, *Heidegger: The Politics of Poetry,* 52. An outline of the resonances between Lacoue-Labarthe's and Nancy's views would require yet another book, and is therefore deliberately avoided in this study. Nevertheless, it should be pointed out that there is often a great proximity between the two thinkers, especially as regards the subjects treated here, and especially in this text by Lacoue-Labarthe.

16. Let us not forget that the Jena Romantics also based themselves on the model of the Copernican revolution, stressing that we should no longer seek external support, a fulcrum outside the earth, but that we should be our own center.

17. For Nancy's view on monotheism, see the two parts of his "Deconstruction of Christianity," *Dis-Enclosure* and *Adoration.* For an elaborate analysis of this theme in Nancy's work see *Re-Treating Religion: Deconstructing Christianity with Jean-Luc Nancy,* eds. Alena Alexandrova et al. (Fordham University Press, 2012).

18. See also: "It is not a question of reviving religion, not even the one that Kant wanted to hold 'within the limits of reason alone.' It is, however, a question of opening mere reason to the limitlessness that constitutes its truth" (*DE* 1).

19. See also: "The world of myth, and of polytheism, is the world of given presupposition" (*CW* 71/94).

20. See *DE* 57 and 189sq. For an elaborate analysis of Nancy's view on demythologization and its traces in language see my "A Demythologized Prayer? Religion, Myth and Poetry in Nancy's Deconstruction of Christianity," *International Journal in Philosophy and Theology* 69, no. 3 (2008); and my "'My God, My God, Why Hast Thou Forsaken Me?' Demythologized Prayer, or the Poetic Invocation of God," in Alexandrova et al., *Re-Treating Religion,* 189–202.

21. Gauchet speaks of a "religion of the exit from religion." Marcel Gauchet, *The Disenchantment of the World,* trans. Oscar Burge (Princeton University Press, 1999). This claim—that Christianity is a religion that understands itself less and

less religiously, and thus *deconstructs itself*—forms the starting point of Nancy's deconstruction of Christianity.

22. Of course, the question of myth is also central in "The Nazi Myth" (with Philippe Lacoue-Labarthe, 1991). This text continues the central theses developed by Nancy in "Myth Interrupted." Because the latter text is both a text with a more general scope *and* a text by Nancy alone, I have decided to take "Myth Interrupted" and not "The Nazi Myth" as my point of reference. In 1986, the original version of "Myth Interrupted" was published, together with the original versions of "The Inoperative Community" and " 'Literary Communism' " in the French collection *La communauté désoeuvrée*, later translated as *The Inoperative Community* and expanded with the texts "Shattered Love" and "Of Divine Places." *L'"Allégorie"* brings together poetic texts by Philippe Lacoue-Labarthe, composed between 1967 and 1968.

23. In "Myth Interrupted," Nancy does not really distinguish between the "mythological" and the "mythical" and the different uses of the word "myth" accumulate. In my own terminology, however, I believe I endorse his interpretation, especially when reading his early texts in the light of more recent ones.

24. Manfred Frank, *Der Kommende Gott*, 211.

25. Raoul Girardet, "L'Age d'or," in *Mythes et mythologies politiques*.

26. Friedrich Schlegel, qtd. in Manfred Frank, *Der Kommende Gott*, 219.

27. Indeed, many of today's philosophical projects (starting with those inspired by Nancy's thought) are dedicated to the search for a *beyond* of politics, or to a *different* politics that renounces precisely such a mythological logic.

28. I will come back to this issue in the final chapter, where I explore the possibility of a *nonpolitical* counter-"power."

29. This is an important distinction, even if it is not without ambiguity. I will develop it further in chapter 4.

30. For Nancy's move away from politics see also his "Is Everything Political? (simple note)," *Actuel Marx* 28 (2000); "Politics and Beyond," interview by Philip Armstrong and Jason E. Smith, *Diacritics* 43, no. 4 (2015): 90–108; or Jean-Luc Nancy and Philippe Lacoue-Labarthe, eds., *Retreating the Political* (1997).

31. The Jena Romantics say something similar about the Ancients.

32. See Schelling, *Philosophy of Mythology* (1857) and *Philosophy of Revelation* (1858).

33. Schelling also opposes allegory to *symbol*. I will return to this on page 148 of chapter 3.

34. This is why the notion of *onomatopoeia* plays a very similar role in Nancy's thinking as the notion of *tautegory*. See page 146 of chapter 3. The notion of tautegory is not unrelated to what Lacoue-Labarthe indicates by the notions of "prosaism" and "literalization." Philippe Lacoue-Labarthe, *Heidegger and the Politics of Poetry*.

35. One unavoidable consequence is that Nancy thus also renounces the postulation of radical otherness, as found, for example, in Levinas's *Otherwise than*

Being, or Beyond Essence or, rather, he inscribes this "otherwise" *in* Being itself. The Copernican revolution instigated by Nancy implies not only that being must be conceived beyond essence, but also that there is *only* being, and therefore no "otherwise" than being. See Jean-Luc Nancy, *Being Singular Plural*: "[W]hat he [Levinas, AvR] understands as 'otherwise than Being' is a matter of understanding 'the ownmost of Being,' exactly because it is a matter of thinking being-with rather than the opposition between the other and Being" (*BSP* 199n37/51n1). As Nancy makes clear elsewhere in this book, it is thus not a matter of thinking the Other, that is, the *aliud*, the *alius* or the *alienus*, but of thinking the *alter* (*BSP* 11/29–30).

36. The fact that there is nothing to bring to the sensible is also the reason why there is nothing to allegorize. Hence the quotation marks in the title of the collection *L'"Allégorie"*.

37. The "Nothing is more misleading" is a quote from one of Lacoue-Labarthe's prose poems.

38. Paul Valéry, cited in Harry Levin, "Some Meanings of Myth," in *Myth and Mythmaking*, ed. Henry Alexander Murray (Beacon Press, 1969).

39. *L'Oubli de la philosophie* ["The Forgetting of Philosophy"] is without doubt one of Nancy's most underrated texts. Compared to *The Inoperative Community*, *The Sense of the World* or *Being Singular Plural*—all of which were conceived as key works—this one seems to have largely escaped the attention of commentators. Significantly, *L'Oubli de la philosophie* was not translated into English until 1997, and moreover combined with the 1991 text "Le poids d'une pensée" ["The Weight of a Thought"] into a volume with a different title, *The Gravity of Thought*. Nevertheless, it is, in my opinion, in *L'Oubli de la philosophie* that Nancy sketches most patiently what motivates his philosophical project.

40. The core distinction made by Nancy between the French *sense* and *signification*, is translated by François Raffoul and Gregory Recco as that between "meaning" and "signification," respectively. Although there is much to be said in favor of this translation, I have chosen to consistently translate the French *sens* with "sense" and the French *signification* with "signification," a choice that is consistent with most other translations of Nancy's work. Though "sense" is less current in English than "meaning" and might lead to slightly awkward phrases, the notion "sense" is closer to the kind of shift that Nancy tries to mark in thinking about "meaning" in general, namely a shift from meaning to be captured in a determinable signification to a more sensual, sensible form of meaning.

41. Page 81sq of this chapter will clarify the fact that this exposure is always a plural exposure, i.e., one shared with others. In "The Forgetting of Philosophy" this is concisely summarized in the section title *"Le sens, c'est nous"* ["We Are Meaning"].

42. This also implies, of course, that Nancy turns away from hermeneutics. Since he focuses on sense and not on signification, there is nothing to interpret. In "The Forgetting of Philosophy," however, he proposes to redefine the notion of

"hermeneutics," indicating that hermeneutics is not the *interpretation* or *translation* of a message, but primarily its *transmission*. The "object" of hermeneutics is thus not, in principle, *what* is said, but the *passage* of a message (*GT* 58sq/88sq).

43. Aristotle, *Poetics*, chap. 4: "Component parts." As already mentioned, I translate *opsis* not as "spectacle" but as "scene," in order to stay as close as possible to Nancy's interpretation of Aristotle, especially in "Scene: An Exchange of Letters" ("Sc," with Philippe Lacoue-Labarthe). I am also taking cue from Esa Kirkkopelto's *Le théâtre de l'expérience: Contributions à la théorie de la scène*, which, in turn, draws on Lacoue-Labarthe's work. In this particular quote, I translate from the French version of Aristotle's *Poetics* used by Nancy, i.e., *La poétique*, trans. Roselyne Dupont-Roc and Jean Lallot (Seuil, 1980). In several translations, including the English translation used here so far, this last sentence is modified or not even translated to avoid any contradiction with what follows. Dupont-Roc and Lallot have, to my mind rightly, chosen to keep the original ambivalence of Aristotle's *Poetics*.

44. Aristotle, *Poetics*, chap. 4: "The ranking completed." Translation modified.

45. The pressing question that nevertheless arises "and weighs heavily on Aristotle's discourse," as Esa Kirkkopelto puts it, is how to decide between good and bad *opsis*, between necessary staging and the spectacular. Kirkkopelto, *Le théâtre de l'expérience*, 85.

46. Chapter 3 will be entirely devoted to this ontological poetics. In another register, we could also say that we are dealing here with an ontological *eroticism*, notably developed by Nancy in *Sexistence*. On Nancy's ontological eroticism see also Boyan Manchev, "Le désir du monde: Jean-Luc Nancy et l'Éros ontologique," *Les Cahiers philosophiques de Strasbourg* 42 (2017). On the relationship between the erotic and the poetic in Nancy see my "Jean-Luc Nancy: A Romantic Philosopher?"

47. See the conversation between Jacques Derrida and Jean-Luc Nancy, published in *For Strasbourg*, where Derrida says: "Yesterday, I was both delighted and in full agreement when Catherine Malabou stated, for example, that the word *existence* does not have the status of a 'fundamental' concept in my work. She is right. . . . My wonderment stems from the fact that Jean-Luc, in a lucid way and without simply returning to the past, took charge so as to treat in a deconstructive, post-deconstructive, manner, these great themes, these great concepts, these great problems, that have as names *sense, world, creation, freedom, community*, and so on. . . . Well, before all these great philosophical concepts of the tradition that Jean-Luc revisits in an incomparable way, I have always had the reflex to flee, as if, upon first contact, indeed merely upon *naming* these concepts, I were going to find myself, like a fly, with my legs glued: captured, paralyzed, held hostage, trapped by a program" ("Res" 58–59/167–68). See also Ian James, *The Fragmentary Demand: An Introduction to the Philosophy of Jean-Luc Nancy* (Stanford University Press, 2006), 148: "Unlike Derrida, Nancy is a philosopher who is happy to deploy the language of ontology or of being without evoking its erasure. Unlike Derrida,

one could argue, he is happy to be a philosopher of existence, of the material and the concrete. . . . Where for Derrida the word being is placed under erasure, for Nancy being or existence is 'exscribed.' "

48. Of course, we might ask whether we should still be talking about an "ontology," as Nancy himself does: "Should one still speak of ontology? You [the interviewer Boyan Manchev, AvR] understand that because of what I said above, I hesitate. I have always talked a lot about ontology until now, trying to make explicit as best I can what I have just tried once again to make clearer; there is no 'ontology' except in a deconstruction of what we old moderns are ready to understand under 'logic' and under 'onto' " ("Mét" 81).

49. See Jean-Luc Nancy: "Nothing behind and, in consequence; everything up front. Everything pushed forward, but a forward with no backward, not even a phenomenon, not even a surface" (*FT* 116/50). Nancy plays with the name Derrida and the words *derrière* and *da*. The "superficiality" of his ontology leads obviously to the main role attributed to the sense of *touch*. See on the role of touch in Nancy's work also Derrida, *On Touching: Jean-Luc Nancy*, trans. Christine Irizarry (Stanford University Press, 2005).

50. Ginette Michaud, " 'La bouche touche' (une 'scène primitive' du corps nancyen)," *Cosa volante: Le désir des arts dans la pensée de Jean-Luc Nancy* (Hermann, 2013). On the theme of the mouth in Nancy's work, see also Andrea Gyenge, "*Fabula, Bucca, Humanitas:* On *Ego Sum*," in *Understanding Nancy, Understanding Modernism*, ed. Cosmin Toma (Bloomsbury, 2023), 88–108.

51. For a more elaborate comparison of Nancy and Derrida's positions, see page 154sq of chapter 3.

52. Catherine Malabou, "Pierre aime les horranges. Lévinas-Sartre-Nancy: Une approche du fantastique en philosophie," in *Sens en tous sens: Autour des travaux de Jean-Luc Nancy*, eds. Francis Guibal and Jean-Clet Martin (Galilée, 2004), 39–57.

53. Malabou, "Pierre aime les horranges," 51. In her text, Malabou places this "ontologization" or "realization" of the ontological difference under the denominator of the "fantastic."

54. It is true, of course, that being is a major category in Sartre's work, especially in *Being and Nothingness*, but his distancing from Heidegger consists precisely in the replacement of the Heideggerian categories of "Being" and "beings" by those of "existence" and "existents." The same holds for Levinas, as is illustrated by his titles *From Existence to Existents* and *Otherwise than Being, or Beyond Essence*.

55. As Nancy states in an interview with Janicaud: "It took me some time to discover that *différance* (with an a) was at work in the body of the ontological difference." Interview of June 23, *Heidegger en France II: Entretiens*. See also Jean-Luc Nancy, "L'être, l'étant, selon Derrida," *Magazine littéraire* 9, hors-série: *Martin Heidegger. Les chemins d'une pensée* (2006). That Derrida is by no means unconcerned about Nancy's attempt to understand the ontico-ontological difference as *différance* is illustrated by the following remark: "[A]re not the meaning or truth of

Being, the determination of *différance* as the ontico-ontological difference, difference thought within horizon of the question of Being, still intrametaphysical effects of *différance*?" Jacques Derrida, *Margins of Philosophy*, trans. Alan Bass (University of Chicago Press, 1982), 22. However, the later Derrida also seems to tend towards the presupposition of a heterogeneity previous to that of language, for example in *Specters of Marx*: "[T]he heterogeneity of a *pre*, which, to be sure, means what comes before me, before any present, thus before any past present, but also what, for that very reason, comes from the future or as future: as the very coming of the event. The necessary disjointure . . . is indeed here that of the present—and by the same token, the very condition of the present and of the presence of the present." Derrida, *Specters of Marx*, trans Peggy Kamuf (Routledge, 1994), 33. On this possible shift in Derrida, see, amongst others, Gert-Jan van der Heiden, *Disclosure and Displacement: Truth and Language in the Work of Heidegger, Ricoeur and Derrida* (Duquesne University Press, 2008), 204sq.

56. In *On Touching: Jean-Luc Nancy*, Derrida characterizes Nancy's thought indeed as "post-deconstructive." See also page 163 of chapter 3.

57. I refer to Friedrich Schlegel's phrase quoted by Nancy and Lacoue-Labarthe in *L'Absolu littéraire* (*AL* 314) and referred to in chapter 1.

58. Nancy also describes myth as "the essential scene of all scenes, of all scenography or staging" (*IC* 44/112).

59. I return to the role of self-deception on page 216 of chapter 4.

60. James, *The Fragmentary Demand*, 198.

61. Nancy already distances himself from a (merely) *political* understanding of communism in "The Compearance": "Communism is an ontological proposition; it is not a political option" ("TC" 378/69). See also "Finite and Infinite Democracy" ("FD" 69sq/88sq). For a comparison between Badiou's and Nancy's views on communism, see, e.g., Daniel McDow, "The Exigency of Thinking: Alain Badiou and Jean-Luc Nancy on 'Communism,'" in *Jean-Luc Nancy: Justice, Legality and World*, ed. Benjamin Hutchens (Bloomsbury, 2012), 204–24.

62. See also Jean-Luc Nancy, *After Fukushima: The Equivalence of Catastrophes*, trans. Charlotte Mandell (Fordham University Press, 2015).

63. See Karl Marx: "[T]he social character of labor is evidently not effected by the labor of the individual assuming the abstract form of universal labor or his product assuming the form of a universal equivalent. [It is clearly community,] on which this mode of production is based, [that] prevents the labor of an individual from becoming private labor and his product the private product of a separate individual; *it [is community that] causes individual labor to appear*" (qtd. in *IC* 74/183–84, my emphasis). For Jean-Luc Nancy's relation to Marx, see, among others, "Literary Communism" (*IC*), "The Compearance," and "Is Everything Political? (a brief remark)."

64. Nancy and Lacoue-Labarthe quote Hannah Arendt from *The Origins of Totalitarianism*. The *Centre de recherches philosophiques sur le politique* was founded

by Lacoue-Labarthe and Nancy in 1980 and culminated in two edited volumes: *Rejouer le politique* (1981) and *Le retrait du politique* (1983, translated as *Retreating the Political*). Among the participants were Jacob Rogozinski, Claude Lefort, Jacques Rancière, Denis Kambouchner, and Philippe Soulez.

65. Nancy refers to Sartre's characterization of Marxism as the unsurpassable horizon of our time.

66. A similar claim is advanced by Philippe Lacoue-Labarthe in *Heidegger, Art, and Politics: The Fiction of the Political.*

67. This last aspect of course distinguishes Nazi mythology from the new mythology of Jena Romanticism, which would be realized above all in *language*, not in blood. Later, in *Proprement dit*, Nancy criticized himself by suggesting that he and Lacoue-Labarthe, in "The Nazi Myth," had not sufficiently realized the "heavily voluntary" and "stupid" or even limpid fabrication of the Aryan myth (*PD* 52).

68. See also Alain Badiou, *The Meaning of Sarkozy* (Verso, 2008); and André Glucksmann and Raphaël Glucksmann, *Mai 68 expliqué à Nicolas Sarkozy* (Denoël, 2008).

69. See among others Claude Lefort, *The Political Forms of Modern Society: Bureaucracy, Democracy, Totalitarianism* (1986); and Jacques Rancière, *Hatred of Democracy* (2005). It is important to note that Nancy does not, in this, associate himself with Lefort's idea of democracy as characterized by an "empty place" of power. According to Nancy, the political should no longer be understood as a *place*, whether occupied or not, but as a spacing, a dynamic in which sovereignty is not concentrated, but always remains *in the act*.

70. How difficult it is to conceive of this position is clear from the large number of commentators who tried in vain to reintegrate Nancy's thought into a political program. See, among others, Todd May, *Reconsidering Difference* (Pennsylvania State University Press, 1997); and Andrew Norris, "Jean-Luc Nancy and the Myth of the Common," *Constellations* 7, no. 2 (2000): 272–95.

71. See also Jean-Luc Nancy, "Is Everything Political?"

72. Jean-Luc Nancy and Philippe Lacoue-Labarthe, "Ouverture," in *Rejouer le politique*, eds. Jean-Luc Nancy and Philippe Lacoue-Labarthe, Cahiers du Centre de recherches philosophiques sur le politique (Galilée, 1981), 28.

73. For elaborate analyses of Nancy's social ontology see, amongst others, Marie-Eve Morin, "Ontology," *Jean-Luc Nancy* (Polity, 2012); and Ignaas Devisch, *Jean-Luc Nancy and the Question of Community* (Bloomsbury, 2013).

74. The title chosen by the editors of the English collection of Nancy's "aesthetic" texts, *The Birth to Presence* (Stanford University Press, 1993), is therefore, in my opinion, very appropriate.

75. Christopher Fynsk, "Foreword: Experiences of Finitude," in Jean-Luc Nancy, *The Inoperative Community* (University of Minnesota Press, 1991), xii. See also Ian James, who speaks of a "total rethinking of Heidegger by way of Heidegger." James, *The Fragmentary Demand*, 103.

76. See for a comparative study on plurality in Badiou and Nancy, Gert-Jan van der Heiden, *Ontology After Ontology: Plurality, Event and Contingency in Contemporary Philosophy* (Duquesne University Press, 2015).

77. See Martin Heidegger, *Being and Time*, §9.

78. Also in "Sharing Voices" and *The Experience of Freedom* Nancy explicitly opposes this humanization or anthropologization of *Dasein*. In *The Banality of Heidegger*, he clearly discerns the disastrous result of this tendency in Heidegger's thought: "Heidegger's *beyng* could be described as that which exceeds being-a-self or being as self. But the Heidegger of these *Notebooks* has led it astray into a kind of Self that is the enemy of every other" (*BH* 39/40).

79. And not to forget the stones. Contrary to Heidegger, Nancy does not want to make a distinction between the existence of *Dasein* and that of Heidegger's famous "stone": "[I]t isn't clear that a stone wouldn't be a body as *we* are a body" (*C* 123/108; see also *SW* 55–56/101–2 and *EF* 157/201).

80. On the theme of intrusion also see *The Intruder* where Nancy indicates that the condition of possibility of a body is to be infiltrated by intruders. This applies not only to those who need a heart transplant to survive—like Jean-Luc Nancy himself—but to us all. I will return to the question of corporality on page 143sq in chapter 3.

81. See Georges Bataille, *Inner Experience*, trans. Stuart Kendall (State University of New York Press, 2014), 100: "[E]xistence *is communication*." Echoes of this claim can be found in Nancy's work: "Being *is* communication" (*BSP* 28/47) and, inversely, "communication *is* being" (*BSP* 93/116).

82. Bataille, *Inner Experience*, 47. According to Nancy, Bataille, for all his merits, has not sufficiently thought community. The reason for this would be that Bataille aims only at the ecstasy of the *subject*, and not that of the community itself. In this sense, community remains outside the subject. Bataille thus maintains the opposition between interiority and exteriority, which must be eliminated if we are to think about the primacy of community. Nancy's approach consists in a radical renunciation of thinking about the subject in favor of thinking about community on an ontological level.

83. In retrospect, this book can be seen as the culmination point of a journey leading, among others, from *Corpus* (2000) and "The 'There Is' of Sexual Relation" (2001) to *Coming* (with Adèle Van Reeth, 2014), *Immortelle finitude: Sexualité et philosophie* (with Mehdi Belhaj Kacem, 2020) and *The Deconstruction of Sex* (with Irving Goh, 2021). In English, some of Nancy's writings on sexuality have been collected in *Corpus II: Writings on Sexuality* (Fordham University Press, 2013). For an analysis of the theme of sex, desire and language in Nancy's work see Boyan Manchev, "Le désir du monde: Jean-Luc Nancy et l'Éros ontologique" and my "Jean-Luc Nancy, A Romantic Philosopher?"

84. Commentators who have noticed this friction are, among others, Robert Bernasconi, "On Deconstructing Nostalgia for Community Within the West: The

Debate Between Nancy and Blanchot," *Research in Phenomenology* 23 (1993): 7; Daniel Hoolsema, "The Echo of an Impossible Future in *The Literary Absolute*," *MLN* 119 (2004): 848; Christopher Fynsk, Foreword in Jean-Luc Nancy, *The Inoperative Community*, 154: 23n; and Leslie Hill, *Nancy, Blanchot: A Serious Controversy* (Rowman & Littlefield, 2018). Although they find Nancy's use of Blanchot's term *désoeuvrement* odd, with the exception of Hill these commentators do not really explain *why* Nancy deviates from it, deliberately or otherwise. For an elaborate answer to this question, see my "La comunidad en obra: Jean-Luc Nancy en diálogo con Maurice Blanchot; Un desacuerdo tácito," *Pleyade* 4, no. 1 (2011): 79–103; and my "*Noli Me Operare*: Reading Nancy (Re)Reading Blanchot" (with Andreas Noyer), in *Understanding Nancy, Understanding Modernism*, ed. Cosmin Toma (Bloomsbury, 2023), 131–46. In chapter 4, I will return to the difference between Blanchot's and Nancy's poetics.

85. Maurice Blanchot, *The Infinite Conversation*, trans. Susan Hanson (University of Minnesota Press, 1993), 357, emphasis added.

86. It is thus necessary, as Paul Davies also remarks, to acknowledge the *oeuvre* in the *dés-oeuvre-ment*. Paul Davies, "The Work and the Absence of Work," in *Maurice Blanchot: The Demand of Writing*, ed. Christopher Bailey Gill (Routledge, 1996).

87. For a more detailed retrospective analysis, see Nancy's *The Disavowed Community*.

88. See Jean-Luc Nancy, *The Disavowed Community*. See on these themes also Jean-Luc Nancy, "The Neutral, Neutralization of the Neutral" (*EPL*) and "Quand le sens ne fait plus monde," remarks collected by Michaël Fœssel, Olivier Mongin, and Jean-Loup Thébaud. *Esprit* 403, no. 3–4 (2014): 27–46. Nancy's interpretation has been contested. See in particular Leslie Hill, *Nancy, Blanchot: A Serious Controversy* (2018). See also my "La comunidad en obra: Jean-Luc Nancy en diálogo con Maurice Blanchot; Un desacuerdo tácito" (2011); several contributions to the *Cahiers Maurice Blanchot* no. 3 (2014) and no. 4 (2015/2016); and Kevin Hart, "The Aggrieved Community: Nancy and Blanchot in Dialogue," *Journal for Continental Philosophy of Religion* 1, no. 1 (2019): 27–42. For an overview of the whole discussion see my "*Noli Me Operare*: Reading Nancy (Re)Reading Blanchot" (2023, with Andreas Noyer).

89. Maurice Blanchot, *The Unavowable Community*, trans. Pierre Joris (Station Hill Press, 1988), 56. I will come back to the issue of attestation in chapter 4. We might say that the divergence between Nancy and Blanchot comes down to their interpretation of Bataille's remark, quoted by Nancy in *The Inoperative Community*, that "language alone indicates, at the limit, the sovereign moment where it is no longer current" (*IC* 25/66, qtd. from Bataille's *Eroticism*). What is at stake here, is the interpretation of the word *language*. For Blanchot, as for Bataille, this remark is, it seems to me, another way of saying that "in order to be silent, it is necessary to speak," that is, the moment when language is *no longer current*, no longer communicates, can only be reached by language. However, Nancy seems to propose

another reading of this remark, one based on a rather Heideggerian interpretation of the word language as *Auslegung*, i.e., as the disposition of things themselves. This disposition, which is always at the limit, is a gesture that prevents it from being put into course or circulation, because it is, in principle, dis-position, going astray. I will return to Nancy's conception of language as *Auslegung* on page 129 in chapter 3.

90. Blanchot, *The Unavowable Community*, 30.

91. Blanchot, *The Unavowable Community*, 14, my emphasis.

92. Blanchot, *The Unavowable Community*, 32, my emphasis.

93. Blanchot, *The Unavowable Community*, 30.

94. Blanchot, *The Unavowable Community*, 32.

95. Blanchot, *The Unavowable Community*, 20, my emphasis. Blanchot joins Bataille here—and defends him against Nancy's attack. In all his projects, but especially in *Acéphale*, Bataille, according to Blanchot, seems to have set himself the goal of *creating* a "negative community," that is, the community of those who have nothing in common, a goal that, according to Bataille, can only be achieved in its failure.

96. As argued by Blanchot in the following passage: "'Without project' . . . it had to be understood not as the totality of social forces, ready to make particular political decisions, but as their instinctive refusal to accept any power, their absolute mistrust in identifying with a power to which they would delegate themselves, thus mistrust in their *declaration of impotence*." Blanchot *The Unavowable Community*, 30–31. The idea of the explicit refusal of power in the form of a *staging* will play a central role in chapter 4.

97. See Jean-Luc Nancy in *The Inoperative Community*: "For Bataille, community was first and finally the community of lovers . . . Bataille's lovers present in many respects the figure of a communion" (*IC* 36/89–90).

98. Blanchot, *The Unavowable Community*, 49.

99. Blanchot, *The Unavowable Community*, 49.

100. See also: "the *lie* of that union which always takes place by not taking place." Blanchot, *The Unavowable Community*, 49. In chapter 4 I will return to the lie as one of the main figures of the deliberate powerlessness or unworking.

101. Blanchot also speaks of *apathy* as the main feature of Duras's community of lovers. Blanchot, *The Unavowable Community*, 49.

102. Blanchot, *The Unavowable Community*, 31. See also Blanchot on Bataille's *Acéphale*: "that attempt made with utmost seriousness, ready to give his whole life to it, left in his memory but the derisiveness of the illusory. And this is exactly one of the traits of the community, when that community dissolves itself, giving the impression of never having been able to exist, even when it did exist." Blanchot, *The Unavowable Community*, 88.

103. According to the crucial formula in "Literature and the Right to Death": "The word gives me being, but it gives it me *deprived of being*." *The Work of Fire*, trans. Charlotte Mandell (Stanford University Press, 1995), 322, my emphasis, trans. modified.

104. Or as Nancy recalls in *The Inoperative Community*: "As Schelling put it, myth is 'tautegorical' (borrowing the word from Coleridge) and not 'allegorical,' that is, it says nothing other than itself" (*IC* 49/124).

105. This is probably also why Bataille says that the absence of myth is itself "a kind of myth" (qtd. in *IC* 47/148). According to Nancy, is it not a matter of filling the thought of myth with a "more human" content, as Thomas Mann proposes: "Thomas Mann wrote to Kcrenyi in 1941: 'Myth must be taken away from intellectual fascism, and its function diverted in a human direction.' This, it seems to me, is exactly what must not be done: the function of myth, as such, cannot be inversed. *It must be interrupted*" (*IC* 160n6/116n37, my emphasis).

106. Ernesto Laclau, "Politics and the Limits of Modernity," *Universal Abandon? The Politics of Postmodernism* (University of Minnesota Press, 1988), 81.

107. Hans Vaihinger, *The Philosophy of "As If,"* trans. C. K. Ogden (Barnes and Noble, 1968).

108. See for an elaborate analysis my "De legitimatie van het alsof: De 'marginale' discussie tussen Lyotard en Nancy" (with Joris van Gorkom), *Tijdschrift voor Filosofie* 67, no. 3 (2005): 527–46.

109. The French text "Lapsus judicii" was first published in *Communications* 26 (1977). A second version, with postscript, was published in *L'Impératif catégorique* (1983), the English translation of the latter is included in *A Finite Thinking*. The French text "Dies irae" was published in Jacques Derrida et al., *La faculté de juger* (Minuit, 1985) and published in English as a separate booklet *Dies Irae* (University of Westminster Press, 2019). The French text "Dies illa" was first published in Dolorès Lyotard et al., eds., *Jean-François Lyotard: L'Exercice du différend* (2001). A second version of this text appeared under the title "De la creation" in *La création du monde ou la mondialisation*, translated in English as "Of Creation" (*CW*).

110. See also Benjamin Hutchens, "Philosophy as Juris-Fiction: Jean-Luc Nancy and the 'Philosophy of Right,'" *Journal for Cultural Research* 9, no. 2 (2005): 119–31.

111. See Jean-François Lyotard, "Introduction à une étude du politique selon Kant," in Jean-Luc Nancy and Philippe Lacoue-Labarthe, eds., *Rejouer le politique*, 95: 3n. Republished and translated in *Enthusiasm* (Stanford University Press, 2009), 71n3: "Considered in this fashion [in the way that Kant's emphasis on judgment is understood as an indication of a reversal of the problematic of origin, AvR], the 'as ifs' in their heterogeneity are not substituted for the ontological phrase whose synthesis would be lacking (*lapsus*), they are 'passages' between 'areas' of legitimacy."

112. See in particular Jean-Luc Nancy, "Lapsus judicii" (*FT*).

113. At first glance, Nancy's reading of the Kantian "as if" is diametrically opposed to Derrida's reading. For Derrida, the Kantian notion of the "as if" is the introduction of literature into the law. Jacques Derrida, "Before the Law," *Acts of Literature*, ed. Derek Attridge (Routledge, 1992), 190. For Nancy, on the contrary, the Kantian "as if" amounts to the introduction of a law into literature. This issue requires further reflection.

114. "[A]lthough we can hear the *fiction* in Latin discourse, this has, in principle, nothing to do with the values that are normally associated with that word—the mixed values of the Greek *poiesis, mimesis,* and *phantasia* which come together in German *Dichtung*" (*FT* 157). Obviously, this remark should not be interpreted too strictly, as elsewhere Nancy often uses the words *poiesis, poetry,* and *Dichtung* in the sense here attributed to *fiction* in Latin discourse. In chapter 4, I will return to this issue and explore the possibility of a "deregulating" fiction.

115. On the death of God in relation to the workings of language in Nancy, see also my " 'My God, My God, Why Hast Thou Forsaken Me?' Demythologized Prayer, or the Poetic Invocation of God."

116. "Myth communicates the common, the *being-common* of what it reveals or of what it recites. At the same time, therefore, as each of its revelations, it reveals community to itself, and it founds it. It is always the myth of community, that is to say that it is always the myth of communion—the unique voice of many" (*PD* 128).

117. By this formulation, I am referring to Nancy's text "Sharing Voices," in *Transforming the Hermeneutic Context: From Nietzsche to Nancy*, ed. and trans. Gayle Ormiston and Alan Schrift (State University of New York Press, 1990), 211–59.

118. In a similar vein, the naked, available body of the woman paralyzes the protagonist of Marguerite Duras's *The Malady of Death*.

Chapter 3

1. All in all, Nancy has published over fifteen books, most of them untranslated, in collaboration with artists. Many of Nancy's essays discussing the works of specific artists are collected in *Multiple Arts: The Muses II*. For Nancy on art in general, see, amongst others, *The Literary Absolute* (with Philippe Lacoue-Labarthe); *The Muses*; *The Ground of the Image*; *The Pleasure in Drawing*; *Portrait*; and *Expectation: Philosophy, Literature*.

2. As Nancy has it in one of his main books on art, *The Muses*: "Generally, it is in the end a matter of initiating a deconstruction of religion, first of all the religion or religions of 'creation' " (*M* 112n63/64–65n2).

3. The only exceptions, to my knowledge, are Martta Heikkilä, *At the Limits of Presentation: Coming-into-Presence and its Aesthetic Relevance in Jean-Luc Nancy's Philosophy* (2008); and Ginette Michaud, *Cosa volante: Le désir des arts dans la pensée de Jean-Luc Nancy* (2013). There are a few edited volumes that also focus on the role of art in Nancy's work: Ignaas Devisch, Peter De Graeve, and Joost Beerten, eds., *Jean-Luc Nancy: De kunst van het denken* (2007); Carrie Giunta and Adrienne Janus, eds., *Nancy and Visual Culture* (2016); and Cosmin Toma, ed., *Understanding Nancy, Understanding Modernism* (2023). In *The Fragmentary Demand*, Ian James devotes a chapter to the question of art, as does Marie-Eve Morin in her book *Jean-Luc Nancy*. In other monographs on Nancy's work, the question of art is simply absent.

4. Since art, in Nancy's view, is a specific form of *doing*, rather than a matter of the beautiful, I speak here, for want of a better term, of a *poetics* rather than an *aesthetics*.

5. Martta Heikkilä, *At the Limits of Presentation: Coming-into-Presence and Its Aesthetic Relevance in Jean-Luc Nancy's Philosophy* (Peter Lang, 2008).

6. Ian James, *The Fragmentary Demand: An Introduction to the Philosophy of Jean-Luc Nancy* (Stanford University Press, 2006), 204.

7. See Esa Kirkkopelto, *Le théâtre de l'expérience: Contributions à la théorie de la scène* (Presses Universitaires Paris-Sorbonne, 2008), 76sq.

8. Denis Guénoun, *Le théâtre est-il nécessaire?*, 23, qtd. in Kirkkopelto, *Le théâtre de l'expérience*, 76.

9. In "Sharing Voices" Nancy speaks of an "active, creative or re-creative *mimesis*" ("SV" 239/71). See also *Proprement dit*, 24 and 42sq.

10. Kirkkopelto, *Le théâtre de l'expérience*, 34.

11. For instance in *The Sense of the World*, where Nancy describes sense as a matter of "[w]riting—and thus also necessarily its *poetry*, which is to say, first of all, its *praxis*" (*SW* 121/187). See also *Being Singular Plural*: "That is why we do not make an economy out of an ontology, but it is also why this ontology must be both an *ethos* and a *praxis*, identically" (*BSP* 65/87).

12. A similar conclusion is drawn by Ian James in the last chapter—entitled "Conclusion: On the Creation of the World"—of his book on Nancy. James, *The Fragmentary Demand*, 232. See on the importance of the concept of "creation" also Boyan Manchev, "Ontology of Creation: The Onto-Aesthetics of Jean-Luc Nancy," in *Re-Treating Religion: Deconstructing Christianity with Jean-Luc Nancy*, eds. Alena Alexandrova et al., 261–74; and my "Intermezzo" to the same volume: "Creation, Myth, Sense, *Poiesis*," 185–88.

13. For a more elaborate analysis of the role and emergence of this issue in Nancy's work, see my "Deconstruction, Dis-Enclosure and Christianity" (with Ignaas Devisch), *International Journal in Philosophy and Theology* 69, no. 3 (2008): 249–63; and my "Re-Opening the Question of Religion: Dis-Enclosure of Religion and Modernity in the Philosophy of Jean-Luc Nancy" (with Alena Alexandrova, Ignaas Devisch, and Laurens ten Kate), in Alexandrova et al., *Re-Treating Religion*, 22–40.

14. In this respect, the titles given by Nancy to his books and texts are often telling. To name a few: *The Birth to Presence*, "In statu nascendi" (*BP*) and *La naissance des seins* [The Birth of Breasts]. In this last book, Nancy plays with the kinship of the French word *sein* [breast] and the German *Sein* [Being].

15. See the interview of June 23, 2000, with Dominique Janicaud, in *Heidegger en France II: Entretiens*, ed. Dominique Janicaud (Albin Michel, 2001).

16. Hegel's aesthetics is analyzed by Nancy in several texts, among which: "Why Are There Several Arts and Not Just One?," "The Girl Who Succeeds the Muses," and "The Vestige of Art," all collected in *The Muses*. For a general introduction into Nancy's aesthetics, see also my "De kunst is dood, leve de kunsten! Over

de enkelvoudigheid en meervoudigheid van kunst," *Algemeen Nederlands Tijdschrift voor Wijsbegeerte* 105, no. 3 (2013): 173–82.

17. See Catherine Malabou, *The Future of Hegel: Plasticity, Temporality and Dialectic*, trans. Lisabeth During (Routledge, 2005).

18. I will return to this intrinsic plurality on page 133.

19. Georg Wilhelm Friedrich Hegel, *Aesthetics: Lectures on Fine Art*, trans. T. M. Knox, 2 vols. (Clarendon Press, 1975), 8, my emphasis.

20. Hegel, *Aesthetics: Lectures on Fine Art*, 45, my emphasis.

21. Hegel, *Aesthetics: Lectures on Fine Art*, 9.

22. On this topic, see also Philippe Lacoue-Labarthe, "The Unpresentable," in *The Subject of Philosophy*, trans. Thoms Trezise et al. (University of Minnesota Press, 1993).

23. It is in this same vein that Nancy introduces the neologism *"Dardichtung"* (*DS* 93/103).

24. Jacques Derrida, *The Truth in Painting*, trans. Geoffrey Bennington and Ian McLeod (University of Chicago Press, 1987).

25. In this respect, the transformation of the French subtitle "littérature *et* philosophie into the English "Philosophy, Literature" is telling.

26. Hegel, *Aesthetics: Lectures on Fine Art*, 165.

27. See also Jeffrey S. Librett, "Introduction: The Subject of the Portrait," in *Portrait*, by Jean-Luc Nancy, trans. Sarah Clift and Simon Sparks (Fordham University Press, 2018), 1–10.

28. Nancy has devoted several books to the art of portraiture: *Le portrait (dans le décor)* (1999); *Le regard du portrait* (2001 [2000], with Federico Ferrari); *L'Iconographie de l'auteur* (2005); *À plus d'un titre—Jacques Derrida: Sur un portrait de Valerio Adami* (2007); and *L'Autre portrait* (2013), as well as several articles. Some of these texts are included in the English volume *Portrait* (2018).

29. In the English translation of Nancy's *Le regard du portrait*, the French *regard* is translated as "look." I have chosen to consistently translate *regard* with the slightly more accurate "gaze," also because this term occurs frequently in many other translations of Nancy's texts.

30. The gaze should be associated not only with touch (as the opposite of grasping), but also with listening (as the opposite of understanding). See Jean-Luc Nancy, *Listening*, trans. Charlotte Mandell (Fordham University Press, 2007).

31. For a detailed analysis of the influence of the Heideggerian *Dichtung* on Nancy's thought, see also Heikkilä, *At the Limits of Presentation*, 92sq.

32. Martin Heidegger, "The Origin of the Work of Art," in *Off the Beaten Track*, trans. Julian Young and Kenneth Haynes (Cambridge University Press, 2002), 19.

33. One could say that Nancy thus links the two extremes analyzed by Heidegger and Hannah Arendt: on the one hand the finitude of existence resonating in being towards death, on the other hand what Arendt calls the "natality" of existence, the emergence of new events.

34. A third aspect is the *anthropocentrism* of Heidegger's thought, already mentioned in the previous chapter. In terms of poetics, this anthropocentrism is demonstrated by the idea that language is always *human* language. Nancy departs from this idea by attempting to think of language as something pre-human or beyond human. See also page 154sq.

35. "But," adds Nancy with great benevolence, "Heidegger also does *not* reproduce these gestures to the extent that he actually says nothing of the sort, or at least does not say it 'in truth'" (*BP* 94).

36. See Ciprian Mihali, *Sensus communis: Pentru o hermeneutica a cotidianului* (Editura Paralela, 2001) with a preface by Jean-Luc Nancy; and Ignaas Devisch, *Jean-Luc Nancy and the Question of Community* (Bloomsbury, 2013), 181–87.

37. For an interesting account of these relations in everyday city life, see Nancy's essay on Los Angeles: *La ville au loin* (Mille et une nuits, 1999).

38. James, *The Fragmentary Demand*, 144.

39. James, *The Fragmentary Demand*, 147. As I will demonstrate on page 161sq, there is, however, a crucial difference between Derrida's and Nancy's views on "writing."

40. This articulation is often indicated by Nancy using the figure of the *mouth*. It is the opening of the mouth, as we saw in chapter 2, that opens into being-there, and as the opening of this being-there that is the condition of possibility of speech. The figure of the mouth recurs frequently in Nancy's work. (See, e.g., "SV" 223/36; *IC* 30/77; *ES* 18/36–37.) I quote from *Ego Sum*: "[T]he Subject had to have itself opened up. In this empty opening—eye and mouth, as we will see, seeing mouth, speaking eye, muted eye, blind mouth—the Subject is *depos(it)ed*, in all senses of the word. The Subject lays down [*dépose*] its certainty on the edge of this open gap." With regard to the theme of the mouth, there is an interesting resonance between Nancy's thinking and the analysis given by Daniel Heller-Roazen in *Echolalies* on the phenomenon of "aglossostomography," that is to say, of a mouth which speaks without a tongue, a phenomenon described in a seventeenth-century pamphlet. Daniel Heller-Roazen, *Echolalias: On the Forgetting of Language* (Zone Books, 2008). I will return to the figure of the mouth in the context of Nancy's reading of Baudelaire's poem "The Desire to Paint" and in the context of the figure of the voice, on page 154.

41. Even literally so by On Kawara in his painting "Location," showing the latitude and the longitude of the exact place of the painting with regard to the equator: "LAT. 31°25'N LONG. 8°41ᴱ."

42. With the exception of Ginette Michaud's *Cosa volante*, the works that (partially) address the question of art in Nancy's work focus explicitly only on the influence of Hegel and Heidegger, and only sporadically name the Romantic legacy. See for an investigation of this legacy in Nancy's work also my "Jean-Luc Nancy: A Romantic Philosopher?"

43. See James, *The Fragmentary Demand*, 202.

44. In French, the two most systematic essays on Hölderlin's poetry are included in the small volume *Résistance de la poésie* (William Blake, 1997). The first one of these essay's, "The Poet's Calculation" is published in English in *Expectation: Philosophy, Literature*, the second one, "Taking Account of Poetry," in *The Muses II*.

45. Jacques Derrida on http://www.editions-galilee.fr/. In addition to tracing the thematic thread of touch in Nancy's thought, and the places where it is tied up or untied from the philosophical tradition, Derrida also highlights the risks of a thinking that starts from the primacy of touch. See page 162 of this chapter. As I intend to demonstrate in the present book, the thematic thread of myth—that is, of touching *language*—forms a path that largely avoids these risks.

46. For an analysis of this metaphysics of vision and its confrontation in twentieth-century French philosophy, with which Nancy is partially associated, see Martin Jay, *Downcast Eyes: The Denigration of Vision in Twentieth-Century French Thought* (University of California Press, 1994).

47. See especially *Corpus* for an implicit discussion of Nancy with Merleau-Ponty.

48. Nancy argues that the desire to paint can perhaps also be understood as "a capitalization of consumption" (*BP* 379/309).

49. Undoubtedly, Nancy enters into an implicit discussion with Lyotard on the theme of the "unrepresentable." As we saw on page 102sq of chapter 2, this discussion between the two was made explicit in their writings on the notion of the "as if."

50. Or as Nancy puts it: "This also means that that which in faith could previously open the world in itself to its *own outside* (and not to some world-behind-the-worlds, to some heaven or hell) closes up and shrivels into a self-serving management of the world" (*DE* 2/10, my emphasis).

51. In line with his renunciation of the connection between ecstasy and poetics, Nancy also renounces the connection between ecstasy and community, as he emphasizes in his discussion with Bataille and Blanchot. See *The Inoperative Community*"; "The Confronted Community"; *Maurice Blanchot: Passion Politique*; and *The Disavowed Community*.

52. For a meticulous reading of "The Sublime Offering" see Heikkilä, *At the Limits of Presentation*, 280–93.

53. Perhaps, as Nancy stresses, this is what Kant himself failed to see, repeating that the sublime would be "indirect presentation" or "negative presentation." For, whether indirect or negative, it is still a presentation.

54. The final formulation "The body is the unity of a being outside of itself" echoes the original French subtitle of Nancy's essay "Borborygmi," i.e., "*Soi de soi débordé*."

55. For instance: "[W]hat isn't body is *mass*, or substance in the sense of mass, without extension, without exposition, a point" (*C* 13/110). Perhaps it is fair to say, in the end, that mass and closed signification are one and the same for Nancy. "The mass," he continues, "we can just as well call this spirit itself, spirit taken as

concentration in itself, which we can call, in a still more terrible way, precisely, concentration as such. I need say no more. What concentration in itself means for us today is effectively the annihilation of bodies, the annihilation of the body as extension, of the body of which there are always several" (*C* 13/110).

56. See especially Nancy's text "Exclamations" (*EPL*).

57. The Greek *sum* is equivalent to Latin *cum* and French *com.*

58. For Nancy on the symbol, see also *Being Singular Plural* (50/79sq); and *The Sense of the World* (134sq/206sq). For an analysis of the theme of the symbol in Nancy's thought, see Anne O'Byrne "The God Between," in Alexandrova et al., *Re-Treating Religion*, 215–28.

59. See O'Byrne, "The God Between," 219.

60. Michel Lisse, "Lire, toucher: D'une main à l'autre," in *Paroles, textes et images: Formes et pouvoirs de l'imaginaire*, eds. Jean-François Chassay and Bertrand Gervais (Centre de recherche sur le texte et l'imaginaire, 2008), 151. A more positive interpretation of the role of touch in the act of reading, is offered by Joni Puranen, "Recitative Voice: Reading Silently and Aloud, with Jean-Luc Nancy," *SATS: Northern European Journal of Philosophy* (2023): 1–17.

61. The notion "living sense" is Hölderlin's.

62. It is important to note that by the *touching* dimension of poetry I do not mean that it is necessarily *emotive*, unless we understand this word in its etymological sense of "e-motion," a movement outwards. Indeed, as we have seen, poeticity is the exposure of a material body to the outside world. It is, in other words, this poetic exposure that results in the body touching and being touched. What touches is not a certain emotional quality, but the naked fact that there is sense. On the touching dimension of poetry, see also my "Poésie haptique: Sur l'(ir)réalité du toucher poétique chez Nancy," *Revue philosophique de Louvain* 107, no. 1 (2009): 127–42. For an analysis of the poetic touch in relation to the legacy of Romanticism, see my "Jean-Luc Nancy: A Romantic Philosopher?"

63. Aristotle, *Poetics*, chap. 5: "Magnitude."

64. Ginette Michaud, *Cosa volante*, 102–3.

65. No doubt it is a courage shared with Lacoue-Labarthe, for whom the song is the exemplary "figure" of defiguration. See, for example, Philippe Lacoue-Labarthe, *Le chant des muses* (Bayard, 2005).

66. See especially Jacques Derrida, *Of Grammatoloy*, trans. Gayatri Chakravorty Spivak (Hopkins University Press, 1974).

67. Texts in which these themes play a central role are "Sharing Voices" ("SV"); "Laughter, Presence," "*Vox Clamans in Deserto*" (both *BP*), and *Listening.*

68. See also the following remark: "[B]efore being verbal, 'language' is the following: the extension and simultaneity of the 'with' insofar as it is the *ownmost power* of a body, the propriety of its *touching* another body (or of touching *itself*), which is nothing other than its de-finition as body" (*BSP* 92/116).

69. See especially §54 of Martin Heidegger's *Being and Time*. While in Heidegger's case the voice of consciousness has the effect of removing *Dasein* from the "they," the sharing of voices is in Nancy's case precisely characteristic of the "they."

70. Significantly, Nancy uses the word *langue* instead of *langage* to describe sense. Meaning both "language" and "tongue," *langue* has the same bodily and material meaning as the *mouth* has.

71. See page 128 of the present chapter.

72. This is also emphasized by James: "The interest and originality of Nancy's thinking of sense, body and eco-technics is that it allows this thinking of 'writing' as originary technicity to be thought in terms of concrete embodiment, a situated and worldly existence." James, *The Fragmentary Demand*, 147.

73. Michel Lisse also underlines that the major point of divergence between Nancy and Derrida would reside in the understanding of *différance*: "The most sensitive point [in the discussion between Nancy and Derrida, AvR] might have been Nancy's rapprochement of *différance* and Heidegger's ontic-ontological difference (See Jean-Luc Nancy, 'L'être, l'étant, selon Derrida,' 96). It seems necessary to begin a reading of *différance* by taking the following question into account: is not 'the determination of différance as the ontico-ontological difference . . . still intrametaphysical effects of différance?' (See Jacques Derrida, *Marges de la philosophie*, 1972, 23)." Michel Lisse, "Literary Creation, Creation *ex nihilo*," in Alexandrova et al., *Re-Treating Religion*, 374:n2. One could say, as Pierre Delayin does in his *Derridex*, that "*différance* precedes metaphysics but also overflows the thought of being, for it is *différance* that makes the sense of being possible and not the other way around." He admits that he is thus radicalizing what Derrida introduces only in the form of a question: Is it necessary to understand *différance* on the basis of the meaning of being (i.e., of the Heideggerian ontico-ontological difference), or is it necessary, on the contrary, to understand the meaning of being on the basis of *différance*? To be consulted on www.idixa.net. With Delayin, I would say that Derrida indeed tends towards the latter option, while Nancy develops the former. See on this topic also Ian James, "Differing on Difference," in *Nancy Now*, eds. Verena Andermatt Conley and Irving Goh (Polity Press, 2014), 110–26.

74. Jacques Derrida, *On Touching—Jean-Luc Nancy*, trans. Christine Irizarry (Stanford University Press, 2005), 255. Derrida expresses this concern in the form of a provisional conclusion to a comparison of Nancy's thinking with that of Jean-Louis Chrétien on Christianity: "Indeed, it does seem as if everything in Nancy's thinking about exscription and the syncope leads back toward this spacing (irreducible even in temporalization itself), which Chrétien would reduce to this phenomenon of finitude, and finite flesh that touching assigns to the interval, to mediatizing interposition, and to the 'medium' and 'distance' that spiritual touching (which is infinite, immediate, etc.) will have first of all *elevated*, and *uplifted* and *relieved*. . . . Two ways of thinking substitution, therefore, but two tangential ways—though no doubt

incompatible. It is a rather troubling, even dizzying, duality, and may lead to the temptation—Temptation itself—to substitute one for the other" (261–62).

75. Derrida, *On Touching—Jean-Luc Nancy*, 46, my emphasis.

76. Although Ian James also points out this "startling claim" of Derrida's, he does not say more than that Derrida "maintains a degree of ambivalence or skepticism in relation to Nancy's refiguring of the figure of touch." James, *The Fragmentary Demand*, 118–20.

77. Jacques Derrida, "Salve: Untimely Postscript, for Want of a Final Retouch," in *On Touching—Jean-Luc Nancy*, 300, my emphasis.

78. I will discuss these questions in detail in the last chapter. A concise coverage of this theme can be found in my "Poésie haptique: Sur l'(ir)réalité du toucher poétique chez Nancy."

Chapter 4

1. Claude Lefort, "The Question of Democracy," in *Democracy and Political Theory*, trans. David Macey (University of Minnesota Press, 1988), 16.

2. To simplify further, one could say that these two extremes coincide with the respective positions of Levinas and Deleuze. In her lecture on March 20, 2008, at the conference "Emmanuel Levinas et la philosophie française contemporaine" organized at the Collège International de Philosophie, Catherine Malabou also tried, and in my opinion convincingly, to bring together the thoughts of these two philosophers regarding the theme of the "face." Although she did not refer to Nancy's work, I have the impression that her conclusions are very close to mine.

3. In the end, these are, perhaps, the philosophical systems of Kant and Hegel, respectively: on the one hand that of an empty transcendence, which creates an impassable abyss between nature and freedom, and on the other hand that of an incarnation of the transcendent movement within the logic of reality.

4. As we saw, also for the Jena Romantics the poetry of the poets is conceived as a continuation of the original poetry already present in nature that, as Friedrich Schlegel indicates in a passage already quoted in chapter 1, "palpitates in plants, radiates in light, smiles in the child, sparks in the flower of youth, blazes in the loving heart of women" (Friedrich Schlegel, cited in *AL* 290).

5. Nevertheless, one may wonder whether there is really only reality for Nancy or whether he is only *interested* in reality. An interesting text in this context is Jean-Luc Nancy, "The Deleuzian Fold of Thought," in *The Deleuze Critical Reader*, ed. Paul Patton (Blackwell, 1996), 107–13. In this essay, Nancy attempts to articulate the "uncanny proximity" (107) of his own thought and that of Gilles Deleuze. He indicates that he and Deleuze have the same philosophical intuitions and address similar questions, but that they do so from "two massifs, two continents, two tectonic plates of philosophy" (113) between which there is no

passage. According to Nancy, these two continents are those of the philosophy of the *virtual* and the philosophy of the *real*: "Gilles Deleuze's philosophy is a virtual philosophy . . . designing a universe entirely formed from images, and not only images as high-quality illusions of the real, but rather those that leave no place for the opposition between real and image. The 'virtual' world is a universe of image-effectivity. . . . Conversely, for the other philosophical strain, thought has to do with the real, it plunges into it, even if this means losing itself there. This is the reason why the former places itself under the sign of play or affirmation, the latter under the sign of care and waiting." Or further: "One might say that Deleuze wants to take things after the fold of being. He wants nothing before this fold. And in fact, there is nothing before. In a sense, the fold is being itself." In a sense, this chapter will be an attempt to move from one continent to the other, by showing that these are not mutually exclusive conceptions.

6. In her book on Nancy's philosophy of art, Martta Heikkilä, too, signals "something equivocal" in Nancy's attitude towards concrete works of art. According to her, the equivocation consists in the fact that Nancy, on the one hand, indicates that art is the presentation of the presentation, i.e., presentation of the fact *that* there is presentation, and in this sense something singular and local, but on the other hand describes concrete works of art in general terms: "The question now arises whether Nancy's account is really capable of approaching the works in their singularity and locality. . . . It is no doubt true that Nancy's descriptions of artworks provide accurate insights into the works and show sensitivity in their specific nature and uniqueness—not as representatives of 'painting' or 'photography,' let alone 'art.' But it is also true to say that he cannot avoid referring to a notion of 'art,' even of 'Art,' when, for example, it comes to explicating the artistic nature of presentation. . . . In other words, does an idea of art as presentation of presentation result in doing justice to the alleged 'singular plurality' of art?" See Martta Heikkilä, *At the Limits of Presentation: Coming-into-Presence and Its Aesthetic Relevance in Jean-Luc Nancy's Philosophy* (Peter Lang, 2008), 303–4 and section 4.4 "At the Heart of the Images. Nancy on the Arts." Heikkilä even goes so far as to conclude that the singular plurality of art deconstructs the ontology proposed by Nancy, because art only presents *"some* world, a facet of it"* whereas ontology is always an explanation of the nature of being in general. Although I agree with Heikkilä that there is something equivocal in Nancy's relationship to art, I do not agree with her conclusion. It should be noted that Nancy's ontology is not an ontology in the sense of an explanation of the nature of being in general, and this is because there is, for Nancy, no being *in general*. In my opinion, the difficulty of Nancy's relation to works of art does not lie in a friction between the particularity of the work and the generality of what he says about it, but to anticipate what will follow, in the ontological status of the work of art. If there is an involuntary self-deconstruction of Nancy's thought, I would say that it is perhaps to be found in the inversion of Heikkilä's argument: It is Nancy's ontology that undermines his notion of art.

7. Jacques Rancière, "The Use of Distinctions," in *Dissensus: On Politics and Aesthetics*, trans. Steven Corcoran (Bloomsbury, 2010), 213–26.

8. See Jacques Rancière, *The Politics of Literature* (Polity Press, 2022), 16.

9. Rancière, *Dissensus*, 219.

10. Rancière, *Dissensus*, 215.

11. Rancière, *Dissensus*, 215, my emphasis.

12. Rancière, *Dissensus*, 215.

13. Rancière, *Dissensus*, 215–16. Note the absence of Blanchot and Derrida, among others, from this "scene," an absence that is obviously explained by their avoidance of assigning "evenemential" power to an ontological principle.

14. Rancière, *Dissensus*, 218, my emphasis.

15. I would like to thank Carlos Perez Lopez for pointing me in this direction. As I shall argue, this aleatory and supplementary character of art implies that the "artistic" is not an immanent characteristic of the artistic object or experience. An artwork can only be an artwork, or rather work *as* an artwork, when we conceive it as art, which we may well not do.

16. Rancière, *Dissensus*, 215.

17. What is at stake here is the rupture, in the aesthetic regime of art, of what Rancière calls the ethical regime. See, amongst others, *The Politics of Literature*; *Mute Speech*; and *Aesthesis*.

18. Nancy quotes Rancière's *Mute Speech*, but isolates the phrase from its context, which is the following: "It [literature, AvR] has the misfortune to have only the language of written words at its disposal to stage myths of a writing beyond writing, everywhere inscribed in the flesh of things." Jacques Rancière, *Mute Speech: Literature, Critical Theory, and Politics*, trans. James Swenson (Columbia University Press, 2011), 175. In my view, what Rancière is indicating in this phrase is more or less the opposite of what Nancy is saying, namely that literature can only speak in the language of written words and for this reason can never be identified with a writing beyond writing inscribed in the flesh of things.

19. In his book on the "politics of resistance," Critchley expresses a similar reservation with regard to authors who understand politics primarily as an ontology: "If we are doing politics we cannot and should not pin our hopes on any ontology." Simon Critchley, *Infinitely Demanding: Ethics of Commitment, Politics of Resistance* (Verso, 2007), 105.

20. See Françoise Proust, *De la résistance* (Cerf, 1997).

21. This is the way he puts it: "In the end it is better not to say that the undecidable is this or that, and even that it is insupportable. Perhaps the least untenable statement is something along the lines of *the same undecides itself.* The same undecides itself: it undoes itself as it constitutes itself" (*DS* 10/13).

22. The image of the desert recurs in *Dis-Enclosure*, where it also indicates the risk of a total absence of sense which could at some point result in a "hyperreligious

upheaval" (*DE* 3/12). See also Ignaas Devisch, "A Trembling Voice in the Desert: Jean-Luc Nancy's Rethinking of the Space of the Political," *Cultural Values* 4, no. 2 (2000): 239–55.

23. Such a sociological and anthropological explanation, however, requires research beyond the scope of this book. This kind of explanation can be found, amongst others, in Benedict Anderson, *Imagined Communities: Reflections on the Origin and Spread of Nationalism*.

24. Maurice Blanchot, *The Work of Fire*, trans. Charlotte Mandell (Stanford University Press, 1995), 62, trans. modified.

25. Rancière, *Dissensus*, 218.

26. I will return to the issue of the "whatever" on page 214.

27. Philippe Lacoue-Labarthe, *Musica Ficta (Figures of Wagner)*, trans. Felicia McCarren (Stanford University Press, 1994), xvii.

28. Quoted in Jacques Derrida, "History of the Lie: Prolegomena," in *Without Alibi*, trans. and ed. Peggy Kamuf (Stanford University Press, 2002), 101.

29. Posthumously, Nancy's book *La vérité du mensonge* (2021, The Truth of the Lie) was published. Its title already reveals that Nancy, there too, emphasizes that there is truth and reality in the lie, as we shall also see below.

30. For a more elaborate analysis of the role of the lie in Benjamin in relation to literature, see my "Interrupting Mythological Politics? On the Possibility of a Literary Intervention," and my "Le cercle mythique: Walter Benjamin sur la politique et son interruption."

31. Walter Benjamin, "Critique of Violence (1921)," in *Reflections, Essays, Aphorisms: Autobiographical Writings* (Schocken Books, 1986), 289, my emphasis, trans. modified.

32. Benjamin, "Critique of Violence," 289.

33. Benjamin, "Critique of Violence," 290.

34. Benjamin, "Critique of Violence," 289.

35. For analyses of community in terms of immunity and intrusion, see, amongst others, Roberto Esposito, *Communitas: The Origin and Destiny of Community*, trans. Timothy C. Campbell (Stanford University Press, 2009); and *Immunitas: The Protection and Negation of Life*, trans. Zakya Hanafi (Polity Press, 2011); and Jean-Luc Nancy, "The Intruder" (*C*).

36. Blanchot, "Literature and the Right to Death," *The Work of Fire*.

37. Instead of saying that this kind of speech has no sovereignty, we could also say, following Bataille, that its sovereignty is "nothing," i.e., that literary speech is sovereign precisely because its sovereignty is empty.

38. Derrida, "History of the Lie," 72. Derrida refers, among others, to Plato's *Hippias Minor* (*On Lying*), Saint Augustine's *De mendacio*, Rousseau's *The Reveries of the Solitary Walker*, Kant's "On a Supposed Right to Lie Because of Philanthropic Concerns," and Alexandre Koyré's *Réflections sur le mensonge*. Derrida's more elaborate

reflections on the lie, the secret, testimony, and responsibility, also in relation to literature, have recently been published in the volume *Répondre—du secret. Séminaire (1991–1992). Secret et témoignage. Vol. 1* (Seuil, 2024).

39. Derrida, "History of the Lie," 34.

40. Derrida, "History of the Lie," 43.

41. Derrida, "History of the Lie," 34.

42. See Immanuel Kant, *Über ein vermeintes Recht aus Menschenliebe zu lügen* (1897), *Werke in zwölf Bänden*, Bd. 8 (Suhrkamp, 1977), 638.

43. Derrida, "History of the Lie," 37.

44. Derrida, "History of the Lie," 45.

45. Hannah Arendt, "Truth and Politics," in *Between Past and Future* (Penguin Books, 1993 [1961]), 27.

46. Arendt, "Truth and Politics," 27.

47. George Orwell, *1948* (Penguin Books, 1950), 41.

48. Derrida, "History of the Lie," 40. For an analysis of Derrida's text, see Martin Jay, "Pseudology: Derrida on Arendt and Lying in Politics," in *Derrida and the Time of the Political*, eds. Pheng Cheah and Suzanne Guerlac (Duke University Press, 2009), 235–54.

49. Arendt, "Truth and Politics," 255.

50. In the past, as Arendt argues, it was rather the authorities who distorted the facts, for good or ill, the archetype of which is perhaps Plato's "noble lie."

51. Arendt, "Truth and Politics," 252.

52. Paul Celan, *Aschenglorie*. See also Jacques Derrida, "A Self-Unsealing Poetic Text: Poetics and Politics of Witnessing," in *Revenge of the Aesthetic: The Place of Literature in Theory Today*, ed. Micheal P. Clark, trans. Rachel Bowlby (University of California Press, 2000), 179–207.

53. Arendt, "Truth and Politics," 256.

54. Derrida, "History of the Lie," 96.

55. Derrida, "History of the Lie," 42.

56. Arendt, "Truth and Politics," 256.

57. Derrida, "History of the Lie," 51.

58. Derrida, "History of the Lie," 51.

59. Derrida, "History of the Lie," 51.

60. Derrida, "History of the Lie," 33.

61. For a more elaborate analysis of what I coin the "forgetfulness of literature," see my *Literature, Autonomy and Commitment* (Bloomsbury, 2019).

62. Derrida, "History of the Lie," 63.

63. Benjamin, "Critique of Violence," 289.

64. For this reason, I do not agree with Simon Critchley, who sees civil disobedience as a form of "anarchic metapolitics." I will not use the words "anarchy" or "metapolitics" because civil disobedience is not an act that stands outside

or annihilates the state, but one that is, as Critchley himself puts it, "as interstitial distance *within* the state." Critchley, *Infinitely Demanding*, 113.

65. Derrida, "History of the Lie," 63.

66. As is so pointedly described by Blanchot in "The Madness of the Day." For a plea for the right to opacity, see also Édouard Glissant, "Right for Opacity," in *Poetics of Relation*, trans. Betsy Wing (University of Michigan Press, 2010), 189–94. Perhaps, as Derrida suggests, the absence of a "veritable problematic of testimony, witnessing, bearing witness" in philosophy has blocked any alternative to the conception of lying as a non-telling or non-wanting to tell the truth. According to Derrida, the absence of a genuine problematic of testimony is one of the reasons that have played "an inhibiting, if not prohibiting, role in taking such a history [of the lie, AvR] seriously." Derrida, "History of the Lie," 67.

67. I agree with Derrida's reservation towards Alexandre Koyré, who—following in Kant's footsteps—regards all secrecy as a threat to the *res publica*. Derrida, "History of the Lie," 63. See Alexandre Koyré, *Réflexions sur le mensonge* (Allia, 1998).

68. Jacques Rancière, "Ten Thesis on Politcs," *Theory & Event* 5, no. 3 (2001), thesis 8.

69. Derrida, "History of the Lie," 66.

70. Arendt, "Lying in Politics," in *Crises of the Republic* (Harvest Books, 1972 [1969]), 5.

71. Jacques Derrida, "The University Without Condition," in Kamuf, *Without Alibi*, 206.

72. In this text, Derrida explains this same theme in terms of a distinction between *justice* and *law*. It is because justice and law are not identical that there is, *in the name of* justice, the right to secrecy, i.e., the right to resistance against the law. Nancy reaches the same conclusion in "Is Everything Political?"

73. Derrida, "History of the Lie," 64.

74. Critchley, *Infinitely Demanding*, 113, my emphasis. See especially Alain Badiou, *Metapolitics* (London: Verso, 2012).

75. See page 182 of this chapter. Manchev formulates his question as follows: "[H]ow, then, can we distinguish between this disastrous world that surrounds, or even suffocates, us today—and the world that emerges *ex nihilo* in the movement of its creation?" ("Mét" 88).

76. See Critchley, *Infinitely Demanding*, 93: "In particular, and this leads back to the arguments about humor in the previous chapter, it is the carnivalesque humor of anarchist groups and their tactics of 'non-violent warfare' that have led to the creation of *a new language of civil disobedience*." My emphasis.

77. Critchley, *Infinitely Demanding*, 124.

78. Judith Butler, *Excitable Speech: A Politics of the Performative* (Routledge, 1997), 141. Butler calls this performative speech "insurrectionary speech" and gives the example of the parodic reappropriation of the word "queer."

79. John Langshaw Austin, *How to Do Things With Words* (Harvard University Press, 1975 [1962]).

80. Drawing on a Heideggerian term, we could say that Nancy's idea of performativity is based on that of a radical *jemeinigkeit*. As Nancy points out in *The Experience of Freedom*, existence is "each time as my own" (*EF* 67/92), that is to say I declare it mine anew each time, just as the performative always *also* declares "hereby in this statement here I am."

81. Austin, *How to Do Things With Words*, 22.

82. Austin, *How to Do Things With Words*, 12.

83. Jacques Derrida, "Signature Event Context," in *Margins of Philosophy*, trans. Alan Bass (University of Chicago Press, 1982), 325. This issue is linked to the issue of mime, imitation, and mimicking analyzed by Derrida in "The Double Session," in *Dissemination*, trans. Barbara Johnson (University of Chicago Press, 1981), 173–96.

84. Undoubtedly, Blanchot has the same reservations about the notion of performativity as Derrida has in "The University Without Condition," namely that a performative act, understood according to speech act theory, implies that "I can produce and determine an event by a performative act guaranteed, like any performative, by conventions" (233). What Derrida, like most contemporary French philosophers, is seeking to think is an eventuality that transcends any horizon of anticipation. My purpose here, however, is to explore the possibility of an *anticipated* or *created* event without it being predictable or controllable.

85. Blanchot, "The Language of Fiction," in *The Work of Fire*, 74–75. For a more elaborate analysis of the workings of the language of fiction in Blanchot, see also my "Kafka Shared Between Blanchot and Sartre," *Arcadia* 55, no. 2 (2020): 239–59.

86. Anne-Lise Schulte Nordholt, *Maurice Blanchot: L'Écriture comme expérience du dehors* (Droz, 1995), 28.

87. Blanchot, "The Language of Fiction," 7, my emphasis.

88. See Schulte Nordholt, *Maurice Blanchot*, 29.

89. In my opinion, one of the most captivating descriptions of this experience is given by Hélène Cixous in her analysis of Clarice Lispector's work. Hélène Cixous, "Clarice Lispector: The Approach. Letting Oneself (be) Read (by) Clarice Lispector. *The Passion According to C.L.*," in *Coming to Writing and Other Essays* (Harvard University Press, 1991), 59–77.

90. Blanchot, "The Language of Fiction," 77, my emphasis.

91. Blanchot, "The Language of Fiction," 80, my emphasis. See on this issue also Daniela Hurezanu, *Maurice Blanchot et la fin du mythe* (Presses Universitaires du nouveau monde, 2003), 32.

92. This is why it is probably a little tricky to present Blanchot's poetics in terms of *performativity*. Tricky, but not incorrect, in my opinion, for the renunciation of every form of doing does not take the form of paralysis or inactivity, but is rather a renunciation or contestation that happens *in writing*.

93. Stéphane Mallarmé, "Crisis of Verse," in *Divagations*, trans. Barbara Johnson (Harvard University Press, 2007), 210.

94. Blanchot, "Literature and the Right to Death," in *The Work of Fire*, 327. Blanchot refers to this phrase of Mallarmé's on several occasions and in several texts. See, for instance, also "The Myth of Mallarmé" in the same volume. The title of this text is telling, as it indicates both Mallarmé's aspiration for mythical speech and the vanity of this aspiration.

95. Leslie Hill is an important exception. See *Nancy, Blanchot: A Serious Controversy* (Rowman & Littlefield, 2018). For an overview of the reception of the debate between Nancy and Blanchot, see my "*Noli Me Operare*: Reading Nancy (Re)Reading Blanchot" (with Andreas Noyer).

96. Blanchot, "Literature and the Right to Death," 322, my emphasis.

97. Maurice Blanchot, *The Space of Literature*, trans. Ann Smock (University of Nebraska Press, 1992), 74. So, for Blanchot, global negation is a suppression of the world, rather than the creation of another world. On the issue of global negation through literature, see also my "Kafka Shared Between Blanchot and Sartre."

98. Blanchot, *The Work of Fire*, 330, my emphasis.

99. Blanchot, *The Work of Fire*, 338.

100. Françoise Colin, *Maurice Blanchot et la question de l'écriture* (Gallimard, 1986), 85. See also Daniela Hurezanu, *Maurice Blanchot et la fin du mythe*, 29sq.

101. Blanchot, *The Work of Fire*, 339.

102. This is not unrelated to the tacit disagreement between Blanchot and Nancy over the notion of unworking (*désoeuvrement*). Whereas in Blanchot's work, this notion refers rather to aporia and vanity, in Nancy's use it has acquired a highly active, even creative connotation, without this shift being really made explicit. On this shift, see also Christopher Fynsk, foreword in *The Inoperative Community*, 154: 23n. We have also discussed this issue on page 93sq of chapter 2.

103. Colin, *Maurice Blanchot et la question de l'écriture*, 32–34.

104. Arthur Cools has approached this theme from the point of view of the phenomenological reduction, arguing that the "space of literature" described by Blanchot is a phenomenological *epoche*. Cools, "Intentionalité et singularité: Maurice Blanchot et la phénoménologie," in *Blanchot et la philosophie*, eds. Éric Hoppenot and Alain Milon (Presses Universitaires de Paris-Ouest-Nanterre, 2009), 137–55. This is not to say, however, that Blanchot does not adopt an ontological point of view. To say that being is suspended in the space of literature also amounts to a certain ontology, even if Blanchot wants to renounce all ontology.

105. In "The University Without Condition" Derrida puts forward the "What if . . . ?" as a radical variant of the "as if." While the notion of "as if" according to him still testifies to a "certain grammar of the conditional," the notion of "What if . . . ?" breaks completely with this grammar.

106. I agree with Derrida in "The University Without Condition," 213: "What I would like to attempt with you is this apparently impossible thing: to link this 'as if' to the thinking of an event, that is, to the thinking of this thing

that *perhaps* happens . . . I will speak of an event that, without necessarily coming about tomorrow, would remain *perhaps*—and I underscore perhaps—to come." Nevertheless, I propose to put the emphasis not on the event that would remain perhaps to come, but on the "perhaps," i.e., the uncertain status of the event that takes place *in the here and now* of the reading.

107. Heinrich von Kleist, "The Earthquake in Chile," in *Selected Prose of Heinrich von Kleist*, trans. Peter Wortsman (Archipelago Books, 2009). The story was originally published as "Jeronimo und Josephe: Eine Scene aus dem Erdbeben zu Chili, vom Jahr 1647," in the *Morgenblatt für gebildete Stände*. Kleist was imprisoned in France when he wrote the story and secretly gave it to his friend Rühle von Lilienstren. In 1810 Kleist published it as a book under the title *Das Erdbeben in Chili*. For an interesting analysis of this story, see Peter Fenves, "On a Seeming Right to Semblance," in *Arresting Language: From Leibniz to Benjamin* (Stanford University Press, 2001). I will come back to this short story later.

108. See page 132 of chapter 3.

109. Derek Attridge, *The Singularity of Literature* (Routledge, 2004), 96.

110. Attridge, *The Singularity of Literature*, 96, my emphasis.

111. This moment of arrest forms the main subject of Peter Fenves's *Arresting Language*.

112. For the importance of this meta-performative for contemporary literary practice, see also the chapter "The Relational Paradigm" of my *Literature, Autonomy and Commitment*.

113. I will return to this theme later in this section when I introduce "authoredness" as a key characteristic of literature.

114. Thierry De Duve, "Do Whatever," in *Kant After Duchamp* (MIT Press, 1996), 357.

115. Rancière, *Dissensus*, 218, my emphasis. See page 175sq of this chapter.

116. See De Duve, *Kant After Duchamp*, 364. In *The Muses*, Nancy quotes De Duve affirmatively when he says that "[t]o make art is to judge art, to decide, to choose" (De Duve, cited in *M* 25/49). Yet, Nancy concentrates only on what he names "the artist's *technical* decisions," i.e., concretely, the decision as to what color to paint, where to put it, etc., and not the decision *for* art, i.e., the decision whether this is art.

117. De Duve, *Kant After Duchamp*, 365.

118. De Duve, *Kant After Duchamp*, 360.

119. Nancy frequently says that he prefers not to pass judgment on art, because that is not his job. See, e.g., "TP" and "Nécessité du sens," in *Yves Bonnefoy: Poésie, peinture, musique, ed.* Michèle Finck (Presses Universitaires de Strasbourg, 1995), 43.

120. I refer to this, earlier quoted, remark of Nancy's in *Dis-Enclosure*: "'[L]iterature' here does not mean 'literary genre' but can, in principle, be any sort of saying, shouting, praying, laughing, or sobbing that holds . . . that infinite suspension of sense" (*DE* 97/146).

121. That this judgment is indeterminate does not imply, however, that there is no need to learn how to express such a judgment. In a way, this is a reiteration of Schiller's idea of aesthetic education expressed in the *Letters on the Aesthetic Education of Man* (1794).

122. Heinrich Von Kleist, *The Earthquake in Chile*, my emphasis.

123. Fenves, *Arresting Language*, 150.

124. Mehdi Belhaj Kacem, *Théorie du Trickster* (Sens & Tonka, 2002), my emphasis. The works of Nancy and Belhaj Kacem are in many ways very close. Not only has Nancy contributed to the journal *EvidenZ* edited by Mehdi Belhaj Kacem, but they have also co-authored the book *Immortelle finitude: Sexualité et philosophie* (Les presses du réel, 2020). Belhaj Kacem has repeatedly expressed his admiration for Nancy's thought, for instance in *Pop philosophie*: "There is someone who has meant a lot to me and whom I have spoken little about in these interviews, who is the philosopher Jean-Luc Nancy. . . . In a way, I am trying to find a sort of balance between Nancy and Badiou." Mehdi Belhaj Kacem, in Mehdi Belhaj Kacem and Philippe Nassif, *Pop philosophie* (Perrin, 2005), 487. This balance, as Belhaj Kacem makes clear, seems to lie in trying to find the answer to the following question: "Can social unworking be called a new site of the event, a site of real resistance and subversion?" (315). In a sense, this is the same question that motivates the present chapter.

125. In similar terms, Nancy declares in "The Unsacrificeable" that "existence can't be sacrificed" (*FT* 74/105).

126. See also: "[T]he *being-feint* of the subject does not imply in any way the 'being-feigned' (the fictitiousness or the fictionality) of the nature of this being, and more specifically of its potential corporeal nature" (*ES* 93/137).

127. Belhaj Kacem, *Théorie du Trickster*, 70.

128. Let us recall one last time the concluding lines of *Truth of Democracy*: "If we first think the being of our being together in the world, we will see which politics gives this thought a chance" (*TD* 34/62).

129. Belhaj Kacem, *Théorie du Trickster*, 69.

130. Belhaj Kacem, *Théorie du Trickster*, 69, my emphasis. Of course, we could also say that the "let's say" with which Belhaj Kacem accompanies his "anecdote" has the same status as the "lie" told "knowing it won't be believed."

131. Derrida, "A Self-Unsealing Poetic Text," 189 and 190.

132. The importance of having faith in the act is also stressed by Thierry De Duve: "It is impossible to choose anything whatever while avoiding that it be this thing by the same token. It is impossible to judge whatever, or the whatever, *while judging.*" *Kant After Duchamp*, 356. My emphasis.

133. Here, a whole new perspective on literary engagement or so-called "committed" literature is opened; one in which literature's engagement is not primarily an engagement with a sociopolitical cause, but with literature itself, i.e., with the specific form of engagement demanded by literature. See also my "Engagement

for Engagement's Sake: An Ontological Rethinking of the Politics of Literature," *Aesthetic Investigations* 5, no. 2 (2022): 129–44.

134. This probably explains the mechanism of *catharsis*.

135. Octave Mannoni, "I Know Well, but All the Same . . . ," in *Perversion and the Social Relation*, vol. 4, eds. Rothenberg et al. (Duke University Press, 2003). At the beginning of his text, Mannoni, too, notices that "something similar occurs in the theatre." Mannoni, "I Know Well, but All the Same . . . ," 68. See also his text called "L'illusion comique ou le théâtre du point de vue de l'imaginaire" in the same volume, where he applies his formula "I know well, but all the same" to the theatrical experience.

136. Talayesva, *Hopi Sun*, qtd. by Mannoni, "I Know Well, but All the Same . . . ," 73–74. Here again, we see the theme of the right to secrecy or opacity. A public secret remains a secret despite the fact that it has been revealed. Slavoj Žižek recognizes this double structure of "I know well, but all the same" in the workings of ideology. He nevertheless gives a critical reading of Mannoni, arguing that self-deception succeeds not because we believe it, but because we believe that *others* believe it: this form of faith, according to Žižek, is therefore external, "interpassive." See Slavoj Žižek, *Sublime Object of Ideology* (Verso, 1989) and *For They Know Not What They Do* (Verso, 1991). I would argue that this intersubjective dimension already follows from the performative structure of the statement. A performative utterance only functions as such if it is generally recognized.

137. See *Julia Kristeva, Powers of Horror: An Essay on Abjection*, trans. Leon S. Roudiez (Colombia University Press, 1982), 37: "It is perhaps unavoidable that, when a subject confronts the factitiousness of object relation, when he stands at the place of the want that founds it, the fetish becomes a life preserver, temporary and slippery, but nonetheless indispensable. But is not exactly language our ultimate and inseparable fetish? And language, precisely, is based on fetishist denial ('I know that, but just the same,' 'the sign is not the thing, but just the same,' etc.) and defines us in our essence as speaking beings." While I do not disagree with this view, it is too general for our purposes here. What interests me is not so much the nature of language in general, but its nature and power in the specific case of language in works of literature. Nevertheless, it could probably be said that literary speech is as fetishistic as any other speech, but in an *explicit* way.

138. Attridge, *The Singularity of Literature*, 101. Attridge adds in a note that he does not necessarily want to restrict his concept of authoredness to the human domain: "The experience of authoredness may at some future date not be limited to the human domain, and literature may already be in the process of undermining the human/non-human distinction."

139. Attridge, *The Singularity of Literature*, 103, my emphasis.

140. See also Samuel Weber, *Theatricality as Medium* (Fordham University Press, 2004), 189: "The 'plot' does not disappear, but its role changes. It is no

longer the *plotting of action*, but the *plotting of acting*, which is also the *staging of the plot*." My emphasis.

Bibliography

Works by Jean-Luc Nancy

Nancy, Jean-Luc. *À l'écoute*. Galilée, 2002.

———. "À la frontière, figures et couleurs." *Le désir de l'Europe* (Paris/Strasbourg, 1991): 41–50.

———. *À plus d'un titre Jacques Derrida: Sur un portrait de Valerio Adami*. Galilée, 2007.

———. "À propos de Blanchot." *L'Œil de bœuf* 14/15 (1998).

———. "*À voix nue*." Interview by Mathieu Bénézet. *France-Culture*, March 22–26, 1993.

———. "Abrégé philosophique de la révolution française." *Po&sie* 49 (1989): 211–17.

———. *After Fukushima: The Equivalence of Catastrophes*. Translated by Charlotte Mandell. Fordham University Press, 2015.

———. *Au ciel et sur la terre: Petite conférence sur Dieu*. Bayard, 2004.

———. *Au fond des images*. Galilée, 2003.

———. "Au lieu de l'utopie." In *Les utopies et leurs représentations*, coll. Le Quartier, 2000.

———. "Autour de la notion de communauté littéraire." *Tumultes* 6 (1995): 23–37.

———. *Banalité de Heidegger*. Galilée, 2015.

———. *The Banality of Heidegger*. Translated by Jeff Fort. Fordham University Press, 2017.

———. *The Birth to Presence*. Translated by Emily McVarish et al. Stanford University Press, 1993.

———. *Chroniques philosophiques*. Galilée, 2004.

———. "Compagnie de Blanchot." *Revue des sciences humaines* 253 (1999): 241–43.

———. *Corpus*. Métailié, 2006 [1992].

———. *Corpus II: Writings on Sexuality*. Fordham University Press, 2013.

———. *The Creation of the World or Globalization*. Translated by François Raffoul and David Pettigrew. State University of New York Press, 2007.

———. "De l'écriture: Qu'elle ne révèle rien." *Rue Descartes* 10 (1994): 104–9.

———. "De la figure politique à l'événement de l'art." *Futur antérieur* 10 (1992): 104–13.

———. "The Deleuzian Fold of Thought." In *The Deleuze Critical Reader*, edited by Paul Patton. Blackwell, 1996.

———. "Dem Politischen mangelt es an Symbolizität: Ein Gespräch mit Jean-Luc Nancy." *Information Philosophie* 4 (2002): 35–41.

———. *Demande: Littérature et philosophie.* Galilée, 2015.

———. "Démocratie finie et infinie." In *Démocratie, dans quel état?*, coll. La Fabrique, 2009.

———. *Des lieux divins* suivi de *Calcul du poète.* T. E. R., 1997. Partly republished in *Demande: Littérature et philosophie.* Galilée, 2015.

———. "Dies irae." In Jacques Derrida, Vincent Descombes, Garbis Kortian, Philippe Lacoue-Labarthe, Jean-François Lyotard, and Jean-Luc Nancy, coll. *La faculté de juger.* Minuit, 1985.

———. *Ego sum.* Flammarion, 1979.

———. "Entretien du 23 juin 2000." In *Heidegger en France II: Entretiens*, edited by Dominique Janicaud. Albin Michel, 2001.

———. *Être singulier pluriel.* Galilée, 1996.

———. *Expectation: Philosophy, Literature.* Fordham University Press, 2017.

———. "Finite and Infinite Democracy." In *Democracy in What State?*, edited by Giorgio Agamben et al., coll., translated by William MCuaig. Colombia University Press, 2011.

———. *The Gravity of Thought.* Translated by François Raffoul and Gregory Recco. Humanities Press, 1997.

———. *Hegel: L'Inquiétude du négatif.* Hachette, 1997.

———. "Is Everything Political? (A Brief Remark)." Translated by Philip M. Adamek. *New Centennial Review* 2, no. 3 (2002): 15–22.

———. *Je t'aime, un peu, beaucoup, passionnément . . . Petite conférence sur l'amour.* Bayard, 2008.

———. *Juste impossible: Petite conférence sur le juste et l'injuste.* Bayard, 2007.

———. *L'Adoration (Déconstruction du christianisme, 2).* Galilée, 2010.

———. "L'art, fragment." *Lignes* 18 (1993): 153–73.

———. *L'Équivalence des catastrophes (Après Fukushima).* Galilée, 2012.

———. "L'être, l'étant, selon Derrida." *Magazine littéraire* hors-série 9 (2006): 96–97.

———. *L'Évidence du film/Abbas Kiarostami.* Yves Gevaert, 2001.

———. *L'Expérience de la liberté.* Galilée, 1988.

———. *L'"il y a" du rapport sexuel.* Galilée, 2001.

———. *L'Impératif catégorique.* Flammarion, 1983.

———. "L'impossible acte constituant." *Le Monde* 29 Juillet 2005.

———. *L'Intrus.* Galilée, 2000.

———. *L'Oubli de la philosophie.* Galilée, 1986.

———. *La communauté affrontée.* Galilée, 2001.

———. *La communauté désavouée.* Galilée, 2014.

———. *La communauté désoeuvrée.* Bourgois, 2004 [first printing, 1986; second, 1990; third, 2000].

———. *La création du monde ou la mondialisation.* Galilée, 2002.

———. *La déclosion (Déconstruction du christianisme, 1).* Galilée, 2005.

———. "La métamorphose, le monde." Interview by Boyan Manchev. *Rue Descartes* 64 (2009): 78–93.

———. *La naissance des seins* suivi de *Péan pour Aphrodite.* Galilée, 2006.

———. *La pensée dérobée.* Galilée, 2001.

———. *La remarque spéculative: Un bon mot de Hegel.* Galilée, 1973.

———. *La vérité du mensonge.* Bayard, 2021.

———. *La ville au loin.* Mille et une nuits, 1999.

———. "Lapsus judicii." *Communications* 26 (1977): 82–97. Republished with post-scriptum in *L'Impératif catégorique.* Flammarion, 1983.

———. *Le discours de la syncope: Tome I: Logodaedalus.* Aubier-Flammarion, 1976.

———. "Le neutre, la neutralisation du neuter." *Cahiers Maurice Blanchot 1: Les Presses du Réel* (2011). Republished in *Demande: Littérature & philosophie.* Galilée, 2015.

———. *Le partage des voix.* Galilée, 1982.

———. *Le plaisir au dessin.* Galilée 2009.

———. *Le poids d'une pensée.* Montréal-Grenoble, Le Griffon d'Argile-Presses Universitaires de Grenoble, 1991.

———. *Le portrait (dans le décor).* Institut d'art contemporain/Les Cahiers-Philosophie de l'art 8, 1999.

———. *Le regard du portrait.* Galilée, 2001 [2000].

———. *Le sens du monde.* Galilée, 2001 [1993].

———. *Les muses.* Galilée, 2001 [1994].

———. "Lecture dérangée." *La quinzaine littéraire* 698 (1996): 22–24.

———. *Listening.* Translated by Charlotte Mandell. Fordham University Press, 2007.

———. "Logodaedalus (Kant écrivain)." *Poétique* 21 (1975): 24–53.

———. *Maurice Blanchot: Passion Politique; Lettre-récit de 1984 suivie d'une lettre de Dionys Mascolo.* Galilée, 2011.

———. *Multiple Arts: The Muses II.* Edited by Simon Sparks. Stanford University Press, 2006.

———. "Nécessité du sens." In *Yves Bonnefoy: Poésie, peinture, musique,* edited by Michèle Finck. Presses Universitaires de Strasbourg, 1995.

———. "Nietzsche: Mais où sont les yeux pour le voir?" *Esprit* (1968): 482–503.

———. *Noli Me Tangere.* Translated by Sarah Clift, Pascale-Anne Brault, and Micheal Naas. Fordham University Press, 2008.

———. *Noli me tangere: Essai sur la levée du corps.* Bayard, 2003.

———. "Of Being-in-Common." In *Community at Loose Ends*, edited by The Miamy Theory Collective and translated by James Creech. University of Minnesota Press, 1991.

———. "On Dis-Enclosure and Its Gestures: A Concluding Dialogue with Jean-Luc Nancy." In *Re-Treating Religion: Deconstructing Christianity with Jean-Luc Nancy*, edited by Alena Alexandrova, Ignaas Devisch, Laurens ten Kate, and Aukje van Rooden. Fordham University Press, 2012.

———. *The Pleasure in Drawing*. Translated by Philip Armstrong. Fordham University Press, 2013.

———. "Politics and Beyond." Interview by Philip Armstrong and Jason E. Smith. *Diacritics* 43, no. 4 (2015): 90–108.

———. *Politique et au-delà*. Galilée, 2011.

———. *Portrait*. Translated by Sarah Clift and Simon Sparks. Fordham University Press, 2018.

———. Preface to *The Inoperative Community*. Minnesota University Press, 1991.

———. "Présentation." In *Cours préparatoire d'esthétique*, Jean Paul. L'Age d'Homme, 1979.

———. *Proprement dit: Entretien sur le mythe*. Interview by Mathilde Girard. Lignes, 2015.

———. "Quand le sens ne fait plus monde." *Esprit* 403, no. 3–4 (2014): 27–46.

———. *Que faire*. Galilée, 2016.

———. "Rancière and Metaphysics." In *Jacques Rancière: History, Politics, Aesthetics*, edited by Gabriel Rockhill and Philip Watts, translated by John Hulsey. Duke University Press 2009.

———. "Rancière et la métaphysique." In *La philosophie déplacée: Autour de Jacques Rancière*, edited by Laurence Cornu and Patrice Vermeren. Horlieu Éditions, 2006.

———. *Résistance de la poésie*. William Blake, 1997.

———. "Rien que le monde." *Vacarme* 11 (2000).

———. *The Sense of the World*. Translated by Jeffrey S. Librett. University of Minnesota Press, 1997.

———. *Sexistence*. Galilée, 2017.

———. "Sharing Voices." In *Transforming the Hermeneutic Context: From Nietzsche to Nancy*, edited and translated by Gayle L. Ormiston and Alan D. Schrift. State University of New York Press, 1990.

———. *Sur le commerce des pensées: Du livre et de la librairie*. Galilée, 2005.

———. *Technique du présent: Essai sur On Kawara*. Nouveau Musée/Institut/Les Cahiers-Philosophie de l'art 6, 1997.

———. "Techniques du présent." Interview by Benoît Goetz. *Le Portique* 3 (1999): 1–10.

———. "Tout est-il politique? (simple note)." *Actuel Marx* 28 (2000): 77–82.

———. "Un certain silence." *Esprit* 32 (1993): 555–63.

———. "Un commencement." In *L'"Allégorie,"* Philippe Lacoue-Labarthe. Galilée, 2006.

———. "Un jour, les dieux se retirent" (littérature/politique: entre deux). William Blake, 2001.

———. *Une pensée finie.* Galilée, 1990.

———. *Vérité de la démocratie.* Galilée, 2008.

———. *Visitation (de la peinture chrétienne).* Galilée, 2001.

———. "What Is to Be Done?" *Diacritics* 42, no. 2 (2014): 100–17.

———. "You Ask Me What It Means Today . . ." *Paragraph* 16, no. 2 (1993): 108–21.

———, and Alain Badiou. *German Philosophy: A Dialogue.* Translated by Richard Lambert. MIT Press, 2018.

———, and Alain Badiou. *La tradition allemande dans la philosophie.* Lignes 2017.

———, and Jean-Christophe Bailly. *La comparution.* Bourgois, 2007 [1991].

———, and Jacques Derrida. "Interview with Nancy." *Topoi* 7, no. 2 (1988): 113–21.

———, and Jacques Derrida. "Responsabilité du sens à venir: Entretien." In *Sens en tous sens: Autour des travaux de Jean-Luc Nancy,* edited by Francis Guibal and Jean-Clet Martin. Galilée, 2004.

———, and Jacques Derrida. "Responsibility—Of the Sense to Come." In *For Strasbourg: Conversations of Friendship and Philosophy,* edited and translated by Pascale-Anne Brault and Micheal Naas. Fordham University Press, 2014.

———, and Federico Ferrari. *L'Iconographie de l'auteur.* Galilée, 2005.

———, and Susanna Fritscher. *Mmmmmmm.* Éditions Au Figuré, 2000.

———, and Irving Goh. *The Deconstruction of Sex.* Duke University Press, 2021.

———, and Mehdi Belhaj Kacem. *Immortelle finitude: Sexualité et philosophie.* Les presses du réel, 2020.

———, and Philippe Lacoue-Labarthe. *L'Absolu littéraire: Théorie de la littérature du romantisme allemand.* Seuil, 1978.

———, and Philippe Lacoue-Labarthe. "Le dialogue des genres." *Poétique* 21 (1975): 148–75.

———, and Philippe Lacoue-Labarthe. *Le mythe nazi.* L'Aube, 2003 [1991].

———, and Philippe Lacoue-Labarthe. *Le retrait du politique.* Cahiers du Centre de recherches philosophiques sur le politique. Galilée, 1983.

———, and Philippe Lacoue-Labarthe. *Le titre de la lettre: Une lecture de Lacan.* Galilée, 1972.

———, and Philippe Lacoue-Labarthe, eds. *Les fins de l'homme.* Galilée, 1981.

———, and Philippe Lacoue-Labarthe. *The Literary Absolute: Theory of Literature in German Romanticism.* Translated by Philip Barnard and Cheryl Lester. State University of New York Press, 1988.

———, and Philippe Lacoue-Labarthe. *Rejouer le politique.* Cahiers du Centre de recherches philosophiques sur le politique. Galilée, 1981.

———, and Philippe Lacoue-Labarthe, eds. *Retreating the Political.* Routledge, 1997.

———, and Philippe Lacoue-Labarthe. "Scène: Un échange de lettres." *La nouvelle revue française* 46 (1992): 73–98. Republished as *Scène*. Bourgois, 2013.

———, and Philippe Lacoue-Labarthe, Bernard Stiegler, and Hans-Jürgen Syberberg. In *Der Ister*. Film by David Barison and Daniel Ross, 2004.

———, and Virginie Lalucq. *Fortino Sámano: Les débordements du poème*. Galilée, 2004.

———, and Anne-Marie Lang. "Traduction et présentation de 'Sur le Witz' de Jean-Paul." *Poétique* 15 (1973): 365–406.

———, Anne-Marie Lang, and Philippe Lacoue-Labarthe. "Traduction et présentation de 'Entretien sur le romantisme' de Brentano." *Po&sie* 8 (1979).

———, and Mathilde Monnier. *Dehors la danse*. Droz, 2001.

———, and Adèle Van Reeth. *La jouissance*. Plon, 2014.

Other Works

Agamben, Giorgio. *The Coming Community*. University of Minnesota Press, 2007 [1990].

———. *Means Without End: Notes on Politics*. University of Minnesota Press, 2000 [1996].

Alexandrova, Alena, Ignaas Devisch, Laurens ten Kate, and Aukje van Rooden, eds. *Re-Treating Religion: Deconstructing Christianity with Jean-Luc Nancy*. Fordham University Press, 2012.

Andermatt Conley, Verena, and Irving Goh, eds. *Nancy Now*. Polity Press, 2014.

Anderson, Benedict. *Imagined Communities: Reflections on the Origin and Spread of Nationalism*. Verso, 2006 [1983].

Arendt, Hannah. "Lying in Politics." In *Crises of the Republic*. Harvest Books, 1972 [1969].

———. *The Origins of Totalitarianism*. Harcourt Brace Jovanovich, 1973 [1961].

———. "Truth and Politics." In *Between Past and Future*. Penguin Books, 1993 [1961].

Aristotle. *Poetics*. Translated by Malcolm Heath. Penguin Books, 1996. *La poétique*. French translation by Roselyne Dupont-Roc and Jean Lallot. Seuil, 1980.

Attridge, Derek. *J. M. Coetzee and the Ethics of Reading: Literature in the Event*. University of Chicago Press, 2004.

———. *The Singularity of Literature*. Routledge, 2004.

Austin, John Langshaw. *How to Do Things with Words*. Harvard University Press, 1975 [1962].

Badiou, Alain. *Being and Event*. Translated by Oliver Feltham. Continuum, 2006.

———. *De quoi Sarkozy est-il le nom?* Lignes, 2007.

———. *Handbook of Inaesthetics*. Translated by Alberto Toscano. Stanford University Press, 2004.

———. *Metapolitics*. Verso, 2012.

Balibar, Étienne. *Nous, citoyens d'Europe? Les frontières, l'État, le peuple*. La Découverte, 2001.

Barnard, Philip, and Cheryl Lester. "Translator's Introduction." In *The Literary Absolute*, Jean-Luc Nancy and Philippe Lacoue-Labarthe. State University of New York Press, 1998.

Bataille, Georges. *Inner Experience*. Translated by Stuart Kendall. State University of New York Press, 2014. *L'Expérience intérieure*. Gallimard, 1954.

———. *Oeuvres complètes*. Gallimard, 1977–1988.

Baudelaire, Charles. "The Desire to Paint." In *Paris Spleen*. Translated by Martin Sorell. Alma Books, 2010 [1862]. "Le désir de peindre." In *Le spleen de Paris*. Garnier, 1985 [1862].

Beiser, Frederick, C. *The Early Political Writings of the German Romantics*. Cambridge University Press, 1996.

———. "Friedrich Schlegel: The Mysterious Romantic." In *The Romantic Imperative: The Concept of Early German Romanticism*. Harvard University Press, 2003.

Beistegui, Miguel de. *Truth and Genesis: Philosophy as Differential Ontology*. Indiana University Press, 2004.

Belhaj Kacem, Mehdi. *Antéforme*. Tristram, 1997.

———. *De la communauté virtuelle*. Sens & Tonka, 2002.

———. *Inésthétique et mimésis: Badiou, Lacoue-Labarthe et la question de l'art*. Lignes, 2010.

———. *Théorie du Trickster*. Sens & Tonka, 2002.

———, and Philippe Nassif. *Pop philosophie*. Perrin, 2005.

Benjamin, Walter. "The Concept of Criticism in German Romanticism (1920)." In *Selected Writings. Vol. 1, 1913–1926*. Harvard University Press, 1996.

———. "Critique of Violence (1921)." In *Reflections, Essays, Aphorisms: Autobiographical Writings*. Schocken Books, 1986.

———. "Fate and Character (1919)." In *Reflections, Essays, Aphorisms*.

———. "Theological-Political Fragment (1920–1921)." In *Reflections, Essays, Aphorisms*.

———. "Two Poems by Friedrich Hölderlin (1914–1915)." In *Selected Writings. Vol. 1, 1913–1926*.

———. "Zur Kritik der Gewalt (1921)." In *Gesammelte Schriften* II.1. Suhrkamp, 1977.

Bernasconi, Robert. "On Deconstructing Nostalgia for Community Within the West: The Debate Between Nancy and Blanchot." *Research in Phenomenology* 23 (1993): 3–21.

Bernstein, Jay M. *The Fate of Art: Aesthetic Alienation from Kant to Derrida and Adorno*. Pennsylvania State University Press, 1992.

Birnbaum, Antonia. *Bonheur Justice: Walter Benjamin*. Payot, 2008.

Blanchot, Maurice. *The Infinite Conversation*. Translated by Susan Hanson. University of Minnesota Press, 1993.

———. *La communauté inavouable*. Minuit, 1984.

————. *Les intellectuels en question*. Fourbis, 1996.

————. *The Madness of the Day*. Translated by Lydia Davis. Station Hill Press, 1981.

————. *The Space of Literature*. Translated by Ann Smock. University of Nebraska Press, 1992.

————. *The Unavowable Community*. Translated by Pierre Joris. Station Hill Press, 1988.

————. *The Work of Fire*. Translated by Charlotte Mandell. Stanford University Press, 1995.

Blumenberg, Hans. *Arbeit am Mythos*. Suhrkamp, 1979.

Butler, Judith. "Critique, Coercion, and Sacred Life in Benjamin's 'Critique of Violence.'" In *Political Theologies: Public Religions in a Post-Secular World*, edited by Hent de Vries. Fordham University Press, 2006.

————. *Excitable Speech: A Politics of the Performative*. Routledge, 1997.

Carroll, David. *Paraesthetics: Foucault, Lyotard, Derrida*. Methuen, 1987.

Cixous, Hélène. "Clarice Lispector: The Approach. Letting Oneself (Be) Read (by) Clarice Lispector. *The Passion According to C. L.*" In *Coming to Writing and Other Essays*. Harvard University Press, 1991.

Colin, Françoise. *Maurice Blanchot et la question de l'écriture*. Gallimard, 1986.

Cools, Arthur. "Intentionnalité et singularité: Maurice Blanchot et la phénoménologie." In *Maurice Blanchot et la philosophie*, edited by Éric Hoppenot and Alain Milon. Presses Universitaires de Paris-Ouest-Nanterre, 2009.

Critchley, Simon. *Infinitely Demanding: Ethics of Commitment, Politics of Resistance*. Verso, 2007.

————. *Very Little . . . Almost Nothing: Death, Philosophy, Literature*. Routledge, 1997.

Culler, Jonathan. "Anderson and the Novel." *Diacritics* 29, no. 4 (1999): 20–39.

Davies, Paul. "The Work and the Absence of Work." In *Maurice Blanchot: The Demand of Writing*, edited by Christopher Bailey Gill. Routledge, 1996.

Derrida, Jacques. *Acts of Literature*. Edited by Derek Attridge. Routledge, 1992.

————. *Dissemination*. Translated by Barbara Johnson. University of Chicago Press, 1981.

————. "Force of Law: The 'Mystical Foundation of Authority.'" In *Deconstruction and the Possibility of Justice*, edited by Drucilla Cornell, Michel Rosenfeld, and David Gray Carlson. Routledge, 1992.

————. "History of the Lie: Prolegomena." In *Without Alibi*, edited and translated by Peggy Kamuf. Stanford University Press, 2002.

————. *Margins of Philosophy*. Translated by Alan Bass. University of Chicago Press, 1982.

————. *Of Grammatoloy*. Translated by Gayatri Chakravorty Spivak. Hopkins University Press, 1974.

————. *On Touching—Jean-Luc Nancy*. Translated by Christine Irizarry. Stanford University Press, 2005.

———. *Poétique et politique du témoignage*. L'Herne, 2005.

———. *Psyche: Inventions of the Other 1*. Stanford University Press, 2007.

———. *Répondre—du secret. Séminaire (1991–1992). Secret et témoignage. Vol. 1*. Edited by Ginette Michaud and Nicholas Cotton. Seuil, 2024.

———. "A Self-Unsealing Poetic Text: Poetics and Politics of Witnessing." In *Revenge of the Aesthetic: The Place of Literature in Theory Today*, edited by Michael P. Clark, translated by Rachel Bowlby. University of California Press, 2000.

———. *Specters of Marx*. Translated by Peggy Kamuf. Routledge, 1994.

———. *The Truth in Painting*. Translated by Geoffrey Bennington and Ian McLeod. University of Chicago Press, 1987.

———. "University Without Condition." In Kamuf, *Without Alibi*.

Devisch, Ignaas. *Jean-Luc Nancy and the Question of Community*. Bloomsbury, 2013.

———. "A Trembling Voice in the Desert: Jean-Luc Nancy's Rethinking of the Space of the Political." *Cultural Values* 4, no. 2 (2000): 239–55.

———, Peter DeGraeve, and Joost Beerten, eds. *Jean-Luc Nancy: De kunst van het denken*. Klement/Pelckmans, 2007.

Domanov, Oleg. *Between Myth and Nihilism: Community in Jean-Luc Nancy's Philosophy*. Verlag Dr. Müller, 2008.

Duve, Thierry De. *Kant After Duchamp*. MIT Press, 1996.

Egginton, William, "The Sacred Hart of Dissent." *The New Centennial Review* 2, no. 3 (2002): 109–38.

Eliade, Mircea. *Myth and Reality*. Translated by Willard R. Trask. Harper & Row, 1968.

———. *The Myth of the Eternal Return: Cosmos and History*. Translated by Willard R. Trask. Harper & Brothers, 1959.

Esposito, Roberto. *Communitas: The Origin and Destiny of Community*. Translated by Timothy C. Campbell. Stanford University Press, 2009.

———. *Immunitas: The Protection and Negation of Life*. Translated by Zakya Hanafi. Polity Press, 2011.

Fenves, Peter. *Arresting Language: From Leibniz to Benjamin*. Stanford University Press, 2001.

Frank, Manfred. *Der kommende Gott: Vorlesungen über die Neue Mythologie*. Suhrkamp, 1982.

———. *Einführung in die frühromantische Ästhetik: Vorlesungen*. Suhrkamp, 1989.

———. *The Philosophical Foundations of Early German Romanticism*. Translated by Elizabeth Millán-Zaibert. State University of New York Press, 2004.

Fynsk, Christopher. "Foreword: Experiences of Finitude." In *The Inoperative Community*, Jean-Luc Nancy. University of Minnesota Press, 1991.

Garrido, Juan-Manuel. *La formation des forms*. Galilée, 2008.

Gauchet, Marcel. *The Disenchantment of the World*. Translated by Oscar Burge. Princeton University Press, 1999.

Geenens, Raf. "La condition politique: Lefort, un penseur normative." *Revue philosophique de Louvain* 107, no. 1 (2009): 98–122.

Giunta, Carrie, and Adrienne Janus, eds. *Nancy and Visual Culture.* Edinburgh University Press, 2016.

Girardet, Raoul. *Mythes et mythologies politiques.* Seuil, 1986.

Glissant, Édouard. *Poetics of Relation.* Translated by Betsy Wing. University of Michigan Press, 2010.

Glucksmann, André, and Raphaël Glucksmann. *Mai 68 expliqué à Nicolas Sarkozy.* Denoël, 2008.

Großmann, Andreas. *Spur zum Heiligen: Kunst und Geschichte im Widerstreit zwischen Hegel und Heidegger.* Bouvier, 1996.

Guénoun, Denis. "Brèves remarques sur la théâtralité du poiétique." *Po&Sie* 120 (2007): 373–78.

———. "Du drame entre poésie et pratique." *Po&Sie* 96 (2001): 105–16.

———. Préface to *Le théâtre de l'expérience: Contributions à la théorie de la scène,* Esa Kirkkopelto. Presses Universitaires Paris-Sorbonne, 2008.

Guibal, Francis, and Jean-Clet Martin, eds. *Sens en tous sens: Autour des travaux de Jean-Luc Nancy.* Galilée, 2004.

Gyenge, Andrea. "*Fabula, Bucca, Humanitas:* On *Ego Sum.*" In Toma, *Understanding Nancy, Understanding Modernism.*

Hanssen, Béatrice, and Andrew Benjamin, eds. *Walter Benjamin and Romanticism.* Continuum, 2002.

Hart, Kevin. "The Aggrieved Community: Nancy and Blanchot in Dialogue." *Journal for Continental Philosophy of Religion* 1, no. 1 (2019): 27–42.

Hegel, Georg Wilhelm Friedrich. *Aesthetics: Lectures on Fine Art.* Translated by T. M. Knox. Clarendon Press, 1975.

———. *Das älteste Systemprogramm des deutschen Idealismus* (1796/1797). *Werke in zwanzig Bänden. Frühe Schriften,* Bd. 1. Suhrkamp, 1971.

———. *Differenz des Fichtischen und Schellingschen Systems der Philosophie* (1801). *Werke in zwanzig Bänden,* Bd. 2. Suhrkamp, 1972.

Heidegger, Martin. *Nietzsche.* Vol. 1, *The Will to Power as Art.* Translated by David Farrell Krell. Harper & Row, 1991.

———. "The Origin of the Work of Art." In *Off the Beaten Track.* Translated by Julian Young and Kenneth Haynes. Cambridge University Press, 2002.

———. *Schelling's Treatise on the Essence of Human Freedom.* Translated by Joan Stambaugh. Ohio University Press, 1985.

———. *Schellings Abhandlung über das Wesen der menschlichen Freiheit* (1809). Max Niemeyer Verlag, 1971.

Heiden, Gert-Jan van der. *Disclosure and Displacement: Truth and Language in the Work of Heidegger, Ricoeur and Derrida.* Duquesne University Press, 2008.

———. *Ontology After Ontology: Plurality, Event and Contingency in Contemporary Philosophy.* Duquesne University Press, 2015.

Heikkilä, Martta. *At the Limits of Presentation: Coming-into-Presence and Its Aesthetic Relevance in Jean-Luc Nancy's Philosophy*. Peter Lang, 2008.

Heine, Stefanie. "*Fort-Pflanzung*: The Literary Absolute's Botanic Afterlife." In Toma, *Understanding Nancy, Understanding Modernism*.

Heller-Roazen, Daniel. *Echolalias: On the Forgetting of Language*. Zone Books, 2008.

Hill, Leslie. *Nancy, Blanchot: A Serious Controversy*. Rowman & Littlefield, 2018.

Hillis Miller, Joseph. "Laying Down the Law in Literature: The Example of Kleist." In *Deconstruction and the Possibility of Justice*, edited by Drucilla Cornell, Michel Rosenfeld, and David Gray Carlson. Routledge, 1992.

Honig, Bonnie. "Declarations of Independence: Arendt and Derrida on the Problem of Founding a Republic." *American Political Science Review* 85, no. 1 (1991): 97–113.

Hoolsema, Daniel. "The Echo of an Impossible Future in *The Literary Absolute*." *MLN* 119 (2004): 845–68.

Hurezanu, Daniela. *Maurice Blanchot et la fin du mythe*. Presses Universitaires du nouveau monde, 2003.

Hutchens, Benjamin. *Jean-Luc Nancy and the Future of Philosophy*. Acumen Publishing, 2005.

———. "Philosophy as Juris-Fiction: Jean-Luc Nancy and the 'Philosophy of Right.'" *Journal for Cultural Research* 9, no. 2 (2005): 119–31.

———, ed. *Jean-Luc Nancy: Justice, Legality and World*. Bloomsbury, 2012.

James, Ian. "Differing on Difference." In *Nancy Now*, edited by Verena Andermatt Conley and Irving Goh. Polity Press, 2014.

———. *The Fragmentary Demand: An Introduction to the Philosophy of Jean-Luc Nancy*. Stanford University Press, 2006.

Jamme, Christoph, and Helmut Schneider. *Mythologie der Vernunft: Hegels Ältestes Systemprogramm des Deutschen Idealismus*. Suhrkamp, 1984.

Jay, Martin. *Downcast Eyes: The Denigration of Vision in Twentieth-Century French Thought*. University of California Press, 1994.

———. "Pseudology: Derrida on Arendt and Lying in Politics." In *Derrida and the Time of the Political*, edited by Par Pheng Cheah and Suzanne Guerlac. Duke University Press, 2009.

Jong, Johan de. *The Movement of Showing: Indirect Method, Critique, and Responsibility in Derrida, Hegel, and Heidegger*. State University of New York Press, 2020.

Kant, Immanuel. *Critique of Practical Reason*. Translated by Mary Gregor. Cambridge University Press, 2015.

———. *Critique of Pure Reason*. Translated by Paul Guyer and Allen W. Wood. Cambridge University Press, 1989.

———. *Critique of the Power of Judgment*. Translated by Paul Guyer and Eric Matthews. Cambridge University Press, 2000.

———. *Über ein vermeintes Recht aus Menschenliebe zu lügen* (1797). *Werkausgabe* Bd. 8. Suhrkamp, 1977.

Kamuf, Peggy, ed. *Jacques Derrida: Without Alibi*. Stanford University Press, 2002.

Kirkkopelto, Esa. *Le théâtre de l'expérience: Contributions à la théorie de la scène*. Presses Universitaires Paris-Sorbonne, 2008.

Kleist, Heinrich von. "The Earthquake in Chile." In *Selected Prose of Heinrich von Kleist*. Translated by Peter Wortsman. Archipelago Books, 2009.

Koyré, Alexandre. *Réflexions sur le mensonge*. Allia, 1998.

Kristeva, Julia. *Powers of Horror: An Essay on Abjection*. Translated by Leon S. Roudiez. Colombia University Press, 1982.

Laclau, Ernesto. "Politics and the Limits of Modernity." In *Universal Abandon? The Politics of Postmodernism*, edited by Andrew Ross. University of Minnesota Press, 1988.

Lacoue-Labarthe, Philippe. *Heidegger and the Politics of Poetry*. Translated by Jeff Fort. University of Illinois Press, 2007.

———. *Heidegger, Art, and Politics: The Fiction of the Political*. Translated by Chris Turner. Blackwell, 1990.

———. "Introduction to Walter Benjamin's *The Concept of Art Criticism in German Romanticism*." In *Walter Benjamin and Romanticism*, edited by Béatrice Hanssen and Andrew Benjamin. Continuum, 2002.

———. *L'"Allégorie" suivi de Un commencement par Jean-Luc Nancy*. Galilée, 2006.

———. "La Fable (philosophie et littérature)." *Poétique* 1 (1970): 51–63.

———. *Le chant des muses*. Bayard, 2005.

———. *Musica Ficta (Figures of Wagner)*. Translated by Felicia McCarren. Stanford University Press, 1994.

———. *Portrait de l'artiste, en général*. Bourgois, 1979.

———. *The Subject of Philosophy*. Translated by Thoms Trezise et al. University of Minnesota Press, 1993.

———. "Sublime Truth." In *Of the Sublime: Presence in Question*, edited by Jean-François Courtine, translated by Jeffrey S. Librett. State University of New York Press, 1993.

———. *Typography: Mimesis, Philosophy, Politics*. Translated by Christopher Fynsk. Harvard University Press, 1989.

———, and François Martin. *Retrait de l'artiste, en deux personnes*. Éditions MEM/FRAC Rhône-Alpes, 1982.

LeBlanc, Charles, Laurent Margentin, and Olivier Schefer. *La forme poétique du monde: Anthologie du romantisme allemand*. Jose Corti, 2003.

Lefort, Claude. "La question de la démocratie." In *Le retrait du politique*, edited by Jean-Luc Nancy and Philippe Lacoue-Labarthe. Galilée, 1983.

———. "The Question of Democracy." In *Democracy and Political Theory*, translated by David Macey. University of Minnesota Press, 1988.

Levin, Harry. "Some Meanings of Myth." In *Myth and Mythmaking*, edited by Henry Alexander Murray. Beacon Press, 1969.

Librett, Jeffrey S. "Between Nihilism and Myth." In Jean-Luc Nancy, *The Sense of the World*. University of Minnesota Press, 1997.

Lingis, Alphonso. *The Community of Those Who Have Nothing in Common*. Indiana University Press, 1994.

Lisse, Michel. "Lire, toucher: D'une main à l'autre." In *Paroles, textes et images: Formes et pouvoirs de l'imaginaire*, edited by Jean-François Chassay and Bertrand Gervais. Centre de recherche sur le texte et l'imaginaire, 2008.

———. "Literary Creation, Creation *ex nihilo*." In Alexandrova et al., *Re-Treating Religion*.

Lyotard, Jean-François. *Enthusiasm*. Stanford University Press, 2009.

———. *Heidegger and "the Jews."* Translated by Andreas Michael and Mark S. Roberts. Minnesota University Press, 1990.

———. "Introduction à une étude du politique selon Kant." In *Rejouer le politique*, edited by Jean-Luc Nancy and Philippe Lacoue-Labarthe. Galilée, 1981.

———, and Jean-Loup Thébaud. *Just Gaming*. Translated by Wlad Godzich. University of Minnesota Press, 1985.

MacLachlan, Ian. "Engaging Writing: Commitment and Responsibility from Heidegger to Derrida." *Forum for Modern Language Studies* 42, no. 2 (2006): 109–25.

Malabou, Catherine. *The Future of Hegel: Plasticity, Temporality and Dialectic*. Translated by Lisabeth During. Routledge, 2005.

———. "Pierre aime les horranges. Lévinas-Sartre-Nancy: Une approche du fantastique en philosophie." In *Sens en tous sens: Autour des travaux de Jean-Luc Nancy*, edited by Francis Guibal and Jean-Clet Martin. Galilée, 2004.

Mallarmé, Stéphane. "Crisis of Verse." In *Divagations*. Translated by Barbara Johnson. Harvard University Press, 2007.

Manchev, Boyan. "Le désir du monde: Jean-Luc Nancy et l'Éros ontologique." *Les Cahiers philosophiques de Strasbourg* 42 (2017).

Mannoni, Octave. *Clefs pour l'imaginaire* ou *l'autre scène*. Seuil, 1969.

———. "I Know Well, but All the Same . . ." In *Perversion and the Social Relation*. Vol. 4, edited by Molly Ann Rothenberg, Dennis A Foster, and Slavoj Žižek. Duke University Press, 2003.

Marchart, Oliver. *Post-Foundational Political Thought: Political Difference in Nancy, Lefort, Badiou and Laclau*. Edinburgh University Press, 2007.

May, Todd. *Reconsidering Difference*. Pennsylvania State University Press, 1997.

McDow, Daniel. "The Exigency of Thinking: Alain Badiou and Jean-Luc Nancy on 'Communism.'" In *Jean-Luc Nancy: Justice, Legality and World*, edited by Benjamin Hutchens. Bloomsbury, 2012.

Menninghaus, Winfried. "Walter Benjamin's Theory of Myth." In *On Walter Benjamin: Critical Essays and Recollections*, edited by Gary Smith. MIT Press, 1988.

Michaud, Ginette. *Cosa volante: Le désir des arts dans la pensée de Jean-Luc Nancy*. Hermann, 2013.

———. "Jean-Luc Nancy's *Expectation*: Rephrasing 'Philoliterature.'" In Toma, *Understanding Nancy, Understanding Modernism*.

Mihali, Ciprian. *Sensus communis: Pentru o hermeneutica a cotidianului*. Paralela, 2001.

Morin, Marie-Eve. *Jean-Luc Nancy*. Polity, 2012.

Nietzsche, Friedrich. *Die fröhliche Wissenschaft* (1882). *Sämtliche Werke, Kritische Studienausgabe in 15 Bänden*. München: Giorgio Colli & Mazzino Montinari, 1980.

Norris, Andrew. "Jean-Luc Nancy and the Myth of the Common." *Constellations* 7, no. 2 (2000).

O'Byrne, Anne. "The God Between." In Alexandrova et al., *Re-Treating Religion*.

"The Oldest Systematic Program of German Idealism (1797)." In *Philosophy of German Idealism: Fichte, Jacobi and Schelling*, edited by Ernst Behler, translated by Diana I. Behler. Continuum, 2003.

Pöggeler, Otto. "Hölderlin, Hegel und das älteste Systemprogramm." *Das älteste Systemprogramm: Studien zur frühgeschichte des deutschen Idealismus*. Bonn, 1973.

Proust, Françoise. *De la résistance*. Cerf, 1997.

———. *L'Histoire à contretemps: Le temps historique chez Walter Benjamin*. Cerf, 1994.

Puranen, Joni. "Recitative Voice: Reading Silently and Aloud, with Jean-Luc Nancy." *SATS: Northern European Journal of Philosophy* 24, no. 2 (2023): 129–45.

Rancière, Jacques. *Aesthetics and Its Discontents*. Translated by Steven Corcoran. Polity Press, 2009.

———. *Hatred of Democracy*. Translated by Steve Corcoran. Verso Books, 2014.

———. *La fable cinématographique*. Seuil, 2001.

———. *Mute Speech: Literature, Critical Theory, and Politics*. Translated by James Swenson. Columbia University Press, 2011.

———. "Plato's Lie." *The Philosopher and His Poor*. Translated by John Drury, Corinne Oster, and Andrew Parker. Duke University Press, 2004.

———. *The Politics of Literature*. Polity Press, 2022.

———. "Ten Thesis on Politics." *Theory & Event* 5, no. 3 (2001): n.p.

———. "The Use of Distinctions." *Dissensus: On Politics and Aesthetics*. Translated by Steven Corcoran. Bloomsbury, 2010.

Redfield, Marc. "Romanticism, *Bildung* and the Literary Absolute." In *Lessons of Romanticism*, edited by Thomas Pfau and Robert Gleckner. Duke University Press, 1989.

Ricoeur, Paul. *Temps et récit I: L'intrigue et le récit historique*. Seuil, 1983.

———. *Time and Narrative, Volume I*. Translated by Katleen McLaughlin and David Pellauer. University of Chicago Press, 1984.

Rooden, Aukje van. "De kunst is dood, leve de kunsten! Over de enkelvoudigheid en meervoudigheid van kunst." *Algemeen Nederlands Tijdschrift voor Wijsbegeerte* 105, no. 3 (2013): 173–82.

———. "A Demythologized Prayer? Religion, Myth and Poetry in Nancy's Deconstruction of Christianity." *International Journal in Philosophy and Theology* 69, no. 3 (2008): 285–304.

———. "Engagement for Engagement's Sake: An Ontological Rethinking of the Politics of Literature." *Aesthetic Investigations* 5, no. 2 (2022): 129–44.

———. "Interrupting Mythological Politics? On the Possibility of a Literary Intervention." *Theory & Event* 12, no. 2 (2009): n.p.

———. "Jean-Luc Nancy: A Romantic Philosopher? On Romance, Love and Literature." *Angelaki: Journal of the Theoretical Humanities* 26, no. 3–4 (2021): 113–25.

———. "Kafka Shared Between Blanchot and Sartre." *Arcadia* 55, no. 2 (2020): 239–59.

———. "La comunidad en obra: Jean-Luc Nancy en diálogo con Maurice Blanchot; Un desacuerdo tácito." *Pleyade* 4, no. 1 (2011): 79–103.

———. "Le cercle mythique: Walter Benjamin sur la politique et son interruption." *Anthropology+Materialism: A Journal of Social Research* 2, special issue, The Persistence of Myth (2014): 2–16.

———. "Le moment révolutionnaire: Sur la temporalité de la littérature chez Maurice Blanchot et Jean-Luc Nancy." *Revue Philosophique de Louvain* 115, no. 4 (2017): 675–90.

———. *Literature, Autonomy and Commitment.* Bloomsbury, 2019.

———. "'My God, My God, Why Hast Thou Forsaken Me?' Demythologized Prayer, or the Poetic Invocation of God." In Alexandrova et al., *Re-Treating Religion.*

———. "Poésie haptique: Sur l'(ir)réalité du toucher poétique chez Nancy." *Revue philosophique de Louvain* 107, no. 1 (2009): 127–42.

———. "Reconsidering Literary Autonomy: From an Individual Towards a Relational Paradigm." *Journal of the History of Ideas* 76, no. 2 (2015): 167–90.

———, and Alena Alexandrova, Ignaas Devisch, and Laurens ten Kate. "Re-Opening the Question of Religion: Dis-Enclosure of Religion and Modernity in the Philosophy of Jean-Luc Nancy." In Alexandrova et al., *Re-Treating Religion.*

———, and Ignaas Devisch. "Deconstruction, Dis-Enclosure and Christianity." *International Journal in Philosophy and Theology* 69, no. 3 (2008): 249–63.

———, and Joris van Gorkom. "De legitimatie van het alsof. De 'marginale' discussie tussen Lyotard en Nancy." *Tijdschrift voor Filosofie* 67, no. 3 (2005): 527–46.

———, and Andreas Noyer. "*Noli Me Operare*: Reading Nancy (Re)Reading Blanchot." In Toma, *Understanding Nancy, Understanding Modernism.*

Rozenzweig, Franz. "Das älteste Systemprogramm des deutschen Idealismus: Ein handschriftlicher Fund." *Sitzungsberichte der Heidelberger der Akademie der Wissenschaften,* 1917.

Schelling, Friedrich. *The Philosophy of Art.* Translated by Douglas W. Scott. University of Minnesota Press, 1989.

Schiller, Friedrich. *Briefe über die Ästhetische Erziehung des Menschen* [1793/1794]. De Gruyter, 2019.

Schlegel, Friedrich. *Dialogue on Poetry and Literary Aphorisms.* Translated by Ernst Behler and Roman Struc. Pennsylvania State University Press, 1968.

———. *Friedrich Schlegel's Lucinde and the Fragments.* Translated by Peter Firhow. University of Minnesota Press, 1971.

———. *Gespräch über die Poesie* (1800). *Kritische Ausgabe*, Bd. 2, Charakteristiken und Kritiken (1796–1801). Schönigh, 1967.

———. *Kritische Friedrich Schlegel Ausgabe*. Band 2. Schönigh, 1967.

———. *Versuch über den Begriff des Republikanismus* (1796). *Kritische Ausgabe*, Bd. 7. Studien zur Geschichte und Politik. Schönigh, 1967.

Schulte Nordholt, Anne-Lise. *Maurice Blanchot: L'écriture comme expérience du dehors*. Droz, 1995.

Smith, Jason. "Introduction: Nancy's Hegel, the State, and Us." In *Hegel: The Restlessness of the Negative*, Jean-Luc Nancy. University of Minnesota Press, 2002.

Sorel, Georges. *Réflexions sur la violence*. Rivière, 1919.

Toma, Cosmin, ed. *Understanding Nancy, Understanding Modernism*. Bloomsbury, 2023.

Tönnies, Ferdinand. *Community and Society*. Translated by Charles P. Loomis. Dover Publications, 2002.

Vaihinger, Hans. *The Philosophy of "As If."* Translated by C. K. Ogden. Barnes and Noble, 1968.

Valéry, Paul. "Petite lettre sur les mythes." *Œuvres I*. Gallimard, 1957.

Voßkühler, Friedrich. *Kunst als Mythos der Moderne*. Königshausen & Neumann Verlag, 2004.

Wagner, Andreas. "Jean-Luc Nancy: A Negative Politics?" *Philosophy & Social Criticism* 3, no. 1 (2006): 89–109.

Weber, Samuel. " 'Ibi et ubique': The Incontinent Plot (Hamlet)." In *Theatricality as Medium*. Fordham University Press, 2004.

Ziarek, Krzysztof. "Reproducing History: Benjamin and Heidegger on the Work of Art in Modernity." In *The Historicity of Experience: Modernity, the Avant-Garde, and the Event*. Northwestern University Press, 2001.

Žižek, Slavoj. *For They Know Not What They Do*. Verso, 1991.

———. *Sublime Object of Ideology*. Verso, 1989.

Index